MODERN ARTICLE WRITING

MODERN
ARTICLE
WRITING

George L. Bird

School of Journalism
Syracuse University

WM. C. BROWN COMPANY PUBLISHERS
DUBUQUE, IOWA

BROWN

JOURNALISM SERIES

Consulting Editor

CURTIS D. MACDOUGALL, PH.D., LITT.D.
Northwestern University
Evanston, Illinois

Copyright © 1967 by
Wm. C. Brown Company Publishers

Library of Congress Catalog Card Number: 67–21313

Manufactured by
WM. C. BROWN CO. INC., Dubuque, Iowa
Printed in U. S. A.

Preface

This book is written for all those who want to learn the techniques of presenting facts interestingly in article form. Such people fall into only two groups — staffers and nonstaffers, or free-lance writers. The latter are by far the most numerous, and their problem in learning how to write articles of professional quality is more difficult because they seldom have competent advisers at hand to help them. The staffers have a few less problems, such as freedom from mailing difficulties and the writing of queries. For these and other reasons, certain portions of this text will be addressed to free-lance writers. It should be obvious, however, that the essential problems of finding good ideas, of outlining, and of writing interestingly are the same for both groups.

The free-lance writer's needs are fully treated in these pages, in which it is assumed that he is a beginner. However, because today's beginners are tomorrow's staff writers, there is much help for young staffers on their writing problems.

The tendency for certain general magazines and a few others to shift from moderate reliance upon free-lance writers to almost complete dependence on staffers is discussed in Chapters I and II. A considerable effort is made to put this tendency and the roles of staffer and free-lance writer into their proper perspective.

Most of the writing done today is on a part-time basis, whether by staffer or by free-lancer. Most free-lance writers will have another occupation, either full or part time. Even the staff writer may have chores other than writing, most frequently in reading or rewriting the work of other writers. Recently a young friend of this author resigned from the staff of a leading magazine to undertake a full-time career in free-lancing because he had grown tired of chores that kept him from creative writing under his own guidance. In general, as far as the production of articles is concerned, the two groups — staffers and free-lance writers — have more in common than their differences.

In either group most of those who fail to write acceptable articles do so because they do not know how to think as professional writers. Not only are they troubled by false notions of what should be done, but also frequently their minds are a complete blank where the steps should be clear and obvious.

Writers at the beginning of their career will be helped if they understand that the process of training a writer is actually the training of a thinker. The writer of articles is first a *thinker* of articles. This book tries to show beginners how to think as an experienced writer thinks. It tries to eliminate the faulty and amateurish ideas and understanding of the inexperienced writer; it tries to replace them with the considered and workable judgments of the mature free-lance or staff writer.

Beginning writers will find two basic steps followed in this book to help them get launched on a successful writing career.

First, the beginner is shown how to write and sell the article known as the "short," or filler. This type of article may consist of one, two, or perhaps three paragraphs. It is easy to write, and relatively easy to sell — if correctly approached through the "inventory" method explained in this book. Later the same type of basic development is applied to the full-length article.

The student writer learns much by beginning with the short item. He starts to get acquainted with the markets, he becomes experienced in uncovering good subjects, and he learns how to handle the paragraph — the building unit of all article writing. The quicker sales of the filler do much to establish self-confidence in the writer.

This approach also has advantages for the instructor who uses this book in an article writing class. He is helped in the shortest time to size up the abilities and needs of his students, early mailing of short material results in more numerous and quicker sales, and the added incentive provided by the actual receipt of checks is of considerable value. Meanwhile, during the second week of instruction, because of the brevity of the academic year, the teacher has put students to work on their first long article.

Second, this text solves the twin problem of *how* and *where* to start writing the long article. If there is a best way of making article writing easier, this book makes use of that method. This it does through three distinct steps that show: 1. how to put down on paper a "free-associational" list or inventory of anecdotes, data, descriptive terms, and all other items likely to be of use in the proposed article, just as they "pop" into the writer's mind; 2. how to rearrange this inventory into a logical pattern to fit the purpose of this article and the needs of the market; and 3. how to pick the easiest place to start.

Further, all the necessary, useful techniques of beginning, slanting, headline writing, querying, rewriting, etc., are introduced as *required* by the writing process, because students most readily learn under the pressure of the need of the particular technique.

All the exercises and suggestions offered at the end of each chapter should be worked out, particularly by the beginner who must learn to write without supervision. It is not sufficient that these exercises merely be read. Having once worked them out, however, any ambitious writer who scans the local field for similar ideas and puts them into professional form will make some sales. This statement has been well proved by the many writers who have sold their very *first* article by following them.

Lists of reference books, guides to the markets, writers' magazines, and other special sources of information are to be found in the later chapters. Special help is also found herein for writers who want to concentrate on science or technical writing.

Other good methods for teaching article writing and other good approaches to this fascinating business of learning to be a successful staffer or free lancer likely exist. But the beginning writer can have full confidence that faithfully following the procedures set down herein will lead him to a workmanlike understanding of the problems of the article writer, as well as to a satisfactory mastery of fundamental article techniques. He should expect that a regular writing program subjected to his own improvement and critical judgment will lead him steadily to better achievement.

Grateful acknowledgment is made to the pioneer teachers in the field, to the editors and students who have contributed to this author's writing education, and to those authors and publishers who have granted permission to reprint professional and student work.

G.L.B.

SCHOOL OF JOURNALISM
NEWHOUSE COMMUNICATIONS CENTER
SYRACUSE UNIVERSITY
May, 1967

Table of Contents

Illustrations

CHAPTER 1

Free-Lance or Staff Writer?

Has the free-lance writer a chance today to make a good living entirely from his craft? Can any adventurous, competent article writer launch himself on the free-lance seas and hope to survive? What are the hazards? Who, if any, can succeed? If success is possible as a free-lance writer, how should a writer go about getting a start?

Or, is the haven of a staff job the best place for a young writer to tie up for a "dock-side" career in writing? What are the latter's advantages? Its disadvantages? How much freedom will the staffer have to write *what* he pleases and in the way he pleases?

Opinions on what the writer of articles can do and what he should hope to accomplish as a free-lance writer are in considerable opposition. Also in disagreement are the opinions on the need for a staff job on a magazine or newspaper if one is going to write articles for that same publication.

Before presenting the two major points of view on the above questions, let the author explain what he means when he refers to the article as a type of writing.

Articles are of many types and lengths, and their characteristics depend upon the requirements of the publications in which they appear.

1

They range in length from the filler of fifty words — more or less — up to three or four thousand words. A few pieces are longer, or may be broken into two or three installments.

After quickly eliminating illustrative material, poetry, and short stories from magazines and newspapers, the beginner wonders whether the remainder should be considered articles. The decision is particularly difficult if he is examining a newspaper. Most magazines use a considerable number of specialized pieces such as editorials, columns of many kinds, departmentalized copy from bolts and nuts to soups and nut bread.

There is a definite tendency today toward specialization by magazines. The newer and growing magazines will be found to be devoted to holidays or illustrated sports in general, or a higher degree of specialization: auto racing, motor boating, guns, camping, outdoor sports, sailing, outdoor cooking, or other similar interests.

The business, manufacturing, and trade magazines also follow this narrowing pathway. This group relies increasingly upon the writing of the literate specialist. Employee journals and external house organs also show this specialization.

The best road to understanding the article and its role is to try to understand what it means to individual publications — magazine or newspaper. Usually the term "article" means different things to different publications.

Remembering that articles do vary from a few score words to a few thousand, we might say, to help us get a central picture, that an average article runs from a thousand to three thousand words. It may be an informal piece, a humorous or serious essay. It may be argumentative. It can be descriptive, but it is seldom devoted to *pure* description today. It is more likely to be an expository piece, or, perhaps, almost pure narration. It is usually thoughtful either in presenting facts or opinion. Recent news facts often are elaborated, "backgrounded," or interpreted until they are no longer news stories but fully-developed articles.

Unless based on personal experience, the article usually is the result of investigation, research, study, and interviewing. Some articles are "tossed off," but the factual piece is not so easily produced. Fully-experienced staff and free-lance writers know that the average piece demands high quality thought, hard work, and much rewriting.

Trend to Staff Writers

Earlier in this chapter it was suggested that opinions did not agree on how rosy the outlook is in the free-lance market. This writer believes that the difference arises because those who disagree are referring to different markets or different groups of similar magazines, such as those in the religious field, or, perhaps, the "food and shelter" field.

Some pessimism has developed in recent years, and with a great deal of justification. Many first-rate, high-paying markets among general magazines have folded with little apparent reason. Among them have been *The American Magazine, Collier's, Coronet, Pictorial Review,* and *Woman's Home Companion.* Some have failed because of too much competition, as occurs in other businesses, and some have folded for the arbitrary reasons of disenchanted publishers.

The failure of these magazines has closed some of the highest-paying markets in America. Article writers and short story writers have had to look elsewhere. They have lost editorial contacts which in many cases were carefully built up and nurtured over the years. These editorial acquaintances can be among an article writer's greatest assets, and their loss is a serious blow to any writing career.

A second force that has tended to close certain markets to free-lance writers has been a trend toward staff-written magazines. This has developed for several reasons. First, the flow of articles from free-lance writers to the magazines has always been unpredictable in quality, quantity, and timeliness. Second, supervision of the work of and cooperation with distant free-lance writers is more difficult than with staff writers. Third, many article ideas are generated within the office, and it is easier to assign them to staffers than to locate competent free-lance writers and frequently carry on arrangements by mail. The matter of illustration also makes work with free-lance writers extremely difficult.

This picture is not entirely black, however, since the work, names, and competence of free-lance writers are usually known by those in charge of magazines that are eager to obtain original articles of first-rate quality.

To these magazines free-lance writers have turned, being forced to explore outlets and opportunities previously passed up. Among these have been *Cosmopolitan* and *Redbook,* which were open to some, and *True, Esquire, Sports Illustrated, Outdoor Life, Field and Stream,* and *Sports Afield* to others.

Further, during this period of decline of general magazines, new, specialized publications of better than average quality were coming onto the market and gaining strength. Among them have been *Holiday* and *Sports Illustrated* at one level of specialization. Other more highly specialized "books" — to be discussed later — were gaining strength.

The trend to the staff-written magazine has opened up new writing positions to which many part-time or full-time free-lance writers turned. The list of staff members on *Reader's Digest* will yield a score and more of such refugees. Dozens of others have moved into permanent jobs on other magazines, big and little.

Outlook for Beginning Free-Lance Writers

What significance does the above trend have for the beginning free-lance writer? How much does it affect his prospects at the start of his career?

The answer is definitely, "Not very much, and certainly not as much as some pessimists have reported."

In the *first* place, the best spot for a free-lance writer to begin has always been from the security of a job that enables him to acquire the necessities of life. This can be almost any sort of position — in trade, business, the professions, housekeeping, or even in manual labor. The basic requirements are that the job allow a bit of time somewhere in the twenty-four hours for writing, that it does not completely absorb his energy, and that it does provide whatever support is necessary. In whatever circumstances, the desire or drive to write must be strong enough to lead the writer to make whatever sacrifices are necessary.

Some advantages exist in having a magazine job, although there are also disadvantages. The staffer usually finds his liberty restricted. He is more likely to have his writing efforts directed by superiors, or to be required to edit the work of other writers. In addition, he may be expected to give his own magazine first chance at whatever he produces in his spare time. This also may limit the range of subjects on which he can write.

Still wide open to the free-lance writer are several broad market fields, although the rate of pay is lower than in the top-flight general field. These include the religious, trade, and outdoor fields. A former student of this writer recently gave up a full-time and well-paying job on *True* magazine to devote full time to free-lancing in the outdoors field. He turns out three illustrated pieces a month, and has pushed his income up nearly fifty per cent. Editors of these magazines say they will always have room for free-lance pieces.

The free-lance writer with demonstrated ability to produce acceptable work can eventually reach the status of contract writer, and can ask and expect to receive definite commitments from editors. These agreements bind an editor to accept any piece *ordered*, provided that the writer has delivered an acceptable article. Editors are not bound to print pieces under these agreements but are bound to pay for them. Additional help can frequently be had under these general circumstances in advances to cover expenses incurred while traveling, photographing or researching a piece.

Unfortunately some editors have closed their columns to free-lance writers, and the latter should waste no time on them. Their names can be found in the article writer's markets listed on p. 357. What they need may be too difficult for the average free-lance writer; to eliminate lost time and energy, they prefer to work with staff writers.

As noted above, however, hundreds upon hundreds of editors are still to be found who welcome work from competent, beginning writers. These men will give sympathetic attention to creditable pieces, to efforts of promising writers to break into print, and to their queries. They need new talent, for many writers do write themselves out, and there are never enough extra good pieces. Many a magazine goes to press containing pieces that the editors would be happy to replace with more useful articles of wider appeal.

The Craft of the Article

Articles sometimes seem so simple that they appear artless. This artlessness is more imaginary than real. The good article must be well crafted, and its author must meet the requirements of his editor in subject, development, style, and choice of details. Many writers who fail have never troubled to find out what editors require. Because magazines are tailored to meet reader expectations, articles themselves must be tailored to staff requirements.

Other writers fail because they haven't learned to write in simple style for better communication. This ability comes with long practice; it is not a gift. Many articles on interesting subjects have been rejected because they were beyond the comprehension or intellectual curiosity of intended readers. A writer of my acquaintance did an original piece on "Push-button Railroading" and had it turned down *twice* by the same magazine with the same condemnation — that it was too difficult. All readers of the magazine were graduates in electrical engineering, but even they wanted pieces that were humanized and simplified.

Simplicity of style and clarity are certain to be stressed more emphatically in the coming years. Communication experts are coming to understand how heavily communication depends on the meaning readers attribute to words, and how widely this varies from person to person. Meanings are in readers' minds, and in order to be understood, writers must try to put themselves in the place of the readers and anticipate how they will react to what is written.

Some articles have not been sold because their grammar was faulty, because they were not interestingly developed, or because the subject was unworthy of magazine space.

Although the craft of article writing includes no mysteries, formulas, or special vocabulary, there are demands for clear writing, an interesting style, competent knowledge, and the ability to entertain. All these attributes of competence can be acquired, but the process is not learned overnight. Steady success demands some years of study, practice, and experience.

Because of these requirements, beginners should direct their efforts in writing and marketing toward the simpler markets and the shorter items. They should not try to market their early work in the country's top-paying markets, because they are not ready for them. The effort to break into them is certain to end in almost complete failure. The resulting discouragement may end what might have been a fine career in writing. Those who start out modestly and gradually raise their sights as their ability grows are more certain to achieve their goals.

To earn the rewards of article writing — recognition, personal achievement, and financial gain — one must expect to serve an apprenticeship. The techniques can be learned through instructors or by reading texts, but high competence can be achieved *only* through continued study, practice, and actual experience with all the problems of the craft.

Full-time or Part-time Writing

Few writers can expect to launch a successful, full-time career in free-lancing until they are thoroughly competent. Beginning article writers have almost no chance at earning even a modest living. Knowledgeable article writers certainly would advise them against such a hazardous launching. The failures are certain to be too numerous, with disastrous results to both hopes and income. Experiences of many hundreds of student writers observed by this instructor fully proved that free-lance writers should start on a part-time basis.

While *any* job that provides support can be used as the haven from which to begin a writing career, one that leaves evenings and weekends free is by far the best. A newspaper job, in which hours are established by the union, is a first-rate place in which to begin free-lancing on a part-time basis. Advertising agency and public relations department jobs are also good because they hold so many people with ambitions for variety in their writing output. While the style and techniques of advertising and public relations copy may be specialized, these occupations do force writing experience upon the novice writer. This author sees very little disadvantage to the restrictions they put upon writers. Style is a matter determined primarily by the writer and the subject matter, and it is certainly under the control of the writer, who may as a free-lance writer write on any subject he settles upon (after getting it approved by an editor) and, hence, in any style that fits his purposes. One advantage to all of these occupations is that they turn up many first-rate subjects that have newspaper and magazine sales possibilities.

The novice, while selecting and getting acquainted with the markets for which he hopes to write, learning to slant his articles, and improving his general writing craftsmanship, also is attempting to market his articles and is learning from priceless, personal experience.

When handled this way, the early years of a writing career are less costly than if a writer were dependent solely upon sales for his income. As in the case of the outdoors writer cited, the day may come when a writer is sure enough of his writing abilities and of his knowledge of the markets to launch out on a full-time career as a free-lance writer. Until then, he will be wiser to hold onto a full-time job with a regular paycheck.

Part-time Writing by Whom?

In addition to those practicing free-lance writers who hope to shift one day into full-time free-lancing, there are countless others who *could* learn — and perhaps *should* learn — to write on part-time basis. Several classes easily stand out: 1. professional workers such as lawyers, clergymen, physicians, and educators; 2. experts in business, manufacturing, and trade; 3. scientists in many areas; 4. experts in such important areas as agriculture, forestry, public recreation, social welfare, and government; and 5. literate citizens in all walks of life.

WHY WRITE? There are good reasons for professional men and women to become writers. Many of them with years of training, education, and experience have important facts to reveal and important stories to tell. Obviously, they have expert knowledge in their own field. If they have been intelligent, imaginative, and observant, they will have priceless conclusions, facts, and observations to pass on. This experience and knowledge are needed by their colleagues and by the public. Because they are often "too busy to write" or because they fear they haven't the training, most professionals turn away from writing.

Here develops what social scientists call a cultural lag. This lag refers to the period between making a new discovery, developing a new process, or formulating a theory, and its coming into general use or understanding. In some cases the lag may be twenty years or longer. The unused discovery and invention are worthless in the undeveloped state. All professional workers should feel compelled to try to bring their creations before the public, and, of course, expression in the mass outlets involves the writing process at various stages.

What is said of professional workers is true largely of experts — scientists, tradesmen, educators, and others. Among the tragic wastes of this interplanetary age are the knowledge and training that are not expressed by these groups, which should be among the most communicative.

Retired trained workers from all of the above professions and trades compose a reservoir of talent, the size of which is impossible to estimate. The wealth of interesting articles that lies therein would fill all the magazines in this country — if it could be tapped. It would be untrue to say that this is a vain hope, for from such people occasionally come articles and even books of great descriptive strength and emotional force — great because they are based upon a lifetime career filled with experience, observation, and thought.

At one time or another everyone asks and answers the question, "What shall I do with my spare time?" or "What shall I do in retirement?" Such questions are asked and answered whether or not individuals are aware of the fact. Each individual answers in his own way.

This author plans a wise investment of his free hours. In looking ahead for a year, or five, or ten, he estimates that hundreds, even thousands of hours, will be completely his own. He can spend some of them on a favorite trout stream, in a thicket where grouse feed, pushing downstream through white-water thrills, at bridge, concerts, dance recitals; at the piano or the organ, over cocktails, in daydreaming; in academic research, original writing, or updating texts. These are among his choices. . .just as they are among yours.

In the disposal of such hours the writer has great freedom. He can turn to hobbies, to sports, to new interests in which eventually he can become an expert and perhaps make important contributions. He can allow the hours to filter through his fingers as if there were no end to them. They can add up to the fading memories of pleasant hours or to important projects undertaken, and, happily, to a sheaf of published articles or a book or several that give continued delight. These are the decisions open to men and women in our society.

HOBBIES.   Many educated, retired workers — professional or otherwise — have paralleled their vocation with a hobby or two, about which they could write adequately with a little instruction or help from the appropriate magazine staff.

While the magazines devoted to hobbies are not always among the best-paying markets, nearly all make some payment. Beyond this is the reward of personal satisfaction in seeing one's own writing in print (properly credited, of course), and, perhaps more important, the prospect of doing a little good in the world. These are excellent builders of morale in any individual who has been "stuck away" on the shelf of retirement while still possessed of energy for creative effort.

The retirement period is an excellent time to become an expert in a new line or to polish up an old hobby. Time, denied to the fully employed, is now abundant and, fortunately, the tools of the writer's craft are few and inexpensive. Paper and pencil are all the basic tools needed, for with them these words are being written at an altitude of 21,000 feet between Rochester and Syracuse, New York.

STEPPING STONES. Many times in a teaching career this writer has seen the value of even a little skill in the writing craft. The printed word has a magic all its own — for the reader as well as for the writer. Between the scribbled manuscript and the printed page some alchemy works to endow ideas both worthy and unworthy with more glamour than is truly inherent in them.

In the office, the factory, research laboratory, or in academic circles the man or woman who can get his ideas into print earns prestige not to be earned in any other way. Extra copies of the printed article or reprints distributed to the right spots have meant "promotion and pay," in the words of Kipling, and even offers of jobs from other concerns. Status often comes more quickly with ability to get into print than in any other manner.

An article or two to one's credit presents an opportunity to promote one's writing career by calling attention to them when querying other editors. A little tact and deftness refers the editor to one's recent article in *Homemaking Magazine* or *Rougher's Life*.

Free-lance Writers and Fiction

If there is anywhere a staff writer for fiction, this author does not recall one. Certainly there are staffers who do write for their own and other publications, but the staffer whose only job is to write fiction is rare, indeed.

But young staffers and free-lance writers alike are interested in the effect of article writing upon their craftsmanship in short story writing, and vice versa. Fact and fiction are closely related. Fact borrows the clothing of fiction to make it more interesting or palatable. Fiction tries to make itself read like fact. In some historical novels, for instance, it is difficult if not impossible to distinguish between fact and fiction. In factual articles, however, while fictional techniques, such as the elements of suspense, are used to arouse interest, nothing should be presented as fact that isn't fact.

Writers of fiction and of fact can profit much from a study of the style and techniques of both crafts. Little if any evidence exists to show that the writing of one type adversely affects the writing of the other. Hordes of writers really do not have a pleasing style and never will have. They simply haven't paid the heavy price of long hours of practice over enough years.

Writing as You Travel

Only a few old-timers can recall the days when newspaper reporters wandered from paper to paper; then six months on a single newspaper was as long as anyone expected to serve. Free-lance writers, too, were almost but not quite as footloose. The crucial difference was between the regularity of the reporter's paycheck and the uncertainty taken by the free-lance writer. The base for operations of the free-lance writer has shrunk; but as pointed out earlier, opportunity is still present for vigorous free-lance writers who are willing to accept a considerable gamble.

Among my former students is a writer with a gift of enthusiasm and a bold spirit. Giving up a first-rate position as staffer on a national magazine, he spotted article ideas in many places, conferred with appropriate editors for the necessary "go-ahead" signal, and then set out on a series of trips that eventually took him to England, Labrador, the St. Lawrence area, Arkansas, the "North Woods" of New York State, Nova Scotia, and other places that fascinated him. In all this there was little or no gamble, because with his reputation as a competent writer, editors were willing to make definite commitments to take what he wrote, provided only that the articles fulfilled their early promise and were adequately illustrated.

Such writers are to be found doing pieces for *Sports Illustrated, Reader's Digest, True, Holiday,* and similar publications. They write pretty much as they *go* and as they *please*, but they do have — or should have — definite commitments before they start out. For those who want to know what lies "around the corner" no more fascinating way of life exists.

Interesting places off the beaten track to be discovered and written about are their meat. They also seek out stories about men and women of accomplishment and achievement for the entertainment of millions of readers. Such writers are generalists in that they are competent to write interestingly of subjects that range from adventure to zoology. The specialist also has considerable freedom when he proceeds carefully and imaginatively within his own narrower field of writing. Take the science writer who can produce readable, accurate articles. He finds that many magazines have a specialized scientific interest. Even such magazines as are devoted almost entirely to religion will reach for science news in their own areas. Among them are *Christian Century, Commonweal, Christian Life, Christian Herald,* and many others — none among top-paying markets, but yet important to a writer's career.

In short, the opportunities for part-time free lancing are almost unlimited in terms of the total market. Opportunities for full-time free lancing are still open to competent and energetic writers, but they have decreased in recent years as many of the top-paying markets folded. It is also true that many markets are now mostly or entirely staff written. But still wide open are opportunities to get into print, to express oneself, and to do a bit of good for society through magazines and newspapers.

Training Steps

1. Take any issue of *Popular Mechanics Magazine* or *Popular Science Monthly.* Note the number of one- or two-paragraph items signed with initials or name. These are free-lance shorts. Note the simplicity of the ideas and the practical style of writing. How many of these could you have written as far as the style goes?
2. Also note in these two magazines the number of different departments that accept material from free-lance writers.
3. Copy one of these short items in your own handwriting, noting how simply they are constructed. This is an excellent way to get the *feel* of these items.
4. Now make a list from your own experience, setting forth ideas that could be handled in one or two paragraphs.
5. Analyze the most interesting experience of your life. Would it make an article? Do you know anyone whose experiences would be worth writing about?
6. Obtain one of the writers' market guides and make a quick estimate of the number of markets that are still open to free-lance writers. What proportion of the markets are known to be closed?

7. In this market guide also look up the magazines in the field of your trade, profession, or special interests. How many use free-lance articles? How many are staff written?

8. Examine the article you like best in your favorite magazine. Does the writing sound as if the author were talking to a friend? If so, you can learn to write like this.

9. Do any of your favorite magazines accept articles from free-lance writers? If not, you should widen your interests and subscribe to some that do.

10. How many short items do you find in your Sunday newspaper?

11. Is there anything in the weekly magazine of the *Christian Science Monitor* that you might have done? This newspaper purchases articles from nonstaff members on occasion.

12. What new magazines have come on the market in recent years? Do they specialize in a restricted field? Or are they very broad in interest? Try to learn whether they accept articles from free-lance writers.

13. Run through a dozen issues of one or more writers' magazines and note what they say about being open or closed to free-lance contributions.

14. Begin to note the length of the sentences and paragraphs in current magazines. Actually make a count of the words per sentence and sentences per paragraph.

CHAPTER 2

Creative Editing

The term "creative editing" is often applied to the process of producing article copy within the offices that later use it. This text will use a slightly broader definition, including also the deliberate effort to direct creative and imaginative processes toward the production of original copy that best expresses the needs of a magazine and the abilities of its staff.

Obviously, the editing of copy is much the same in any office, regardless of the source of the copy or its content — so long as we refer to checking of such items as accuracy, clarity, grammar, punctuation, spelling, typographical style, and other such editing concerns. Magazine rules, public or other demands or pressures, and typographical requisites are fixed by precedent and necessity and leave little freedom of choice in these items. For an excellent text on this subject see Robert Root's *Modern Magazine Editing*[1]. This chapter will not concern itself with matters related to rudimentary editing but rather to production of ideas, their acceptance by editorial authority, assignment to whatever staffer is to produce the material, research for the necessary data, background

---

[1] *Modern Magazine Editing*, Robert W. Root, Wm. C. Brown Company Publishers, Dubuque, Iowa, 1966.

and interpretative material, the writing process, subsequent changes in editorial conferences, and other final editorial adjustments.

The free-lance writer has a small role in the editing processes referred to. Exceptions occur occasionally when he works on assignment, since at those times he becomes the equivalent of a staffer. We shall not consider the editing processes at this time, but will discuss them at their appropriate places in Chapters 6, 8, 12, and 13.

Restrictions on Staff Writing

The staff writer is nearly always a member of a team that works (writes) together. The finished article may be, but more frequently is not, entirely his own. He must exchange pride in his own originality for pride in a group effort. Many factors bring about such situations: first, the basic idea may not be his own; second, other staff members may have contributed important ideas for development; and third, another staff member may be given the task of rewriting the finished piece, cutting it to shorter length, digesting it, elaborating it, or changing angle or emphasis.

Staffers may not have to write on subjects or develop angles to which they are morally or ethically opposed, but they certainly will have to handle subjects in which they are not interested or which actually bore them. Furthermore the pressure on them to meet deadlines is great and frequently applied.

A greater degree of income security exists on magazines than in dependence upon free-lance checks. Yet even top positions disappear, as staffers on *The American Magazine, Collier's, Coronet, Pictorial Review, Woman's Home Companion,* and *Country Gentleman* — to name a few — found out in years still remembered. Further, anoyne can be discharged from an apparently secure job for a variety of reasons, not necessarily connected with his competence.

STAFFERS' ADVANTAGES. Among the numerous advantages that staff writers have over free-lance writers, in addition to more regular pay and fringe benefits, may be quicker access to research sources in the office library or local public, private, and university libraries, since most editorial offices are in large cities. In addition, expenses for research, including travel, are paid from publications' budgets, a tremendous help to any writer.

The staffer has a greater opportunity than the free-lance writer to confer with his editorial associates as his concepts or perspective change on a developing article. The staffer has the editor's ear in suggesting changes or new ideas. He also is very early aware of plans for future holiday, seasonal, or special editions, and knows what future needs will be without reference to writers' magazines, literary agents, or queries — all of which can be helpful, but also slow and frequently out of date.

Subtleties of magazine policy are often unknown to free-lance writers and difficult to learn. Free-lance failures after "go-ahead" signals may be due to editorial whims or policy changes, but they are truly discouraging. The staffer is usually spared these rejections. Intimate knowledge of a magazine's point of view on what it stands *for* and what it is against — its pet peeves, taboos, or favorite topics — is the daily bread of the staffer. Of course he is first to know of any changes in the policy of his magazine.

In addition to knowing what his magazine has printed in the past, or already has on hand through purchase or staff assignment, the staff writer will know how to handle the complications of advertising tie-ins, publicity plugs, and various other types of free editorial mention beyond the ken of the free-lance writer. While some magazines allow no free advertising, many actually use it as part of their policy of help to advertisers. In certain magazines in which circulation is restricted to users of products advertised in the magazine and where the practice is understood by all concerned, no ethics are violated. The "hidden plug," in which the relationship of advertiser to publisher is obscured or deceives the reader, may be unethical.

While the articles staff writers produce must meet editorial criteria, staffers have a much easier time in bringing them up to standard because of easy editorial conferences or proximity to office advice. The free-lance writer in the field has fewer such opportunities. Further, the reader who handles a free-lance article first may be inexperienced or lacking in good judgment. One of this author's graduate students not long ago got a job in New York City with the publisher of a chain of magazines and presently wrote that she was "first reader" for five of the magazines. One can only pray for the writers whose work comes into such inexperienced hands.

Editorial Conferences

The heart of creative editing is in the editorial conference in which two or more staff members seek out or discuss new ideas, analyze for purposes of improvement items already on hand, or plan future issues. Many other types of conferences are held, of course, to decide whether to buy certain new items, how a recent issue could have been improved, or possibly to survey what competing magazines are doing.

The "brainstorming" conference holds the greatest fascination for most staffers, for it gives each of them a chance to pit his imagination, memory, or general creativity against the others. On a magazine with good morale this can be both exciting and stimulating. Chapter 26 describes the eight methods that can be used in a brainstorming effort to produce new ideas from old. Student writers ought to make such efforts a regular and basic part of their writing program. Some minds do not respond well to the open competition of brainstorming, apparently working best in a quiet study or under other circumstances. Nevertheless, when these eight methods are applied persistently to what the writer himself reads, they will produce far more ideas than any writer can find time to use!

Where Ideas Come From

Few article ideas — if any — are entirely new; they are nearly always adapted from or suggested by ideas already in print in fully-developed articles or perhaps indirectly from suggested articles.

These ideas may come from the writer's unconscious use of one of the eight methods previously cited. However, most new ideas come from articles already printed in competing magazines or newspapers, from scientific papers or government bulletins and similar sources, or from datebooks or "future" books in which ideas are set down against the date upon which they can be used. Experience and observation also are productive sources for anyone who keeps his eyes open and is curious about all new or strange occurrences, situations, scenes, or developments.

Free-lance writers also supply ideas to magazines, a few of which are said to buy ideas from them for exploitation by staff writers. Other magazines, as in the outdoors field, rely almost entirely on articles they arrange for with free-lance writers.

Staff Conferences

How often staff conferences are held depends entirely upon the need for them. This in turn depends upon the magazine and how it operates; nearness to deadline; or even upon such emergencies as the failure of one or more articles to be completed or cancellation of an advertising contract. Some staffers meet daily, some twice a week or weekly, and some only on the editor's call.

Assuming that a meeting is to be held to make preliminary plans for a future issue of a monthly magazine, the call may go out from six to eight months in advance of the publication date. Earliest plans are made at least twelve months in advance. Staff writers and free-lance writers alike have to anticipate these dates, and may plan ahead as far as twelve months.

Magazines are usually divided into departments. For instance, a typical food and shelter magazine may have the following departments: furnishings, food, decoration, architecture, gardening, family life, and special features. Each editor will report on the material he has on hand for the issue and what is planned, and also upon such other items as color or art requirements, space needed, and the state of readiness of all times.

A completely free hand is seldom given to any department head. Compromise is a common practice, and nobody gets all the color process he wants nor as frequently as he wants it — the cost is too high. Color rights often are handed around a bit, although obviously food and fashion requests carry greater weight than the average general feature piece. Often there is a spirited argument over who gets what and how much, or what article or department gets the prize of front-cover billing, the lead-off position, a two-page spread, or such special art treatment as hand-lettering of titles.

Hundreds of details of typography, article length, cutting, fitting, cropping of pictures, accuracy, clarity of style, arrangement, titling, total number of pages, and almost countless other items can come up at any staff meeting. Many articles are sent out for examination by experts: lawyers look for libel and scientists and other professionals may check articles in their fields.

Issues just off the press are usually checked by each editor in the area of his responsibility. His first duty is to produce a creditable unit in the magazine. Eventually, the entire "book" is taken apart and evaluated: compared with past issues, with competing magazines, and with the recognized goals of the magazine. The editors want to know how closely they came to producing the best magazine possible and how to improve.

How Staffers Work

The writing staff worker may write in any one way or in a combination of many ways. Since there is a multitude of trades, professions, and specialized interest fields, each magazine that represents any one of them develops its own organization and aims and methods of achieving these goals. For instance, on a trade magazine a staffer may hit the road like a roving reporter to visit stores or factories in search of news that will interest his magazine. On the other hand on the same magazine he may spend his time writing or rewriting publicity releases or news items for such papers as the *Wall Street Journal.*

A former student of this writer does endless reading in natural history to develop brief but accurate articles about nature and science for a magazine that circulates to fourth and fifth graders in the public schools. A second student, on the staff of an outdoors magazine, does little but edit copy, plan layout, and judge the acceptability of free-lance offerings. His is a top-flight job in this field, but it includes little original writing. A third student with an excellent job on a similar magazine became bored with office inaction and resigned to do full-time free-lancing, which he finds to be more fun and pays him considerably more.

No pat answers exist to questions on how magazines handle article ideas or how staff writers produce copy. Every magazine has its own methods because its problems usually are peculiar to itself. Staff writers proceed in different ways also. The goal is the same in all cases: to produce a magazine acceptable to the public and an article acceptable to top staff members.

It would be obvious from these remarks that anyone who wishes to train himself for work on a magazine in editing or writing should have a broad journalistic training. Probably it is the experience of every school of journalism that some of its trained reporters enter public relations or advertising or magazine editing; its magazine trainees get jobs on newspapers, in advertising or in public relations; and so on for all the other possible shifts in employment. The result is that any capable graduate — if well trained — usually succeeds in whatever branch of mass communications he enters.

Two main reasons exist for this adaptability. *First* is the core training required in most schools of journalism. This usually consists of basic training in graphic arts, news writing and reporting, and editing. The *second* reason is that success in the areas mentioned rests chiefly on ability to write, general intelligence, and a relatively few simple techniques.

ROVING EDITORS. Many a beginning writer longs to step into the role of roving editor, with salary assured and expenses paid. These rare jobs are alluring to any young writer who is still footloose and hasn't a family to tie him down. The average roving editor is ready after the first year of wandering to stick closer to home with an occasional jaunt to distant places. The job of a *Reader's Digest* roving editor may carry a basic salary, but each writer still has to produce articles. He is paid so much per article, and a high and fairly constant rate of production is required to bring his salary into top income figures in the magazine world. Other magazines employ roving staff members, but these jobs prove tiring as the writer grows older, and the desk job takes on added glamour. Anyone who has a yen for this sort of write-as-you-run ought to undertake it early in his career.

FREEDOM OF CHOICE.   As one who has free-lanced for more than forty years on a part-time basis, it seems to the author that the part-time basis offers greater freedom of choice in what one can write about than either full-time free-lancing or full-time staff writing. From the security of a full-time job such as this teacher-writer has, one need not grind out hack work to keep the free-lance income high, nor do hack writing for an editor boss. In either position a writer can usually expect to grind out many pieces in which he hasn't the slightest interest, or which he may, in fact, actually detest. As a part-time, free-lance writer, he need write only what appeals to him or about the burning causes he wishes to support.

Training Steps

1. What is meant by "creative editing"? Examine a number of magazines until you have located what you believe to be a number of examples of creative editing. Check these with your instructor if you are in an article writing class.
2. You have already taken a look at the magazines published in your field. Now from a market guide ascertain the number of magazines that take an occasional article in your field. How many are there?
3. What types of articles and what kinds of subjects would be easiest to place with these publications?
4. If your local newspaper has a Sunday edition, find out from the editor whether he would be willing to buy well-written pieces that his staff members have overlooked.
5. If you have a hobby or avocation, examine the magazines devoted to these fields. Visit your public library so that you won't have to buy them, or go shopping at a secondhand magazine store.
6. If you have not studied a book in the field of magazine editing, either borrow or buy one and read it thoroughly. This will help start you thinking like a professional writer, and perhaps save you months or years in your writing apprenticeship.
7. Get or borrow the back issues of the *New Yorker* with the articles on the *Reader's Digest*. How much of the *Reader's Digest* is staff written and

how much is contributed by free-lance writers through other magazines? If you can find a book on *Reader's Digest,* read about the manner in which roving editors work and are paid.

8. What are your real ambitions? To become an editor or a writer? Are you truly creative? Or are you not very original in your thinking? Do you have a real gift or curiosity? If you are not original, creative, nor curious, give up the idea of becoming a writer. You had better stick to editing.

9. Can you drive yourself; are you a self-starter; do you like to meet and quiz people; are you aggressive? If not, don't try to free-lance on a full-time basis. Get an inside job editing other people's articles.

10. Watch the writer's magazines for announcements of new publications and determine whether they are open to free-lance writers. Note their rates of pay and the type of articles they need. Try to fit yourself into their pattern. Be among the first to query the editors if you can.

CHAPTER 3

Finding Article Ideas

Ideas for articles are likely to be found almost anywhere, but even the writer of long experience may have difficulty keeping a supply of first-rate subjects on hand. Not every individual, shop, or manufacturing concern is worth writing about, though the writer of articles never knows in which shop, street, or corner he will find an idea, person, or process worthy of his abilities.

Ideas are Elusive

Many a prospective subject will be found, studied, and discarded before one completely suitable turns up. Some must be discarded because they have been used, others because they lack substance or because no editor would be interested in them. Among the certainties for the writer is the fact that he cannot afford to wait until he stumbles over subjects. He must have a regular plan for searching them out. Fortunately, the pathways usually are well marked.

One other fact should be noted. While good subjects are by no means numerous, some excellent opportunities will be seen by one individual and overlooked by a second. The writer has but one pair of eyes, and before going far in his career he will find that he must employ his eyes and ingenuity constantly to keep his name in print. It is unlikely that he ever will suffer from too many subjects.

Specializing

The article writer with a special field of interest is fortunate. Experienced writers unite in urging the beginner to concentrate his efforts as soon as possible. It may be well for a short time to work in several areas, but the writer who sells regularly is always an expert on his subject. Life is too short to become truly proficient in more than one or two fields. This advice is not meant to discourage avocations or hobbies or writing about them. Actually, such interests are commendable, but only the unusually versatile and tireless individual will find the hours in which to master more than one profession and one avocation.

The writer's chances of selling increase as his name becomes known to editors and to the public. Neither is inclined to trust completely the person who steps into too many fields. It takes time — years, in fact — to establish oneself in a particular field. The reputation and good will that attach to a writer's name comprise almost his greatest asset. He cannot afford, therefore, to discount it by trying to establish himself in several other realms.

Let the beginner keep these facts in mind when exploring the following suggestions for finding material. Let him choose carefully the field in which he intends to stay, as well as the group of publications for which he hopes to write. He may become a writer for or about business, for or about children, about gardening, home building and construction, science, politics, or art. He should hesitate, however, before he tries to establish himself as an expert writer in more than one such field.

Ideas From the Newspapers

No one knows the local field better than the newspaperman. The interests of his readers lead him to write of retail trade, manufacturing, accidents, and lawbreaking; of housing conditions, fires, civic improvements, the schools, hospitals, the museums, and other institutions. Often illustrated, these stories or articles appear in the newspaper columns, most often in the Sunday or weekend edition.

Such articles may be fully developed and need little work to make them suitable for the magazines or for use in some other noncompeting newspaper. For example, a newspaper carried the story of how a farmer and his four sons remodeled their house, streamlining the architecture so that the house became modernistic. Their neighbors were so impressed that the farmer and his sons were hired to repeat the process on three other houses. Pictures of the homes together with 800 words of copy made an interesting Sunday article. The man who wrote this story, or another writer, could have reworked it with little effort for *Successful Farming, American Home,* or *Better Homes and Gardens.*

Another illustrated article told of a ceramics exhibit at the local museum. *Time* magazine printed several hundred words on the show. The trained writer would find in such an exhibit material for a half-dozen articles in as many magazines: a how-to-make pottery article for handicraft magazines; a critical article for one of the art magazines; articles on the use of ceramics in decoration for a home magazine, on the use of ceramic cooking utensils for the same type of magazine; on freak ceramic exhibits for *Popular Science Monthly* or *Popular Mechanics Magazine;* or on ceramics as a profession for *Mademoiselle.* This list could easily be doubled.

In addition to such fully developed articles, requiring only slight additional work, are items more briefly mentioned. On these the writer may have to do all the research. Typical items, most of which would make good full-length newspaper articles, are cited below.

1. A man has built a bird sanctuary on his property. This item has several possibilities: a how-to-do article for a handicraft magazine; a personal experience story for *National Wildlife* or *Audubon Magazine.*
2. A family has constructed a combined rock garden and lily pool. The story of how it was done might be well received by *American Home* or *Better Homes and Gardens.*
3. A university professor has invented a new device for measuring distance through the use of binocular cameras and microscopes. Different articles could be sold simultaneously to *Scientific American, Popular Science Monthly,* and the newspaper syndicates.
4. A salt museum is opened to the public. This shows the development and history of a local industry of wide interest. The museum itself may be worth an article, but the story of the national salt industry might be purchased by the *Magazine of Wall Street* and *Business Analyst.*
5. A college newspaper carries a story telling how a senior paid his expenses with his camera. The story would interest *Camera 35, Popular Photography,* and *Modern Photoraphy.*

6. Letters to the editor may provide good ideas. One woman wrote to tell how she averted the possible disastrous effects of polio by massaging her child's body with oil and alcohol, beginning as soon as the pain had gone. Market suggestions: *Parents' Magazine, Today's Health,* newspaper syndicates.

7. A photograph in an advertisement shows how a store is using a collection of old valentines to promote the sale of modern valentines. A photograph of the exhibit (possibly supplied by the store itself) and the necessary explanation might interest *Department Store Economist, Department Store Journal* or *Notion and Novelty Review.*

Sometimes the specific item may not be worth an article, yet may suggest a similar idea that is. For instance, the valentine advertisement might suggest a display of pots to show how coffee has been made at different periods. A collection of antique coffee pots would make a fascinating window display and suggest an idea that could be sold, perhaps, to a restaurant magazine or department store magazine.

Magazines as Sources

Other important sources of ideas are the magazines with national circulation and wide appeal. Editors of these magazines are alert for new ideas in their respective fields. They constantly scour the sources from which new ideas come — contributions in the mail, competing magazines, the newspapers, scientific bulletins, and technical publications. The ideas so garnered are presented later for the benefit of their readers. Because of the keen competition among magazines in the same field, articles based on these ideas must present the soundest and most expert advice. Anyone trying to write will find in such magazines the best examples of what the editors want as well as stimulating ideas for other articles.

OTHER ARTICLES. For instance, suppose a young woman wishes to handle problems of interior decoration. If she is qualified by professional training so much the better, though study and experience in her own home may be sufficient. She should start with simple ideas.

Looking through *American Home,* a logical source of ideas (and a logical market), she finds an illustrated article on the use of plates as decorative objects. The photographs show two especially attractive plates hanging on the living room walls, and others lined up on a molding around the dining room. The writer asks herself how the idea can be adapted to other items. After some thought she decides that books may be equally decorative. Out they come from the customary shelves and cabinets. She tries them on the mantel, above a certain door, on a special rack along the stairway, or in the bedroom. Behold, the colorful jackets or the rich green and red of lovely bindings transform their new setting!

Her own good sense and the judgment of neighbors tell her that she has an interesting decorative feature — not a big idea, but one of the small, salable kind. Four or five pictures, showing what she was able to do, and a concise explanation with well-chosen suggestions for further expressions of the idea — perhaps only 800 or 1,000 words of copy — would merit a check for seventy-five dollars or more. Many articles found in current popular magazines, trade journals, and newspapers originate in this fashion.

The story of a game room built in an attic suggests an article about a neighbor's basement game room. How one woman modernized a living room suggests an article on modernizing a bedroom. An article on antique furniture suggests a further one on new and different uses for old-fashioned sugar boxes, wooden bowls, coffee grinders, or old glass.

TITLES. The titles of published articles often suggest other articles. For instance, the title "Safe At Home — But Are You?" from *Better Homes and Gardens* suggests this one for *Parents' Magazine*: "Mother Knows Best — But Does She?" Often an article can thus be built around a title. After all, an article is but the elaboration of an idea. Take this popular phrase: "Sweet Sixteen — Never Been Kissed." It might suggest an article for *Seventeen*: "Sweet Seventeen — Never Been Missed." This would be an article on how to be popular. The idea has as much substance as most of those found in articles on self-improvement.

This technique for finding ideas can be applied in practically any specialty and in any type of publication. It is likely to prove highly useful, because many adaptions can be turned up in the course of the routine study of the markets that every writer must make.

LETTERS FROM READERS. Don't overlook letters from the readers. Often they tell what the subscribers wish the magazine would do. When you find such a tip, drop a query to the editor and ask if he would be interested in an article covering the point.

Personal Experience and Observation

A free-lance writer must be a doer and a seer. Most beginners will quickly write themselves out if they depend upon past experience alone. From this type of writing probably come most of the items by those individuals who never produce more than a single article. The fact that they are numerous is good news for the free-lance writer, because competition with persistent writers is cut by this amount.

From personal experience and observation come some of the best articles. Generally they are good because the individual has been deeply stirred by what he has seen or done. Perhaps he has had an unusually exciting deer hunt in Maine and is moved to tell it for readers of *Field and Stream*. He has been thrilled by trout fishing and can't rest until he has sent a story and pictures to *Outdoor Life*. A young woman may have seen a friend, back from a camp for young men, making an attractive leather pocketbook. Interested, she studies the process and writes it up with illustrations for *Mechanix Illustrated*. This is another fifty-dollar item. Many Sunday newspapers are equally good markets, though for such items they pay less than the magazines.

A farmer's wife, a talented writer, tells of her experience in the Dust Bowl, another of living on the lonely wheat praries of western Canada, another of fighting locust hordes in South Africa. A professor's wife tells of the difficulties of life in academic circles. The professor himself relates his side of the story two months later. A salesgirl explains what girls in trade learn about customers. A vacationer writes about the youth hostel movement and the joys of life in the wilderness. For every moving experience there is a market.

Scientific and Technical Sources

SCIENTIFIC REPORTS.   Scientific discoveries usually are first announced at conventions of scientists. An announcement most often is made in a paper read by one scientist to his colleagues. The language is technical, and the training required to understand it is great. Hundreds of such papers are read each year. Usually they are first published in professional journals. For example, a paper on the making of artificial rubber might appear in *Chemical Processing*, later in *Popular Science Monthly*, and still later might be distributed by newspaper syndicates.

The process of progressive popularization extends from the most scholarly down to the most popular magazines, forming a ladder between science and the masses. Here is an example: A paper appears in *Science*, is rewritten for *Scientific American*, next for *Popular Science Monthly*, and finally for *This Week Magazine*. Roughly, the typical reader of *Science* is highly educated, with scientific training; the reader of *Scientific American* is also an educated man but with less specialized training and broader interests; the reader of *Popular Science Monthly* is a man of average education and training; while the reader of *This Week Magazine,* although of average education, is very likely to be a woman or a child. Below is a diagrammatic representation of this pyramid of readership.

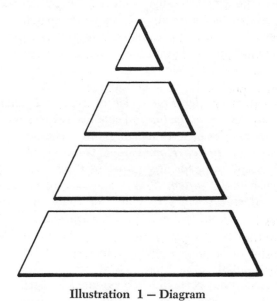

Illustration 1 — Diagram

It matters little whether the writer scanning the scientific magazines for possible subjects is a free-lance journalist or a scientist with a desire to popularize scientific news. What is important is the fact that such magazines form an excellent source — an almost inexhaustible source — of articles, and certainly one into which no writer can hope to dip more than briefly.

GOVERNMENT BULLETINS. Bulletins that come from the United States Department of Agriculture contain a wealth of good articles. Most of them are already popularized to such an extent that the article writer need only rewrite them (with proper credit) for his own choice of market. Such bulletins cover a thousand different subjects: how to do home canning, reupholster furniture, refinish old furniture, cook new dishes with new and improved foods, plant gardens, grow fruit, improve the farm, or recognize the grains in various woods. Many of them are free. Others cost only a few cents.

Numerous other departments of the federal government issue bulletins, books, and monographs that contain usable materials. Various divisions of the state governments are sources almost as good. Most of this material can be used by free-lance writers. Of similar types are the reports of private and public charities, educational groups, and numerous special-interest groups. Literally hundreds of organizations publish reports that contain the information from which articles are made. Frequently these groups will aid the writer by supplying photographs or in other ways help get an article into magazine or newspaper columns.

TRADE JOURNALS. Trade papers contain much that can be rewritten for other magazines or for the newspapers. In this group are such journals as *American Builder, Practical Builder, The Exchange, American Druggist,* or *Furniture Manufacturer.* Technical articles on home building in the *American Builder* or in *Practical Builder* should suggest items for *American Home* or *Better Homes and Gardens.* Articles from *The Exchange* may inspire tips for newspaper features and articles for magazines like *House and Garden.* News items on furniture appearing in *Furniture Manufacturer* will give clues for follow-up articles for such topflight home magazines as *Ladies' Home Journal;* articles to be found in *American Druggist* may well supply the facts for later articles in *Parents' Magazine.* The possibilities of this type of rewrite are so great they can be but hinted at.

CURRENT BOOKS. Books should be examined. It isn't necessary to buy them. Your public or college library probably purchases more than you can use. Biographies yield data for birthday and anniversary articles. A new account of any noteworthy character has possibilities, although the fact that a man is somewhat obscure may be more reason for a good sale. A biography of Opie Read, once one of America's best-known humorists but now forgotten, would provide material for good articles on life on the early traveling Chautauqua, reminiscence about itinerant printers, suggestions on public speaking, how to write humor, and the like. Autobiographies are in the same class. Travel volumes furnish ideas for the vacation sections of magazines and newspapers such as *The New York Times, Ford Times,* or *Holiday.* Books on history, economics, psychology, and many other subjects contain material for worthwhile subjects.

Ideas from Experts

The man who has achieved eminency in his field is usually one who knows something the public would profit from hearing. Take a medical specialist. The eye specialist can tell the public how to protect precious eyesight. The child specialist can tell parents how to protect their children from childhood disease. The specialist may be an expert automobile mechanic who can give advice on proper operation and maintenance. He may be the county agricultural agent giving advice on city gardening or rural planting. One would have to exhaust the list of trades and professions to mention all possibilities.

These experts can be approached in several ways. In each case one or several interviews will be necessary. The free-lance writer may have an order from a magazine or newspaper, or he may only hope to sell the proposed article. Through a series of questions the writer draws enough material from the expert to support the theme of the article. It should be stated that the writer usually has in mind a definite idea for an article before he sees the expert. The subsequent article may be signed by the writer alone, by the two jointly, or by the expert alone.

A somewhat different idea is that of asking certain types of experts for tips on possible articles. The free-lance writer will find that librarians, historians, curators, and others can often point out feature subjects, such as individuals, landmarks, or institutions worthy of a write-up. Among other sources where feature material accumulates are hotels, trade associations, institutions of learning; public bodies, such as boards of health, offices of city and county legislators, and waterworks; and factories and distribution agencies.

Anticipating Coming Events

A casual examination of the newspapers and magazines will show that numerous articles are written about recurring events. These can be said to be tied to the calendar and can be classified as seasonal, anniversary, fads and crazes, or holiday articles. While tips for such pieces need not come from the newspapers or periodicals, these publications do show what is considered important and how the subject is customarily handled. In Chapter 21 a more complete treatment of this type of writing is offered. Almanacs and books of dates are aids to anyone wishing to write in this excellent field.

Copyright and Libel

Because article writers need to quote from published works or the words of private and public individuals, they should get acquainted early with the laws governing copyright and libel through such a book as that by Wittenberg (see Chapter 23). Though many government and social agencies seek popularization of their publications, if extensive quotations are to be used, one should obtain permission to quote. For brief quotations, reference to the original source is sufficient.

A published article may be copyrighted in the author's name if so agreed at time of purchase by the editor. Blanks can be secured from the Copyright Office in Washington; registration costs $4.00. Secondary and other publishing rights can be reserved at the time of selling first rights. Most magazines transfer reprint and similar rights on request, but one should make clear what he is selling.

Facts, titles, ideas, and names of characters cannot be copyrighted, but a writer's way of saying anything can be. Any number of free-lance writers may retell the same event from published accounts — such as stories about the recovery of a lost hydrogen bomb off the coast of Spain. But in describing any event it is not lawful to use the expressions and terms another has originated. A sentence or two may be quoted with credit to the creator, but a writer cannot help himself to whole sections.

Writers and Editors

Because editors must keep up with what is new, they are best informed on promising subjects for their publications. While some editors depend entirely upon their own staff, hundreds buy from free-lance writers. Occasionally an editor will ask a competent, established writer to handle a subject. The assignment may go to someone who has previously contributed to the publication. Conferences follow, either by mail or in person, and eventually the article appears.

Magazine editors should not be expected to furnish ideas for articles, nor should free-lance writers go to them seeking such help. Relations with city or Sunday newspaper editors and editors of country weeklies are different. There is no good reason why a writer should not call on such persons to ask if they have ideas for articles or know of individuals worth interviewing. Nothing is lost if the editors have no ideas to pass along.

Within One's Loves and Hates

There remains one other approach to the matter of finding subjects for salable articles. This is the neglected but highly successful trick of writing about the objects and circumstances of everyday life that cause the writer to be deeply moved. Every reader recalls coming across

articles by writers whose passionate interest has lifted the pieces out
of the dull class into which many articles fall. Such articles are so outstanding that they appear to have been done by a different species of
writer. The secret appeal is the writer's great urge to record a highly
charged situation or deep emotion.

AN EXTRA QUALITY. Out of such emotion grows an extra quality
that suffuses the article and makes it better than it would have been
otherwise. Many a commonplace subject has been elevated because
of some writer's zeal for it. Furthermore many first-rate subjects have
been turned into superlative articles by the burning interest of a writer.

Readers easily recognize this quality in an article. So do editors.
Like sincerity and honesty, interest is difficult to feign. When a writer
has no interest in his subject, he is under a handicap. Fortunately, one
trait of human nature can be brought to this aid. This is the trait that
leads people to become interested in those subjects into which they
penetrate deeply. This fact can be made one of the greatest props of
the article writer. More will be said of it later on.

The manner in which interest is manifested is difficult to point out.
Primarily it is in the choice of words. A writer will find that more
expressive terms come to mind on a subject about which he feels deeply
than on one about which he is indifferent. The nouns he uses will be
more descriptive, the verbs more vivid, and the adjectives more frequently of the superlative degree. The writer's interest will lead him to
work harder and longer, and he will be less likely to be satisfied with
the first ideas that occur. The tendency to do better work and to exercise more care contribute to the success of articles written with
enthusiasm.

WHAT OF DULL SUBJECTS? At times a writer may be faced with the
problem of doing an article on a subject that bores him. If he is a staff
writer, he may have to set to work against his inclinations. Other choices
are offered to the free-lance writer. As his first alternative, he can drop
the troublesome idea and turn to one about which he is enthusiastic.
The raw material from which articles are made is sufficiently plentiful
so that no free-lance writer need write about facts that hold no interest
for him.

The second alternative — to study seriously in order to promote a
greater interest — holds a world of help for the free-lance writer.
Suppose a person has an opportunity too good to pass up. An editor has
asked him to write an article on a notable stamp collection. The fact
that tens of thousands of people find the subject fascinating means

little or nothing to the writer. Stamps have always been a boring subject to him.

Actually, no subjects are dull. There are only dull ways of looking at them. In this case our writer has a dull approach. He needs to become a temporary expert in the field. He should read a number of articles or a book or two on the subject. He should learn what the encyclopedias say, and talk to a number of serious collectors. When he discovers that as much as $50,000.00 has been paid for a single stamp, and becomes acquainted with the lore in this field, he is very likely to be able to write with enthusiasm — if not with the devotion of a collector.

Once having experienced the growth of interest in a field through study, a writer can approach other seemingly dull subjects with the hope of finding his interest aroused by the time he has buried himself in the subject matter.

A second technique for uncovering the interesting phases of any subject is to interview opponents and proponents. The stronger their beliefs, the more certain are the interviews to be interesting. A few such encounters are likely to provide colorful opinions and facts that any writer could take pleasure in working into an article.

DUAL NATURE OF INTEREST. The writer driven by interest may move in either of two directions. He can take action on behalf of something, or he can take action against the same idea, principle, or thing. The latter attitude probably will be backed by the emotion of anger or indignation.

Examples of enthusiastic embracing of ideas are many. A writer may be thrilled by traveling, sea bass fishing, riding, the making of ceramics, leatherworking, hunting, sailing, remodeling of old homes, collecting old glass, herb gardening, or any one of a thousand other hobbies. If he writes about them, the fascination they hold for him will inevitably appear in his article.

The free lance should beware of becoming bored with what he sees, hears, and does. He faces a more difficult problem than the newspaper reporter, whose need it is to be objective about what he writes. Being receptive to new ideas and keeping alive the ability to be carried away by new experiences are requisite in every writer.

Antipathies also are numerous. They are seen in the many "Letters to the Editor" printed in the daily papers. Someone writes against juvenile delinquency, another decries the high cost of medical attention, a third complains of reckless driving, still others want lower taxes, better refuse collection, more parks, or reform of the public schools. The writer who feels the same antagonisms might turn some of these into first-rate pieces. Being human the writer will have his own "pet peeves" or antipathies. And he might do better to capitalize on them than to waste his wrath on thin air.

WHILE THE IRON IS HOT. The moment to capitalize on enthusiasm or antagonism is while the mood is at its peak. Don't wait to outline the article or to perfect a title or introduction. Talk it all out on paper as you would tell it to a good friend. Don't spare the adjectives the *first* time through. Write the way you feel, and don't try to perfect punctuation and grammar. Just remember you are doing this for a publication that will send it into thousands of homes with differing tastes, and be good natured in what you say.

Experience will teach that it is wise to keep on writing until you have written yourself out on the subject. Then will be time enough to start rewriting. Probably the first paragraphs will have to be thrown away, and the order of the rest shifted. Ways will have to be found to tie the paragraphs together, but such mechanical details will not prove difficult. Simply be careful in the grooming process not to eliminate the qualities of sincerity and enthusiasm that should pervade the article. Their presence may be the factor that persuades an editor to buy your piece. Probably you will want to tone down statements that are too laudatory or condemnatory. A little restraint is a good thing.

REWARDS OF ANGER. What are some of the subjects on which it has paid to get "burned up" when writing? What have been some concrete results of writing while rage was at white-hot point?

One free-lance writer, a southerner by birth, who knew true southern cooking, grew indignant at the tasteless imitations passed off by restaurants here and there. She wrote an indignant piece for the *Atlanta Journal,* using fictional techniques. The newspaper was glad to buy the patriotic defense of southern cooking.

Your present author broke into the outdoor magazine field years ago in the same way. Finding that the mourning dove was being shot, in certain sections of the South, far in excess of the legal limit, he wrote an article demanding reduction of the limit and enforcement of the law. The article, called "Must the Dove Go, Too?" was printed by *Outdoor Life.* In sending the check, the editor wrote, "We are buying your article because you so obviously put your heart into it."

Using the same approach and psychology, the author has sold numerous articles more because they carried conviction than because they covered important subjects. Many writers have had the same experience, and out of such has grown the maxim "To interest other people, you must first be interested yourself." To capitalize on dynamic interest is one of the secrets of successful article writing worth remembering.

Other fields of exploration for the free lance exist among the under-privileged and handicapped people and in some obscure and lost causes. The deaf, the mute, the defective in speech, the blind, and the crippled need someone to plead their cause repeatedly. So do the orphans, the juvenile delinquents, and the criminals trying to "go straight." Public understanding of neurotics, of habitual drunkards, and of the mentally ill needs to be furthered. A thousand causes wait to be pleaded by the writer with knowledge and insight.

Above all, watch for opportunities in the field of your own specialty. If you are a writer on child training, perhaps one day you will become indignant at the way some parents leave their infants in baby carriages on zero days while doing their shopping. If your indignation compels you to write, *Parents' Magazine* may buy the resulting article. Or you may watch an immature parent nag a youngster to distraction, and turn out a fine piece on "Bringing up Parents." Or, if you doubt the wisdom of parents in general, you may want to do a piece on "Does Mother Know Best?"

To whatever you turn your hand, remember that nothing succeeds like a white-hot, passionate reaction — either *for* or *against*. It pays occasionally to get vehement if you write about it later.

Training Steps

1. Examine your daily newspaper for local items. Has any manufacturing concern recently put a new product on the market? or modified an old one? If so, clip these items. With a little rewriting, they can be sent to the proper trade journal. Or perhaps you can do a piece with pictures for the local newspaper.
2. Has any local department store recently redecorated? or rearranged its interior? If so, a story may be marketable.
3. Make a careful tour of your shopping district. Has any new window display been presented? If it is original, striking, and effective, an article on it is salable.
4. Has any store or service shop of your acquaintance offered a new service to its customers? If so, it is likely worth an article.
5. Do you know any outstanding engineers, physicians, psychologists, in-ventors, or other interesting personalities? There's a market for articles on every type of individual.
6. What are your favorite magazines? See if they use articles about people, processes, places, or things. Jot down a list of similar items within your own experience. Put them in your permanent file of prospective subjects.

7. In your radio listening and TV viewing, watch for programs presenting individuals who might be written up for a magazine.

8. Ordinary conversations often produce suggestions for articles. Learn to keep your ears attentive for these valuable tips. Jot them down at once for later transference to your permanent file.

9. Have you ever devised a gadget or a new way of doing an old process? Jot it down. There is a market for it if no one has written of it before.

10. What would you like to know that you don't know? Perhaps about a process — say, how gloves are made? or what salt is used for? Go to *Readers' Guide to Periodical Literature*. Has any article been written on it in the last two years? If not, perhaps thousands like yourself would like to know about it. You can read up on it, become a temporary expert, and do an article on it for a magazine that has approved the idea.

11. Ask your acquaintances what it is that they would like to know about, or see in their favorite magazines. If the subjects have not already been well handled, here are new possibilities.

12. Take a trip through the ten-cent stores, the department stores, or other shops. What new products are being offered? what old ones in new colors or shapes? There is a market for these new ideas in the women's magazines and the popular science field.

13. Since *Reader's Digest* is the most important magazine for the study of general articles, read an issue from cover to cover. Mark every article that shows the writer felt deeply about his subject.

14. Select three of the above articles. Now mark every noun, verb, and adjective that gives color to these articles. Make a careful comparison of the words so marked. In them will be found the secret of why the three articles were interesting.

15. Examine copies of *True Story Magazine* and *True Confessions*. Note how the emotional quality differs from that of the items used above.

16. Compare the editorials of *The New York Times* with the items found on the same page in the column "Topics." The writing of which was enjoyed more by the writers?

17. Study a few issues of *Popular Mechanics Magazine* and *Popular Science Monthly*. Do the articles give evidence of being "ground out"? Or did their creators enjoy the writing?

18. Make a list of the subjects that interest you intensely. Could you do an article on any of these now? If not, why not?

19. What things "burn you up"? What would you like to do something about: the price of haircuts, the number of strikes, or the way some salesgirls chew gum? If any "pet peeve" sufficiently annoys you, it is probably the source of a marketable article.

20. Did you ever write a letter to a newspaper or magazine editor? Could this have been turned into a salable piece by proper handling?

21. Study the "Letters from the People" column of your local press. Some of the practices complained about may yield an idea for an article.

CHAPTER 4

Evaluating Article Ideas

How does a writer know when he has a salable idea? He can submit the idea to the editor of the magazine for which he works or might wish to write. This takes time, though it is far better to have an idea rejected than the finished article. The expert knows that about eight out of ten ideas should be discarded. Submitting mediocre ideas is a reflection upon the writer, as well as a waste of effort and time. No author can afford to create a reputation for shallowness or hasty thinking. The letter to the editor therefore should be used with caution. The writer has a duty to himself to protect his own reputation, as well as an obligation not to waste the editor's time.

The free-lance writer comes upon scores of possible subjects as he reads, observes, listens to others, and reacts to his own experiences. Some are outside his field of interest, or beyond his experience or ability to handle. Some he recognizes as trivial; others are not timely enough to be marketable.

Reasons for Discarding Ideas

Reasons for discarding subjects are about as follows:

1. Too late because of previous handling
2. Too late to be put into print by necessary date

3. Outside of writer's experience or ability
4. Lacking in merit
5. Insufficient material available
6. Lack of suitable illustration
7. Contrary to magazine policy

Previous Handling

Every mature writer knows that article subjects are often "in the air." Circumstances and events create the need for certain articles, and at least the possibilities for others. The first angle that suggests itself under these conditions is also likely to suggest itself to other writers. Study of *Reader's Guide to Periodical Literature* will reveal whether the subject has been used and by what markets, with the exception of recent months. The same research should reveal what angles have been utilized by various writers.

A creative free-lance writer may be able to develop an entirely new angle and get a go-ahead signal after writing a careful query to the prospective editor. This will depend on finding the new angle and enough new facts to make a substantial article. In this connection refer to page 391 for a list of eight ways of creating new ideas from old ones. Mere imitation of previously printed articles is not a good way to get an idea accepted. It would be wiser far to avoid ideas that are "in the air" and likely to suggest themselves to scores of writers. Let the free-lance writer dig up his own new ideas from his own experience and observation.

The writer must expect that other scribes will hit upon the ideas that occur to him. Some articles will have been completed and sold, perhaps even put into print, before he comes upon his idea. This is to be regretted, but it is a warning to think ahead, to anticipate magazine needs and trends, and to act quickly when ideas occur.

No one should submit an article or a query on a subject that has been recently handled in the prospective market. On a controversial subject one might be allowed to present another side; but generally a magazine hesitates to duplicate its subject matter until considerable time has passed. This is particularly true of personality sketches, or subjects capable only of limited treatment. These remarks do not refer to seasonal articles, which are used by some magazines every year in the same issue. Nor do they refer to similar articles on the same subject, such as articles on how particular homes were remodeled. *American*

Home, for instance, is likely to print one or more articles on this subject in every issue.

Occasionally, before the arrival of an article or query another manuscript on the same subject may have been recently purchased, or purchased at an earlier date and put away in the safe for later scheduling. These are circumstances that can be learned only by consulting with editors. There is no excuse for submitting a single-treatment article to a magazine that has recently printed something on the same subject. The writer must study the current issue and back files of his prospective market in order to eliminate such blunders.

Time Is Too Short

Some subjects must be dropped because there isn't time to write about them and get into print by the day the publication must go to press. There are frequently seasonal items, or other events, that are tied to the calendar. When writing such articles for monthly magazines, the writer should start working at least six months ahead of date of publication. For weekly magazines the period is about six to eight weeks in advance of publication. For both types of periodicals exceptional circumstances may alter cases, but the writer cannot build a successful career on exceptions. If the free-lance is to begin writing so far in advance of publication, he will naturally have had to do some thinking, planning, and querying even earlier. A more complete discussion of the point will be found in Chapter 21.

Other articles not of the seasonal type may be discarded because their timelines will be lost before they can be put into print. These are the articles that must reach the street or newsstands within a few days, or at best a few weeks, of some news event. All except a very few magazines are automatically ruled out by this requirement. The best markets for such topical articles are the Sunday or daily newspapers. Further reference to these is made in Chapter 18. Included in this type of article are those based upon such disasters as floods, cyclones, explosions, or fires. Personality sketches based upon the passing of a prominent person or the recent success of another may also fall in this class.

Outside Writer's Experience

When a writer comes upon a good subject outside his experience, he may be wise to discard it. Scientific subjects such as those in the fields of chemistry, physics, medicine, or industrial research may be too difficult. At times the difficulty can be overcome by persuading the scientists involved to collaborate with the writer. Or the manuscript may be gone over for accuracy by those who supply the information. The latter instance implies a degree of scientific training on the part of the writer before he undertakes to interpret discoveries for publication.

The writer should beware of supplying either incorrect or superficial information to the readers. The danger is threefold: it is harmful to the public, dangerous for the writer's career, and harmful to the scientist's reputation.

The alert person will soon find that he must specialize in a limited field. He must concentrate his efforts upon establishing his own reputation as a writer on architecture, perhaps, or upon gardening, or upon scientific discoveries. He cannot forever be instructing himself in new fields. Nor do magazines care to buy from jacks-of-all-subjects. The names of such writers are not likely to carry confidence to magazine and newspaper editors or to the public.

The names of certain men are associated with articles on scientific discoveries and developments. They are not found in the sports field, the trade field, or in interior decoration. A writer may shift from the writing of general news items to specialized reporting, or from the writing of shorts to the production of articles in limited fields. Once the change is made, the writer should stick to it as closely as possible, for there is an accumulative value to a writer's name as it becomes more and more closely associated with meritorious articles in the same field.

Lack of Merit

One of the most difficult abilities to develop is the ability to weed out weak or doubtful subjects from the "sure-fire." Study of the markets, analyses of good articles, and practice in writing will eventually prove of much help to the writer, but at the outset of his career he will accept many a subject that ought to be passed up.

Among the tricky possibilities are the personality sketches. First, and even second, glance at the individual may lure one on, particularly if the subject is an interesting conversationalist with a gift for oral narration and description. The great difficulty is in transforming this personal charm into an equally interesting article. It is well to consider seasoned judgment if there is any doubt. This is where the query may be used, though it is also possible to get help from others who may be able to say whether this person's accomplishments are truly out-standing.

Most people are not sufficiently interesting to be worth a write-up. The writer simply must take the cream from among his prospective subjects. What is true of personality sketches is true, in almost as great a degree, of all other kinds of articles. There will be prospective subjects that should be discarded because of their fundamental lack of interest for the journals to which the writer is accustomed to contribute. Others must be ignored because they are not sufficiently helpful to readers.

Insufficient Data

Occasionally a promising subject may present itself, but investigation may show insufficient data to develop a full-length article. This will occur frequently when the prospective article is based upon hearsay information or secondhand acquaintance. A friend may meet an inter-esting stranger and pass his information on to the writer. Or a friend may visit some foreign spot, rich in untouched lore, and suggest it as article material. Generally such efforts will fail. The details have faded, the facts are meager, and only generalities are left. It is almost useless to attempt to supply the missing information through correspondence, for nine times out of ten the writer will fail to get enough facts to make the correspondence worthwhile.

There is no substitute for firsthand knowledge; the writer must write about people he has met and about places he has visited. Standard works of reference may supply part of the missing background, but the editor wants articles that treat authoritatively of the subject at hand. It will be time saved to discard prospective subjects when the data are insuffi-cient. Padding generally leads to a weak article.

Lack of Illustration

Some articles require illustration. Among them are those that tell how someone remodeled a house, converted a barn into a home, re-decorated a room, went on a hunting or canoe trip, or visited foreign countries. When it is impossible to procure illustrations from any source, such subjects should be dropped. Most writers soon get acquainted with the numerous photo syndicates that exist for the purpose of supplying photos to newspapers and magazines, and so save many an article. Some syndicates are glad to supply a selection of photographs from which the writer may choose proper illustrations. Methods of illustrating the article are discussed in Chapter 11.

When rejection of an idea looms as a possibility, that idea should be discarded before the facts are lined up on paper. The writer's time is a priceless possession, and it must be used to advantage. One cannot afford to devote long hours and great energy to writing a piece that intelligent investigation would have revealed to have little or no chance of sale.

Against Editorial Policy

Nearly all subjects that violate established editorial policies should be discarded. The novice ought not to expect a journal that derives a large part of its revenue from advertising cosmetics to buy an article telling of the danger or uselessness of cosmetics, how to get along with safe and cheaper substitutes, or how to make one's own. In short, editors do not print articles that offend their advertisers. In saying this, the author recognizes the well-known fact that many editors exercise a censorship over the kind and quality of advertising admitted to their columns.

Newspapers and magazines have policies on many subjects. *Parents' Magazine* is a staunch supporter of the American family and the American home. Articles submitted to this office that advocate programs tending to break down either the family or the home would come straight back to the sender. Probably the writer would never learn why the article was rejected. The writer must study his markets, must learn their principles, and must give up the idea of writing articles contrary to that for which they stand.

Fortunately, there are enough periodicals so that many points of view are represented. The wise course to follow is to write upon those policies with which the individual is in accord. Somewhere he will usually find an editor who believes as he does.

Training Steps

1. Select from your list of prospective subjects, prepared after reading Chapters 1 and 2, about five of your best prospects. Go to your city or college library and check them in *Readers' Guide to Periodical Literature*. How many have been dealt with in the past two years?
2. If some have been written about, can you find a different slant? Would an opposite point of view produce an article? If someone tells how to grow a flower garden indoors, can you tell how to grow herbs indoors?

3. Discard from your files any subjects that have grown stale or appear trivial. Don't let deadwood clutter up files.

4. Choose prospective markets for your five subjects. If the content of these magazines is not listed in *Readers' Guide to Periodical Literature*, see if you can find a set of recent issues at the city or college library. Cross off any subjects that prove to be dead, unless you can get a new angle.

5. Are any of the five in the seasonal or anniversary class? If so, they can be used another year if the time is now too short. Don't discard them. Put them back into your files for a later try.

6. Now list your five subjects in order of preference, putting in first place the item most likely not to have been touched upon or discovered by anyone else.

7. Take your favorite magazine, or the one that represents the field in which you work. Decide why the articles they contain were printed. How wide is their appeal? Will your own prospective articles be likely to interest as many readers?

8. Compare two issues of *McCall's* and *Good Housekeeping* for the same month. These are competing magazines. Which prints the more articles? Which has the wider appeal? How do their articles compare for breadth of subject matter?

9. Does *The New York Times Index* indicate use of seasonal material?

10. Study the files of your local newspaper. What kind of subjects does it like to use? Can you parallel any of them?

CHAPTER 5

Slanting for Editors and Readers

Before putting the first word on paper, the writer should take certain analytical steps to make sure that what he proposes to do will meet the requirements and whims of his market or editor. He will do this for both newspapers and magazines. Because greater care is required for the latter, most of the remarks in this chapter will be directed toward writing for magazines. For analysis of special newspaper problems see Chapter 18.

One of the first steps the writer should take is to determine, to the best of his ability, whether his idea is important enough to use. If it is to become a long article, he will query by one or another means. He will proceed to compose the article only if he receives a go-ahead sign from the editor. For his own protection he will make sure that he does not duplicate recent subjects in the same journal.

Splitting the Data

Most magazines expect exclusive rights to articles. Exceptions exist in the religious and trade areas, but duplicate articles or those with close resemblance should be offered to two or more editors only with the knowledge of all concerned. Duplicates may be submitted — if so indicated — to newspapers in different circulation areas. Otherwise, once a writer has marketed an article on a particular subject, he never submits the same facts to a competing magazine. To do so is to take a short cut to an unenviable reputation, and perhaps to blight the writer's entire career.

It is permissible for a writer to present different aspects of the subject to competing or to noncompeting magazines. In the case of noncompeting periodicals, he may even use some of the same facts, but he prepares a different article for each.

A person might visit a modern farm and be impressed by the possibilities for a number of articles. He could well submit to *Successful Farming* an article on how this farm controlled soil erosion and gullying through cover crops and contour plowing. To *National Live Stock Producer* might go a second article on how the farmer used artificial insemination to build up his dairy herd. And a third on how the farmhouse was modernized might sell to *American Home* or *Better Homes and Gardens*. These three examples by no means exhaust the possibilities for items to different markets or to the same market. A keen observer might find a dozen articles in one such spot. It has been done.

Editorial Point of View

Generally, you will find it easier to write for those journals with whose philosophy you are in harmony. As a matter of fundamental honesty, a writer should not contribute an article in which he doesn't believe. To do so is to violate the unwritten ethics of the writing profession. Furthermore, it is likely that articles will lack the ring of honesty and will fail to convince when prepared for a publication in which the writer has no faith. Articles done against one's convictions are unlikely to bring much pleasure or profit in their wake.

VARIATION IN PHILOSOPHY. Magazines and newspapers vary in their philosophy. Some are conservative or ultraconservative; others are middle-of-the-road; while still others are liberal, or radical. The same journal may differ in its degree of liberalism or conservatism on various points. The *Ladies' Home Journal* would probably rank on most subjects as a conservative publication, yet some years ago it broke old traditions to wage a fight against venereal diseases. *Parents' Magazine* is conservative in its handling of many family problems, but in the field of education it reflects the fact that on its board of advisers are to be found some of the leading exponents of so-called progressive education. Many newspapers show similar variations.

LEFT OR RIGHT? In the author's opinion, the *Saturday Evening Post* would be considered conservative; *The Reporter* would be slightly more liberal; *The Nation* and the *New Republic* would be considerably more to the left; also on the left are *The Progressive* and the *New Leader*. To the right of the *Saturday Evening Post* would be many if not most of the women's magazines. Because acceptance of generalizations is dangerous, the intelligent writer must study his publication to know what stand it takes on the issue with which he is concerned. The *Saturday Evening Post*, for example, was a leader in conservation of natural resources. Its early articles on reforestation, reclamation, contour plowing, and the like were highly progressive.

SUPPORTING THE STATUS QUO. The writer, then, will consider the economic, social, and political philosophy of his prospective market. Most American editors — but not all — support private enterprise for private profit, competition in business, and federal regulation of interstate commerce. They believe in the general beneficence of the capitalistic system, and few of them would publish an article that advocated any other system. Some editors support one set of political beliefs; others adhere to something different. One journal will stress a specific treatment for a social problem, and a second — perhaps just as important and well edited — will promote the opposite solution.

Find out what the philosophy of your market is. Don't expect it to use an article that advocates contrary beliefs, or one calling for great modification of its point of view. Instead, find a publication that believes as you do. It will be an easier, quicker market. But don't expect to discover attitudes stated in so many words. You may find them expressed on the editorial pages — if they exist — though they are more likely to be found elsewhere, both in what is and what is not printed.

Attitude toward Reader

Editors differ a great deal in their handling of the reader. They try to reach him through the adoption of certain devices and attitudes. They may assume a friendly, chatty manner of address. This is the customary style of a great many journals. It is similar to the manner in which two well-bred, educated friends might address each other. Good breeding prevents either from assuming greater familiarity than actually exists. There is an element of reserve that reflects the good taste of both.

Notice the manner in which customers are treated by saleswomen in different stores. In the cheaper stores untrained saleswomen may call the customer "dearie," but there is no such familiarity in the exclusive shops. A parallel is to be found in the way magazines and newspapers treat their "customers." The best manner for the writer to take is a friendly one that does not presume too much of an acquaintanceship.

Magazines are generally cheerful in tone, because they are cheerful in outlook. This is not to say that pessimistic articles cannot find their way into print. A magazine may have an optimistic look and still find itself condemning the crime problem and the way lawbreaking is handled. Magazine tone is seldom sarcastic. Sarcasm is left to the lecture platform or to the radio and TV. Nor is the tone frequently ironic, for irony is quite likely to be misunderstood.

Only a few magazines can be said to be wholly critical, and even in these exceptions would be numerous. The *American Mercury* in its early years was as clear an example of the iconoclastic magazines as could readily be found, though in later years it changed its formula. *The Nation* and *New Republic* will take critical articles that otherwise meet their policies. Either might take a highly critical article on advertising in general, though no free-lance writer should expect many of the other magazines or newspapers to do so.

Editorial Taboos

Within the framework of a publication's philosophy are set up certain policies. These form a platform — generally unwritten — upon which the publication stands. Magazine policies include various ideas, concepts, and notions. They are of two types: those favored, and those opposed. Innumerable examples of each type could be cited.

The religious publications naturally bar profane language. The fact is so obvious that the beginning writer should not need to be warned. On the other hand, he might well need to be told that these same magazines do not admit the goody-goody youth to their columns.

Each magazine and newspaper has a list of taboos — those policies that must not be violated. The fact that these taboos exist in the heads of editors rather than in printed lists does not decrease their potency, or lessen the certainty of rejection of articles or stories that violate them.

Earlier it was noted that editors do not offend their advertisers. This is not a criticism of these workers. It is evidence of the application of common sense to everyday economics. These same editors will refuse the use of their columns to those advertisers whose products are known to be unworthy of public favor.

Furthermore, editors do *not* offend any great group among their readers. Antiracial, antireligious, and antisectional articles are generally barred. Let us be specific. You will not find *Look* or *The Saturday Review* attacking any racial or religious group within this country. However, you could assume that either one would print an article on the low quality of Negro education in America, because the inadequacy of educational facilities for Negroes is no reflection upon the Negro.

Offenses against Good Taste

Matters that offend good taste are generally kept out of print, and the free lance will do well to avoid them. From time to time editors do risk offending some of their readers. Such an example is to be found in the action of the *Ladies' Home Journal* in its campaign against venereal diseases. This was a program upon which the magazine embarked after long thought and careful planning, and, no doubt, it was prepared to take some losses in circulation. The lone writer cannot expect to persuade a magazine to begin a campaign, nor is he likely to find a place in one.

Finally, editors will not buy articles that encourage lawbreaking, though markets are numerous for articles on the apprehension and punishment of wrongdoers.

Quality of Writing

Anyone who counsels a writer to submit less than his best gives bad advice. Nevertheless, it is a fact that not all publications offer the same quality of entertainment or information. Most editorial staffs would admit that a few magazines like *Harper's Magazine* and *The Atlantic* are of first-rate quality. And most newspapermen would admit the merits of the *Christian Science Monitor* and *The New York Times*.

The great group of newspapers and general and trade publications falls into a class somewhat below these mentioned above. In still a third group are such publications as the confession magazines, the true detective story magazines, and some of the more sensational Sunday newpaper magazines.

Writing One's Best

The beginning writer should by all means make use of the markets where competition is least keen. He will find them more hospitable and easier to break into than the first-class general markets mentioned earlier, but he should never offer them less than the best writing of which he is capable. As his work improves, he can try the more difficult markets. It is well to point out, however, that first-rate writing is to be found in even the unpretentious journals. They know good writing and are quick to reject slovenly work. But they do not require the highly polished style of the more exclusive publications.

Among the better magazines with simple demands are the juvenile and religious publications. They welcome new contributors, and often give far more help to a novice than he can obtain elsewhere. The necessity for simplicity and objectivity is great, and the free-lance writer actually improves his style by trying to write for them. Some of the country's best writers can be read currently in these publications. Others quite as well known got their start in this market and continued to contribute, because of the benefit to their style, long after they had broken into better-paying markets.

Economic Class of Readers

In many ways the average reader's income determines the nature of an article, and it may also settle negatively the question of whether an article should be written for a certain publication. This is true even when the market buys the type of article under consideration. Let us look at a few examples.

If a writer contemplates doing an article on game rooms — the so-called rumpus rooms — he may write for *Better Homes and Gardens* or for *American Home.* Both are circulated to the same income group; consequently, they are interested in items that involve the same financial outlay for readers. However, neither would purchase an article that involved expenditures beyond the means of the readers.

Perhaps the writer has material on building an unusual and beautiful private swimming pool. The cost is about $25,000.00, which is far too high for readers of these two magazines. The average house and lot owned by their subscribers could not exceed that figure by much, and the building of such a pool would not be practical. Good judgment would suggest that the article be slanted for *House Beautiful* or to *House and Home.*

A number of signs point out the income group in which a publication circulates. Among them are 1. the cost of advertised items; 2. the price of the magazine; 3. the extent of circulation; 4. the quality of paper and illustrations, and 5. the type of subject matter in the articles.

ADVERTISING.   Advertisers are shrewd enough not to advertise merchandise priced beyond the income of the readers of the journal in which their products are presented. The highest priced automobiles, the largest country estates, and the finest in home furnishings are displayed for sale in magazines that circulate in the highest income brackets. Products of modest price may be offered to higher brackets, but the middle income group is the one that represents the greatest market.

PRICE AND CIRCULATION. Price is a good index to reader income. The highest priced magazines generally are bought by the highest income group. The limited number therein tends to put limits on the circulation of magazines that cost 50 cents or more, which is but a fraction of that of periodicals selling at lower prices (*Good Housekeeping* and *McCall's*).

Circulation itself thus becomes a direct guide to whether a magazine has mass appeal (*Good Housekeeping* and *McCall's*), or class appeal (*The Atlantic, Harper's Magazine*). Data from Ayer's annual *Directory* show the great gap between these groups: *Good Housekeeping*, 5,435,000, and *McCall's*, 8,545,000; *The Atlantic*, 285,000, and *Harper's Magazine*, 290,000. Similar differences exist between *Better Homes and Gardens*, 6,582,000, and *American Home*, 3,360,000, on the one hand, and *House Beautiful*, 978,000 on the other. Such differences exist in even highly specialized fields.

ILLUSTRATIONS, PAPER. The quality of illustrations and paper is another guide, though perhaps not so good as circulation or advertisements. The tendency is for mass-circulation periodicals to make use of medium grade paper, and this in turn permits use of only medium fine engraving and color processes. Those magazines which carry fine illustrations extensively use the highest quality of paper. The delicate tones of fine, half-tone engravings cannot be produced on poor or medium grade papers.

TYPE OF ARTICLE. The writer must not overlook the articles that a magazine prints. They are the best guide to what it wants and buys. Most magazines are edited according to a pattern or formula, which the editorial board believes the public wants. In *Redbook Magazine* there is so much fiction, consisting of serials and a number of short stories; so much factual material; so much humor, and so much miscellany. Sometimes in recent years such formulas have changed, usually to admit a greater percentage of articles.

The home-improvement magazines present about the same pattern of information on new house construction, remodelling, decoration, equipment, cooking, landscaping, and gardening year after year. Their continued operation and steady or rising circulation figures prove the success of their formulas, and they fear to change them greatly lest a declining circulation result.

Vocabulary

Magazines are divided into classes within the fields of their interest. There are publications in the fields of agriculture, of home interests, and of science. Within each of these, as well as in many other fields, an attempt is evident to reach different groups that vary in education and experience, as suggested briefly in Chapter 3.

If we examine magazines devoted to the field of science, among the numerous journals we will discover *Popular Science Monthly, Scientific American,* and the *Engineering News-Record.* The language of the last is highly technical and beyond the training of the average writer. The language of *Scientific American* is neither too technical nor too popular. *Popular Science Monthly* comes a step below *Scientific American* in its simplification and popularization and may be said to be more popular than scientific. *Scientific American* is more scientific than popular, while *Engineering News-Record* makes no effort to be popular. A considerable distance beyond these three in popularization is the Sunday magazine, *This Week,* distributed by a number of newspapers.

TECHNICAL TERMS. When the free-lance writer prepares an article for *Engineering News-Record,* he is writing for men of the engineering profession. Unless the writer is a highly trained specialist, he is unlikely to understand problems of engineering as well as his readers do. Except in unuual circumstances, he will not need to explain scientific terms. In writing for *Scientific American,* he writes for a well-educated audience, probably of college level. This audience, like that of the former magazine, is capable of independent thought and of a high degree of technical assimilation. It will not in a great percentage of cases have the specific vocabulary of the trained engineer, and will expect some explanation or definition.

Readers of *Popular Science Monthly* are men of average education; that is, they have somewhat less than a high school education. They will need a complete interpretation of the data, and a full explanation of scientific terms. In fact, only terms in everyday use should be included in articles for this magazine. The writer need not, however, underestimate these readers' ability to think.

EDUCATION VERSUS ENTERTAINMENT. Readers of *This Week Magazine* are in another class. They are more interested in being entertained than in being educated, and they take greater interest in entertainment and less interest in a well-rounded article than readers of the other three magazines cited above.

The writer must have a good idea of how much technique his readers can grasp. He must know how extensive is their vocabulary, and he must know something of their reading habits. These considerations will determine whether his article should be popularized and, if so, to what degree. They will also determine the range of vocabulary, the kind of illustrations, and the choice of anecdotes and incidents.

Typographical Considerations

The field of the writer for popular magazines and newspapers is different from that of the writer of books or of scientific monographs. One of the chief reasons for the difference is the type of audience each writer reaches. The newspaper reader usually gives material but fleeting attention. He is seeking brief entertainment. The reader of fiction may likewise desire entertainment, but generally he is less hurried. These facts influence the style of the writer of popular articles.

COLUMN LIMITATIONS. Still another factor is the narrow columns to be found in most magazines and newspapers. Scientific reading tests have proved that columns can be printed too wide for easy reading. The human eye tires quickly from pursuing small type across wide columns. Also, it tires from paragraphs that are too long. Part way through a long paragraph it gives up the effort and drops to the beginning of the next paragraph, a fact that influences writers to keep sentences and paragraphs short.

AVOIDING MONOTONY. The writer must study the length of sentences and paragraphs in the magazines for which he wishes to contribute. It is better for him to err on the short side than on the long. He will vary the length of sentences and paragraphs for the sake of avoiding monotonous style, but no one can lay down exact limits for either. Too many short sentences give a staccato or telegraphic pattern that is undesirable, except to create special effects.

Probably the average sentence length for general magazines should be about 17 words; for newspapers, 15 words. Confusion sets in shortly after this point is passed. Paragraph length might average about three sentences, though some paragraphs and sentences may be no longer than a single word. Each sentence and paragraph must do the task intended for it, as simply and briefly as possible.

Article length is important. The free lance should make a careful estimate of the lengths used by his market, finding the maximum and minimum. It is wiser to approach the minimum than the maximum, because more short than long articles are used. In the case of an unknown writer, risk to the editor is less on a short contribution. Also the writer's investment of time and energy is kept to a minimum.

Length of Titles

A good title is a great help in selling an article. The writer must outdo himself on this point. But the title must be of the kind used by the publication. If the magazine has a limit of five words, then the writer should be guided by that limit.

The tone of the title should follow the tone of the magazine. If the editor seems to like breezy titles or those that play on words, then the writer may set his fancy to work on something suitable. If *Modern Bride* likes this type, send it an article entitled "Early to Wed." This, incidentally, suggests what might be the beginning of an article on teen-age marriages.

What of the Subtitle?

Whether or not to write a subtitle is a somewhat different matter from composing the title. All magazines use titles, but many do not use subtitles. Experience and judgment must settle this point for the writer. Unquestionably, it gives him one more chance to sell the magazine on the contents of the article.

On the other hand, indiscriminate inclusion of this unit might suggest that the writer is not familiar with magazine practices. However, since it is an easy matter for an editor to strike out the item, it is difficult to believe any article would be rejected for bearing a subtitle. If used, the subtitle should follow the pattern set by the magazine in length, capitalization, and tone.

Editors' Changes

One must expect editors to change titles, subtitles, or subheads as they see fit, particularly on pieces submitted to the newspapers. These items must fit into the pattern made by other articles in the same issue. No free-lance writer can know in advance what these will be. Also, staff members like to put their own stamp upon an article, and at times do it by writing a new title. A title that is obviously a good one is not likely to be changed.

Illustrations

If your market uses illustrations, then by all means supply them if you can. Many an article is rejected because of lack of illustrations. On the other hand, do not offer them to publications that do not use illustrative material. Illustrations should conform to magazine or news-paper practices and should be of sufficient size and quality to create a favorable impression. Poor illustrations can kill a good article.

CUT-LINES. Be sure to write cut-lines or captions for each illustra-tion. All newspapers and magazines use one or the other. Some maga-zines and some newspapers occasionally use both. The caption is the brief title that appears over the picture. Cutlines usually appear at the side or below. They are longer than titles, and frequently attempt explanation not possible in a title. The style of cut-lines and captions prepared by the free-lance writer should be as near as possible to that of the periodical he has in mind. This frequently saves a laborious effort by the editor. Also the contributor is in a far better position than the editor to know what is in the illustration.

PAGE SIZE. The size of page is an important item to note, because it is a determining factor in the number of illustrations used. The smaller the page, usually the shorter the article. Small pages normally mean smaller illustrations, affecting the type (but not the size) of illus-tration to be submitted. Bigger pages allow for better dramatization through larger and more powerful illustrations. The beginning writer should acquire a working knowledge of how photographs and other illustrations are handled by the art and engraving staffs.[1]

Back Files

In examining a magazine to discover what subjects are wanted and how they should be treated, the writer should make a thorough study of the back files. In the case of a monthly, he should read the table of contents for a score or more issues; of a weekly, he should take one issue a month for two or three years. He should examine carefully the articles that interest him. This scrutiny will give him a general idea of what he should do, though slavish imitation of style and development is not desirable. He should let the printed contents set the general pat-tern; then bring in dialogue, analysis, and anecdote that are original.

Only after he has made such an analysis of the magazine is the writer ready to begin. The more carefully he has made the examination,

---

[1]For list of works on this subject, see Chapter 22.

the greater are his chances of selling the finished article. Hours of careful study are required the first time this analysis is performed on a particular magazine, but the second effort requires only a fraction of the initial effort. Finally, the writer should keep up with current issues of all his prospective markets. This exercise should be made a fixed part of his writing program. After the original study, a few hours a month will take care of the brush-up — a period that the writer will find to be highly profitable.

Training Steps

1. Take two consecutive issues of *American Home*. Select five articles of the longer variety from each. Make an accurate estimate of the word length of each. What are the average length and the range of length for this type of article in this magazine?
2. Count the number of words in every fifth paragraph in each article. What is the average paragraph length?
3. Count the number of words in twenty sentences selected at random from each article. What is the average sentence length? Be prepared to apply your findings to your own future writings for magazines in this field.
4. Now examine several issues of *Better Homes and Gardens*. Is there a definite difference in article length? paragraph length? or sentence length?
5. Read portions of an article in a magazine of your own choice. What is the tone? Is it aloof? or friendly? Is it chatty and informal? or distant and formal?
6. Obtain copies of *Harper's Bazaar* and *Vogue*. Do you find differences between the style of these magazines and that of the two magazines above?
7. Examine an issue of *Successful Farming*. Do you find evidences that the special problems of its readers have been studied? Are there any how-to-do articles that would be of little use to the average farmer?
8. Do you find articles *anywhere* that offend general good taste or public morals?
9. Are there articles that would be offensive to a particular religion, race, or nationality?
10. Are any of the articles likely to offend the advertisers?
11. What difference in appeal do you find between *House Beautiful* and *American Home*?
12. Can you tell anything about the income group to which a magazine appeals by looking quickly through it? What? Be specific.
13. Do the aviation magazines differ materially in style from those in the popular mechanics field?

14. How does the sentence and paragraph length of your local daily differ from that of *Atlantic Monthly?*
15. Compare the tone of the Sunday magazine of *The New York Times* and *This Week.* Which is more familiar? Which has longer sentences and paragraphs? Which is more sensational?

CHAPTER 6

T

Writing the Short Item or Filler

The best way for the novice to begin learning the techniques of article writing and to break into print is to start with the short or filler. There are many kinds and qualities of shorts, but the more advanced are as difficult to handle as the fully-developed article. Until some progress has been made, the beginning writer should attempt the specialized short that appears in such magazines as *Pageant, Reader's Digest, McCall's,* and *Good Housekeeping.*

The so-called elementary short used by the homecraft magazines, many trade journals, and newspapers is the most useful training unit for several reasons. 1. Every individual can find a number of such items within his knowledge if he consults with himself. 2. He can pick them up readily from friends and acquaintances. 3. He can find in published matter countless items that can be rewritten for other markets. 4. He has a wide market at hand. 5. He can learn the appropriate style quickly. 6. His investment of time in each item is small, and mailing costs are light. 7. He can use the same structure for the short or filler that he uses for the ordinary paragraph or explantion or development.

In many ways, every paragraph can be said to be a short article. A well-organized long article consists of a series of these short articles, joined by linking words and phrases, or sentences that tie the parts together.

Analysis of every well-written article will reveal the underlying structure upon which the writer has built the superstructure of words and ideas. Absence of formal signs of an outline does not mean that none was used. Experienced writers generally can dispense with most of the formality of putting outlines on paper. But you may be sure that some process of arrangement has been going on in the mind of the writer — a process of which the writer was well aware.

The ultrashort paragraph, the narrow column, and the desire to make magazine and newspaper articles appear readable and typographically attractive have led many writers to break up their paragraphs into smaller units than those generally used two or three decades ago. At times this has been done without reference to the structure of the paragraph. More properly it has been accomplished by making an additional paragraph of such a natural subdivision as a final emphatic sentence.

Topic Sentences

Teachers of English have made use of the device of topic sentences plus subsequent elaboration as a means of developing unified paragraphs. These topic sentences stated a fact or a conclusion, or expressed a point of view. It was customary to begin with such a statement, and to make all the following sentences within the same paragraph explain or elaborate the idea expressed in the first sentence.

In Chapter 6 the author proposes to use this method as the most logical way of preparing short items for print. And it is upon such an approach to writing that he bases the statement that anyone who can learn to write simple English can learn to write and sell certain types of articles.

Style of Short Articles

The general style of the short item is much the same as that of longer articles. It should be free from useless words and sentences. Extra-careful pruning will eliminate what is unnecessary. When editing these items, ask what is accomplished by each word, or by each sentence. If the sentence element is not important, try leaving it out. Sentences and paragraphs should be shorter, perhaps, than in long articles. The sentences are terse and exact — to the point. *The first sen-*

tence must state the main idea to be explained or illustrated. Later sentences merely add the details or make specific applications. If the item consists of a single sentence, make the first five words or the first line give the gist of the idea.

Avoid long words and technical words, unless they are explained. Use the common, everyday words on the tongue of everyone. Because the result will be good grammar, it will most likely be understod by the mass of readers.

Item One

Examine the following sentence.

1. An ordinary pocketknife makes a good candleholder when no other is available.

This is simple English. There is nothing startling about it, nothing difficult, nothing magical. Anyone could have written it. Many could, perhaps, improve upon it. For let it be stated here that *there are countless ways of setting down on paper the same general idea.* In the sentence above one could have dropped the last five words and still have had a clear meaning.

Let us write some more sentences about this pocketknife.

2. Open the knife with the large blade fully extended.
3. A smaller blade should be half extended.
4. Thrust the large blade into a tree trunk, tent pole, or other upright with the small blade straight up.
5. Push the candle down upon the point of the small blade.

Inspect these last four sentences. Obviously, each could have been written differently. Yet they do well enough, and they are so simple a sixth-grader could write any one of them. Now let us put them together.

An ordinary pocketknife makes a good candleholder when no other is available. Open the knife with the large blade fully extended. A smaller blade should be half extended. Thrust the large blade into a tree trunk, tent pole, or other upright with the small blade straight up. Push the candle down upon the point of the small blade.

Would you recognize these 57 words as worthy of a place in a magazine of national circulation? Are they an article? Yes, indeed, this simple paragraph is worth publishing, and it is an article if we include shorts in our definition of articles. Actually, it was published by a leading homecraft magazine, and it was the first work of a student writer.

The first sentence was our old friend, the topic sentence. The other four explained the "how" of the first. Together they make a five-sentence how-to-do-something article.

Item Two

Examine the following sentences.

1. Owners of wooden boats should not overcaulk their boats.
2. Overcaulking — that is, pushing the seams too tight — will pull the screws, and also cause the boat to leak.
3. A small, even space should be left to allow for the natural swelling of the wood.
4. The boat will be more serviceable, last longer, and be dry throughout the season if caulking is not done excessively.

The first sentence is the topic sentence. The second tells the result if the advice of the first is not followed. The third tells how. The fourth affirms the advantage of the step explained in the third. The last three sentences are somewhat repetitious, but generally tend to explain the topic sentence. However, a simpler explanation would have been better.

Item Three

1. Pearls are more easily restrung when placed on a pleated piece of material or cardboard, according to size of bead.
2. This prevents them from rolling around and getting mixed in size.

The first sentence is the topic sentence; the second is a statement of why the step mentioned in the first should be taken. An item such as this can be written half a hundred different ways. Its 29 words might have been stretched to several hundred. Or it might have been cut about one half. Generally, the more condensed a short is, the more likely it is to be purchased. The magazines that buy such items do not pay so much per word, but according to the merit of the idea. The rate generally figures at from five to fifteen cents a word.

Item Four

1. If the ends of a chest or dresser become marred and unsightly, paint the entire piece an attractive color and cover the ends with wallpaper to match that used in the room.

Note that in Item Four our entire piece consists of but a single sentence. This is cutting down writing to its simplest terms. Yet the item is good writing. It accomplishes its purpose in simple, direct English. It is perfectly clear and well suited to the readers it seeks to reach. What form of writing can do more?

You have probably noted that the four brief items above presented patterns of increasing simplicity. Item One was composed of five sentences; Item Four, of only one. The beginning writer can easily believe that a salable article may consist of as few as five sentences. But he may hesitate to believe it can be composed of but a single sentence.

Yet, each of the four examples cited above was the work of a beginner. Each was the first piece of writing done for sale by the student, and each was sold to a nationally-known magazine. Two were bought by *Popular Mechanics Magazine,* and two by *Popular Science Monthly.*

The fact that items like these four can be sold holds out to the average aspirant much hope for breaking into print. The reader should remember that each of the four was the result of a first attempt to do something for publication. Their writers had no special training for writing, though each had had a good general education. Examples such as the above could be multiplied a great many times. Later on the author will cite full-length articles done as first efforts, which sold on their first trip to market.

Why Write Short Items

The production of the short items affords a great deal of good training and the beginning writer should not scorn to do them.

To handle these items well, the writer must study the markets, particularly the magazines and syndicates. Suppose he begins with *Popular Science Monthly.* He examines it thoroughly and, in the process, becomes acquainted with the table of contents, staff, nature of the advertising, and the general quality, character, and method of display of the content. He not only learns about this magazine as a market for short items, but also as a market for full-length articles. He should garner a number of suggestions for similar articles for this or some other magazines.

Many a subject discussed in *Popular Science Monthly* will hold possibilities for articles that might appear in other magazines. Consider this example: *Popular Science Monthly* prints an illustrated article on the invention of a huge, portable machine that can pour a complete concrete home in twenty-four hours. It takes little imagination to see that the subject should be of interest to magazines like *Better Homes and Gardens.* A completely different article, properly slanted, should interest *House and Home, Progressive Architecture,* and other magazines, as well as individual newspapers or the syndicates.

The writer will not stop with *Popular Science Monthly,* but will go on to examine the other dozen or so magazines in the same field — all of which use these short items. He will branch out into such other fields as the home magazines and trade publications. The latter group is an almost insatiable user of shorts. He should also study the Sunday newspapers, some of which are first-rate markets.

In the process of this study the writer will learn much that has little to do with the markets for shorts. He will increase his knowledge of markets in general. He will become acquainted with outlets for all manner of articles. He will sharpen his point of view on his own specialty. He will learn to recognize prospective subjects at an early date. In effect, he will become a more experienced and a better writer than he could without this study.

Writing the short article affords excellent training in the handling of effective grammar. It teaches simplicity, which is one of the fundamentals of good style in any kind of writing. It shows the necessity for *condensation,* generally considered a requisite throughout the magazine and newspaper fields. And it forces the writer to strive for *clarity,* because most short items deal with facts, which the writer must explain to his readers.

Should a short item come back from one market, there are usually a number of others that might take it without further slanting. The writer may wish to retype it when he prepares his new envelopes, but this task will require only a few moments. His investment of time, effort, and stamps will not add up to a great deal. The encouragement a young writer gets from selling such items will more than offset his rejections.

Working with Ideas

IDEAS IN THE RAW. Every professional writer has had the experience of seeing in print articles that he could have written. "Why didn't I write that?" he asks himself. The reason is that he didn't recognize the merits of the idea in its raw state.

A book such as this might devote an entire chapter to the subject "The Magic of Print." Not only practice makes perfect. Print makes perfect, too. Words put into cold print have a magic quality. They assume a power beyond themselves. They pass for truth when they may be guesswork. They have a roseate hue in print that they never had otherwise. The magic of the written word is great, indeed, and for some of its power there is no accounting.

Good print makes plain what otherwise might be ignored. That is one of the satisfactions a writer gets out of his craft. He becomes a self-appointed Columbus, bringing new (if tiny) worlds to the attention of those too busy to explore for themselves.

But writers must drill themselves in the techniques of finding and recognizing article material. They must question every experience of their waking — yes, and sleeping — hours. Everything they hear, every thought, every act may be the beginning of an article. They must eat article writing, dream about it, and live it. They must study every friend and every new acquaintance for his possibilities as magazine or newspaper material. Every newspaper they read may hold a first-rate idea. But ideas will best be found when they are sought by a writer who is looking for them.

THE STUFF ARTICLES ARE MADE OF.   In the next few paragraphs this book presents some examples of the ideas from which short items are made. Would you recognize them as being salable?

A. Colorless nail polish can be used to protect the edge of shoe soles, shoe heels, and metal objects.
B. Adhesive tape has a variety of uses.
C. A bit of screen will protect household drains from lint on wash day.
D. Maps make attractive wall decorations.
E. Vinegar can be used to dissolve old glue.
F. Old walnut picture frames can be converted into useful footstools.

These six items are typical of the ideas that a person may discover in his own house, or in the homes of friends and acquaintances. When driven by need, the average individual can invent or devise solutions to many of his difficulties. Probably each of the six suggestions mentioned above has been "invented" a thousand times by different individuals, each devising his own solution independently of the others. Probably not one of the thousands of amateur Edisons even thought of telling a magazine or newspaper audience about his device.

To the average person the writing would appear more difficult than the creation of the device itself. Nevertheless, no writer should hesitate, because they are well-known to himself, to put into article form his own inventions, and others he comes across. The author has watched scores of such items sell when every reasoned judgment predicted that they would not. While it should not take ten minutes to do any one of the six items above, if it does, the minutes will have been spent in creative writing. And they will be followed by days of pleasant anticipation, which in turn may bring a check.

The Finished Idea

Now let us see how the ideas will look when put in manuscript form without titles.

A-1. A thin coat of colorless nail polish may be applied to the outer edge of the sole of a white shoe to provide a smooth, hard surface from which surplus white polish may be wiped after the shoe has been polished.

A-2. Colorless nail polish applied to the dark heels of white shoes protects heels from scuffing. Additional coats may be applied as often as needed.

A-3. Metal lamps, candlesticks, trays, and other treasured pieces can be protected from rust and tarnish by applying a coat of colorless nail polish.

B-1. When waste fats are stored in tin cans, a tab of adhesive tape will protect the fingers from cuts and burns.

B-2. Strips of adhesive tape sewed sticky side out upon an old glove are excellent for removing lint from woolen clothes.

C-1. A small piece of wire screening placed in the drain of an electric washer or in the rinse tubs will catch the lint and prevent clogging of sewer connections.

D-1. Maps make attractive wall decorations. Use maps like those supplied by *National Geographic Magazine*. Coat the back with glue, and apply one layer of cheesecloth for reinforcing. Fit an attractive molding around the map, and tint the molding to fit the color scheme of the room. The map itself should be shellacked for protection.

E-1. Vinegar can be used to dissolve hardened glue on old furniture when it is desirable to take the pieces apart. The vinegar will not discolor the wood.

F-1. The deep, old-fashioned walnut picture frames can be converted to first-rate footstools. Cut an oval-shaped board to fit inside the frame. The upholstery fits over this board and inside the frame. Add four short wooden legs about 8 inches long and stain to match the walnut.

There are now nine items based on the six ideas. The process of composing any one of them should not have taken longer than ten minutes. The first eight were purchased by magazines in the popular mechanics field. The ninth has at least fifteen possible markets.

Hunting Marketable Shorts

While short items may be turned up in one's own home or in the home of friends, the most prolific source are shops, stores, banks, manufacturing plants, and other businesses of all kinds. Not only are these items more numerous in the aggregate among such places, but also the total possible markets are greater. For every trade and business there are from a half dozen to a score of ready markets. Most of these pay from two dollars to ten dollars per item for shorts of 25 to 100 words. For somewhat longer items up to 400 words, the rate is about one to fifteen cents a word.

Thousands of these short items remain undiscovered, or perish by going out of date because writers do not know they can be sold. If you will go with me on a ninety-minute walking tour through my home town, I shall point out a score or so of items that could be sold to the proper trade journals.

1. Our first store is a drugstore. The proprietor has a huge sign across the entire front above the window. He has it repainted every second month because the freshness and smartness of the sign suggest that his store possesses the same qualities. Market: Retail drug magazines.
2. Across the street is a florist who makes many of his own vases and decorative figurines. This is good for a short or for a long article in a florist's journal.
3. On the next corner is a restaurateur who is opening his second restaurant in the same block. The fact is good for a short news item or a longer "success" article for the restaurant journals.
4. A second drugstore continued its home delivery service when help was scarce by organizing a corps of neighborhood boys and girls to handle the task. This item has the same markets as No. 1.
5. Continuing to the central business district, we find a bank that has bought an adjoining parking lot and is putting up a combined office building and parking garage for use of its customers. Market: A banker's journal.
6. The same bank gives free use of its front windows a. to local concerns for display of their products, and b. to townspeople for

display of their hobbies. The main idea goes to the banker's journal, but a. goes to the manufacturer's trade journal, and b. goes to the magazine *Antiques*. Here are four items at one step. A little digging would uncover material for a long article.

7. Across the street is a pet shop. The proprietor has put in a new feed department. Market: *The Feed Age*.

8. Two blocks up the street a sporting goods store has moved one block to new quarters. An item for *The Sporting Goods Dealer*.

9. On the main street a ladies' shoe store has moved to new quarters with doubled floor space. A natural for *Boot and Shoe Recorder*.

10. A department store is capitalizing on St. Patrick's Day by advertising a collection of Irish pipes. Market: Any one of many retail journals.

11. A toy shop has a novel window display that would interest department store journals.

12. A florist is moving into an abandoned but attractive gasoline station. Market: A florist's journal.

13. A select women's wear department store has put in the latest type windows and swinging plate-glass doors. Market: The department store journals.

14. A jewelry store has opened up a new department for antiques. This item goes to a jewelry journal.

15. A hardware store window shows a new type portable sanding machine equipped with a dust bag like a vacuum cleaner. It is made locally. Market: The popular mechanics field.

16. A second department store window is advertising coffee by showing a historical collection of coffeepots. Market: The department store journals. Also a good many other places.

17. A baked goods store in an area where there are two other similar stores sells more goods than the other two combined. Why? The answer is either a short or long article for a baking journal.

18. Another department store has installed a self-service shoe department. It is an item for the department store journals.

19. A book store has its windows full of art work from the public schools. Books for children and books on art are prominent in the background. This goes to a book trade magazine.

20. A supermarket has installed a number of old-fashioned grocery store devices, such as pickle and olive barrels, because its customers like to see them. This item is salable to the grocery trade journals. The same store has a complete old-time country store set up in a special wing — nothing for sale.

21. In a certain beauty salon at 3:30 each afternoon customers' orders for refreshments are taken. While the customers wait for their hair to dry, they are served with sodas, tea, or "cokes," according to their orders. Market: *American Hairdresser.*

22. Ex-servicemen are attracted to one large department store by an offer of a free photograph and an 8 x 10 enlargement upon showing their discharge papers. Market: department store journal.

23. A new bar and grill opened up with a doorway that simulates a huge brass keyhole. Curious spectators pause to gaze inside, and are attracted to enter. Market: *Restaurant Equipment Dealer.*

24. The most attractive bookstore in town has a real fireplace that burns wood in cold weather. Around it are easy chairs and benches, and nearby are stacks of books. Customers are rested and warmed while they decide what to buy. Market: *Saturday Review.*

25. The jewelry business is going the way of the drug trade. An enterprising jewelry store is opening up an electrical appliance department. Entrance is through the jewelry division. Market: *National Jeweler.*

26. Using the phrase "Out of This World" to advertise its hats, a hat shop has decorated its windows with characters out of Oriental fairy tales. Market: *Hats*

27. For the "teen about town" young women, a department store has decorated a special department with high school banners and the like, and has installed a "coke" machine, a juke box, and easy chairs. Market: Department store journal.

28. The leading music store has devoted its windows and showcases to photographs of composers on the faculty at Syracuse University. Copies of their books, music scores, and records are displayed. Market: *Music Trades.*

29. A chain store group is opening a local branch of the "Three Sisters." Market: *Chain Store Age.*

30. In a leading hotel, murals made from very old photographs show Syracuse as it was years ago. The "Old Syracuse" room is the haunt of old-timers. Market: *New York History.*

Illustrated Shorts

The illustrated short will nearly always be easier to sell than the unillustrated item. Some magazines will not buy unillustrated matter. Among them is *Mechanix Illustrated,* which has long been a good market for the free-lance writer. *Popular Mechanics Magazine* and *Popular*

Science Monthly will buy items without illustration, but prefer them illustrated. The items on pages 63 to 64 were sold to these publications in an illustrated state. Those capable of illustration should have been so treated by the writers, though in these cases they *were* illustrated by the magazines.

Illustrated items may be of two kinds: 1. articles of a paragraph or more, illustrated with one or more photographs or drawings; 2. articles consisting of one or more illustrations carrying short but complete explanations in the form of cut-lines.

Illustrations should be slanted to the market. Some markets prefer photographs; others will use drawings, charts, or photographs, or a combination. The details of illustrating an article are set forth in Chapter 11 and need not be anticipated here. The writer will examine one or more — preferably more — copies of his proposed markets to see exactly what they do use. He will make his article conform as closely as possible to the length used in the market of his choice. It is wiser to aim at the minimum rather than at the maximum length. Space is more easily found for shorter items, and the investment is less should they become valueless before they can be put into print.

In many cases the free-lance writer can procure illustrations without cost to himself. When stores move to new quarters, enlarge their premises, or create an unusual display — perhaps in a window — they are quite likely to call in a commercial photographer to record the event. If so, the writer may be able to obtain a photograph from the store by explaining why he wants it. Or the local newspaper may have taken one for its own use. By acting immediately, the writer can usually get one at little or no cost.

PHOTOGRAPHIC ILLUSTRATION. Photograph illustration is best for several reasons. 1. The photograph is proof positive of the existence of the item discussed. 2. It shows proportions and relationships in a way that cannot be done by drawings. 3. A good photograph is easier to reproduce than a good drawing. 4. It gives the editors more detail than a drawing, even when a drawing will eventually be used. 5. It is likely to be more striking in quality and more likely to sell the idea to the editors than a drawing.

GRAPHIC ILLUSTRATION. Drawings have some advantages over photographs. It is easier to show dimensions on them than on photographic prints. And when, occasionally, the writer cannot obtain a photograph, a drawing is the only substitute. Also, the so-called ghosted drawing, which shows interior as well as exterior, is superior for some purposes.

The beginner will be tempted to say, "I can't draw." The answer to this statement is that it is unnecessary to be a good draftsman. Except in unusual cases, a magazine will not use and does not want free-lance drawings in its columns. But the magazine does want sketches that will guide its own artists. It does not expect expert work from the amateur, though the better the drawing, the more likely is the article to sell. Generally, the writer can draw well enough to direct staff workers. Or the free lance may find it possible to get a friend or acquaintance to make a few drawings for him. Sometimes a single illustration is all that is required.

Do not allow your lack of skill as a draftsman to prevent you from becoming a successful writer. A number of substitutes can be found for drafting skill. It is the merit of the idea that counts most in these short items — not the way they are written, nor the illustrations provided by the writer.

Headlines for Shorts

When the short consists of a photograph or drawing with a few words of explanation, it probably will not require a headline. However, in this case the cut-lines should be so written as to take the place of the headline. That is, the first few words should be written with consummate care. Each word should be vital. Together the group should tell the entire story. These few words must sell the editor on your idea. If they don't interest him, the rest probably won't. Editors decide by their own reactions to an article whether their readers will be interested in it. To sell an article, however small, you must first interest the editor. Eliminate all unnecessary words from cut-lines. Confine them to vivid, specific words.

Headlines should be no longer than those used by the market. If the headlines are designed to fit the space they may later occupy and are otherwise worthy, they are likely to be kept. While editors usually write their own headlines, they welcome those that do not require rewriting. Get a verb in every headline if you can. Use vivid adjectives and live-wire nouns. Make the headlines tell why your items are interesting or helpful. Keep them short.

Here are some headlines that might have been written for the four items beginning on page 58.

> Item One: Pocketknife Makes Good Candle Holder
> Item Two: Overcaulking Ruins Boats

Item Three: Cardboard Helps Restring Pearls
Item Four: Wallpaper Improves Old Dresser

In each case the headline tells the story. The editor can judge from it whether sufficient readers of his magazine would be interested in it to pay him to make the purchase. Each item will have a slightly different audience. Few items, indeed, will interest all readers. The best an editor can do is to give his followers a variety of reading and hope that they will find enough therein to keep them returning to his columns.

Don't Tell All

If you will turn back to the series of items that begins on page 63, you will note that the same basic idea has been used in three different items: Colorless nail polish has been utilized as a protective agent in a new role. Instead, however, of presenting in one short all possible uses of the polish, the writer has written a separate item for each new use. He was paid as much for each one as he would have been for a single item that combined them all.

It takes some judgment to know when to split such items. Writers should beware of giving too little for their money either through cutting down or padding out. Either thins the offering. On the other hand, he is a foolish writer who pours two articles into one when each might have been sold separately.

Locating Trade Magazines

Only a few of the trade magazines are to be found on the news-stands. You may find a few in your local city library or in college or business school libraries. The best way to obtain them is to borrow them from subscribers. Your department store manager will have copies of *Department Store Journal* or *Department Store Economist* in his office, and will be glad to let you study them. The druggist will have *American Druggist* or *Drug Topics*. Your florist probably subscribes to *Florists' Review* or *Flower and Garden Magazine*. Most of these can be studied in the shop that takes them. If unavailable there, get the address from a market guide, and write for sample copies. Pay, if you have to, of course.

The writer eventually will specialize on contributing to a limited number of publications — this means in a very few fields of interest. He will also become acquainted with the sources of ideas. Store owners, department managers, and window trimmers must become his friends. He will call on them again and again. Keeping these facts in mind, the young writer will understand why it is possible occasionally to borrow and examine the journals to which they subscribe.

Training Steps

1. Rewrite the following short sold to a national magazine by a student writer. (*a*) Eliminate unnecessary sentences, if any. (*b*) Strike out useless words. (*c*) Rearrange if necessary.

    Film spools discarded after the films have been exposed make useful cores to hold bits of string and cord. They are especially useful in holding lengths of ribbon, because the ribbon is held flat and taut. Most of the creases thus disappear after a time. A rubber band can be used to hold the ribbon flat.

2. Rewrite Item Three on page 59 so that all the necessary facts are included in the single sentence. Is it now more, or less, easily understood than in its original form?

3. Take the six items from page 62. Write your own shorts. Time yourself to see how long it takes to produce such items. Compare your versions with those in this book.

4. Send yourself on a walk about town. Do you see anything unique, new, strange, or different? If it interests you, it will interest others. Write it up for the appropriate magazine.

5. Study carefully the long list of items beginning on page 64. Do any of these ideas suggest other items to you? If so, write them down now. Then go on a fact-gathering trip. Get the facts, and write them for the correct markets.

6. The ideas beginning on page 64 are not salable in this form. Study No. 2. What facts are needed to complete this item?

7. Examine the entire list. How many items would be improved by photographic illustration? by drawings or charts?

8. For how many items could you provide a rough drawing if photographs were not obtainable?

9. Study No. 10, page 65. Can you see how this item might be adapted to the window displays of a tobacco shop? Look through a market guide. Are there any journals for tobacconists?

10. Make a list of the items found on our joint tour. Go to the best available libraries. Get out the appropriate magazines. How would these magazines have handled the items that naturally fall in their field?

11. Do any of the magazines use date lines similar to those that head newspaper stories? Example: SYRACUSE, N. Y., The Blank Shoe Store, of 432 S. Salina Street, etc. Note the magazines that do or do not use such date lines.

12. Study a week's issues of your local newspaper. How many "tips" are there for short features about local concerns? Rewrite three of these, each for a different market. Are additional facts needed?

13. Call on your local newspaper editors. Find out whether they will buy from you shorts based on items picked up in your rambling about town.
14. If your local paper has a Sunday edition, investigate possibilities of a weekly column based on a group of these shorts.

CHAPTER 7

How and When to Query

Every professional writer knows that he does his best work when he has a definite market in mind. No two reader audiences are alike. Magazines differ particularly in the educational level and the income group to which they seek to appeal. The story or article that may be a credit to *The Atlantic* usually will fail to meet the tastes of the editors of *True* or *Good Housekeeping.* Consequently, it is a mistake to write an article aimed at all markets in general. The writer should not sit down and merely pen an article. This is like going into the woods with a gun to fire into the trees, hoping some creature will be in front of the charge and thus be bagged. A hunter goes to a certain area with *selected* ammunition to shoot a specific *type* of game. In selling his articles a writer is very much in the position of the hunter.

Since the above is generally true, how foolish it is for a writer to do an article for a magazine or newspaper that is in no position to buy his offering! The argument has been used that if the free-lance writer does submit a few articles, he will sell some that otherwise might not have been sold. Again the writer is like the hunter. When he goes into the woods, he ought to know whether he goes for squirrel, grouse or deer.

Writers usually will conserve time, energy, and finances if they query before they begin their articles. While an editor's reaction may be sought by telephone or personal visit — either procedure may be highly desirable where opportunity permits — this chapter restricts itself to the written query, which is most frequently used in connection with writing for magazine editors.

The written query is merely a letter that asks an editor if he would care to look at an article that some writer contemplates doing — all without obligation to the editor. The query is not a request for an order. No editor will buy unseen an article from a writer about whom he knows little or nothing. But he will frequently tell the query writer to go ahead and submit the article in question. And this implies that the subject is attractive to the editor.

When to Query

What are the circumstances that lead a free lance to send a query to an editor? Perhaps they shape up like this: 1. when the market is strictly limited; 2. when the writer will have to spend considerable time in research or travel; 3. when there is noteworthy expense involved; 4. when other income must be forfeited while the article is being prepared; 5. when the possibility is great that some one else might do the article before the writer finishes his own version; 6. and when time to get the article into print is short.

Many an article has but one or two possible markets. Where, for instance, would you sell an article on the falsities of certain kinds of advertising? If and when the market is restricted, the writer cannot afford to gamble a week or two weeks of time on the possibility that some editor *may* want it. The writer must know that — with few exceptions — the magazine's columns are not already closed to his subject.

Professional writers may invest from two to six weeks' time in an article, particularly when travel is necessary. The sums of money spent during this period may run into several hundred dollars. No writer can afford to make this investment of time, energy, and money unless he has not only a nod from the editor but also a definite commitment. The writer's chief commodity for sale is his time. He will not dispose of it without careful forethought. Nor will he give up other sure income to take a "flier" on a possible sale to a market unacquainted with his plans.

Articles are sometimes inspired by conditions or circumstances that are obvious to many. Subjects of this sort are said to be "in the air." The idea of writing about them is likely to occur to a number of writers simultaneously. When a writer decides to do an article of this type, he ought to learn whether his prospective editor has contracted for or already purchased something on the subject.

Another time when the writer should query is when the article must get into print quickly, or lose its value. This may be the case with anniversary or seasonal articles. The facts may have been unknown to the writer sufficiently far enough in advance to permit leisurely development of the article. Generally, magazines contract for seasonal articles far ahead, or have a staff member do them. If a writer uncovers something of pressing importance — particularly if he has a "scoop" on the facts — he should reach his market at once. Monthly magazines may be of little or no help in such cases, though the weekly general magazines or the newsweeklies may be glad to get the facts. The newspapers and syndicates are of more help to writers who have uncovered material that must be put into type in a hurry. If necessary, these agencies can get items into print within a few hours.

When Not to Query

When the writer is dealing in shorts he need not use the query. The investments of time and energy in the query are hardly less than those in the short item. While the query is being written, the item itself can be produced and sent out. Furthermore, it is not worth the editor's time to answer such a query, and the writer's judgment should lead him to protect the editor on this point. Again, the query supposes that the writer has something to sell. He must be able to produce an article, or he should not write the query. Until the writer has demonstrated that he can turn out a satisfactory article, he may defer using the query. The success of a short will be some indication of his ability to write salable long articles.

How to Query

The length of query depends upon the subject and the tastes of the editor — if the writer knows them. It should reflect his best writing ability, because it is a sample of his literary ability. An outline one page in length can be included to show the proposed content and how the article is to be developed. Finally, a first page can also be sent, complete with title (and subtitle, if used by the market), a strong, interesting introduction, and a carefully thought out, logical development in later paragraphs.

WHAT NOT TO DO.   1. Do not write long queries. Try to conserve the editor's time. 2. Do not bring in irrelevant matter of any kind. To do so is to waste precious space and perhaps your opportunity to give the editor a good impression of your ability. 3. Do not boast of your knowledge of the subject at hand. 4. Do not send a query that looks unbusinesslike. 5. Do not be flippant, long-winded, or exhibit poor taste.

WHAT TO DO.   1. Use standard 8½" X 11" typewriter paper. 2. Type your letter, neatly arranged and accurately spelled and composed. 3. State the point of your letter in the first line if possible. 4. Outline in three or four sentences what you propose to do. 5. Indicate whether you have illustrations if they are called for. 6. State simply what your qualifications are for writing the article. 7. Indicate your willingness to submit the article entirely on speculation.

Below are cited some queries sent in by student writers, together with the answers they received. The queries were not always perfect, but they indicate the general approach that should be taken, as well as the points to be covered. You will note that some favorable and some unfavorable answers were received. Unfavorable answers were received when the article would not have fitted into the plans of the magazine. Had the article been submitted without query, the writer's loss of time and effort would have been measurably greater. These negative answers reveal important facts, and are worth careful study. They show why articles are *rejected*.

Not all of those writers who received favorable replies were able to produce satisfactory articles, but the number was high enough to mark the technique as successful.

These Said "Go Ahead"

1. *To a Department Store Magazine*

Dear Madam:

Would you be interested in seeing an article about two original window displays, one showing a color harmony between chintz dresses and wallpaper, and the other showing the new "powder blue" yard goods shot from a wooden cannon?

These unusually attractive windows were designed by a local department store. The ideas were original with the store manager, who has told me that they brought a great deal of favorable reaction from the customers.

I have in mind an article about one thousand words. Two photographs are available, and I shall be glad to submit the article on speculation. If you are to make any suggestions for developing it, I shall carefully follow them.

Sincerely yours,
MARGARET HOLLORAN

(The Reply)

Dear Miss Holloran:

We would be interested in seeing from one hundred to two hundred words on each of the two ideas which you suggested in your letter of May 6th. The first was "relation between chintz dresses and wallpaper," and the second, "displaying powder blue by means of a cannon."

However, we would want these stories and whatever photographs you might send with them, submitted on speculation.

Thank you.

Very truly yours,
THE EDITOR

Analysis: Note that the editor welcomed the query, but suggested a treatment different from that planned by the writer. Instead of one long article, she suggested two short ones, which were later bought by the editor.

2. *To a Well-Known Monthly*

Dear Sir:

In this city is a grocer who has created two giant stores on old-fashioned principles in the face of the keenest chain-store competition.

He is a leading citizen in a population of 220,000, a far-famed antique collector, a man widely-known for his campaigns for civic improvement, and a wit quoted around this part of the state. Do you think your readers might like an article of about 1200 words on this self-made leader, stressing his originality and wit?

May I submit an article on speculation to you, following whatever suggestions you care to make?

Very truly yours,
JACK GILSON

(The Reply)

Dear Mr. Gilson:

The article you suggest sounds an interesting subject for us. However, I always find it quite impossible to defnitely commission articles simply from suggested ideas, particularly when dealing with writers with whose work I am not familiar.

If you care to submit the finished manuscript on speculation, I would be very glad to read it and give you a prompt answer. The usual length of our character sketches is about 1500 words, but if you can do this in less, so much the better.

With many thanks for your interest, I am,

Sincerely,
THE EDITOR

Analysis: In this letter the writer suggested the multiple aspects of character that made his subject a fascinating person. Note that the editor was interested, but careful not to give a definite order for the article. He also increased the proposed length.

3. *To a Science Magazine*

Dear Editor:

Do you think your readers would be interested in learning how to do decorative sandblasting on glass panels for home use?

I have in mind an article of about 1000 words, based on my own experience in making glass panels for a game room. The article would be illustrated by several photographs and drawings, showing:

a. How to make the cartoon sketches.
b. How to cut away the unwanted parts.
c. How to paste the cartoon cutouts upon the glass.
d. A sandblaster in operation.
e. Several finished panels in place.

The various steps are so simple any average handy man can do them. Sandblasters are available at most glass firms, and often can be found elsewhere. If you would care to see such an article, I would be glad to submit it entirely on speculation.

Yours sincerely,
CLARENCE DAVIS

(The Reply)

Dear Mr. Davis:

We cannot promise to buy your article, but if you care to submit it on speculation, we shall be glad to look it over.

Our readers appreciate simple language and clear explanation. Keep your article as short as possible, as we try to present a great variety of useful information. We are a little skeptical about the availability of sandblasters. Can this work be done by the acid-etching process? If so, be sure to tell how.

Your illustrations sound interesting.

Very truly yours,
THE EDITOR

Analysis: The writer has itemized his group of illustrations. This is the best feature of the query. But note how this query (and the two preceding) get to the point in the first sentence. Also note the brevity of the entire letter. In this third letter the editor has pointed out a weak spot. If the writer does not eliminate it, he may face a future rejection.

4. *To a Home Magazine*

Dear Madam:

I have recently spent some weeks investigating ways of making closet space more useful, and have incorporated the best of them in a remodeled closet in my own home.

It is possible to triple the usefulness of the average closet by putting in more drawers, more shelves, and rearranging hangers. In the process the closets are made dustproof and more attractive.

If you would care to see an article incorporating a score of good suggestions, illustrated with drawings and photographs, I would submit it on speculation. The article would probably run perhaps 1200 words. Would you care to suggest whether this is about right?

Sincerely yours,
MARTHA A. PRESTON

(The Reply)

Dear Miss Preston:

Thank you for your interest in writing to us about a possible article for our decoration department. We shall be pleased to have you send us the story for consideration, and if photographs are available they should accompany the manuscript. Our usual length of time to report on material submitted is two to three weeks.

We would prefer to leave the length of the manuscript to your own judgment. Some of our articles are 700 or 800 words; seldom do we exceed 1000 words for feature articles according to our new style of make-up. Our rates vary according to length of manuscript, number of photographs used, merit, etc.

Cordially,
THE EDITOR

Analysis: The writer indicates that she has experience on what she plans to say. She also has photographs to show what was accomplished. The editor's reply gives some valuable information on article length that may have escaped the writer's eye. Note what is said about rate of pay.

5. *To a Food Magazine*

Dear Sir:

Few people know that the choicest secret of good cooking is in the use of appropriate herbs.

I have been making a study of the use of herbs, singly and in combinations, and have tested many recipes calling for herbs. Certain conclusions have become clear to me, and I believe they would make an interesting article.

Would you care to see such an article, embodying what I have learned? I would write it on speculation.

If you would care to make any suggestions for developing the article, I would be glad to follow them. What do you think of about 1000 words?

Sincerely yours,

ANNE RICHARDSON

(The Reply)

Dear Miss Richardson:

We are always glad to read any literary contribution to good living, under which heading a short article on practical cooking herbs and how to grow them, would fall. One thousand words, however, would be too short. Between fifteen hundred and twenty-five hundred words would be necessary.

The only suggestions we would like to offer for the writing of such an article, without any obligation on our part, is that it should be informative, but at the same time, light and entertaining.

Thanking you for your letter,

Very sincerely yours,

THE ASSOCIATE EDITOR

Analysis: This is all a writer can ask for. The editor suggests a longer article, and wants it in a light and entertaining style. He is definitely interested and will give the article careful study when it reaches his desk.

Why Some Ideas Are Rejected

The following answers to student queries reveal some of the reasons why certain ideas fail to hold interest. The queries are not included because the answers are self-explanatory.

1. *From a Farm Journal*

Dear Mr. George:

The idea of part-time farmers is one that we naturally have thought about at various times but have practically abandoned the idea of doing anything on it for two reasons. One, of course, is the fact that the trend is away from small farms, and second is the fact that such a large percentage of our readers are full-time farmers.

Cordially yours,
THE ASSOCIATE EDITOR

Analysis: The idea was good, but the wrong market was chosen.

2. *From a Home Economics Journal*

Dear Miss Kister:

Articles for our publication are already scheduled for the next six months, and the clothing picture may change so radically during that time that I hesitate to make any commitments for fall articles.

Sincerely yours,
THE EDITOR

Analysis: This query was based on the type of idea that dies quickly. The magazine could not take a chance on long-time buying when current needs were already filled. Articles on style are usually done by experts.

3. *From a Magazine for Young Women*

Dear Miss Westmiller:

In reply to your letter, we have a great deal of material on hand which deals with the type of article you suggest, so we will not be able to accept yours. We wish to thank you for submitting the idea.

Sincerely yours,
THE EDITOR

Analysis: This market was already stocked. Some subjects are written about too frequently by too many people.

4. *From a Leading Outdoors Magazine*

Dear Mr. Teller:

We have read with interest your suggestion for an article on the Kentucky rifle — its origin, history, and qualities. While we haven't had an article on this subject in recent years, several magazines devoted exclusively to guns have dealt with it and at least one general magazine.

Our gun editor says that two recent books on the subject have pre-empted public interest in this rifle. Good luck with it if you try elsewhere.

Sincerely yours,
THE EDITOR

Analysis: Gun articles for the "big three" in outdoors magazines are usually done by the gun editor. The free-lance writer must have a highly original idea in order to sell an article on this subject.

5. *From a General Magazine*

Dear Mr. Berment:

Your idea for an article on "Death on the Highways" is a topic we've treated several times of late — which automatically disqualified it from our magazine. But thank you for writing about your idea.

Sincerely,
THE EDITOR

Analysis: There should have been no need for this type of answer. The writer had not studied his market.

6. *From a Leading Weekly Magazine*

Dear Mr. Earle:

We see no opportunity for the article you offer on the sport of gliding. May we suggest that your idea might interest an aviation magazine?

Cordially yours,
THE EDITOR

Analysis: A good idea, but the query did an inadequate sales job. Perhaps one of the aviation magazines would be interested.

7. *From a Women's Second-Class Magazine*

Dear Miss Gaylord:

Your letter suggesting an article on making gloves at home has been turned over to me. The idea sounds very interesting, but I am afraid we have no place for it at present.

Thank you for thinking of us nevertheless.

Sincerely yours,
Fashion Editor

Analysis: Good idea but market was stocked. Writer should send out more queries. Some magazine will want to see the article.

8. *From a Farm Journal*

Dear Mrs. Black:

Though we have several times had suggestions similar to yours on the use of discarded fats, we have always decided that it was not

possible for us to present such an article. I am very sorry that we
still feel it is a subject we cannot use.

We do want to thank you for thinking of us.

Sincerely yours,
WOMEN'S EDITOR

Analysis: Apparently crashed head-on against a magazine policy. Might
have offended the advertisers of soaps.

9. *From a Woman's Magazine*

Dear Miss Basford:

Interesting as your proposed article on giving a party for college
men sounds, I cannot encourage you to submit it to us. Articles of
that nature for our magazine are always staff written.

We appreciate, however, your thinking of us and wish you good
luck in placing your article elsewhere.

Very truly yours,
THE EDITOR

Analysis: A narrow idea bumped into a magazine largely staff written.
Free-lance writers have little chance here.

Editorial Contacts

By using the query a writer saves much lost motion, and he gets to
know editors who would otherwise be outside his acquaintance. This
is a two-way process, for the editor also becomes acquainted with the
query writer.

Where personal contacts are absent, the editor's most lasting impressions may come from the inquiry. The writer will be repaid manyfold
if he turns out a businesslike letter. He will find it an excellent idea
to get a book on business letter writing. so that he can follow the proper
form — though composing his own remarks.

The careful writer will edit the first versions of his queries. The last
copy should be correct in all details of style, grammar, and punctuation,
and it should be well arranged on the page. The writer will remember
that this query is a *sample* of his work. If it is poor, the editor will most
certainly believe that the article suggested will be of the same quality.

In doing the exercises that follow, complete each query so that it is
ready to drop into the mail except for the envelopes. Look up the
editor's name and the editorial office. Write letters in keeping with the
policies of the magazine.

Training Steps

1. Take any issue of *Esquire, True,* or *Reader's Digest.* Select an article done by a nonstaff writer. Now formulate a query to the editor setting forth the main idea, the ground to be covered, and your qualifications for writing the article. Assume that you have had the same experience as the actual writer of the article.

2. Write a complete query to the proper staff member of *Popular Mechanics Magazine* about a proposed article on how to make an item of your own choice, in which you include a list of illustrations to be sent with the manuscript.

3. Assume that you are a teacher in a country school. Write a query to *The Atlantic* or *Harper's Magazine* asking if either would be interested in an article entitled "Confessions of a Country Teacher."

4. Your local police department has solved a strange and involved murder mystery. What magazine would be a natural market for an article on the solution of the killing? Write a query to the proper magazine, addressing the editor by name.

5. Select a subject with which you are familiar. Write the necessary query to a carefully selected market.

6. After studying *Musart* or *Music Journal,* write a query about the interest of college students in the battle of classical versus jazz music.

7. Write a query to an aviation magazine on the organization of a college glider club or on the practice of joint ownership of pleasure planes.

8. What distinctions should be kept in mind when writing queries to *Flying* and *Aero News International?*

9. Upon what subjects might you query *This Week?*

CHAPTER 8

Putting Long Articles Together

Before the article writer sits down to put the first word of his article on paper, he has already completed a number of carefully planned moves. 1. He has chosen what he believes to be a first-rate subject. His choice is backed by all his experience, his keenest judgment, and all the tests he is able to muster. 2. In addition, he has selected as a market that publication most likely to purchase his finished work at the most favorable rates. 3. He has written a query, and has received the green light from the proposed market. 4. Finally he has tentatively determined the length of the article.

His decision upon the last-named point was probably influenced by a. the amount of data available, b. the importance of the subject, c. the general policy of his market, and d. any hints from the editor in answer to his query.

Other points, perhaps some of them important, may also have been settled. He may already have procured illustrations. This would be a wise step if the article is the type that calls for graphic or photographic illumination. At least the writer should know that illustrations are available. Perhaps, too, he has hit upon a striking title, a perfect opening, or a strong conclusion. He may have worked out other details. But now comes the time when he must put words on paper.

The Writer and His Moods

Shall a person wait until he is in the mood for writing? until he feels ready to unburden himself?

There are obstacles to writing, such as the demand of duty or other responsibilities. But the one who waits for "mood" or "inspiration" is the one who will do little writing. The writer with available time can usually get himself in tune for his work by a study of his data, by further research, or through revision of work done earlier. Eventually the mental machinery gets warmed to its task, and the writing process can be gotten under way.

The writer who feels he hasn't time can make time by giving up those unimportant activities that are unlikely to advance his literary career. He also can plan his waking hours efficiently. Or he can give up a few hours of sleep. Remember that the free-lance writer is a self-made and self-sustaining man, with no one behind him to drive him on, to give him assignments, or to check upon his use of the passing hours. He succeeds because of his own drive, initiative, and intelligence. And so, more credit to the writer who succeeds.

Assembling the Data

All, or nearly all, the material to go into the article should be on hand before actual writing begins. This material includes the statistics, anecdotes, incidents, and quotations — if any. The facts are brought together from one or more sources, perhaps including interviews, research in libraries or newspaper offices, and visits to shops, factories, farms, or other cities. The writer may find later that he will have to dig up additional information to find a hole he has overlooked. But when he begins to write, he should be convinced that he has all the facts in hand.

Articles are seldom done piecemeal — a bit now and more later. They can be done that way, but usually the process creates confusion. It is better to work days or weeks in gathering the data, and then to sit down when an unbroken period of a few hours is known to be ahead. This continuity of effort tends to ease the task of composing.

Avoiding Return Trips

Some years ago the *Saturday Evening Post* presented a series of articles on soil erosion. The writing was preceded by a trip that carried the staff members into many different states. A return to Georgia, from which came a portion of the facts, would have been expensive and time-consuming. Let the writer get the facts while he is in the area being considered! Let him get more than he is likely to use! It is far better to have too much than too little. If more data have been gathered than can be used immediately, perhaps they may be made the basis for a later article or series of articles.

Here is an important fact known to nearly all professional writers, but to only a few beginners: The editor or intelligent reader can invariably tell whether a writer has mastered his subject. Sometimes the telltale evidence may be in what the writer includes; sometimes it is in what he omits. It may be in the wonder he shows at certain facts that a more experienced person would take for granted, or in his inclusion of details that should have been omitted.

No writer wants to reveal an inadequacy of knowledge. Therefore let him overprepare, and, if necessary, submit his article to someone more expert than himself for additions and corrections. In every case the article done from an abundance of material and from a wide knowledge of the subject is better than the one squeezed out from scanty facts and superficial acquaintance.

Taking Accurate Notes

Just as more notes should be taken than ever appear in print, so should a writer exercise far greater care in jotting down the data he plans to use.

Suppose the writer is doing part of his research in a library. Whatever items he chooses to copy, he should check back line for line, or fact by fact, to make certain he has copied everything correctly and has omitted nothing he wants. Also, he should put down the name of the book or magazine, name of the author, the page, exact date of publication, and volume number if a magazine or other periodical is used. He may later have to use the source again and will waste valuable time finding the exact reference unless the data are complete and accurate.

In obtaining facts though an interview, the writer would be wise to jot down important items and quotable phrases. At times it is well to avoid taking too many notes while the conversation proceeds, as certain types of interviewees may stop talking when they see their words being recorded. But as soon as possible, the writer should set down everything he remembers of the conference. He can do this at the first drugstore counter or the first restaurant. One never regrets such forethought.

Clarifying the Notes

Some authors like to type out their penciled notes. When typewritten, the notes are clearer and easier to judge, because they more closely resemble the finished manuscript. They are also more permanent. Some effort at rearrangement and clarification should be made at an early moment. This will increase mastery of the subject, and, perhaps, reveal weak points while there is yet time to do something about them. Either 3 X 5 or 5 X 8 cards are satisfactory, though the latter handle easier in the typewriter. The advantage of cards is in the ease with which they can be shuffled or rearranged. Supplementary notes, such as illustrative anecdotes or incidents, are readily inserted when the card system is used.

Nature of the Data

Novices will wonder what makes up an article. Unless they read with an analytical eye, they may never learn *what* and *how much* it takes to make an acceptable piece. Most reading is done for pleasure or information, and the pattern and framework of the article are overlooked. This is as it should be in a good article, but the process of reading only for pleasure will not promote the growth of the individual as a writer. Any article worth the writer's reading is worth reading twice — once for pleasure and again for purposes of analysis.

The material that goes into an article is composed of 1. incidents; 2. examples that are factual, or anecdotal; 3. statistics; 4. descriptions or processes, both technical and scientific; and 5. formulas, recipes, and the like.

INCIDENTS. There are the adventures, the human dramas, the incidents, encounters, and conflicts that bring life to what might without them be a boring article. Suppose you are doing a personality sketch of a railway engineer. The story of a wreck in which he was involved would be an incident — dramatic or colorless, depending upon the circumstances.

Perhaps you are writing on the building of outdoor fireplaces. A neighbor has constructed one, but forgot to put foundations below the frost line. Such incidents as this, both of good practice and bad, may become the high light of almost any article, because through them the article comes to life.

Naturally, the most interesting incidents are the ones to use.

EXAMPLES. The examples that go into articles are likely to be physical objects, whereas the incidents are probably processes or actions. To use the hypothetical case of the poorly constructed fireplace; the fireplace, when completed, is an example; the building was a process; but the mistake with the foundation was an incident. The recently constructed St. Louis arch is an example of contemporary architecture. The manner in which it was built was a process. Examples, also, are likely to be static in character, while incidents are fluid or concerned with motion. These distinctions may become somewhat arbitrary. The main point to remember is to have enough of each element in the article to keep up the interest.

At this point it should be mentioned briefly that incidents and examples, like anecdotes, may be hypothetical or fictional. But the reader should be made aware that the writer is inventing imaginary individuals and situations. The practice, borrowed from fiction writers, has been a standard device in developing articles for many years. Apologies for using the technique are unnecessary.

STATISTICS. Statistics are more commonly known as figures. They may be few or many, complicated or simple, actual or estimated. Sooner or later the writer must learn how to handle them. He must know how much to use and how to make them interesting. This method of popularization is discussed more fully in Chapter 15, "Humanizing the Facts."

Too much care cannot be given to the accuracy of the writer's data. When possible, he should seek out the original sources. For instance, a book from which the writer wishes to quote may cite figures from the U. S. Census volumes. It is best to go to these works for the original figures, because numerous factors cause errors to creep into published work. Among the many bodies of statistics the writer is likely to handle are those dealing with different aspects of population, farm crop production, manufacturing, income, memberships in various associations, tax rates, community chest budgets, etc. Prices, dimensions, temperatures, distances, racing times, and the like also fall into this classification.

PROCESSES. Because people like to know how things are done, descriptions of processes are frequently found in magazines. The *Satur-*

day Evening Post in a color-process article told how glass is made by the Corning Glass Company. *McCall's Magazine* told women how to make a suit of clothes. *Popular Science Monthly* explained how to make a set of sectional bookcases. *Farm Journal* explained artificial insemination among dairy herds. *Department Store Economist* printed the details of a new credit system for customers involving metal identification stamps usable in a number of coöperating stores.

The general magazines are rare that do not devote a portion of their space to process articles. Scores of trade journals, of course, are largely devoted to material of this kind. There will never be too many well-written, helpful articles telling how certain processes can be done more quickly, more easily or cheaply, with less hand labor, or with greater precision.

FORMULAS AND RECIPES. These two are skeletonized forms of the recipe. The recipe for a cake is but a shorthand version of an exposition telling how the job is done. The same is true of chemical and physical formulas. Both types are useful — perhaps invaluable at times — but they should be used with caution. There is always the danger that a greater or smaller portion of one's readers may not be able to interpret them.

The Point of View

The point of view is often what makes the article a success or a failure. A college student might wish to treat the subject of college politics. His point of view might be that of the freshman, sophomore, junior, or senior, depending on the class to which he belonged. His point of view would differ from that of the professor or the university administrator, and certainly from that of the professional politician viewing the amateur efforts of the undergraduate. Not only would the point of view differ between these broad jumps, but also within each group. The point of view, and hence the opinions, of political scientists would likely differ from those of sociologists or journalists. And doubtless there would be differences within each of these three groups, depending on age, experience, wisdom, and personal philosophy.

Before starting an article, the writer should become aware of his own point of view. This understanding puts him in a better way to emphasize the strength of his position, as well as to improve the weaknesses. Who, for instance, can speak as well on the point of view of the college student as the student himself? Who else can write "Confessions of a College Politician?" There is an obvious strength in the open admission of this writer's identity. Readers will recognize that he is in a position to know whereof he speaks. Moreover, he will not be expected to handle the subject with the mature and perhaps disinterested point of view of the middle-aged writer.

Whether he is a teacher telling what his colleagues think of rising prices, or a physician telling what fellow medicos feel about campaigns for socialized medicine, the individual who writes as one on the inside is more likely to get an audience than one who tries to give the *same* point of view from the outside. Another advantage rests in the fact that he who writes from a stated point of view is not expected to give opinions on the other side of the question. He can consolidate his position and get his arguments or facts across quickly and powerfully. In an argumentative article a frank announcement of position and affiliations is desirable.

Objective articles that give all sides of a debatable matter are in another class. These must be truly what they purport to be — be impartial and well balanced. Here the writer's qualifications, affiliations, and background are important matters to the reader, though, unfortunately, these are by no means always made clear.

Purpose of the Article

The writer should ask himself at least two questions before he begins his article: "What am I trying to do?" and "Why am I trying to do it?" Though the first is the more important, the writer should be able to answer each in a single sentence. When he cannot do so, it is likely that his purposes are not clear to himself. He should take stock of his intentions. It is an excellent idea to do this before beginning the composition of the article. Below are a few typical statements of purpose:

A. This article is planned to show that participation in college politics is (or is not) good training for honest citizenship.
B. My purpose is to prove that contour plowing, winter cover crops, and increased reforestation will nearly eliminate soil erosion on the average farm.
C. I want to convince the reader that unions should not be forced by congressional action to publish statements of their financial condition.
D. This article intends to show how one bank is winning new friends by offering to customers services never before presented by banking institutions.

E. The purpose of this article is to show that the so-called cloistered academic halls are in no wise separated from the normal stresses and strains of everyday living.

A writer is in no position to begin writing until he can set down his own purpose quite as clearly as in the above statements. It may not be expressed on paper, but it should be crystal-clear in his mind. Then all the purposes, or cross-purposes, should be put aside. At best the average article is a short affair. There is insufficient room in it to accomplish several different purposes. It should have a single aim and a single goal. And the more a writer learns about writing, the more truth he will find in this statement. The novice may believe 1,500 words comprise a long piece, but not the experienced writer. In that space he hardly finds room to turn around.

Adhering to the Purpose

All matter unassociated with the writer's purpose should be ruthlessly excluded. Part of this task can be done before the first paragraph is begun. If by chance irrelevant material does creep in, it should be taken out in the rewriting process. The preliminary outline, explained later, will prove to be an excellent device for revealing data, incidents, or anecdotes that are unrelated to the writer's purposes.

Greater choice among details will be afforded in some types of articles than in others. Considerable leeway is offered in personality sketches, humorous essays, and narrative accounts. Articles that relate processes have less flexibility, because the details must be accurate and complete, although some freedom is given in pieces done for advanced readers. Argumentative articles are similarly restricted, a fact that makes condensation and selection imperative.

The writer might query himself further now. What is it that makes this article worth doing? Will it entertain? Will it provide useful information? The second and third questions yield the answer for the first one. If the article is likely to be neither entertaining nor helpful, it should not be undertaken. There can be no pride in writing such an article. The writer who does only an occasional piece is well advised to drop pale subjects for those with greater vitality.

Planning the Article

An article should be planned for the same reason that a house should be planned. Only by planning can mistakes be prevented and the proper relationship between the parts maintained. If the reader of this chapter will follow the four simple steps explained in the next few pages, he will find that the difficulty and confusion have been removed from the outlining process. This four-step approach can be used on every type of article, except the collective article, which lacks the continuity of other types.

The first step is simplicity itself. Make a list of the items you intend to put into the article. Don't concern yourself with the order of arrangement. Just write them down, and number them as you do. Include every anecdote, every incident, bits of conversations, the names, dates, humorous facts and ideas, all the data — in short, everything. In the case of anecdotes and incidents, a one-line reminder will be sufficient.

After this step has been taken, let us call the results a "working list" or inventory. This working list serves several useful purposes. First, we can now almost tell at a glance whether we have adequate material from which to build an article. The practical writer knows that it will take 50 words to explain or describe one idea; 25 to do the next; a third will need 75. By setting these estimates at the side of each item, and later adding them, the writer can arrive at a fairly accurate estimate of the length of his proposed article.

The second advantage of the working list is that it is the *first* step in outlining. Once this list is jotted down, a large part of the work of outlining has been completed.

FIRST STEP. Suppose you were to write an article on building a rumpus or game room in the basement. You are relating your own experience, or that of a friend or acquaintance. The first step is to jot down and number a list of everything done in the transformation of the basement, including the task of cleaning it up — if that was necessary. Omit nothing. Put in the cost of new materials, the decorations, the mistakes you make, the troubles you had (and the fun), where you got advice, how much help you had, how long it took, the paint, the wallboard, the waterproofing, the new pipes, the nails. Perhaps this list will total fifty or sixty items. If so, it certainly is big enough for a full-length article.

SECOND STEP. The second step is as simple as the first. We look for a useful classification for grouping similar items. The purpose of the article and the inherent nature of the data largely determine what the groupings will be. Examples are given below.

1. In the article about our game room the classifications might include these items: a. the cleaning process; b. building supplies purchased;

    c. cost of all the supplies; d. actual work of remodelling; e. the decorations and furnishings.
2. Facts to be included in the confession of a college politician would fit into these divisions: a. how the college machine operates; b. examples of questionable practices; c. comparison with professional machines; d. student attitudes on college politics; e. carry-over into postcollege period.
3. A character sketch of an interesting person could be classified in the early stage under these groups: a. ancestry and parentage; b. education; c. professional career or adult experience; d. achievements; e. description of the person; f. quotations from the individual, his friends, and other sources; f. human interest items (likes, dislikes, peculiarities).

Each of the three outlines suggested above is different from the others. A dozen subjects might produce a dozen different groups of classifications. This variation is not important. It is important, however, that there be logic in the sorting process and that the final grouping be usable by the writer.

When the topics for grouping the material are chosen, then proceed to set down under each heading the items that properly belong there. Some items may fall under two (or more) headings. That is all right. Later on when you are doing the actual writing, simply do not repeat what you say about these items. Present different aspects each time they come up.

THIRD STEP. This is the shortest and quickest of the three steps. It consists of deciding upon the order in which the major divisions selected in Step Two are finally to appear.

But the material thus arranged *does not necessarily include either the beginning or the ending of the article.* Actually, the article beginning may be the last item worked out, while the ending may be the first. Either a good beginning or a good ending may be the result of inspiration, of hard work, or of both. If you by chance hit upon a satisfactory beginning or ending, put it down on paper at once before it slips into the realm of the forgotten. And so with all other good ideas that come along.

FOURTH STEP. The fourth step consists of eliminating those items which for one reason or another should not be included. This elimination process includes the dropping of weaker elements, as well as the selecting of those that might be used in a second article for another market. Again a word of caution: Do not put all your facts into one article when the chances are good for multiple sales. This is logical advice for another reason. Because an article is a short piece of writing, it should have a single point of view. It should not try to cover too much ground. Like the well-written short story, it should strive for a single effect. This is done in part by asking yourself whether the particular market in mind would be interested in this and that detail. If not, put them aside for a different article.

Creating the Article

Since instruction in writing should be accompanied by examples, suppose we take a subject and put it through the four steps that lead to a complete outline. Let us see what the working list of inventory looks like. Then we shall group the material under certain logical headings, rearrange it, and finally weed out those items in which our market would not be interested.

THE INVENTORY. As previously stated, the *first* step is to put down every single item the writer has been able to discover about his subject. He does this in no particular order, because an effort to establish order at this point would slow up and interfere with the jotting down process. He puts down one idea. It leads to a second, the second to a third, and the third to a fourth. These processes of recall and association are in themselves rather fascinating to the analytical writer. However, while he may be intrigued by the way his mind works, he is usually wise to give it a free rein, so that the subconscious processes will function to better advantage.

The subject we have selected is an ordinary garden pool in which grow various acquatic plants. It is a good subject because everybody has seen such pools, and because it is a prospect for several markets. The particular pool that we shall discuss is one the author saw in Florida.

Our experience in the writing field tells us that *American Home, Better Homes and Gardens,* and *House and Garden* might be interested in the pool as a landscape feature, and hence might buy an article telling how to build it. *Natural History* might like to see an article that told of the relationships of the plant, insect, and fish life in the pool. *Parents' Magazine* might accept an article that told why the pool could be used to instruct children in natural history, perhaps with reference to propagataion among the creatures that live in or visit the pool.

This last line of reasoning was followed by the author in preparing the article under discussion. *Parents' Magazine* published it after making some editorial changes, which included a request for information on how to construct the pool. The complete data and actual steps taken in writing the article are fully set forth below.

THE INVENTORY

1. Water lilies, 3 types
2. Dragonflies
3. Snails
4. Goldfish
5. Moths
6. Butterflies
7. Orchids
8. Arrowheads
9. Snakes
10. Turtle
11. Bees
12. Hornets
13. Muck pocket
14. Water supply
15. Water hyacinth
16. Water lettuce
17. Fresh-water clams
18. Spirogyra
19. Bass
20. Spider vs. hornet battle
21. Irregular contours
22. Quail
23. Cardinals
24. Plywood forms
25. Mockingbirds
26. Rock garden background
27. Waterfall
28. Difficulty finding rock
29. English sparrows
30. Brown thrasher
31. Cement
32. Reinforcing steel
33. Cinders, sand, gravel
34. Drain
35. Bream
36. Blue jays
37. Hummingbirds
38. Home picnics
39. Use of books, etc.
40. Waterproofing
41. Snails clean walls
42. Clams purify water
43. Keep plants, animals out 3 weeks
44. Earth makes one wall of form
45. How frequently drained
46. Dragonflies have "hawking places"
47. Hornets use anesthetics
48. Anopheles minnows
49. Minnows eat wrigglers
50. Dragonflies catch mosquitoes
51. Wild life interdependence
52. Digging excavation, etc.
53. Putting in drain, etc.
54. A miniature world
55. Use of books, etc.
56. Pool easily adapted
57. Gain wild life knowledge
58. Family united in play
59. Garden improved
60. Struggle for existence
61. Place for picnics
62. Dragonflies deposit eggs

Before we are through putting down what we learned of the construction and use of this pool, we find more than half a hundred items on our list. And, doubtless, as we proceed to deal with the subject, other items will occur to us and we shall include them, for article writing is a flexible process.

CLASSIFICATION. A number of different classifications might be devised for our sixty-two items. The final test will be whether or not the one we select helps us produce a good article. Here is a first attempt, then, at classification: 1. migratory wild life; 2. materials used; 3. how the pool was built; 4. useful applications and benefits; 5. preparations; 6. dramas involving the pool's inhabitants and visitors.

We might have used a series of narrower classifications in place of the item "migratory wild life." For example, we could use a. insect visitors; b. bird visitors; and c. unwanted intruders. And the third item "how the pool was built" also could have been further subdivided.

THE CLASSIFICATION

1. *Migratory wild life*

Dragonflies	Butterflies	Bees
Snakes	Moths	Wasps
Spiders	Mockingbirds	Blue jays
Quails	English sparrows	Hummingbirds
Cardinals	Brown thrashers	

2. *Materials used*

Muck	Cement	Drain and intake pipe
Plywood forms	Reinforcing steel	
Rock	Cinders, sand, gravel	

3. *How the pool was built*

Muck pocket	Rock garden combined	Waterproofing
Water supply	Waterfall	No planting for 3 weeks
Irregular contours	Difficulty getting rock	Earth makes one wall
Plywood forms	Putting in drainpipe	Frequency of draining
		Digging excavation

4. *Useful applications and benefits*

Shows wild life interdependence	Use of books
Knowledge of natural history	Garden more attractive
Family united in recreation	Room provided for picnics
A miniature world	Struggle for existence

5. *Preparing for use*

Waterlilies, 3	Arrowheads	Fresh-water clams
varieties	Turtle	Spirogyra
Snails	Water hyacinths	Bass
Goldfish	Water lettuce	Bream
Orchids		

6. *Poolside dramas, etc.*

Spiders battle the wasps	Dragonflies, their "hawking places"
Hornets anethetize spiders	Minnows eat mosquito larvae
Snails clean walls	Dragonflies catch mosquitoes
Clams purify the water	

REARRANGEMENT. With few changes, the items are as they were in the original inventory. As the analytical and writing steps proceed, other points may be added. But now, as we examine the items above in terms of what *Parents' Magazine* would like in an article, we see that most of the notes dealing with stray birds and the like probably should be put in an article for *Audubon Magazine*. At least we would not start our article with these facts. Perhaps our most interesting group is number 6. Then might come, in order of interest, numbers 5, 1, 2, 3, and 4.

ELIMINATION. What to leave out is always a problem. Sometimes those ideas that a writer finds most interesting must be omitted for lack of space. When there is a choice between two ideas of about equal interest, the writer must try to put himself in the place of his prospective readers. What will most interest them? What is likely to prove most helpful?

Included in our list of data was a reference to snakes. Possibly some of our prospective readers would find repulsive the thought that children might be confronted by such reptiles. Because it is not vital to our subject and because we must omit much of our data, let us drop this item.

Also, some of our material too closely duplicates other items in our list. There are times when repetition is necessary to emphasize an important point, but generally it is best to avoid too close parallelism. Variety improves the article and keeps the reader interested.

When the various groups are carefully studied and weighed with respect to the problem of teaching children some of the facts of natural history, it becomes clear that the details of how to build the garden pool could be left for an article for, perhaps, *House and Garden* or a homecraft magazine. And the complete list of birds and insects is more properly in the field of *Audubon Magazine*. We really have material for several articles here.

Having reached this decision, we can eliminate the wild life and the how-to-do facts, which would thus cut out classifications 1, 2, and 3. Of the groups that remain, number 6 is best at the beginning, followed by 4, and then by 5. Perhaps we will not be able to get along entirely without numbers 1 and 3. We may have to borrow a few ideas, but in the main we are rid of them in so far as this article goes.

The completed outline, together with an introduction and a conclusion, follows.

COMPLETED OUTLINE

I. Question lead
1. Outdoor days bring new attractions for children
2. Play at home is difficult to devise
3. A solution may be found
4. Natural processes are demonstrated

II. Poolside dramas
1. Dragonflies' egg laying may be observed
2. Hornets are interesting

III. Useful applications
1. Necessity of understanding what takes place
2. Mating should be explained
3. Shellfish, a lesson in blindness
4. Snails help keep pool clean
5. Struggle for food always present
6. Interrelation of life demonstrated
7. Bird life may be attracted

IV. Preparing for use
1. Useful books should be at hand
2. Libraries often much help
3. Other equipment, if available
4. Cost is low
5. Animal life may be added
6. Plant life from countryside
7. Shrubbery may be changed

V. Summary conclusion
1. General benefits
2. Low cost

Recapitulation

If we stop now, to look back, we note that all our data are in hand. We have selected a market, and presumably have received an affirmative answer to our query directed to *Parents' Magazine.* Our purpose in writing the article if stated in a single sentence would be about like this: We want to show parents how garden pools can be used to give children worth-while instruction in plant, animal, and insect life. Our article should be somewhere around 1,800 words in length. It is addressed to parents — not to their children. And our readers will be intelligent, educated parents in the upper half of the middle-income group. Our data have been grouped and tentatively selected.

Before beginning to write this piece, let us take a look at the fundamental unit of the article — the paragraph. This unit when presented in a magazine article should not, on the average, exceed 70 words. Nor should the sentences, on the average, be longer than 17 words. Each paragraph should be independent in thought.

Because articles of this type do not attempt to create dramatic suspense, we can start to write anywhere. We can begin in the middle of the article, or at the end. The best point at which to begin is that point which looks easiest — the aspect about which you must feel like writing. Begin where you feel most sure of what you say. Later on, when warmed to the task, you can tackle some of the harder ideas.

How Paragraphs Are Developed

A number of methods are available for developing the paragraph — that is, ways of getting facts and situations expressed on paper. The desired result can be accomplished 1. by exposition, narration, or description — all in the writer's own words; 2. by use of dialogue; 3. by expanding or explaining through an interview; 4. by using direct or indirect quotations from various sources; or 5. by using charts or other graphic presentations. Any or all of these methods may be employed in the same article.

Just as the paragraphs are units in themselves, so are the sections of the article. It should be possible to write any section of the article first — or last. These sections, too, are frequently shiftable. They can be picked up bodily and moved to a later or an earlier place in the article if this move is wise. The editing process occasionally reveals that an article needs to be strengthened at some weak point. One remedy is to shift good material from another section to the weak point. A better way is to bring in new material not previously used.

Malleability of the Article

Because the article is a *malleable* form of writing, it can be condensed or expanded. Paragraphs and sections may be excised and better material inserted. These facts are far less true of other types of writing. And the secret is to be found mostly in the *interchangeability of the paragraphs and sections*.

The young writer should recognize these facts. And when he does, he will lose his awe of the writing process as applied to articles. All respect is due a worthy subject ably handled — but the free lance should be able to look at such an article and mentally to take it apart, seeing what "made it tick." He should be able to tell what were the techniques used in developing the article, whether they were the proper ones to employ, and whether they were well used.

In the article we shall prepare from our facts above, we shall employ exposition, narration, and description in the writer's own words. Other methods of paragraph development, such as the quotation, could be used. The writer always has a choice of methods.

Starting to Write

Where shall we begin? That depends upon what seems easiest or perhaps most interesting at the moment. Memory tells us that the item about the dragonflies' egg-laying act once fascinated a group of young children. We can begin with it as well as with any other item on our list.

At the west end of the pool behind a screen of orchids and arrowheads, a blue dragonfly flirted with a greenish-blue female. Having mated in air, they sank to the water. The female dip-dip-dipped her tail, sometimes into a thin layer of water atop a lily pad, but more often wherever she happened to be. Scores of eggs would become food for fish long before they hatched; perhaps a few would live to perpetuate the next generation.

Other dragonflies came and went. A green female with a black and white striped tail, unaided, laid her eggs carefully inside the stem of a lily pad. Occasional packs of brown-winged dragonflies hunted in gregarious hunger for mosquitoes or gnats. An insect guide would have given a key to a score or more varieties of these "mosquito hawks."

We saw one catch and devour a mosquito not three feet from our eyes. Later a stubby-winged creature, looking like a cross between a dragonfly and a horsefly, sailed past us, taking a "mosquito hawk" on a one-way ride.

Pining Down New Ideas

These three paragraphs will do for the present. Perhaps we shall have to change them later. Certainly they will require additional explanation, as well as some linking words or phrases to tie them into the rest of the article.

While the above three paragraphs were being written, they suggested that similar episodes in the life of the hornets might fit in here. Let us see how they would look, for these sudden inspirations should not be allowed to slip away.

Black-bodied hornets were landing a few inches away on the damp muck and taking off with a load several times the size of their heads. The weight of the mud bore them down, and they rose slowly, barely clearing the ground as they headed homeward. One loaded carrier crashed into a spider web that was strung between an arrowhead stalk and the leaf of an orchid.

The head-on collision carried the hornet part way through the net. It clung tenaciously to its load, thrusting vigorously against the net that imprisoned it. Strand after strand became looped about its legs, wings, and neck. Back in a silken tunnel a grey spider watched the struggles of the hornet grow weaker.

We wondered if the hornet's building instinct would be strong enough to cost its life. Presently it dropped the load that was taking its strength, but it had released the mud too late, for the torn and tangled web was wrapped around it with unbreakable hold.

Slowly the spider moved out along a main guy thread. The drama was too near a tragic end to please us, and so we released the enmeshed hornet. In a moment it tore the net from its body and flew back to the mudbank as if its life had not been nearly forfeited.

Life streams by thickly in a constant series of little dramas, some of them humorous but many of them tragic. Much of interest depends on the spectators' being able to understand them; otherwise they are as if presented in a foreign language.

Phrasing the Beginning

These two *incidents* are entertaining in themselves, but they should also be instructive, for that is the purpose of our article. Readers of *Parents' Magazine* do not expect to be entertained. They come to this magazine to find the answer to definite problems that perplex them in bringing up their children. Among these problems are those of keeping the children entertained, of keeping them at home, of creating wholesome interests that will develop their personalities. It is to the parental interest in these problems that we must address our article. If we can now create a favorable beginning addressed to this interest, it will assist us in choosing and slanting the rest of our facts. To the readers, of course, it would appear that such an opening was actually written first.

When children transfer their games to the out-of-doors, it becomes difficult to supervise their activities. New interests draw them into the street, down the block, and around the corner.

Outdoor play that keeps children at home, that fosters wholesome interests, that teaches the essential mysteries of life around the child, and in which the parent can participate to just the right degree, is difficult to devise.

Few among the thousands who have constructed a garden pool as part
of their landscaping have discovered that it can be used as a fascinating
instrument for the entertainment and education of their children. The birds,
the insects, the fish, the mollusks, and the plants that can be brought here
will in the course of their lives set up a never-ending series of dramas in
the realm of natural history.

Because these dramas involve conception, birth, life, and death, they
afford an unexcelled opportunity to help the child develop an interest in
things outside of himself, to teach some of the facts of propagation, as well
as to enrich greatly the child's personality through inculcating a love for
the out-of-doors.

Tens of thousands of these pools have been constructed in recent years.
How easily they can be transformed into a combined zoo and botanical
garden, and the fascination and instruction they then afford are illustrated
by the experience with the pool shown in the accompanying photographs.

The incidents that follow indicate how much interest such a pool may
hold for children. Similar episodes may be discovered by the children for
themselves. But a parent may well use some of them to point out desirable
object lessons.

Sharpening the Purpose

Now let us go back to our first two items (p. 100) and point out how
these contribute to the purpose of our article. Every stroke we make
must be directed to keeping the ball moving in the predetermined
direction.

Parents may with complete frankness speak of the mating of dragonflies
and other insects. Children will observe the ritual and will ask questions.
They deserve a truthful answer, for the time has long since passed when a
truly educated person believes a child's questions on these matters should be
turned aside.

A great many other lessons are to be learned from close observation of
the inhabitants of the pool itself.

Children will watch the slow progress of clams or mussels along the sandy
bottom. Their tiny furrows and blind, aimless gropings will prompt many
questions concerning their obscure purposes.

The snails that feed on the moss covering the sloping concrete walls,
like cows gazing on a green hillside, will catch and hold a child's interest.
Their movements, like those in a slow-motion picture, flow evenly and effortlessly. So thoroughly covered with green moss are they that a few inches
depth it is difficult to distinguish them from the concrete wall. Here is a
lesson in camouflage.

Chief competitors of the snails are the tadpoles, which in recurrent cycles
hatch from eggs of garden toads, feed on the moss, grow up, and move to
new homes. While in the pool, they battle with the snails for the available
food.

Some of this struggle for existence should be explained to children. They should know that throughout the world it is man's lot to work for his daily bread. They should know that there is competition for food and for jobs. What is happening in the pool should be pointed out.

The pool itself is a world in miniature, restricted, of course, but rather self-sufficient. It produces green moss to feed goldfish, tadpoles, and snails. The microscopic life that grows in all such water feeds the mussels and the minnows. Soil in the bottom of the pool supports lilies, which provide green fodder for the larvae of certain insects.

Visiting birds remove these larvae. Still other insects are trapped by spiders, which in turn are caught by black hornets to feed their own young.

Bird life is one of the most instructive and pleasurable aspects of Nature. A pool developed like this may persuade a dozen or more birds to spend the season nearby. Increased ease of procuring food and drink are irresistible attractions.

The natural history of the pool visitors forms a field in which much-simplified writing has been done for those with interest but little experience. Moreover this study offers a field of interest that is quickly picked up or put aside.

The investment of time, effort, and money may possibly repay the costs a hundredfold. The wholesome character of the entertainment offered is the same basically as that afforded by Boy Scout and Campfire Girl activities, garden clubs, and the like. Much is to be gained, and at little expense for those who already possess the pool.

Public libraries everywhere are ready to suggest the names of books that will be helpful. Those done on the child's level will be best. It would be wise to purchase copies of those for home use. And they should be kept on hand for quick reference whenever new specimens come to visit the pool.

A home-owned bird guide, a moth and butterfly chart, and an insect book will contribute greatly to the pleasure of time spent at the pool. Something more than the exhilaration of crossword and jigsaw puzzles is inherent in the rush to identify a passing bird or butterfly or moth.

This development can be brought about by any one with a slight degree of effort. The transformation costs practically nothing. It involves no more than two or three dollars beyond the original expense of the pool, which itself was built by an inexperienced beginner.

The materials are simple: a half dozen fresh-water clams or mussels, a handful of snails from a florist or pet shop, a dozen or so minnows from any brook, stream or lake, and a few assorted frogs. Only the snails and goldfish need be purchased. Most gardeners who have built a pool or a rock garden will know where to obtain the rest.

Nearly all of the plants were found near some stream or swamp. Among them were the arrowhead, various ferns, several varieties of orchids, wild lotus, mint, hyacinth, water lettuce, and others. And of the animal life only the goldfish and the snails were purchased.

In addition some shrubbery should be set close to the pool, and one spot keep constantly wet where the mud-carrying hornets can come for material for their abode homes.

Additional plantings can be made from time to time. The effort to obtain the plants will take the plant hunters to the fields and woods. This is opportunity for a family excursion, which itself should be one of the most pleasurable of parties.

Completing the Article

Here, then, is the first draft of our article. We do not yet have a conclusion, nor have we begun to edit our manuscript. Before we finish an article, we probably will rewrite it three or more times. Some writers revise their manuscripts a half dozen or even a dozen times. This may be necessary in fiction, or during the early years of an article writer's career, but it should not persist past the third or fourth year of consistent writing. If it does, then the writer should examine his methods of work — they are somewhere at fault.

Below is the finished article with a conclusion.[1] While good writers seldom, if ever, are satisfied with what they write, a time comes when they must cease rewriting so that the manuscript can be sent to its market. Thus, we present this article, knowing we would continue to work on it if time permitted. The title and subtitle have not been completed at this point.

THE COMPLETED ARTICLE

I. QUESTION LEAD

1. Outdoor days (*Introducing a common problem*)

When children transfer their games outdoors, new interests draw them into the street, down the block, and around the corner. How can a parent then, keep an eye on their activities?

"I want to go over to Buddy's to play" is the familiar song of the average boy. And what can a parent say to that?

2. Play at home (*Uses multiple appeal*)

Out-of-door play that keeps children home, that fosters wholesome interests, that teaches some of the mysteries of life, and in which the parent can participate to just the right degree is difficult to devise.

3. A solution (*Previously overlooked*)

Few among the thousands who have constructed a garden pool as part of their landscaping have discovered that it can be used as a fascinating instrument for the entertainment and education of their children.

---

[1]Reprinted by permission of *Parents' Magazine*, in which it appeared under the title "We Built a Simple Lily Pool."

The birds, insects, fish, mollusks, and plants that can be brought here will set the stage for a study of natural history.

4. Natural processes (*What children may learn*)

Because this study involves conception, birth, life, and death, it affords an unexcelled opportunity to help the child develop an interest in things outside himself, to teach some of the facts of propagation, as well as to enrich greatly the child's personality through implanting an appreciation of the out-of-doors.

(*An effort to improve salability of article*)

Tens of thousands of these pools have been constructed in the past ten years. How easily they can be transformed into a combined zoo and botanical garden, and the fascination and instruction they then afford are illustrated by experiences with a pool I recently observed.

(*Used for human interest*)

"You wouldn't believe so many dramatic events could happen around one small pool," said the prideful builder.

II. POOLSIDE DRAMAS

1. Dragonflies' egg laying (*Used because a common sight*) (*Emphasis on natural history*)

At the west end of this pool, behind a screen of orchids and arrowheads, a blue dragonfly flirted with a greenish-blue female. Having mated in air, they sank to the water. The female dip-dip-dipped her tail, sometimes into a thin layer of water atop a lily pad, but more often wherever she happened to be.

(*Numbers indicated*)

Scores of the eggs would become food for fish long before hatching; perhaps a few would live to perpetuate the next generation. Thus is Nature wasteful at the lower levels of life.

Other dragonflies came and went. A green female with a black and white striped tail, unaided, laid her eggs carefully inside the stem of a lily pad. Occasional packs of brown-winged dragon-flies hunted in gregarious hunger for mosquitoes or gnats. An insect guide would have given a key to a score or more varieties of these daring "mosquito hawks."

(*Another incident added*)

We saw one catch and devour a mosquito not three feet from our eyes. Later a stubby-winged creature, looking like a cross between a dragonfly and a horsefly, sailed past us, carrying a "mosquito hawk."

(*Used to forestall reader's objections*)

"He's being taken on a one-way ride," my host explained.

"What do your children think of such accidents?" I asked.

"They take it as a matter of course. It doesn't bother them the slightest."

2. Hornets
   (*Dramatized
   by airplane
   comparison*)

Black-bodied hornets were landing a few inches away on the damp muck and taking off with a load several times the size of their heads. The weight of the mud bore them down, and they rose slowly, barely clearing the ground as they headed homeward. One loaded carrier crashed into a spider web that was strung between an arrowhead stalk and the leaf of an orchid.

(*Life-death
struggle*)

The head-on collision carried the hornet part way through the net. It clung tenaciously to its load, thrusting vigorously against the net that imprisoned it. Strand after strand became looped about its legs, wings, and neck. Back in the silken tunnel a grey spider watched the struggles of the hornet grow weaker.

We wondered if the hornet's building instinct would be strong enough to cost its life. Presently it dropped the load that was taking its strength, but it had released the mud too late, for the torn and tangled web was wrapped around it with unbreakable hold.

(*Dramatic
episode*)

Slowly the spider moved out along a main guy thread. The drama was too near a tragic end to please us, and so we released the enmeshed hornet. In a moment it tore the net from its body and flew back to the mudbank as if its life had not been nearly forfeited.

III. USEFUL
    APPLICATIONS

The incidents indicate how much interest such a pool can hold for children. Similar episodes may be discovered by the children. But a parent may well use some of them to point out desirable object lessons.

1. Necessity of
   understanding
   (*Analogy
   makes point
   clearer*)

Life streams by thickly in a constant series of little dramas, some of them humorous, but many of them tragic. Much of interest depends on the spectators' being able to understand them; otherwise, they are like stage plays in a foreign language.

2. Mating
   (*Explanation
   always a
   problem*)

Parents may with complete frankness speak of the mating of dragonflies and other insects. Children will observe the ritual and will ask questions. They deserve a truthful answer, for the time has long since passed when a truly educated person believes a child's questions on these matters should be turned aside.

(*Many readers
would ask this
question*)

"Do you ever refuse to answer your children's questions?" I ask my host, knowing him for a con- servative-minded father.

"Certainly not. My wife and I make it a point to speak frankly, but sometimes we try not to speak before the children of other parents. Also we don't volunteer more information on breeding habits than is requested."

(Connective paragraph)   A great many other lessons are to be learned from close observation of the inhabitants of the pool itself, it became evident.

3. *Shellfish*   Children will watch the slow progress of clams or mussels along the sandy bottom. Their tiny furrows and blind, aimless gropings will prompt many questions concerning their obscure purposes. Religious or philosophical interpretations may be introduced according to parental desire.

4. *Snails*
   (Examples of camouflage)

   (Any parent is able to explain this)

The snails that feed on the moss covering the sloping concrete walls, like cows gazing on a green hillside, will catch and hold a child's interest. Their movements, like those in a slow-motion picture, flow evenly and effortlessly. So thoroughly covered with green moss are they that at a few inches depth it is difficult to distinguish them from the concrete wall. Here is a lesson in camouflage.

Chief competitors of the snails are the tadpoles which in recurrent cycles hatch from eggs of garden toads, feed on the moss, grow up, and move to new homes. While in the pool, they battle with the snails for the available food.

5. Struggle for food
   (Advice to parents)

Some of this struggle for existence should be explained to children. They should know that throughout the world it is man's lot to work for his daily bread. They should know that there is competition for food and living space. Parents can show this by pointing out what is happening in the pool.

6. Interrelation of life
   (Multiplicity of examples)

The pool itself is a world in miniature, restricted but rather self-sufficient. It produces green moss to feed goldfish, tadpoles, and snails. The microscopic life that grows in all such water feeds the mussels and the minnows. Soil in the bottom of the pool supports lilies, which in turn provide green fodder for the larvae of certain insects.

(Using commonly known facts)

Visiting birds remove these larvae. Still other insects are trapped by spiders, which in turn are caught by black hornets to feed their own young.

7. Bird life
   (Broadens appeal of article)

Bird life, also, is one of the most instructive and pleasurable aspects of outdoor study. A pool developed like this may persuade a dozen or more birds to spend the season nearby. Increased ease of procuring food and drink are irresistible attractions to many bird varieties.

IV. Preparing
for Use
1. Useful books

(*Comparison
with well-
known facts*)

The natural history of the visitors forms a field in which much simplified writing has been done for those with interest but little experience. Moreover this study offers a field of interest that is quickly picked up or put aside.

The investment of time, effort, and money may repay the costs a hundredfold. The wholesome character of the entertainment offered is the same basically as that afforded by Boy Scout and Campfire Girl activities, garden clubs, and the like. Much is to be gained, and at little expense for those who already possess the pool.

2. Libraries
(*More advice*)

Public libraries everywhere are ready to suggest the names of books that will be helpful. Those done on the child's level will be best. It would be wise to purchase copies of these for home use. And they should be kept on hand for quick reference whenever new specimens come to visit the pool.

3. Other
equipment
(*An attempt
to aid
parents*)

Home-owned bird, moth, and butterfly guides, an insect net, and a pair of field glasses will contribute greatly to the pleasures of hours spent at the pool. It will be found that something more than the exhilaration of crossword and jigsaw puzzles is inherent in the rush to identify a passing bird or butterfly or moth.

4. Cost
(*Appeal of
inexpensive-
ness*)

This development at the poolside can be brought about by anyone with a little effort. The transformation costs practically nothing. It involves no more than two or three dollars beyond the original expense of the pool, which, in the case referred to, was built by an inexperienced beginner.

5. Animal life
(*Where
found*)

The materials are simple: a half dozen freshwater clams or mussels, a handful of snails from a florist or pet shop, a dozen or so minnows from any brook, stream or lake, and a few assorted frogs. Most gardeners who have built a pool or a rock garden will know where to obtain the rest.

6 Plant life
(*Where
found*)

Most of the plants were found near some stream or swamp. Among them were the arrowhead, various ferns, several varieties of orchids, wild lotus, mint, hyacinth, water lettuce, and others. And of the animal life only the goldfish and snails were bought.

7. Shrubbery

Some dwarf shrubbery should be set close to the pool, and one spot kept constantly wet where the mud-carrying hornets can come for material for their adobe homes.

(*Suggested to make work easier*)	Additional plantings can be made from time to time. The effort to obtain the plants will take the plant hunters to the fields and woods. This is opportunity for a family excursion, which itself should be one of the most pleasurable of parties.
V. SUMMARY CONCLUSION 1. General benefits	If the pool holds the attention for one or two summers at the right stage — between the sixth and ninth years — it will have done a good job. How much children learn will largely depend upon the guidance and interest of the parents.
2. Low cost	Nothing yet devised about the home is likely to yield quite the wholesome and general education as inexpensively as the garden pool.

In order to keep our article within prescribed limits, unnecessary characters were omitted. The presence of one or more children in the article would have been interesting, and more conversation might have brightened it. But our problem is not one of entertainment. Rather, it is one of instruction. The broad outlines have been sketched, and the proper suggestions for developing the pool have been made. An intelligent parent will be able to carry on from this point.

With envelopes correctly prepared and photographs captioned and protected by cardboard, the manuscript is now ready to seek its market. How the title and subtitle were written is told in Chapter 10.

Training Steps

1. Select from your notebook the subject you consider most salable. Next, write down and number all the data, incidents, anecdotes, and other items available on the subject.
2. Under what logical headings could these be classified? Make such a list of headings.
3. Select a market for this article. Now cross out the items that would not interest this market. Decide whether enough remains for an article within the limits of the market.
4. State what would be your purpose in writing the article.
5. Make an outline suitable for carrying out your objective.
6. Select two articles from *Reader's Digest* and two from the *National Geographic Magazine*. Write out the purpose of the author of each article. Do each in one sentence.
7. Prepare an outline based upon one of the four articles.
8. Alongside this outline state briefly the purpose of each paragraph, or division of the article.
9. Count the number of paragraphs of conversation or dialogue in each. Count the total number of paragraphs in each. What percentage is found within quotation marks?

10. Count the paragraphs in which data (figures) are used. What is the percentage of the total?
11. How many incidents are used in each article? How many examples?
12. Cross out in two of these articles every sentence or paragraph that *does not* contribute to the purpose of the article.
13. How have the statistics been given life? Are they enlivened by specific examples, by break-downs, by translation into other terms?
14. State the point of view of each of the four articles examined. Did the writer of each represent the best point of view? Could someone else have done a better job with a different viewpoint?
15. Can you point out the "tricks" or devices used to develop each article?
16. Is there evidence that the subjects have not been completely covered? Any angles left untouched?
17. Name two other possible markets for each of the four articles.
18. Does the title of any of the four articles appear as a phrase within the article itself?
19. Do the conclusions add to the force of these articles? Or do you feel that they weaken them?
20. Examine several issues of *American Home* and *Better Homes and Gardens.* In general do the articles show evidence of planning? Or do they appear to be thrown together? Do not give a hasty opinion. Be sure of your facts.
21. Does either magazine use articles whose purpose is to entertain? What is the general purpose of these articles?
22. Select an article in which the purpose is vague. State how the article could be improved.

CHAPTER 9

Types of Beginnings

The writer of articles has a twofold sales problem. His article must persuade an editor to use it. Once set up and in print, it must convince the reader that it is worth reading. These two facts must be kept in mind from the moment a subject is selected until the finished article is dropped into the mail.

Artistic sensibilities and temperament may reside in the writer, and they may be assets of considerable value. But they are not enough alone to determine the success of an ambitious writer, who must remember that he is also a businessman. In this latter capacity he will need to exercise keen judgment in selecting subjects about which to write and in preparing his articles for sale.

Sales Opportunities

Beginning writers have five chances to sell an article to an editor and his readers. Established writers may add a sixth — their name. These chances are like show windows in which merchants display their wares. Naturally they use their best merchandise — best from the point of view of attracting customers into the store. Items exhibited therein are carefully selected and carefully dressed. For the young writer these five show windows consist of 1. the title, 2. the subtitle, 3. the illustrations, 4. the beginning and 5. the appearance of the manuscript. While the ultimate consumer, the reader, will not see the manuscript, he will likely see the writer's name and be attracted according to the drawing power of that name.

Value of Good Beginnings

In magazines and textbooks much has been written upon the necessity of a good start. Agreement is nearly unanimous that few readers will stick by an article if the beginning is uninteresting. This statement should be qualified by the fact that a good title or a subject of impelling interest may carry a reader along for a few paragraphs in spite of a lame start. It should also be qualified by the fact that the title supplied by the writer may not be the one used by the editors, who frequently rewrite titles to suit their own tastes. Yet it is still true that some readers will be lost if the beginning is weak.

A few editors give a manuscript a careful reading from beginning to end. Most do not. The first reader, usually an assistant staff member, merely samples the article. He sees the title and subtitle (if any), the illustrations, the general appearance of the manuscript, the writer's name, and the beginning. But he may read only the title, subtitle, and beginning. Unless these are of high quality, he may read no further. The theory that it is unnecessary to eat all of an egg to know it is bad has been frequently applied to manuscripts.

Editors look upon the beginning as a sample of what the writer can do. They expect the writer to know that a good beginning is important, and to do his best work with it. In fact, they accept as a matter of course that the beginning *is* the writer's supreme effort. And, naturally, when it proves to be inferior, they accept as a fact that the rest of the article also will be poor. That is why articles with dull beginnings usually get only one reading when they go to market.

The good beginning has three purposes: 1. to catch the reader's eye; 2. to arouse his interest; and 3. to entice him to read further into the article. At times a single, short sentence is sufficient to accomplish all three. Upon occasion a single word may be made to do the work. Generally, the writer will need at least two sentences — one to catch the eye and a second to tie the first to the body of the article. Not infrequently the acceptable beginning may be the last part of the article to be written. It may also be the result of inspiration, or of careful thought and rewriting, usually the latter.

What to Do

Good beginnings are characterized by the presence of certain desirable qualities. They are simple, short, a vital part of the article, and they embody a skillful transition. To put these in an affirmative way, the writer 1. must keep the beginning as simple as possible, 2. must keep it as short as possible, 3. must make it an integral and vital part of the entire article, and 4. must link it adeptly to the rest of the article.

Drafting of an article should not be considered complete until the beginning cannot be improved in any of these four respects. A dozen or more beginnings may be written before one completely satisfactory is found. Even then it is likely to embody parts of several different efforts. The writer should not consider his work done when he has composed the first beginning. Let him try another totally different approach, and let him continue writing additional beginnings until he is convinced he has one that accomplishes its purpose.

All the devices and skill of the fiction writer should be called upon to weave the beginning. This author has purposely avoided calling this beginning a "lead" after the newspaper fashion, because the newspaper lead is usually a stilted, clumsy, tricky device. While it requires considerable skill to compound, it offers little opportunity for the play of literary talent. Here, again, is another advantage article writing has over the writing of ordinary news stories.

Beginning Types

The best and simplest classification of beginnings was worked out by Bleyer several decades ago.[1] Subsequent writers have added to it, but have never improved upon it. The list appears in the order of importance of the various types. They are as follows: 1. striking statement; 2. summary; 3. direct address; 4. question; 5. narrative; 6. description; and 7. quotation. Over a period of years the first and second will probably be used more than all others together, though on occasion any one of the seven may prove to be the best for a particular article. The writer

---

[1]Bleyer, W. G., *How to Write Special Feature Articles*, p. 132.

should know and be master of all types, experimental examples of which are cited below.

The Striking Statement

Striking statements made good beginnings because readers like to be startled. They like to be jarred by the "gee-whiz" element in the news. Shocking news may be used, but is best when it is about others than the readers. New and unusual ways of stating old facts are particularly good, because they breathe new life into what may be dull but important.

Most magazine readers are also readers of the newspapers, in which they are trained to expect the startling. It becomes a habit for them to read the exciting events and to pass over the dull ones. Such reading habits are transferred to the magazines to the disadvantage of reader and writer. Many a worth-while article has been skipped by its prospective readers because the beginning was not sufficiently interesting to catch their attention.

Whenever an article writer finds that he is doing a piece about anything in a class by itself, he might well use this fact as a beginning. If it is the first or the last, the largest or the smallest, the most or least numerous, the most expensive or the cheapest, the oldest or the youngest — if any of these, he may be sure the reader's eye will be halted long enough for him to see whether the subject holds further interest for him.

Striking statments will vary in the degree of interest they arouse. But you should not exaggerate the facts merely for the sake of attracting attention. As always, stick to your facts. Avoid anything that is likely to be misunderstood or considered ridiculous. Your editor won't like it, and your readers, therefore, may be deprived of your article.

Which striking statement will eventually be chosen will depend upon the ingenuity of the writer. He may read his already written article, and from it select the most interesting statement for rephrasing and display in the opening paragraph. Or he may put himself in the place of his readers to discover what would move him most if offered as a beginning. This calls for exercise of the imagination. The writing of a striking-statement opening is not difficult, for there are numerous possibilities in every article. Be sure to keep the beginning accurate and closely related to the subject, as in the examples below.

A.

GAMBLING WITH HOMES

What Is Happening and Is Likely to Happen to
Those Who Buy Homes on Today's Market?

The family without a home might just as well throw away $3 every day for the next five years as buy the average house on today's inflated market.

If the statement sounds strange, let it be said that it is exactly what today's home-buyer is doing.

Throughout the nation prices already have risen from 45 to 75 per cent on the average home. On a house that cost $8,500 ten years ago, the inflationary rise is now about $5,000. In some cases the increase has been over $13,000, or more than the original cost of the house. . . .

B.

CAN YOU TRUST YOUR GROCER?

Seven out of ten grocers cheat their customers by small amounts, a recent survey in five large Eastern cities reveals.

Though the butcher counter leads all individual departments for sheer brazenness, the most deadly thievery is done where customers line up at the cash registers. Impatient shoppers with multiple purchases make overcharging almost impossible to detect — and if caught, the cashier admits to an "error" but goes quickly back to. . . .

C.

AMERICA'S GREATEST HARPIST

Without peer, without equal, Melville H. Clark truly had all the techniques of the world's great harpists at his fingertips.

Marie Antoinette's harp, the harps of early Irish bards, an Egyptian harp so old no one dares guess its age sang for him with a perfection they never achieved under the plucking fingers of the original owners.

Among the unique instruments that. . . .

D.

DEATH ON THE HIGHWAYS

Is America Really Callous to the Mounting Slaughter
on the Nation's Traffic Lanes?

If the first four months of this year are a safe index, more Americans will be injured in traffic accidents on city streets and country highways in the next three years than in any period of similar length in our history.

E.

MEDICAL COSTS FACE AN OPERATION

There Are Free Clinics for the Poor, and the
Wealthy Don't Need Help, but No One Aids
People of Moderate Means

The great middle class is the underprivileged orphan when it comes to medical care.

Free clinics, free dispensaries, and free operations are available for much of the country's low income groups. But in spite of health and hospital insurance, for which the sufferer usually pays, most members of the middle income brackets cannot get the skilled medical attention they need.

Three chief reasons account for this. . . .

F.

TICKET FIXING DELUXE

More than 4,500,000 traffic tickets are given to American automobile drivers each year. But in numerous cities less than half of the violators are required to pay the penalty prescribed by law.

The answer is the traffic "fix." . . .

The Summary

The summary beginning resembles the summary lead of a news story. It presents a synopsis of the entire article for the reader. Because of this fact, it quickly selects its readers, who can tell at a glance whether they wish to read farther.

The greatest advantage of this type of beginning is that it permits display of several interesting points in the first paragraph. Instead of concentrating on a single point, as in the striking statement, the summary beginning includes as many "sales points" as possible. This beginning offers a multiple show window for presenting the most attractive or impelling items in the article. There are more chances, therefore, to attract and hold the attention of the editor — and other readers.

Most subjects have different facets of interest. Putting as many relevant ideas as possible into the beginning assures a wider group of readers. Yet the opening must not be clumsy or overburdened. Perhaps three or four points will be sufficient. When the opening has been set down, the writer should judge its merits. If too long, or complicated, it should be trimmed to the proper point.

Some of the examples below might also be classified as striking statements.

A.

FUN AT HOME

How Amateurs Built a Game Room Out of Waste
Space in the Basement

Unaided, our family has just built a rumpus room at a cost of $65 in
what was waste space in an unsightly basement. . . .

B.

SHE COULDN'T KEEP OUT OF BUSINESS

Mary Alice Burlingham, a contented housewife, became a successful
manufacturer doing business on a national scale in spite of herself — all
because she gave away half a dozen jars of mint jelly.

A department store buyer tasted, became enthusiastic, and asked her to
put the jelly on the market, giving him exclusive local rights in the upstate
New York city where she lived.

Within a few months one of New York City's largest department stores
begged her to send them a shipment. She did, and that was the beginning of
her growing success. . . .

C.

THIRD-GENERATION FARMER

Charles Towne Carries On Until His Son
Gets Back from College

Charles Towne, of Onondaga County, New York, a successful dairy
farmer, has operated for 27 years the 169-acre farm which his father and
grandfather built into one of the finest estates in Central New York.

"When my son, Albert, gets through Cornell, I aim to turn the hard
work over to him," says Mr. Towne. "Right now I work from 5 A.M. to 8 P.M.,
including Sunday. . . ."

D.

CHALK TALKS

A few bits of chalk, a pad of paper, and a homemade easel were the sole
items of equipment with which Edgar Dowley, self-trained chalk-talk artist
of Buffalo, started the hobby that has become a profitable and interesting
sideline . . .

Direct Address

The appeal of the direct address beginning is instantaneous. It is the
shortest path between writer and reader. There is no better way to get
an article off to a quick start than to use this type of opening. Further-

more, it is far more intimate than most other types. For this reason, it is excellent when used with articles discussing personal problems or personal revelations.

As with other beginnings, some dangers are to be avoided. It is well to avoid overuse of the word "you." Employ it occasionally, but don't permit the technique to become monotonous. Also, don't become too familiar with the reader unless circumstances warrant — which they seldom do. Don't presume to know the reader too well, or to scold, or talk down to him. He will quickly resent it.

Often, too, when a subject discusses errors which the reader himself may have made, it will be wiser to impute the mistake to other individuals. This can be done very easily, and the reader will get the point. For instance, don't say, "The chances are, Mr. Reader, that you are dishonest in some things." Say, "Surveys reveal that sixty people out of a hundred admit that they are dishonest at times." The psychology of the individual is such that he can scarcely avoid making an application to his own conduct.

Note whether the following examples overwork the word "you."

A.

WORLD'S LEADING CERAMIST

You probably wouldn't have given a second glance to Adelaide Robineau had you met her by chance. She was slight of build and undistinguished in appearance.

Yet within her lifetime she became recognized as one of the world's greatest ceramists. . . .

B.

HOMEMADE ACCIDENTS

The house where you now live probably holds more menace from serious accidents than the streets where you walk or the highways upon which you travel.

The bathtub, the cellar steps, the light plugs, the kitchen stove, the stepladder, and scores of other items in everyday use are potential sources of maiming or fractures, even of death itself. . . .

C.

HOMES BY MAIL

If you are among the more than 10,000,000 Americans now planning to construct or buy a home of their own, you probably have already considered the prefabricated house.

Included in the advantages of prefabricated houses are cheapness, ease of construction, the latest type conveniences, and a variety of plans to suit many tastes.

Already being made in all sections of the country. . . .

D.

BAD MEDICINE

When you adopt another person's remedy, or perform any of the other dangerous acts of self-medication, you are putting yourself in the place of the trained specialist who is required by law to have a minimum of four years of medical instruction and a year of hospital interneship. . . .

The Question

Question beginnings are good because they cannot be avoided. The reader will formulate an answer in spite of himself. Some questions, of course, are uttered for rhetorical effect. They are not meant to be answered. But even with such questions the formulation of some answer is almost automatic.

If you wish to "put the reader on the spot," if you wish to force him to take a position, the question is the best weapon. This lead, however, has the same disadvantages as has the direct address. It must be handled with good sense and in good taste. Occasionally the writer must take care to frame the question so that it will elicit the answer he desires.

Although the openings cited here are examples of direct questions, indirect questions may also be used.

A.

TREASURE FOR THE FINDING

What has become of the ancient buried treasures, the sunken galleons, the pirate gold of past centuries, and the hidden hoards of countless misers?

Few years have passed, except war years, that have not seen some expedition set off for Cocos Island. . . .

B.

THE MISSING MUSICIAN

What happens to dance band and orchestra players when they grow old?

Puzzled because practically no band of any repute, not even the local orchestras, contains a member beyond the mid-forties, I recently set out to discover what becomes of these musicians when they begin to lose the stamina that permits long jaunts, irregular hours, and the strain of an exacting profession.

Symphonic orchestras are an exception. . . .

C.

COURTESY IS OUT OF DATE

Are good manners disappearing? Is old-fashioned courtesy really a thing of the past? If so, what are the causes, and what can be done about it?

Next time you make a trip, or go shopping, or visit another city, note the indifference to your comfort and welfare of your fellow travelers and those who serve you.

And it might not be unfair to ask, "What are you doing to perpetuate the ideals of good breeding?"

D.

HAS THE MELTING POT CEASED TO MELT?

Is it true, as is frequently printed of late, that racial and religious antipathies are on the increase in this country?

The newspapers report incidents in Boston of anti-Jewish attacks by youngsters not yet out of their teens, of anti-Negro assaults in New York City. Labor and capital seem farther apart now than in many a year.

Have the forces which once appeared to be creating a homogeneous population in America ceased to function?

E.

MAP MAKING BY AIR

What is photogrammetry?

This relatively new science that makes possible the accurate mapping and measuring of all terrain, regardless of its contours, can cut to less than 1 per cent the time formerly required to make maps of mountain and wooded areas.

Roughly, photogrammetry produces three-dimensioned photographs, taken by air, from which depth, height, length, and breadth can be read directly through a system of grids and. . . .

The Narrative

Long before the written word was invented, men were telling stories of adventure, love, and achievement. Interest in the narrative goes far beyond man's ability to record that interest. Hence, the first crude writings and drawings were frequently attempts to record what men had done. Most short stories and novels are fictional records of adventure in one field or another.

Articles that recount what has been done are, therefore, based upon an ancient interest, and the narrative beginning drills in a proved field. The narrative, or story, beginning is best when used to introduce a narrative article, but it may be used on all types of articles.

Stories of personal experience, confession tales, and adventure stories in the third person are common examples of types of articles to which narrative beginning are well suited.

Among the types of narrative beginnings are incidents and anecdotes, which must be interesting to draw readers further into the article. Action is the key to a vital and effective narrative opening. Make characters move; have them do or say something. Dialogue also makes a good beginning if it contributes action to the article, as in examples A and C below.

A.

PINK-TAILED DEER

Two hunters from Philadelphia recently were deep in the Adirondacks on a deer run not far from Lake Placid. They had driven up the day before to be on hand when the deer season opened.

"Bless my eyes," said one. "Is that a pink-tailed deer, or am I crazy?"

"You're not crazy," said the other, "—that is, unless I am, too. If that deer didn't have a pink tail, then I'm back at Brennan's Bar."

That was how word leaked out of the studies being made on the feeding and ranging habits of wild life in. . . .

B.

IN HOSTEL COUNTRY

An Old European Custom Has Been Introduced
to American Youth

We set out on our bicycles from Hartford shortly after sunrise, intending to follow the level road that parallels the winding Connecticut, until we could turn northward into the Berkshires.

This was our first adventure in youth hosteling, and we were embarking without knowing entirely what to expect.

On our bicycles we had loaded a frying pan, coffee pot, and enough food for two meals for each of us. We were also carrying a raincoat and a change of clothing apiece. . . .

C.

WHEN A LAWYER TURNS BANKER

At the Merchants National Bank one rainy day a customer grumbled about the difficulty of opening doors if one's arms were full of packages when stopping to cash a check.

"We'll take care of that," said a man standing near.

"I hope you do," the customer said.

He didn't know it, but he was talking to Marcus A. Holt, president of the bank, a reformed lawyer, as he puts it, who makes a habit of mixing with his depositors to find out what they actually think of the services his bank offers.

Within a few weeks' time the doors were gone and in their place were jet streams of warm air, making it possible for customers to walk directly from the street into the bank while cashing checks or making deposits. . . .

The Descriptive

Variety is given to an article through the descriptive beginning, because it is used infrequently. To be good it must be vivid. It should yield a swift, clear picture of the scene, the individual, the article, the emotional state, or the perception which the writer wishes to set forth.

Remember that readers tend to skip lengthy passages of description. Limit descriptive matter to a few short paragraphs. Inject action when possible. Try to make the language picturesque, and keep away from hackneyed figures of speech. Give the total picture with as few strokes as possible. Avoid technical terms and definitions.

Few articles made up entirely of description are used by the magazines or newspapers. Consequently, the writer must shift quickly into expository or narrative writing. Dialogue and quotation also are good as follow-ups. Item A below is an example of this type of development.

A.

TEACHER EXTRAORDINARY

Harold D. Myer was the most extraordinary teacher I have ever known.

His thinning hair was red, his features florid. He stood about five feet nine and was on the stout side. His features were inclined to be pudgy, but he had an engaging smile that made you forget his other characteristics.

Vivid with words, vital in action, he never left a classroom without having impressed his students with his personality.

"My, my," he would say in tones of slight chagrin, "I never thought a student of mine would be guilty of racial or religious intolerance. . . ."

B.

PRAIRIE FISHING

Flower's "prairie," as the native Floridians call certain types of swamp, was like a circular meadow three miles across.

It was emerald green at all seasons of the year, for the grass grew thickly over its shallow waters. Yet here and there were tiny lakes — some only a dozen feet long and half as much across. "Pot holes" the Florida crackers called them.

These pot holes were chuck-full of black bass — so big and fat it was worth the back-breaking work of poling a boat over the grass for a chance at them. . . .

C.

BURIED TREASURE OF RHEIMS

A hundred feet beneath the gray chalk soil three miles outside of Rheims there rests one of the greatest treasures in all France.

Twenty-five million dollars would be a low estimate of the value of this liquid gold. Perhaps 40 million would not be too high.

The dimly-lighted, vaulted roofs of the treasure-holding caverns seem to stretch endlessly. Actually they are perhaps a quarter of a mile long, but they number into the scores.

Here built against the walls are racks with slanting shelves upon which from 12 to 15 million bottles of champagne are groomed for the market. . . .

The Quotation

To be effective the quotation beginning should be sufficiently striking or interesting in itself to arrest attention. If it is the work of a well-known author, it should not be hackneyed from overuse. Some excellent bits of writing have been so frequently cited that they now bore the average reader. The old maxims are likely to fall into this category. Unless the writer can paraphrase them clearly or give them a new twist (as in Item A below), he should shun their use.

Quotations hold a fascination all their own. Anybody can prove this by noting how in reading short stories or novels he jumps from one patch of dialogue to the next. Descriptive passages, even by the best of current writers, are likely to be slighted. Quotations also usually carry the action in any piece of writing, whether fact or fiction. Continued reading trains readers to appreciate this fact. Consequently, the average individual is likely to sample any beginning that makes use of quotes. Note how the following beginnings get away to a quick start.

A.

DOES MOTHER KNOW BEST?

Mother doesn't know best in this scientific age — unless she is possessed of a training and skill unknown in the days when that parental "answer-all" was first coined, according to the best of scientific opinion.

Intuition and other forms of guesswork. . . .

B.

"NOTHING SUCCEEDS LIKE WORK"

"All work and no play" is the surest way to success in almost any field, says Charles P. Todd, noted industrial psychologist of New York City.

"Competition for top positions in industry, the professions, and even in politics is too keen for anyone to take time out for wasteful play hours. . . ."

C.

TRAINING CHAMPIONSHIP DOGS

Famous Trainer Tells How He Schools Winners for the Tennessee Field Trials

"I never whip a dog, or otherwise abuse him," says Bert Noonan, trainer of more Tennessee field-trial winners than any other dog handler in America. "A scolding or a sharp order is enough for any intelligent dog.

"If a pointer or setter is smart enough to place in field competition, he's got enough brains so he doesn't need to be whipped. If he isn't intelligent, training of any kind is a waste of time."

Bert Noonan was pointing out the pups from which he expected to make champions.

"That dog will make a good hunter, but he'll never get a ribbon in a field trial," Noonan declared. "He lacks showmanship, an' he's got a bad stance."

D.

REFORMING OUR COLLEGES

"Cafeteria courses and purely vocational education must be dropped from the curricula of institutions aiming at cultural education," declares President Thomas P. Bryant of Nottingham University.

"Too many elective courses produce Jacks-of-all-trades, while less than 20 per cent of college and university graduates ultimately follows the vocations for which they are trained.

"What is needed is an education conceived. . . ."

Multiplication of Types

Types of beginnings may be multiplied through further subdivision and combination. For instance, we might have a striking statement in the form of quotation, or perhaps even description. A quotation beginning might appear in the form of an anecdote, and so forth. These seven, however, are the basic forms, and all others are special adaptations.

Writers are more interested in creating effective introductions to their articles than in producing this or that variety of beginning. For this reason you will frequently find two or more of the above types combined. Always, the test of a beginning is, "Does it accomplish its purpose?" Combined types may make excellent beginnings, but they are likely to run longer than the single type. Extra care should be taken, therefore, to prune them to their minimum length.

Training Steps

1. In an issue of *Pageant,* classify all of the article beginnings according to our seven types.
2. Make a tabulation of the various types. How many of each are there? Which are the most numerous? How many combination leads do you find?
3. Try these same steps on an issue of *Reader's Digest.* What types of beginnings are preferred by each magazine?
4. Make the same analysis of an issue of the *Catholic Digest.*
5. In these three magazines mark off the point at which the beginning of each article ends. Count the number of words in the beginning of every other article. What is the average length? Which magazine has the shortest and which has the longest beginnings?
6. In the same issue of the *Catholic Digest,* compare ten of the beginnings of articles with the originals from which the condensations were made. What are the actual differences in length of beginning? Have these ten articles lost in appeal because of the condensation?
7. If you find evidence of loss of appeal in any article, what was the cause? If appeal is improved, state how it was accomplished.
8. Take two or three issues of your favorite magazine. What types of beginnings does it use? How long are they? Could you condense any of them?
9. Examine a magazine that you consider dull. Would you say the beginnings of articles are uninteresting? If so, why?
10. Now take a different copy of the *Catholic Digest,* or of either of the other two magazines used above. Give free rein to your interest. Mark each article that you would probably not read. When you have gone through the entire issue, go back and study each article that failed to catch your interest. How many had weak titles? How many had weak beginnings? How many did you pass by because of subject matter?
11. Select a subject with which you are perfectly familiar. Write for it a beginning in each of the seven types. Which is the strongest? Is it good because of type, because it fits the subject, or because of inherent merit?
12. Examine an article in which you find the beginning uninteresting. Is there material elsewhere in the article that would have made a better introduction? Now write a beginning based on this hidden material.
13. The *Reader's Digest* is said to have a standard style. How long are the introductions to its articles? Are they longer than those in the *Catholic*

Digest? Try an editorial pencil on the *Reader's Digest.* Can you shorten the beginnings of its articles?

14. Select an interesting *Reader's Digest* article. Can you write a more interesting beginning?

15. Have you found descriptive beginnings as interesting as narrative? As interesting as striking statements? Wherein lies the fault?

16. Compare a half dozen beginnings in a Sunday newspaper magazine with those in a general popular magazine. What differences of length and style do you note?

17. Compare the beginnings of a number of news stories with those of articles in the same newspaper. What differences are there?

CHAPTER 10

Handling the Title

The sale of an article often depends upon the merit of the title. In the nonillustrated article the title is the first part to catch the eye. In the illustrated piece either photographs or drawings may seize first attention, but from these the eyes turn to title and subtitle — if any. According to the routine of most offices, the editor seldom sees more than a small percentage of the manuscripts addressed to him, because between him and the writing fraternity stand one or more readers and perhaps a departmental editor or two.

If, then, you want to reach the editor, your unpublished title must be good enough to shine among a score or a hundred others and persuasive enough to convince these assistants that the article is worth reading with a view to passing it on to the editor.

No Good Title is Wasted

Since every writer hopes to make the best impression upon his editor, no effort is too great to spend in devising the best possible title. If the title is good and suitable for make-up plans, the editor will use the one that comes with the article, should he buy it. Frequently titles are good, but not quite good enough; if the article is purchased, the title must be redone. Editors, like other purveyors of competitive goods, are bound to make their products as attractive as possible. But whether or not the writer's good title is used, it will have measurably aided in presenting the article to the prospective market.

In articles submitted to newspapers and newspaper syndicates, the writer will be wise to include first-rate titles. His titles will not be used, of course, for he cannot know in advance the column width his article will finally have. The sales job of these titles is the same, nevertheless, as that of titles submitted to magazines.

Marks of a Good Title

Since the editor probably will do some rewriting if he buys the article, a good title from the point of view of the writer is 1. accurate, 2. attractive, 3. exact, and 4. concise. Good titles may have other desirable traits. But if a title meets the four specifications above, it is a good title.

ACCURACY. When a title is said to be accurate, the implication is that it accurately describes the subject matter. The writer may have used his imaginative powers, but they will have been exercised within the natural boundaries of the facts. He will not advertise an item as unique, unless it is the only one of its kind. Nor will he use the superlative degree in any manner, unless the subject matter warrants it. If he writes about the largest dairy barn in the state, it must be a matter of record that the structure is actually the largest. Anything else is untruthful, and that is sufficient reason to demand a change in the title. If an editor misses an exaggeration, some reader is almost certain to nail the error. And the writer's relations with the magazine may end there.

Some facts are matters of opinion. A writer may describe as his "most unusual experience" an incident that is routine for someone else. *Reader's Digest* pursued the theme of personal opinion in its series, "My Most Unforgettable Character." In such cases, the writer is not taking liberties when he uses the superlative.

ATTRACTIVENESS. The attractiveness of a title varies with the reader. It may be said to excel in this respect when it halts the roving eye of the reader, and compels him to read the first paragraph. At that point the beginning becomes responsible for the continued attention of the reader. Yet the finest titles will be passed over by some readers because of previously developed antagonisms to the subject. The best the writer can do is to show how his material affects the reader's success, health,

or personal affairs — if it does. Many magazines are built around these
three items, which serve as a formula for attracting the reader's interest.
Each issue contains one or more articles intended to promote the reader's
comfort, his health, his financial affairs, or his personal relations. Titles
that bear on these points when "dressed up" are likely to meet magazine
needs.

EXACTNESS.   When it is said that a title should be exact, it is meant
that it should be to the point. Far-fetched allusions and vague references may either confuse or offend. Both are adverse reflections upon
writer and magazine. Unless there is reason for mystifying a reader, it
is better to let him know at once what the article is about. This is one
advantage of the title that merely labels an article.

CONCISENESS.   This quality is always appreciated by editors and
readers. Theoretically, at least, the best title is a one-word title. Yet
most titles must be qualified for the sake of accuracy, and they must be
brought to life through choice of words. Conciseness, or brevity, is
achieved by careful selection of words, which must be exact, as well as
accurate and attractive. Then when put together, a very few will do
the work. Conciseness is achieved at times by using the blue pencil on
unnecessary words or phrases. The writer should ask himself whether
the title can get along without each word or phrase. Among words contributing little are "a," "an," "the," "very," and "that." Frequently these
can be omitted with considerable improvement to the title.

Slanting Titles

Titles inappropriate to the columns to which the article is submitted
are poor salesmen for the article. They suggest at once that the writer
has not examined what the publication uses. Obviously, by implication
the writer is unfamiliar with the policy of the staff upon other matters.

What are the points to be considered in slanting the title toward
selected markets, particularly the magazines?

LENGTH.   First, there is the matter of mechanical limitations, or
length of title. Some magazines never use a title that runs to two or
more lines. Others may set the maximum limit at 5 or 6 words — or less.
Most magazines use both one- and two-line titles, looking for variety
rather than uniformity. In recent times hand-lettered titles and freak
arrangements — particularly in magazines interested in any phase of
design, decoration, and clothing — have become more common. Some
titles stretch across two pages, and others pile up line upon line on a
single page. While the writer can do nothing about the typographical

arrangement or decorative angle, he can follow the pattern in other particulars.

STYLE. In the second place, most magazines have some policy on content of titles. *Popular Science Monthly*, for instance, frequently uses the paraphrase. Some magazines like the pun, some the question; while still others seek a sprightly style. Many use alliteration, such as "The Cults of California" from the *Reader's Digest*, though this latter publication almost invariably follows a matter-of-fact, objective style in titles, as in "The Scandal of Our Traffic Courts." Generally, a magazine with wide appeal will be found to use titles without adornment, and the wider the appeal, the more likely is this to be true.

TASTE. Third, the question of taste is important. Titles should lean to the conservative side when matters of taste are involved. If the title seems doubtful, it should most certainly be dropped for one about which there is no question. No journal wishes to offend against public taste or morals, nor will any wish to risk offending a large segment of its readers on racial, religious, or moral grounds.

TABOOS. Last, many magazines have pet ideas, taboos, or sanctions that should be understood and followed. If *Parents' Magazine*, for instance, supports the idea of summer camps for children, don't submit a title "Beware of Summer Camps." Instead, if there is danger in the summer camp idea, find a way to explain without bumping into almost certain rejection. Write, "Improving Summer Camps," or "Latest Aids for Summer Camps." Approach the title and the rest of the article from the positive angle.

The Title-Beginning Unit

The opening paragraphs, the title, and the subtitle (if any) should be considered and handled as a unit. Within these two or three subdivisions of the article, there should be a well-developed coherence. This is achieved by a limited repetition. Repetition is of two kinds: of idea and of word, or group of words. Used with judgment and restraint, repetition develops an introduction as nothing else can do. Variety is maintained by changing the descriptive words and by using synonyms.

Subtitles, almost without exception, are longer than the titles they accompany. Where the average title is probably no longer than five words, the average subtitle is about 12 words. This enlarged space gives room in which to expand or qualify the main idea expressed in the title. Amplification and qualification are more important between these two units than repetition of ideas. New ideas should be brought into the subtitle. This is nearly always possible. Remembering that the subtitle represents an additional window in which to display his wares, the writer will dig out some new and interesting facts to attract and hold the reader's eye.

The opening paragraphs should be the amplification of what was stated, revealed, or promised in the title and subtitle. Most of the repetition should be handled through synonymous words and parallel ideas. Except for emphasis, repetition of the exact wording should be avoided. In this beginning the reader should find a hint at least of what was promised earlier, as well as new hope for additional entertainment or information.

Subheads

Some writers and editors consider subheads an extension of the idea in the title. Not all magazines use them. When used, subheads serve several purposes. They break up long passages of monotonous type; they catch the eye of the reader and lure him to further reading; and they tell what is in the passages ahead.

Subheads may be used about every 200 words. One or two will be sufficient on any page. Almost invariably they will be found to consist of one line, which limits the length to three or four words. A noun, verb, and object make a good combination. Vivid, action words are best. Probably the first page of the manuscript should have no subhead. Page 2 might use two, and page 3 a single subhead. The content of the article will determine this point.

If a magazine does not use subheads, it may be of questionable value for the writer to insert them. If it appears that valuable items might otherwise be overlooked by the fleeting eye of a first reader, probably little harm can come from employing them.

Types of Titles

Various classifications of titles have been made. Most writers on the subject recognize the existence of certain basic types, and then add a few variations that appeal to their own judgment. Classifications of types of titles and types of articles and the like are useful to the student of writing. They form the basis for a system of dissection through which he can take articles apart to see what makes them tick.

According to some teachers of writing, excellent titles often suggest themselves to the writer. This is but a manner of speaking. Some titles are recognized because they are obvious. Some are merely quotations from the article itself. Some are adaptations. But the ones that "pop" into the mind are the result of considerable thought on the part of the writer, whether he knows it or not. The subconscious mind has a way of being helpful to writers sometimes when they least expect it.

The following list of twelve types of titles has been arranged as far as possible in the order of their usefulness to the writer, in regard to ease of composing and frequency of use by standard magazines: 1. striking statement; 2. provocative statement; 3. label; 4. paraphrase (including pun); 5. declarative sentence; 6. how, why, and what; 7. question; 8. direct address; 9. quotation; 10. exclamation; 11. rhyme and alliteration; 12. balance and contrast.

Striking Statement

Almost without effort writers seem to create striking-statement titles. Perhaps they know that readers like to be startled. And perhaps they also realize that striking statements make good sales arguments for the article itself. When the writer can dip into his article and bring forth a statement that will jolt a sizeable percentage of readers, he has the making of a good title. He should, of course, avoid exaggeration and offenses against good taste. Examples of titles consisting of the striking statement from standard journals are as follows:

A. *Reader's Digest*

THEY'RE FREEZING ULCERS TO DEATH

A New Procedure Gives Promise of Lasting Relief
from the Misery of Peptic Ulcer

B. *Life*

SPARE PARTS FOR THE HUMAN BODY

Recipient of a Lung Transplant Dies, But
Surgery Takes a Leap Forward

C. *Time*

THE GENTLE GORILLA

D. *Popular Science*

LIVING BENEATH THE SEA

E. *Reader's Digest*

LIVE LIKE A KING—
IN A CASTLE

F. *Look*

DO WE NEED THE DRAFT?

G. *Field & Stream*

PICKUP CAMPER PARADISE

Some of the Most Spectacular Fishing
in the World Is Yours in Mexico

H. *Outdoor Life*

LIONS ALMOST ANYTIME

Provocative and Mysterious Statement

Curiosity probably has killed more human beings than cats. In fact, the trait is one of the strongest manifested by mankind. How many inventions and discoveries are due to man's insatiable curiosity no one will ever be able to say. But we do know that whatever arouses curiosity is likely to be investigated. Relying upon this well-known fact, some nationally known magazines and newspapers have used the following titles:

A. *Pageant*

FOUR WOMEN IN ONE BODY

B. *Field and Stream*

THE KING AND YOU

C. New York *Herald Tribune*

MUSICAL CAKE RETURNS TO PERK UP BIRTHDAYS

Tinkles Lilting Melodies
as Knife Severs Layers;
Photos Decorate Pastry

D. *Sports Illustrated*

THE VALLEY OF DEATH

The Best Basketball Conference
in the Country Offers Visitors
Nothing but Trouble

E. *Popular Mechanics Magazine*
UNLOCKING THE UNIVERSE

F. *House Beautiful*
KEEP LIFE WITHIN THE REACH OF YOUR HAND

G. *Reader's Digest*
THE SHEPHERD
WHO WOULD NOT GO

H. *National Geographic Magazine*
REVOLUTION IN EATING

Machine Food Age — Born of Roads, Research, and
Refrigeration — Makes the United States
the Best-Fed Nation in History

I. *Outdoor Life*
WALK THE PLANK

I Wasn't Blindfolded but There
Was a Time When I Just Went
Ker-plunk

J. *Popular Science Monthly*
LOST: A GENERATION OF SCIENTISTS

Label

The label title sets forth the obvious. That is its weakness and its strength. The type is weak because it is limited to the subject of the article. Its strength lies in the fact that it quickly selects readers. Unlike oher types, it does not seek to lure readers by promises of excitement, but states its case quickly, letting those read who wish. If a subject is sufficiently interesting, it will need little advertising. Examples of this type are as follows:

A. *Antiques*
NEW ENGLAND PAINTING
1700-1725

B. *This Week*

THE THREE R'S — PLUS ART

Students at the High School
of Music and Art Aren't Odd
—— They Just Hate Vacations.

C. San Francisco *Chronicle*

COLLEGIATE BABY CLINIC

Life Changes Down on the Farm —
Families Added to Vets' Curricula

D. *Time*

PRESIDENTIAL HOLIDAY

E. *Mademoiselle*

LATIN AMERICANS IN NEW YORK

F. *Hobbies*

ANTIQUING IN THE KENTUCKY MOUNTAINS

G. *McCall's Magazine*

YOUR NEW HOME FREEZER

H. *Life*

UMPIRE SCHOOL

I. *The New York Times*

CHILDREN WHO HAVE KNOWN NO CHILDHOOD

Paraphrase or Pun

Few editors can resist paraphrasing a well-known quotation, because it is certain to attract those who recognize the original. Occasionally a well-conceived pun may be used, but it must be good. Punning is not in good standing with particular editors. The play on words is somewhat better. What may be done is suggested in the following examples:

A. *Look*

INSTANT NEIGHBORHOODS

Where Do the Hosts of Home-Hungry
Middle-Income People Live — Those Who
Can't Afford Luxury Housing?

B. *American Home*

HOME, HOME OFF THE RANGE

Hate to Turn on the Oven on a Hot Day?
You're in the Market for an
Electric Skillet

C. *Reader's Digest*

HERE COMES THE DYNA-SOAR

A Preview of an Amazing Aircraft Which,
in just a Few Years, will be
Rocketing into Space

D. *House and Garden*

TO LIVE HAPPILY EVER AFTER

E. *Time*

TALE OF TWO EMPIRES

F. *The New Yorker*

WAS NOT ALL SHE USED TO BE

G. *American Home*

TIME MARCHES BACK

Treasured Pieces from the Past from
the Georg Jensen Collection

H. *House and Garden*

CUT YOUR TREES AND HAVE THEM TOO

Declarative Sentence

One of the easiest types of titles to write is the declarative sentence. Because the subject and verb lend themselves to easy manipulation, it is easy to get action into titles of this type. Of all types this one is the most flexible. That is why it ranks high on the list. Following are some examples:

A. *Christian Science Monitor*

UTAH SAGA UNFOLDS IN GRANITE

Connecticut Man Carves Figures

B. *Life*

EVERYBODY BLOWS UP!

C. *Mademoiselle*

WOMEN ARE GOOD NEIGHBORS

D. *This Week*

THEY CHASE TRAIN ROBBERS

Catching Con Men or Protecting Presidents,
Our Railroad Dicks Are on the Job. They
Have to Think Fast — and Move Fast, Too

E. *National Civic Review*

CALIFORNIA CLEANS ITS COURTS

F. *Harper's Magazine*

WASHINGTON IS WHAT WE MAKE IT

G. *Family Circle*

SCHOOL VACATIONS SHOULDN'T WEAR YOU OUT

H. *Life*

MOBY DICK IS MISSING

Movie Model of White Whale
Eludes Its Pursuers

How, Why, and What

The how-to-do-something article is often headed by the "how" title.
"Where," "who," "what," "why," and "when" are other varieties. Numerous applications are possible, but this kind of title is commonly used on articles of advice. Some examples are as follows:

A. *Reader's Digest*

WHY JOHNNY CAN'T GET A JOB

B. *Woman's Day*

HOW TO MEND CHINA

C. New York *Herald Tribune*

WHEN YOUR CHILD IS HURT

Here Is Advice from a Babies' Hospital
That May Save a Life in Your Family — a
Prescription for a Healthy Childhood

D. *Reader's Digest*

WHAT THE ATOM BOMB WOULD DO TO US

E. *School and Society*
> ## HOW GEORGIA'S TEACHERS GOT A RAISE

F. *Better Homes and Gardens*
> ## HOW TO RESTORE OLD FURNITURE

G. *TV Guide*
> ## WHAT TELEVISION CAN — AND CANNOT — DO
>
> It Will Homogenize Us, Says a
> Distinguished Critic
> — and That's Not All

H. *U. S. Lady*
> ## HOW I LEARNED TO BE AN EXPERT BARGAINER

I. *Popular Mechanics Magazine*
> ## WHAT TO DO BEFORE YOU PAINT

Question

When the reader comes upon a question title, he is forced to seek an answer whether he wishes to or not. If the question is sufficiently interesting, it is almost certain to draw him further into the article. Psychologically it is one of the soundest types to use. Examples of question titles follow:

A. *Mademoiselle*
> ## WHO KILLED ROMANCE?
>
> One Good Old-Fashioned Love Affair
> Is Worth at Least a Dozen Ultra-
> Modern "Relationships"

B. *Family Circle*
> ## ARE YOU KILLING YOUR HUSBAND?

C. *Reader's Digest*
> ## IS YOU DOG SAFE FROM DISTEMPER?

D. *Maclean's Magazine*
> ## IS THE U. S. FIT TO LEAD THE WORLD?

E. *The Atlantic*
> ## WHAT DO STRIKES TEACH US?

F. *Woman's Day*
WHY MUST A REAL BOY BE TOUGH?

G. *The Denver Post*
WHAT'S HAPPENED TO MOTELS?

The Kozy Kabins Have Become Motor
Hotels where the Traveler Can
Find Every Modern Luxury and
Convenience at a Price

H. *Harper's Magazine*
WHO'S GETTING THE MONEY?

I. *Better Homes and Gardens*
IS NOW THE TIME TO BUY OR SELL?

If You Have to Buy to Get a Place to Live,
Buy; You Likely Won't Save a Lot by
Waiting, Because Costs Are
Going Up

Direct Address

Direct address is about as effective as the question. Either is difficult to dodge. Because the method is completely inclusive, the reader can exclude himself only by a deliberate act of the will. He is less likely to do this with the question than with most other types. Common sense and reasonableness are necessary qualities of this type of title. Both indirect and direct address may be used, though the latter is usually more effective. Examples are as follows:

A. *The Atlantic*
DON'T BELIEVE ALL YOU HEAR

B. *Outdoor Life*
DON'T BET ON ROOSTERS

C. *American Home*
WHEN YOU HAVE A GOOD PLAN LEAVE IT ALONE

D. *McCall's Magazine*
DO IT BY HAND

E. *Holiday*

SAIL THE SOUND IN DINGHIES

F. *Mechanix Illustrated*

FOLD YOUR FISHING POLE

Toting That 15-Foot Bamboo Pole Will Always
Be Troublesome — Unless You Fold It into an
Easy-to-Carry Bundle — Here's How

G. *Popular Science Monthly*

PAINT A CARPET ON YOUR FLOOR

H. *House Beautiful*

MAKE ROOM FOR SUMMER

Give Your House an Uncluttered Look

I. *Pageant*

YOUR HANDWRITING CAN GET YOU A JOB

Quotation

While lacking the current twist which can be given to the paraphrase, the quotation may be effective, particularly when used with subtitle and illustrations. Occasionally, excellent titles are made from recently-coined phrases after they have gained wide recognition. Such a title heads the list below. Avoid using the phrase that is lacking in essential merit.

A. *The National Geographic Magazine*

"BLOOD, TOIL, TEARS, AND SWEAT"

An American Tells the Story of Britain's War
Effort, Summed Up in Prime Minister
Churchill's Unflinching Words

B. *Mademoiselle*

"ET TU, BRUTE!"

C. *Good Housekeeping*

"REST YE MERRIE GENTLEMEN"

D. *House Beautiful*
HE PRACTICES WHAT HE PREACHES

A Man Whose Business Is Linoleum Uses It
Freely, Decoratively, Personably in
His Home in Woodside, Calif.

E. *Time*
"THE TIME HAS COME"

F. *Popular Science Monthly*
THERE'S NO PLACE LIKE HOME

G. *Better Homes and Gardens*
"I WAS ONLY TRYING TO HELP"

A Dizzy Dissertation on Plain and Fancy Ways
of Getting in Your Builder's Way

H. *National Geographic Magazine*
"THE GLORY THAT WAS GREECE"

I. *Kiwanis Magazine*
HOW DEAR TO MY HEART

Exclamation

Editors sometimes develop a fad for a certain type of title, or for a certain style. As this is being written, *American Home* is using numerous titles of the exclamation type. In most magazines it is one of the rarer types, because readers are not so much startled by form as by content.

A. *The New York Times*
I SAY IT'S DOUBLE TALK!

B. *Popular Science*
SLOW DRIVERS CAN KILL YOU!

Columbia University Researchers Take a Look
at Your Driving Habits — and Come up
with Some Startling Findings

C. *American Home*
STAY IN YOUR OWN BACK YARD AND TAKE IT EASY!

D. *Reader's Digest*
LEAVE ME SOME ILLUSIONS!

E. *House and Garden*
SO YOU'RE BUILDING IN THE COUNTRY!

F. *American Home*
GREAT GRANDFATHER WHITTLED HIS OWN!

G. *Good Housekeeping*
LET THE OLDER MEN ALONE!

Rhyme and Alliteration

Too frequent use of alliteration by the newspapers has almost destroyed its usefulness to the magazines. It is one of the easiest types of literary adornment, and one which becomes boresome quickly. Few magazines will use more than one title of this type in the same issue. Rhyme is another tool which must be handled carefully. Like the girl in the well-known poem, when these two are good, they are very good; but when bad, no one wants them around. Some of the better examples are quoted below.

A. *The Rotarian*
FACTORY FOR FORGOTTEN MEN

B. *Time*
POTSDAM PRODUCT

C. *Mademoiselle*
MEXICO'S MOVIES

D. *Chatelaine*
MIDDLE-AGED MOTHERHOOD FOR ME

E. *Holiday*
MONTREAL'S "MILLIONAIRES"
The Spectators Are as Good a Show
as the Hockey Players

F. *Better Homes and Gardens*
CARPENTRY CAPERS

G. *Ford Times*

BELOVED BUMS OF THE BLACK HILLS

H. *Woman's Day*

BOYS AND TOYS

I. *McCall's Magazine*

SUN FUN

Balance and Contrast

Titles that make use of the principle of balance or contrast simply set one idea against a second. Occasionally alliteration is employed in the same title. Grammatically, the commonest type consists of two nouns and a conjunction. The type is frequently a variation of the label title. *Atlantic Monthly* uses the principle of balance on numerous articles. Some of the variations of this form are as follows:

A. *The Atlantic*

THE AUSSIE AND THE YANK

B. *The New York Times*

BETTER MINDS FOR BETTER POLITICS

Columbia Dean Says We Must Train Our Young
Men to Take a More Active Role in Public Affairs

C. *Reader's Digest*

STRONG MEDICINE FOR CARELESS GUESTS

This Week-end Guest Left His Shoes
in the Spare Room — He'll Never
Do That Again

D. *Ladies' Home Journal*

THE HARD PRICE OF SOFT COAL

E. *Harper's Magazine*

ARABIAN OIL AND AMERICAN IMPERIALISM

F. *McCall's Magazine*

CHRIST OR CHAOS

G. *The Atlantic*

THE SCHOOLS AND THE WAR

H. *Mechanix Illustrated*
BOATS AND BOATING

I. *Popular Gardening*
SOIL CONDITIONERS AND SOIL FUMIGANTS

Multiple Classification

Some titles may be classified under two or more headings. For instance, whether a certain title is a striking statement or a label is a matter of degree. The title "One World or None" is certainly a striking statement, but it is also of the contrast type. And as pointed out above, alliteration may be used with the principle of balance and contrast. This should not disturb the writer, for his purpose is to compose an effective title. Let him do that regardless of type.

Composing a Title

If a writer hasn't a satisfactory title on hand when his article is otherwise finished, his next step is to put one together. The quickest and easiest course is to make a list of the outstanding features or items of interest in the article. In number they may run from three or four up to a dozen or more. Within this group should be all that is needed for a good title.

By way of illustration, consider the article written in Chapter 8. A list of the items of interest in it might be set down as follows:

1. Natural attractivenes of a garden pool.
2. Use as a family project.
3. An instrument to teach natural history.
4. Place to replant wild flowers.
5. An attraction for birds, insects, and so forth.

Perhaps at another writing we would have prepared a different list, or would have put the items down in a different order, for writing is not a mechanical process, but an intellectual process, subject to the rules of the imagination. As we study the list above and attempt to uncover the most interesting association, we recall that for children and adults a zoo is one of the most interesting places in the world. Why not use this idea in a title? Here, then, are several titles, any one of which might be the proper one for which we are searching.

1. Backyard Zoo
2. Homemade Zoo
3. Child's Silent Teacher
4. Understanding Life
5. Backyard School

Here is an assortment of titles, emphasizing various angles in our article. Since the article developed the idea that the garden pool could be used to teach natural history, we should emphasize the same point in the title. The first and second appear to be the best, because they are shortest and most interesting.

Adding a Subtitle

This title should be elaborated with a subtitle that adds a few more details and arouses additional desire to read the article. Something like the following would do. The third was the one used by *Parents' Magazine*.

How a Garden Pool Entertains and Instructs
Children in the Absorbing Facts
of Natural History

(*or*)

Equipping the Garden Pool to Entertain and Instruct
Children in Their Own Yard

(*or*)

Properly Equipped, the Lily Pool Is a Guide
to the Beauties of Nature for
Parent and Child

Some writers make a practice of offering a choice of titles when they submit an article. Alternative titles are shown on the cover page. It is not a common practice, though little objection to it can be offered. The title and subtitle submitted with the article done for *Parents' Magazine* are shown below.

BACKYARD ZOO

Properly Equipped, the Lily Pool Is a Guide
to the Beauties of Nature for
Parent and Child

Training Steps

1. Examine an issue of *Time*. How frequently do quotations appear as titles? In your magazine studies have you found any other magazines using this type so frequenlty?
2. Study also several issues of *Woman's Day*. Note the Table of Contents. Is the label a frequent type of title?
3. Take any three issues of *The Catholic Digest*, or some other digest magazine. Classify the titles as to type. What is most frequent?
4. In Question 3, do you find any titles that can be classified in more than one group?
5. Select five examples of label titles. Rewrite these as striking statements, using material from the body of the article.
6. Choose 15 titles from *Reader's Digest* and 15 from *Catholic Digest*. Give each 1 point each time it rates high according to the list of four qualifications for a good title (p. 128). If a title rates high on all four points, give it a rating of 4, etc. Add the total for each magazine. Which is higher?
7. What general differences do you note between the titles of the two magazines.
8. Select three examples of articles in which the title, subtitle, and beginning are not satisfactorily unified. What is the cause?
9. Make a rapid survey of twenty magazines. Which use subheads? Do you find the device effective in calling attention to important ideas?
10. Select an article in any current magazine. Classify the title. Then write as many other types of titles as possible for the same article.
11. What type of title do you find most frequently in your own reading experiences? Is this a characteristic of a special field of interest, or of a group of magazines of general appeal?
12. How do newspaper headlines differ from magazine headlines? What is the purpose in creating a good title when submitting an article to a newspaper?

CHAPTER 11

How to Use Illustrations

Universal experience testifies to the value of illustrations with the printed word. It is no accident that the largest circulations among magazines and newspapers are found among those with liberal illustrations. *Better Homes and Gardens* and the New York *Daily News* owe their front rank as much to their illustrations as to any other single factor.

The success of *Life* and *Look* and similar magazines is based primarily on the variety and quality of their photographs, charts, diagrams, and pictographs. Similar claims could be made for *Time* and *Newsweek*.

In another category are *The Atlantic* and *Harper's Magazine*, both limited in appeal partly because of meager illustration. The nonillustrated magazine, almost without exception, numbers readers by thousands, whereas the illustrated periodical counts in the tens of thousands.

When to Use Photographs

The point is obvious to every student of article writing. If you want an article to be attractive, understandable, and widely appealing, provide ample, first-rate illustration of appropriate type. Many writers have experienced the rejection of meritorious articles because the illustrations were inadequate. Conversely, excellent illustrations have frequently sold articles in which the copy was below average. If an editor expects illustrations from the writer, the latter should spend at least as much care in procuring them as he does in writing the article.

As indicated above, some magazines do not use illustrations. The first observation for the writer to make is whether or not his market uses illustrations. If not, he may ignore the matter.

Who Provides Illustrations?

Some magazines use only pen-and-ink sketches or other drawings by their own staff artists. Experience will help to direct the writer. Market guides give some information on the point. And the writer can frequently decide by direct observation of credit lines whether the illustrations were purchased with the article, or whether the magazine itself did the work.

The query is the best place to handle the question of illustration, and the writer should make every effort to cover this subject in his correspondence with the editor. If the writer is providing illustrations, he should list and enumerate them. When the editor does not want either article or illustrations and the latter have not yet been obtained, the query will save the cost of providing them.

Among the magazines that frequently supply photographic illustration for free-lance articles is *Better Homes and Gardens.* The editor of *Woman's Day* also has written this author that free-lance articles need not be illustrated for her magazine, since the staff prefers to provide its own illustrations. On another occasion the editor of *American Home* wrote a student writer that they would be glad to send a photographer to the Adirondacks to obtain photographs for an article the student had written about a remodeled summer camp.

Most magazines that use illustrated material prefer to have the illustrations come from the writer. The latter is generally in a better position to obtain them, presumably being closer to the subject. Then, there are those narratives of personal adventure, such as hunting and fishing trips, for which only the writer could supply actual photographs.

Nearly all editors pay for photographs supplied by the writer. The price varies from five to twenty-five dollars. Some few do accept photographs without paying for them separately. If they first must be purchased by the writer, their cost will cut his net returns. If he is selling a short or filler, the fact may make it unprofitable to do the item.

Taking Your Own Photographs

If the writer can take good pictures, he is frequently wise to do so. He can take them when need arises, without depending upon the convenience of another photographer. And he usually will save considerable money. If a first effort fails, the writer can better afford to try a second time himself than to secure another photographer or to rehire the first one.

Also the writer who is his own photographer is more likely to get what he wants. His knowledge of the subject will exceed that of any photographer he may engage, and he will have greater interest in getting exactly what is needed.

The possibility of obtaining photographs from other persons concerned with the article should not be overlooked. In personality sketches, interviews, various narratives, or how-it-was-done articles, the individuals involved may have first-rate photographs or other illustrations. Often these can be secured without cost to the writer. In numerous cases the subject will be willing to have photographs taken at his own expense. Articles about merchants and other tradesmen are in this class.

Since magazines and newspapers rarely return illustrations, it is not wise to send photographs or other illustrations that are irreplaceable. It is far better to send photographic reproductions of such material.

Other Photographic Sources

There are five chief sources of photographs for the writer who is not taking them himself. They are 1. the local newspapers, 2. professional photographers, 3. amateur photographers, 4. the syndicates, and 5. manufacturers, tradesmen, and agencies.

LOCAL NEWSPAPERS. These can be used in several ways. First, the free-lance should watch them for subjects which he can rework for magazines, other newspapers, or newspaper syndicates. When these newspaper features are illustrated, the writer may be able to obtain prints by acting quickly. Let him call the city editor as soon as the article is discovered. He should ask for the photographer's name, and then should make arrangements with him to get the desired prints. The acquaintance with this photographer should be valuable in connection with future articles, and the writer should cultivate his friendship.

Copies of prints from negatives already used should not cost more than $5 per print. On occasion also a newspaper photographer may be willing to go on special assignment in his spare hours.

PROFESSIONAL PHOTOGRAPHERS. Studio or commercial photographers are willing enough to help the free-lance writer at a price. Occasionally they have in their files photographs which may be purchased reasonably. Some studio photographers will not leave their place of business, but the so-called commercial photographer is usually willing to go anywhere, and is equipped to take most types of indoor and outdoor pictures. His price should be sought in advance, so that the writer can accept or reject his help before incurring too great expense. Ordinarily the writer can afford to use such services only when he is fairly certain of a sale.

AMATEUR PHOTOGRAPHERS. The skill of this group often exceeds that of professionals, who sometimes have less to offer in other ways than have amateur photographers. Not only are charges of the latter likely

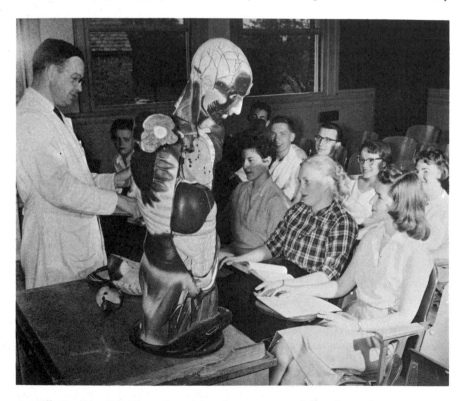

Illustration 2 — If a picture is taken at a carefully planned moment, it can tell more than many paragraphs — and far more quickly. Note how intent spectators are in watching lecturer explain the model. (Photo by Karas)

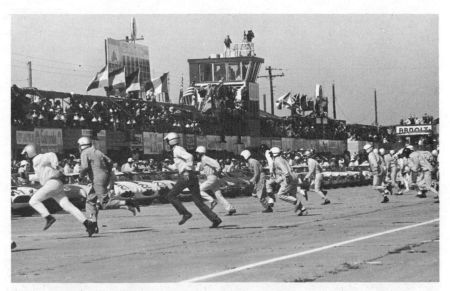

Illustration 3 — Auto race. One of the easiest and most successful ways of making a picture a real hit is to pick a well-known subject at a crucial moment with plenty of action and with all interest focused on its chief actors. (Photo by Bob Kerns)

to be lower where a cash arrangement is made, but also they frequently will work on a speculative basis. If a sale is not made, there is no charge. Or a compromise between the two may be worked out. This includes a minimum charge in advance, plus an additional sum if the article is sold. The writer will work only with competent amateurs, and pay only for satisfactory pictures. He should not pay for photographic failures.

SYNDICATES. The syndicates with millions of prints in their files make a business of furnishing pictures to writers and editors. For instance, when a writer wishes to do a piece on Mexican handicraftsmen, following a trip to that country, and finds his own photographs lacking, he can make contact with one of the syndicates. After stating what his purposes are and the type and subject matter he wishes portrayed in the photographs, he can ask what the syndicate has to offer and what their terms are. Eventually, he will find a syndicate willing to submit a number of prints from which he can select those best suited to his needs.

Syndicates operate in various ways. Some charge a flat price per print. Others ask for the full amount paid for the illustrations by the

Illustration 4 — Athlete in Gym. Pictures are usually better if they tell a story. The lone athlete suggests the exhaustion that comes from athletic competition, as well as its loneliness. This is an example of how back-lighting aids a picture. (Photo by C. J. Wistala)

magazine. And still others are willing to permit their prints to be submitted on speculative articles. All unused prints are returned to the syndicates, and the writer pays only for those retained by the magazine. It is not uncommon for a writer to pay five dollars each to a syndicate for prints for which a magazine pays him twice that much. The shrewd writer ought in the long run to be able to make a profit on the photographs he supplies the editors.[1]

NEGLECTED SOURCES.   Manufacturers, tradesmen, advertising agencies, and publicity directors form one of the most helpful groups, yet one of the least used by writers needing photographs. The advantages in using photographs and other illustrations from these sources are striking: 1. they are always authentic; 2. they are usually of highest excellence; 3. they are often supplied free to the writer; 4. where illustrations are

[1] A list of syndicates supplying photographs to writers and editors can be found in Editor & Publisher's *International Year Book*.

Illustration 5 — Characters in any scene may legitimately be posed, but they should be engaged in a normal action or routine if naturalness is to be achieved. It should appear obvious to the viewer that no attempt at deception has been attempted. (Photo by Norman B. Moyes)

not currently on hand, these sources frequently are willing to have them made for the writer if he has legitimate grounds for believing they will be used.

Photographs without Cost

The method of procuring photographs free of charge is simple. The writer should get the go-ahead sign from an editor. Then while the article is being prepared, an inquiry is directed to the most likely source of photographs. In this letter the writer states that he is preparing an article on a certain subject, and that the editor of *Blank* magazine has indicated his interest in it. The writer asks whether photographs can be supplied, and promises that full credit will be given with each print when used. Managers of advertising or public-relations departments usually handle such arrangements.

Following is a list of typical subjects with which this technique can be used, as well as the source of the necessary photographs.

1. An article on traveling in Canada. Source: the Canadian National and Canadian Pacific Railroads.
2. An article on modern kitchen design. Source: Cornell University Extension Service; any manufacturer of such equipment.
3. An article on glassware for table use. Source: the Corning Glass Works; other manufacturers of glassware.
4. An article on selecting silver for table use. Source: Gorham, Community Plate, Wallace, or similar manufacturers.
5. An article on youth hostels. Source: American Youth Hostels, New York City.
6. An article about some aspect of university life. Source: the publicity bureau of the institution concerned.
7. An article about a local merchant. Source: the store management.
8. Expansion of a national business concern. Source: the publicity director or the advertising department or agency handling the firm's account.
9. A sketch of a theatrical or motion-picture star. Source: the artist's agent or employer.
10. The story of the accomplishments of a state or federal bureau of department. Source: the bureau itself, or its official publicity representative.
11. A feature story about a zoo, library, or museum. Source: the publicity representative or the management.

This list suggests a few of the possibilities of securing photographs without cost. There are hundreds of kindred sources of which writers might make greater use than they do. Numerous students in the author's classes have used such sources successfully. Occasionally prints are not available, but the request is seldom refused when prints are on hand. The writer must keep his promise to the agent supplying the illustrations and must handle all arrangements with strictest professional ethics.

Types of Pictures Wanted

Magazines and newspapers are united in desiring photographs of first quality. Only in rare circumstances will second-rate prints be accepted.

The writer will remember that the pictures that illustrate his own article must compete with those intended to illustrate articles submitted by other writers. He will seek to obtain those of highest excellence, not merely illustrations good enough to "get by."

Almost invariably, magazines and newspapers want prints made on glossy paper, because they reproduce better than those on dull paper. When ordering, specify glossy prints, which cost no more than the others.

Size is also important, but this may vary. The author has always used prints 5 X 7 inches in black and white, but larger prints are more satisfactory to the average writer in the long run. Sizes 6 x 8, 7 x 9, and 8 X 10 are all good. Prints larger than 8 X 10 are seldom, if ever, necessary. The 8 X 10 print costs more, but is generally better bceause editors are accustomed to handling this size and because it may more easily be trimmed if it is not the right size. The photograph in Illustration 9 was enlarged to 7 X 9 from a negative 1¾ X 2⅝. It was used as one of the illustrations for the article cited in Chapter VIII.

When submitting color prints, you must know the editor's precise needs because of the greater cost to yourself as well as to the magazine. Some editors will accept 35mm transparencies, but for many a 4 X 5 inch print is the acceptable minimum, and larger sizes may be required. Know your markets; inquire first, if necessary.

Dynamic pictures and those that tell a story are most sought after. Close-ups of individuals are usually better than more distant views. Unposed, characteristic attitudes are also more desired than studied sittings. Action shots at crucial moments are far better than those taken at less crucial moments, and are better than static poses. For instance, a photograph of the finish of a race is better than one taken at the start or midway along the course. A shot of a vaulter as he soars over the pole is better than one taken at the start or at the moment he hits the earth.

Posed Pictures

Posed pictures are legitimate devices. They are particularly good in showing what-to-do or what-not-to-do, as in an article on accident prevention. In an article on hunting accidents a what-not-to-do photograph of a hunter pulling a gun through a fence with the muzzle aimed at himself should make an excellent illustration. "Before" and "after" photographs are almost a necessity in tracing the course of a house remodeling job.

Other Illustrations

YOUR OWN SKETCHES.   The writer who can illustrate his own articles is in an enviable position. His chances of selling are greatly enhanced even if his market later assigns the job to a staff artist. The combination of writing and drawing talent is unusual, but the better for its rarity.

While some editors do not use sketches by nonstaff members, others are glad to get them. The point can be settled in the query. Eventually, the freelance writer learns which markets in his own special field do or do not use sketches.

For the writer who does not draw well, there is the possibility of finding someone locally who does. High school art teachers in the small towns may be able to help, or to recommend another who can. In larger centers, of course, commercial artists are usually available and can be found through the classified section of the telephone book.

Some magazines also are glad to receive rough sketches by the writer. These sketches serve as a guide to staff artists. Accompanied by accurate dimensions, they can frequently be turned into excellent representations of what the writer would have drawn had he been able. Among the magazines welcoming such visual aids are *Popular Mechanics Magazine* and *Popular Science Monthly.*

Almost any magazine that uses illustrations will be glad to accept suggestions for illustration and decoration, with or without accompanying sketches. Good ideas are always at a premium in the publishing world.

CHARTS, DIAGRAMS, MAPS.   Such magazines as *Life, Time,* and *Newsweek* are quick references to the types of hand-drawn illustrations of this kind. Other examples will be found on the financial pages of the daily and Sunday newspapers. The various forms and variations in which these illustrations appear are available to anyone who wishes to use them. The basic design cannot be copyrighted or patented, though a specific application may be protected. Any writer is privileged to follow as a model any basic form he can find, using his own figures.

Weekly movements of the stock market are depicted by *The New York Times, Wall St. Journal,* and *Time* on graphs that are almost identical. Each uses a somewhat different group of stocks in establishing an index to price ranges. They could, if they chose, use the same selection. Such basic forms are the property of everyone. To the form may be added a style or manner, which is the property of the inventor. This should not be imitated. The writer should create his own style, or rely on standard designs.

The *pictograph* has come into widespread use. It is usually composed of a group of objects or small pictures drawn to scale, each related in size and significance to other items in the composite drawing. In a pictograph on gainful employment in various occupations the overall-clad figure of a working man carrying a dinner pail might stand for 1 million day laborers. Ten and a half such figures would represent 10,500,000 day laborers. The artist tries to select a tool or uniform typical of the trade or occupation. The farmer may be shown with a hay fork, the brick layer with a trowel, and the professor clad in cap and gown.

"Ghosted" *drawings* of homes show the skeleton or phantom walls. The observer sees through them into the interior, where furnishings and furniture or the inhabitants are in place. These drawings are unexcelled for giving the complete picture of a home, or in affording an acurate idea of size dimension, and relationship.

Bird's-eye views of interiors and *airplane views* of widespread terrain, as of a city, are other effective applications of special points of view.

Floor plans and *elevations* of new houses or of proposed changes are widely used by many magazines such as *House Beautiful, American Home,* and *Better Homes and Gardens.*

Blueprints and *working plans* are used by all of the craftsmen's magazines, including *Popular Science Monthly* and *Popular Mechanics Magazine.* Plans for the layout of vegetable and flower gardens and of landscaping design are similar. In the same class would be working plans for crop rotating, contour plowing, or digging drainage ditches, such as are used by *Farm Journal* and other agricultural publications. The aviation magazines also use profuse illustrations of this type.

Maps, showing the routine of automobile, bicycle, or canoe trips, frequently yield more information at a glance than do hundreds of words of explanation. Maps that locate boundaries, topographical features, cities and villages are almost indispensable in articles on distant states or foreign lands. *National Geographic Magazine* has carried such illustrations to the highest development in this country, but scores of other publications also use them.

Drafting Supplies

Black india ink is best for nearly all sketches and map making, because it reproduces better than other inks. Paper used with pen and ink should be a good white drawing board. Any art store can furnish

SPECIFICATIONS ON CARS TESTED

	Chrysler 300H	Buick Wildcat	Thunder-bird
Retail price*....................	$5,461	$4,357	$6,141
Wheelbase (in.)	122	123	113.2
Length (in.).....................	215.3	214	205
Height (in.).....................	55.7	56.3	53.3
Width (in.)	79.4	78	76
Weight (lb.)	4,324	4,328	4,400
Turning diameter (ft.)	42.7	45.9	40.2
Steering ratio (:1)	19.2	19.9	20.3
Axle ratio (:1)	3.23	3.42	3.00
Tires...........................	7.60x15	7.60x15	8.00x14
Fuel capacity (gal.).............	23	20	20
Crankcase capacity (qt.).........	5	5	6
Lube interval (mi.)..............	32,000	1,000	6,000
Oil change (mi.)	2,500	4,000	6,000
Radiator capacity (qt.)	17	18.5	20
Piston displacement (cu.in.)......	413	401	390
Compression ratio (:1)	10	10.25	9.6
Carburetion.....................	Two 4-bbl.	4-bbl.	4-bbl.
Horsepower	380	325	340
Weight of car per hp. (lb.).......	11.3	13.3	12.9
Torque (lb./ft.)	450	445	427

Illustration 6 — A simple chart that could have been made by a student writer. (Reprinted by permission of Popular Science Monthly)

satisfactory materials and give general advice on these points. Pencil sketches are adequate when meant only as a guide to the editors.

Graph, or coordinate, paper for bar charts and graphs can be obtained at art or stationery stores, or other stores furnishing school supplies. Before making his own charts and graphs, the title. The cut-lines should be longer, more detailed, and more comprehensive.

The best guide to follow is the practice of the magazine or newspaper, or syndicate to which the illustrations are being sent. Captions should be no longer or shorter than the limits set by the proposed market. They should be interesting and terse. The style may be sprightly or serious, but it should be in harmony with the nature of the subject.

Sample Captions

To illustrate some of the desirable characteristics of captions, suppose we think of how we might label photographs accompanying an article on accident prevention in the home.

1. This photograph shows a woman reaching to turn on an electric light switch while one hand is in the wash tub.

HOW THE WORLD'S BIGGEST LINERS STACK UP

	Gross Tons	Length	Beam	Decks	Propulsion	Horsepower
QUEEN ELIZABETH	83,673	1,031	118	14	Steam turbine, quadruple screw	158,000
QUEEN MARY	81,237	1,019 1/2	118	12	Steam turbine, quadruple screw	158,000
FRANCE	66,000	1,035	110	12	Steam turbine, quadruple screw	160,000
UNITED STATES	51,987	990	101 1/2	12	Steam turbine, quadruple screw	Not available

Illustration 7 — This chart was staff prepared from data presented by the writer. (Reprinted by permission of Popular Science Monthly)

Don't write a label title:

A DANGEROUS ACT

Write an action title:

THIS MAY MEAN SUDDEN DEATH!

2. In this photograph the model is reaching too far out from the top of a ladder to dust a picture.

Don't write a vague title:

MANY SERIOUS ACCIDENTS START
THIS WAY

Be specific:

IN 1946 MORE THAN 100 DEATHS AND 1583
SERIOUS ACCIDENTS BEGAN LIKE THIS

3. This photograph shows a two-year-old child reaching for a pan, the handle of which protrudes over the top of a stove.

Don't write a general statement:

ANOTHER DANGER SPOT

Be concrete:

KITCHEN STOVES RANK SECOND AS A
SOURCE OF HOUSEHOLD ACCIDENTS

All the qualities of a good title for an article should be found in the caption of a photograph. Like the title, the caption should be carefully tied into the article, possibly by using a specific idea or quotation from the article. Also a special section about a good illustration can be written and inserted in the article itself. Occasionally articles are thus built around the illustrations.

Substitute Photographs

There are times when the exact photograph wanted by the writer cannot be had at any price. This may be true also for other types of illustrations. The author has circumvented this difficulty by a device that has saved numerous articles from the wastebasket.

This practice might be called the "technique of opposites." Basically, it utilizes the idea of contrast. Examples of its use are numerous. For instance, in an article on civic planning, if a photograph of a well-planned city is not available, use one showing poor planning as an example of what not to do. An illustration of bad landscaping, bad plowing, or bad plumbing may be just as effective as one showing good procedure. In an article on posture an illustration of how-not-to-sit may be more effective than the how-to-do-it-correctly. Used in emergencies the device is sometimes invaluable.

Training Steps

1. The next time you examine magazines on a newsstand, note what attracts you to a particular publication. Is it the type display or the illustration?
2. When you run through a magazine, do you devote more time to titles or to illustrations?
3. What section of your daily newspaper do you seek out first, the graphic sections or the solid reading matter?
4. In an issue of any illustrated magazine, read the article that appeals to you most. Then rewrite the cutlines. Were the cutlines accurate, condensed, and interesting? Have you improved them?
5. Examine an issue of *Life*. Note that some articles consist solely of a series of photographs, each of which has a long explanation without other text matter.
6. Also examine issues of *American Home* and *Better Homes and Gardens*. Do you find any articles consisting mostly of pictures and cutlines?

7. Do you note any difference between the cutlines of these two magazines in form, style, or content? In which of these magazines do you think the cutlines are more successful?

8. Watch the daily newspapers. Do you find any photographs that suggest articles to you?

9. In Question 4, can you suggest other and better illustrations for the article that you read?

10. Study your own writing carefully. Go over your current or recent articles. Could you have suggested or can you suggest illustrations to the editor? Make such suggestions in the next query submitted. Also on the next article.

11. Examine an issue of *House Beautiful* or *House and Garden*. For how many articles in each could illustrations have been secured from the offices of manufacturing concerns?

12. How many charts, maps, and diagrams are used in an average issue of *Time magazine?* How many of each?

13. How many different types of illustrations can you find in current magazines? Clip interesting examples of each and place them in your files for future use.

14. Study several issues of current photography magazines. What are the qualities in the prize-winning pictures?

15. Analyze the pictorial page of one of the newspapers. What is there about each picture that made it worth printing?

16. Examine copies of *Popular Mechanics Magazine*. What type of blueprints or working plans does it use?

17. The magazine *Flying* is a good market for photographs. Classify the subjects to be found in several issues.

18. What type of photograph is most frequently used in *Look?* Do you find informal snapshots?

CHAPTER 12

Editing and Preparing the Manuscript

Polishing and preparing the manuscript involve two distinct processes. First, the editorial content must be reworked until no more can be done to improve its clarity, interest, and conciseness. Second, the envelopes, illustrations, and copy must be put into professsional form.

Articles are items of merchandise offered in a highly competitive market. Some of the leading magazines and newspapers receive hundreds of manuscripts daily. These are dumped by the sackful on the desk of the first readers. Some are travel-worn, some are crudely prepared, some are neat and professional in appearance. If you were a first reader, which would you most likely be tempted to reject at first sight?

Some publications give every article a careful reading. Others reject as soon as it becomes obvious that the article is at fault in any important respect. This may be at first glance. The following paragraphs tell the writer how to check on every detail of his article in order to minimize chances of rejection.

The Business of Rewriting

Because every writer is impatient to get his article into the mail, hoping thus to speed the acceptance of an article and the receipt of a check, he is likely to slight the business of revision. Yet few, if any, articles are published without revision, and it is certain that every article can be thus improved. Most articles that get into print have been revised and retyped at least three or four times. Between these retypings the writer may have skimmed through a score of times to make changes here and there.

This rewriting, changing, shifting of order, and retyping is part of the trade of being a writer. And it is a very important part. To neglect it is to cripple the writer's certainty of improving his work. Only by constant effort to improve and to bring forth the very best within him can the writer speed his growth as a craftsman. Rewriting probably plays the most important single role in this process of growth.

Checking for Completeness of Development

Perhaps the first question to ask when considering the article in its entirety is this: Is this article fully developed?

ALL DIVISIONS PRESENT. When *is* an article fully developed? It is fully developed when all parts are present, and when those parts need no further explanation. In a how-to-do-something article it is easy to discover whether important steps have been omitted. The writer can determine the clarity of each step by trying out the article on a friend with limited previous knowledge of the subject. If the latter, after a reading, can relate what was intended in each step, the writer can assume that the explanation will be clear to other similar readers. Such guinea-pig readers should be as nearly like the members of the prospective market as possible in education, age, and experience.

In a more general article, such as one on soil erosion, the question of completeness may be more difficult. Here the writer will ask himself whether he has given a true picture of what is happening in the areas encompassed in his article. It is not sufficient that articles of this type be interesting. They must also present an accurate picture.

ALL FACTS PRESENT. In the second place, a writer should ask whether his article requires more facts. An article may cover or touch upon all important aspects of a subject without adequately handling any one of them. Where the writer seeks to prove a point, he must present enough data to convince the reader. It is better to have too many facts than too few. The superficial article gets scant welcome in any office. Since the writer expects to be paid for his work, he should see to it that he gives the reader his money's worth.

COMPLETE CONDENSATION. In checking development, the third item is whether the article needs condensation. It may be too long for the limits set by the market. Or the subject itself may be unworthy of the space allotted in the first version. Also it may be too thin. One way to improve a seemingly superficial article is to condense it. Wordiness is always a liability to an article. The writer should go through it repeatedly with heavy pencil. Each time he should try to eliminate every word, phrase, and sentence that can be omitted. Most articles can be improved by this boiling-down process. Under it the style becomes firmer, the meaning clearer, and the interest greater.

NOT TOO TECHNICAL. Another point is whether the article is too technical. Except for the professional periodicals, written for the highly-trained specialist, an article may be too technical. It should be substantial and authoritative, but its message should be translated so that readers can understand without having to puzzle it out. Too many facts and figures will ruin the average article. This statement is quite as true for "highbrow" publications as for the more popular magazines or newspapers, though in different degree. Readers of *The Atlantic* no more wish to bog down in an article than do readers of *Sports Illustrated* or the Baltimore *Sun*. If the writer is in doubt, let him try out his article on a carefully-chosen reader.

FULL OF SPARKLE. An article may be free of the curse of being too technical and yet lack life and sparkle. Wit, humor, and human interest are appropriate in nearly all articles. Discussions of politics, religion, or race relations may be improved by appropriate touches of human interest and humor. If the article lags in interest at any stage, right there is the spot to introduce a pointed anecdote or a bit of human interest.

COMPLETE HUMANIZATION. Most articles need to be humanized. Human beings should be introduced. Data should be shown in relation to people. Names are important. Characters and their conversation bring life to dull facts. Most facts are interesting only in their relation to people who are or might be affected. Articles should be checked to see whether specific references and applications are made. Our article on soil erosion can be humanized by showing what happened on the farm of John Bottomland. His remarks and his reactions will bring life into the discussion.

OPINIONS WEIGHED. Perhaps the sixth item to be considered is the matter of *opinion*. Ask yourself, "Is this article too opinionated?" Opinions must be based on facts, and they should be backed up by facts cited in the article. Just as intelligent people dislike opinionated individuals, so do they dislike opinionated articles. It will pay the writer to support his statements with carefully-sifted evidence. He should be judicious in making claims. Statements should be qualified where there is room for doubt. There is no sense in trying to convince readers of untrue statements, or in using those of which the writer is uncertain. His errors will find him out, and possibly end his writing career.

GRAMMAR CHECKED. The matter of grammar must always be present in the writer's mind. Through training he will naturally come to write correctly. However, errors and slips of the pen and typewriter will occur. This fact is one of the nightmares that trouble conscientious writers. The only way to avoid errors in print is to examine every sentence. Agreement in number between subject and verb must be checked, as well as agreement between pronouns and their antecedents. Tense sequence must be put in order. All the points that ordinarily give trouble must be tested, and made right where necessary.

This examination must be carried on not only during the first writing, but also during the process of revision. Sentence by sentence and paragraph by paragraph, the article must be scanned. If any sentence is questionable, rearrange it or leave it out. The written word is so much a part of its creator that here again it is wise to have the assistance of an experienced second person whose criticism can be more objective.

CONNECTIVES USED. The coherence of the whole article will be greatly promoted by a studied use of connecting words and phrases. Their use is important where the reader needs to be guided. Connectives are signposts that point out where the reader is bound. They promote clarity and unity by indicating the relationship between paragraphs.

These connectives are numbered by the hundreds. This paragraph, for instance, began with one. It indicated that the word "connectives" had been used recently above. Actually, without taking thought the writer will link many paragraphs. It is usually wise during the rewriting process to examine the use of connectives and to insert as many as may be necessary to carry the reader along with clarity and comprehension. To knit an article into a coherent whole, nothing else serves so well as a judicious sprinkling of connectives of the right type. Whether they be such simple connectives as "but," "or," "nor," and the like, or the more elaborate kind, such as "on the other hand" and "along the same line," they serve the same purpose — to assist the reader in understanding the writer's message.

Checking the Beginning

When the writer believes that he has done his best with the article as a whole, let him re-examine the title, subtitle, and opening paragraphs. He should check each for the desirable qualities listed in earlier chapters. Is the title arresting, accurate, and specific? Does the subtitle add other important facts? And it is it free from useless repetition? What of the first few paragraphs? Do they read as if the article offered helpful and interesting information?

Some or all of these parts may need rewriting — a discovery that most writers make in every article. The final title, for instance, may be hit upon only after a score have been tried and discarded, though the subtitle is usually easier. Also the opening paragraphs may require many rewritings before they satisfy the writer. Experience teaches that there is no perfect title, subtitle, and opening; rather there are scores of excellent versions for each of these parts. The writer's problem is merely that of composing a satisfactory unit for each division.

Having checked these three items individually, the writer should next judge them as a unit. Do they work together harmoniously? Are they free from contradictions and unnecessary repetition? Do they sell the article in a satisfactory way? This last question cannot be answered affirmatively unless the most interesting or persuasive aspects of the subject have been incorporated. The three-part unit should include at least a hint of the interesting facts to follow.

Judging the Conclusion

Often a conclusion in the form of a summary is unnecessary. It may be only a space-filler and a waste of words. Similarly an introduction to an article is unnecessary. The first paragraphs serve to attract the reader — not to explain why the writer has undertaken to do an article. Likewise, the last few paragraphs should not be used for apologies. They should be an integral and necessary part. A final word of admonition or encouragement may be appropriate. If it makes the writer feel better, perhaps it will do no harm. But it should be brief, and in harmony with the rest of the article. There is a final point: it should avoid moralizing.

Dressing the Article for Sale

Before the article is ready to be dropped into the mailbox, careful attention must be paid to at least seven different divisions of the manuscript. The items will be fewer if there are no illustrations, or if the article is a short or a filler.

Beginning on the outside, the various items are as follows: 1. the outside envelope; 2. the inner or return envelope; 3. the return stamps;

4. the cardboard protector (if illustrations are used); 5. the cover page; 6. the illustrations; and 7. the physical aspects of the manuscript. Because quality of paper and typing first impress the editor, let us see how they should be handled.

Standards for Paper and Typing

PAPER. Only white business-letter stock is used. This should be of one size — 8½ X 11 inches. The use of anything else is eccentric, and editors do not like to deal with the "freaks" of the literary world. It is economical to buy by the ream, or box of 500 sheets. An expensive grade is unnecessary, but the paper should be sturdy enough to permit erasing. Typographical errors will be made and must be corrected or removed without spoiling the appearance of the sheet. The paper should be neither too thin nor too thick.

TYPING. Editors assume that all articles will be typewritten regardless of their length. It would be an impossible task to examine the heaps of manuscripts that reach the desks of larger publications if these manuscripts were written by pen. Custom and common sense have established the typewritten page. No writer should permit himself any variation. It is as much an advantage to the writer as to the editor, for the plain typewritten page reveals to the writer the errors, inconsistencies, and other weaknesses far better than does handwriting.

In general, all manuscripts should be double-spaced to permit editorial changes. Single-spaced work tells the editor that the article is the product of a beginner, thus creating an unfavorable impression at the start. A few minor exceptions to the above rule may be noted. These include long, quoted passages, the subtitle, and information supplied on the cover page.

Margins should be about an inch on all sides, A little more at the top or a little less at the bottom is permissible. There are no hard and fast rules covering margins. The writer's intention should be to present a neat, attractive page.

The first typing of the manuscript may be somewhat rough, but each subsequent draft should be nearer professional standards. As his experience grows in typing and manuscript preparation, the writer will find that the details are becoming less and less bothersome.

The typing occupies only one side of the paper. There should be no exceptions to this rule. The typewritten impression should be clear and crisp. This means using good ribbons. Black is always preferred. Though ribbons should be discarded before they become frayed, double service can be secured from them by reversing the position of the ribbon on the reels. From time to time the typewriter keys should be cleaned with alcohol or other cleaning fluid. The letters "a," "e," "o," "b," "d," "p,"

Illustration 8 — Illustration of "Backyard Zoo" with cut-lines. The picture was taken to show as many details of planting and construction as possible. In this way photographs and articles can be made to work together. (Photo by the author)

and a few others are prone to become clogged. They should be cleaned as often as necessary. An ordinary needle is a handy aid in keeping the keys free of lint.

CARBONS. Carbon copies of all manuscripts should be made. No manuscript should ever be put into the mail unless there is a duplicate copy. Some writers do their first draft with pencil or pen. Carbons are difficult at this point, though each typing thereafter should be made in duplicate. In order to understand this point, the writer need lose only one manuscript when time does not permit replacement. If the work is specially valuable, it is wise to keep the second copy at some distance from the first during the writing process. The consequences of fire, theft, or misplacement will thus be circumvented.

Illustration 9 — Children lend human interest when used in photographs to illustrate an article. They are naturally photogenic, and are often best when taken unaware. This picture can be enjoyed without further knowledge of what they saw. (Photo by Thomas A. Richards)

Handling Illustrations

Manuscripts may be accompanied by a variety of illustrations, including photographs, maps, charts, diagrams, blueprints, pictographs, and the like. It may be necessary to fold blueprints, but the practice should be avoided whenever possible. Photographs must not be folded, because folding produces cracks, which may reproduce if a photoengraving is made. Very large photographs are usually undesirable.

Captions are typed on a separate sheet and pasted with rubber cement to the back of the illustration at the bottom. They are best when narrower than the illustration to which attached. It is an excellent idea to fold the caption over the front of the illustration to save wear and tear. The writer's name and address should be written in *pen and ink* on the back of each photograph. Typing should never be done on a photograph.

Illustrated manuscripts usually need to be protected by plain or corrugated cardboard for mailing. The writer should experiment with the possibilities until he works out a system that suits himself. This writer usually folds manuscripts horizontally across the middle with the typing on the outside. Size 5 X 7 photographs are used for illustrations, which fit neatly with captions inside the folded manuscript.

Handling Envelopes

The rigors of mailing the average manuscript call for good, strong manila envelopes, which can be bought at stationery stores or bookstores. Postoffices do not handle them. Since manuscripts should be carefully mailed, envelopes must be of a type that can be sealed. Metal clasps, found on some types, are unnecessary. For a manuscript that has been folded once, as described above, a 6½ X 9½ inch *return* envelope is best. The outgoing envelope should be a half inch larger in each dimension, or 7 X 10 inches. Unillustrated shorts may, of course, be mailed in standard postoffice envelopes.

PROTECTING PHOTOGRAPHS. Manuscript, photographs, and cardboard should be inserted in the *smaller* envelope, to assure that returning photographs will be protected by the writer's cardboard. This would not be possible if the cardboard fitted only the outer envelope. Protection requires fitting the cardboard to the *inner* envelope. When the latter is 6½ X 9½ inches, the cardboard should be exactly 6 X 9 inches. These dimensions permit the greatest ease in handling all items involved in the mailing process.

The author has experimented with all other systems, and has found the foregoing to be safest as well as easiest. It will take care of all manuscripts up to 15 or so pages. Few magazines use anything much longer, except in booklength. However, if photographs 7 X 9 inches, or 8 X 10 inches, or larger are used, then larger envelopes must be purchased. In this event, the manuscript should be mailed flat. Since the standard paper is 8½ X 11 inches, a *return* envelope of 9 X 12 inches and an *outgoing* envelope somewhat larger will be needed. In all cases the cardboard should be fitted to the return envelope. For the envelope of 9 X 12 inches, the cardboard should be 8½ X 11½ inches.

OUTER ENVELOPE.   The *outer* envelope should carry, toward the lower right section, the name of the journal to which the manuscript is being sent, the city and street address, and the *name of the proper editor*. It is a mistake to send a manuscript addressed blindly to "The Editor." Articles should not be written (except in practice classes) unless a favorable answer has been received to the writer's query. And then the manuscript should be mailed to the person who answered the query. In the case of an article aimed at a particular department, the article should be sent to the departmental editor by name.

In the upper left-hand corner of the *outer* envelope should be the writer's name, and his street and city address. It may also be well to have the postmaster stamp "First Class Mail" on both envelopes and to weigh the package. The stamps should be *pasted* on the outer envelope and *clipped* to the inner envelope. When photographs accompany the manuscript, it will do no harm to print or type on each envelope, "PHOTOS — Do Not Bend."

INNER ENVELOPE.   The *inner* envelope receives as careful treatment as the outer. The journal's name and address go in the upper left-hand corner; the writer's name and his street and city address go toward the lower right. Other pertinent data should also appear on it. If the inner envelope is half an inch smaller than the outer, it will not be necessary to fold or crease the former at any time on its journey.

Return stamps should always be clipped — never glued — to the inner envelope. Otherwise, if the manuscript is purchased such stamps could not be used. Magazines usually deposit return postage in a general stamp fund, from which sufficient postage is later withdrawn if the manuscript is to be returned. Failure to send adequate postage may mean that the manuscript will be held until added postage is sent. This delay may be expensive if the article is particularly timely.

Manuscript Check list

Because the properly-prepared manuscript creates the most favorable impression, the writer will study the various details that mark the efforts of a professional worker. Eventually, it is well to evolve a system that pleases the writer and fits his own needs. Once this has been worked out satisfactorily, the writer should stick to it. The details of manuscript preparation are discussed below.

INSIDE ADDRESS. The inside address — that is, the writer's name and complete address — should appear on the cover page and on the first page of the manuscript. The best location is in the upper left-hand corner. This item may be single spaced, because the editor will find no occasion to change it. The standard margin should be observed. The last name may be written first, but this is not necessary.

TO WHOM SUBMITTED. The name of the publication should be put in the upper right-hand corner on the cover page and on page one. This item should consist of three lines: a) Submitted to (or Written for), b) *Blank Magazine,* c) About, 1,150 words. If the article is being done in answer to a query, the first line of this part should read, "Written for." Spacing between lines should follow the practice adopted for the inside address.

WORD COUNT. An exact word count is not required, but a close approximation should be made. Where a market buys on a *per word* basis, it will make its own count. The simplest way to make a word tally is to count the number of words in any three typical full lines, and divide the total by 3. Then multiply this average by the number of full lines in the entire manuscript. Anything less than half a full line should be ignored. Those over a half should be counted as full. In an article of 1,500 words this method should not miss by more than 50 words, which is close enough.

CONTINUED PAGES. The word "more" has been used by the newspapers so long to warn of a continued item that the sign has become standard practice. The word "continued" is also used. The practice is to put either of these words in the lower right-hand corner on every page except the last. The final page should bear the words "The End," or some other accepted symbol. The figure 30 is mostly used by students of journalism.

TITLE SPACING. While the standard spacing between lines is two units, this does not apply to spacing in titles. It is wise to develop an eye for proportion and to adapt spacing to the circumstances. Usually it is well to write the title completely in capital letters with double spacing between lines. If there is no subtitle, the title may be written in capital and lower-case letters. Every word must be capitalized.

When a subtitle is used, it should be started three spaces below the title. In this unit only important words are capitalized though there is no universal rule covering the point. Since the subtitle is usually a complete sentence, standard rules of punctuation may be followed.

The title (and subtitle when there is one) should be centered near the top of the page. A little practice will enable the writer to accomplish this without elaborate counting. A good style to follow, also, is to place both units three spaces above the first line of the article. If, then, the manuscript of the first page is typed so that two or three lines of copy occur *above* the center of the page (previously determined by creasing the page in the middle) a series of excellent proportions will be set up. Examination of the sample page one, accompanying this chapter, will reveal what has been done by using these same directions.

SUBHEADS. Whether or not subheads should be used is a matter to be decided according to the practice of the prospective market and the needs of the manuscript. Some subjects are so complicated, or embrace so many interesting points, that it is difficult to refer to all of them in title, subtitle, and beginning. The writer may then find it wise to insert subheads in the body of the manuscript at the appropriate points. These are always units of one line and they are usually centered. Two spaces should be left both above and below. Capitals should be used for the initial letter of each word, or of all important words, according to market practice. If the entire subhead is then underlined, sufficient contrast will be provided. Staff readers will be unable to pass them up — provided that they read beyond the first page.

PAGINATION. The numbering of pages is simple. Neither cover page nor first page bears a number. All pages thereafter are numbered in the upper left-hand corner. The cover page is omitted from the total count. In addition to the number of the page, either the writer's name or the title of the article should be added. It is unnecessary to use both. For page two the complete information would be as follows: *John P. Smith* — 2.

COVER SHEET. A cover sheet is useful on most manuscripts, particularly long ones and those accompanied by illustrations. It is unnecessary on shorts. The upper half of the cover page should be identical through the subtitle with the upper half of the first page.

The space below the title may be used in place of a note to the editors. It should be carefully arranged and spaced. Items that may be included are as follows: 1. the writer's qualifications for writing the

Fred E. Pew
1167 Genesee St.
Syracuse, N.Y.

Written for
Parents' Magazine
About 1,750 words

BACKYARD ZOO

—

Properly Equipped, the Lily Pool Is a Guide
to the Beauties of Nature for
Parent and Child.

—

When children transfer their games outdoors, new interests draw them into the street, down the block, and around the corner. How can a parent, then, keep an eye on their activities?

"I want to go over to Buddy's to play" is the familiar song of the average boy. And what can a parent say to that?

Out-of-door play that keeps children home, that fosters wholesome interests, that teaches some of the mysteries of life, and in which the parent can participate to just the right degree is difficult to devise.

Few among the thousands who have constructed a garden pool as part of their landscaping have discovered that it can be used as a fascinating instrument for the entertainment and education of their children. The birds, insects, fish, mollusks, and plants that can be brought here will set the stage for a study of natural history.

Because this study involves conception, birth, life, and death, it affords an unexcelled opportunity to help the child develop an interest in things outside himself, to teach

(More)

Illustration 10 — A typical first page

Fred E. Pew
1167 Genesee St.
Syracuse, N. Y.

Written for
Parents' Magazine
About 1,750 words

BACKYARD ZOO

—

Properly Equipped, the Lily Pool Is a Guide
to the Beauties of Nature for
Parent and Child.

—

This article is based upon the personal observation and experience of the writer. The basic ideas suggested will apply with some variations to all sections of the country.

Five photographs are enclosed as follows:

1. Excavation for the pool with forms in place.

2. The completed pool and combined rock garden before landscaping.

3. The garden pool one year after completion, showing growth of plantings.

4. A family picnic by the pool.

5. A dragonfly poised on a lily stem ready to deposit her eggs.

Illustration 11 — The cover sheet

particular article; 2. the sources of data used, if the article is not a part of the writer's own experience; 3. a list of illustrations with their captions.

This information should not be elaborate. The style should be telegraphic, and the form that of the outline. Because the editors may study this page even before they examine the illustrations, the importance of careful preparation is obvious. Although the first staff member to examine the article may not see the envelopes, he will inspect the cover page. Here is the writer's first chance to exercise salesmanship. He should rework this section until he cannot improve it. Any fact that will enhance the apparent value of the manuscript should be stated. Among such items would be the reputation of persons interviewed, whether the facts have not been printed before, the value of advice offered, the number of people affected, and the writer's special fitness for handling this subject.

APPROVAL SHEET. Occasionally a separate sheet may be included, upon which persons interviewed for the article sign their names below a typed statement that the article has been read and approved by them. Such statement is of value when unusual or controversial facts are included, but ordinarily is unnecessary. Professional writers depend upon their reputation to guarantee the accuracy of their work.

PEN NAMES. Upon occasion a writer may wish to follow the common practice of using a *nom de plume*. Departmental editors may use the device to disguise their own contributions. Free-lance writers use it occasionally when their names are to appear more than once in the same issue. And any writer may adopt it to conceal his identity in such writing, for example, as a confession article. The writer's name is typed in the upper left-hand corner of the cover page and the first page. The pen name appears below the title, thus: "By John Doe." The writer will select a name that meets his fancy or needs. The check will be made out in the writer's real name, but the article will carry the pen name as supplied. The writer may include on the cover page a brief explanation of why he is using a pen name.

AUTHOR'S RIGHTS. A good article may have extensive reprint rights that the young writer has never considered. This writer once sold to *Nature Magazine* a piece later reprinted in a book called *This is Nature*, a collection of articles from the magazine. Somewhat later it was purchased for inclusion in a nature text for public schools. The third check was five times as large as the first.

Some magazines buy only first print rights and assign back all other rights upon request. Others buy all rights, including foreign rights, radio and television, and all other reprint rights.

To protect himself the writer simply types on page one what rights are offered or what rights are reserved. This legend should correspond to the likely value — if any — of such rights, sic. "First magazine rights only. All others reserved." Find out from a market guide or the magazine what it usually expects and act accordingly. Also see page 310 for suggestions on multiple sales.

CORRECTIONS. Corrections on manuscripts should be made as neatly as conditions permit, on the typewriter if possible. Occasional typographical errors may be corrected in ink. If numerous enough to call attention to themselves, the entire page should be retyped. Errors are corrected with standard copyreading symbols, inserted at the proper point in the manuscript. They should not be put in the margin, which should be reserved for proofreading signs. A set of copyreading symbols will be found in Appendix C. Frequent use of these should be unnecessary. It is usually possible to correct errors so that the text will read as if originally errorless.

Training Steps

1. From a copy of the *Catholic Digest* select an article and compare it with the original in the magazine from which it was derived. Underline each word, phrase, and sentence omitted. Has anything essential or important been dropped? Count the words in each version. What was the percentage eliminated?
2. Now take one of your own articles and subject it to the same rigid boiling-down process that the *Catholic Digest* uses. What was the percentage of elimination in your article?
3. On the average, what is the minimum of revisions through which an article must go before it is in shape to be mailed?
4. Read any article that appeals to you in a current magazine. Does it leave important questions unanswered? Would you say the writer was at fault, or was the omitted information really unnecessary?
5. Study an article in which a writer has liberally expressed his opinion. What devices or techniques has he used to avoid antagonizing his readers? If you can detect them, copy them and save them for your notebook.
6. What devices do you find in use to make articles come to life? Name as many as you can.
7. Using any of the articles studied above, count the number of paragraphs in which connectives are found in the first two lines. What percentage

of paragraphs do not have them? Do these connectives actually join paragraphs only, or do they join major divisions of the article?

8. Examine an entire issue of *Reader's Digest*. In how many articles is the beginning unified with title and subtitle?

9. In this same issue see if you can find any articles that would be improved by omission of concluding paragraphs.

10. What is the advantage of inserting cardboard protectors in the inner rather than the outer envelope?

11. Write a page of single-spaced manuscript. Now try to make interlinear corrections. Is it clear why all manuscripts should be double-spaced?

12. Make a rapid survey of a dozen magazines. How many use subheads?

13. Examine an issue of *The National Geographic Magazine* and the editorial page of *Life*. What differences do you find in subheads, typographically and editorially?

14. How many magazines that you know use the device — "By John Doe. . . . As Told to Arthur Roe"?

15. In your local Sunday newspaper how many unsigned articles do you find? Do you consider the magazine practice of printing signed articles an advantage to the writer?

16. What differences do you note between preparing an article for a syndicate and preparing one for a magazine?

CHAPTER 13

Free-Lance Marketing

A free-lance writer's program for selling an article actually begins before the final choice of subject. A writer seldom tries to develop an article out of the first possibility that comes to his attention. Considerable picking and choosing take place. And this selective process is done in terms of the needs of specific magazines and newspapers. The writer asks himself, "What market would take an article on this subject?" He asks also, "Is there a salable article in this idea?" If not, another must be found.

Arranging for Articles

As magazines and newspapers are conducted today, most articles and feature materials are arranged for or planned *in advance*. An editor cannot take a chance on what *may* come in the morning mail. Usable articles may or may not arrive. Hundreds of thousands and even millions of invested dollars depend upon publications that continuously please the public. Hence the editor has to make sure (as nearly as he can) *in advance* that he will have sufficient first-rate articles on hand for every issue.

This calls for planning, so the editor can take several obvious steps. First, he can maintain a staff of salaried writers or editors who can be depended upon to produce acceptable articles when assignments are given them, as discussed in Chapter 2. These writers will turn out a substantial portion of the articles used. Second, he may develop a group of regular contributors, who submit articles more or less frequently and are paid at so much an article. These contributors probably will also be asked occasionally to do articles on assignment for forthcoming issues of the magazine. Third, the editor may keep in the safe a supply of articles against the day when an unexpected "hole" occurs. And, fourth, he may continue to scan the mails for whatever help the postman may bring from free-lance writers. The newspaper editor has a fifth alternative. He may patronize the syndicates to make use of the wealth of material they can supply.

Knowing that an editor must arrange in advance for most of his articles, the writer will inject himself into this process through the *query*. Use of the query has already been discussed, but it should be repeated that many editors welcome a query that gives promise of producing a good article. A writer can turn out an amateurish query, as well as an amateurish article. He must learn to operate at professional levels with both.

Planning the Campaign

Because the writer is not only a manufacturer but also a salesman, he should plan a definite campaign to sell his article even before writing the query. The query is not the first step by any means. Before this the writer has mentally at least lined up a number of prospective buyers.

Also, being a specialist, the writer will know almost at once what the possible markets are. Much knowledge of newspapers and magazines is carried in his head, but the exact details must come from study of market guides, and recent issues of the publications themselves. Perhaps it would be well to repeat here that editors prefer the work of specialists, because their work is likely to be more accurate and up-to-date. Editors reveal this preference by requesting the specialists now and again to do pieces in their field. The requests come unsolicited and usually are akin to definite orders. Therefore, let the writer limit his contributions to one or more major fields in order to establish his reputation as a specialist.

Single Versus Multiple Sales

In planning a sales campaign, the free-lance writer will remember that multiple sales to the general markets should not be attempted, because the circulation is likely to overlap and the editors naturally don't want to publish what their competitors are printing.

In some instances, however, the trade and religious publications are an exception to the above statement, especially where the circulations are unduplicated or noncompetitive. The free-lance writer can find out by writing directly to the editors involved. He may then submit duplicate copies to consenting editors with a release date and a list of the other markets to which he is submitting his article.

Rating the Markets

The experienced free-lance writer has a general understanding of the markets before he considers an idea. He may also turn to the writer's guides which list magazines by approprite classifications, for instance, recording approximately twenty-five magazines in the building field. The writer now examines these and considers possibilities of sales to such a leader as *Architectural & Engineering News,* which might be interested in an article on a home-building boom in America. Having read what the market guides say, the writer tentatively lists the magazines in order of preference as possible buyers. However, examination of the newspapers themselves must be made if they are to appear in the writer's list, for the market guides are of little help on this point. Further explanation on working with the newspapers is contained in Chapter 18.

Next the writer studies current and back copies to discover which publications have recently dealt with his ideas. Since magazines do not like to repeat themselves, he will eliminate (or put low on the list) any magazine that has published an article within the year on the same idea. Actually, it would be better if back issues for two or three years were studied. The *Readers' Guide to Periodical Literature* and other indexes listed in Chapter 23 will be of some assistance in shortening this search.

The factors that cause a magazine to be rated high on the list are as follows: 1. high rate of pay; 2. payment on acceptance; and 3. likelihood of interest in the idea. The writer should beware of magazines that pay on publication, for the author has more than once sold articles to magazines that kept them longer than three years before publishing.

Since it is difficult to tell how long a magazine may have to retain an article before the proper spot is found, the writer will give preference to those editors who pay on acceptance.

When the order of preference is finally worked out, it should be set down, so that the study will not have to be repeated if the first market rejects the query or the finished article. A more permanent record of the actual travels of the manuscript should be kept. How to do this is explained later in this chapter.

Using Standard References

The free-lance writer is fortunate in having available much classified information that is of help in his writing. In general it is found in three sources — writer's magazines, periodical indexes, and yearbooks. Selected lists of each will be found in Chapter 23. Although there is no substitute for a study of the magazine itself, the writer should not have to go beyond these other sources to get the introductory information he needs.

Many or most of the works cited are shelved in the average library. Others can be located in newspaper offices, college libraries, and similar places. It should not be necessary to purchase any of the indexes mentioned. Every beginning writer, however, should subscribe to at least one good writer's magazine and regularly purchase a comprehensive market guide.

The First Query — and After

After the first-choice market has been selected, the writer sends out his query. If the answer is favorable, he proceeds to write the piece, slanting it as carefully as he can. The slanting may call for further analysis of the market if the writer is beginning his trade. The final draft of the article will be typed and arranged with as great care as the writer can summon.

Receipt of the favorable answer is a signal for the writer to start work. It is not time then to "rest on the oars," for something else may arrive in the mail to take the place of the projected piece. The timeliness may disappear, or changes in advertising schedules close the hole the editor had in mind. Quick return of the article also is an index of the writer's ability to deliver the goods.

It is inevitable that some queries will not meet with favor, and that some articles written in response to a favorable nod will be rejected.

If the first query is rejected, the next step is to write the editor of the magazine in second place on the writer's list of possible markets, and so on down the list until it is exhausted. If the idea is carefully chosen and timely, the list should not need to be pursued too far.

Many editors disapprove of sending the same query to more than one magazine at a time. The best rule is to send only one query when dealing with magazines that do not use syndicated articles. When a writer learns which editors in a particular field may be willing to use a syndicated article, then there can be little objection to multiple inquiries sent to them.

When a query or article is submitted, it should be addressed to the department editor concerned. An article on house remodeling should be sent to the architectural editor of *Better Homes and Gardens* — not to the editor-in-chief. Only when the department editor is unknown should the articles be sent to the editor. Then the editor's name should be obtained either from the magazine or from a market guide.

Keeping Articles on the Move

If an article is rejected by the magazine of first choice — even after favorable response to a query — the next step is to consider the magazine second on the list.

The next campaign should begin *the same day the article comes back*. Time is precious to a writer. His ship never comes in unless it is sent voyaging, and his article can't sell while it is on his own desk. A writer in looking back over his manuscript record can tell how wasteful and inefficient he has been by comparing the date his manuscript returns with the date of its subsequent mailing.

The young writer is likely to be hurt and discouraged by a rejection. He must overcome these attitudes to as great a degree and as early in his career as possible. Both attitudes are handicaps to his progress as well as to his income. The best aid to recovery is to restudy the article and to look for additional interesting angles.

Before sending the manuscript out again, the writer should review what he knows of the second market. He should decide whether to *query* this second market before submitting the article, possibly with respect to details now of new significance such as length, tone, or angle. In some cases a query would reveal that the market is closed, and so save time and expense. However, the writer may decide not to query, but instead to send it in unannounced "over the transom."

Some retyping will be required. The cover page and first page will always demand redoing. Unless other pages are soiled, the rest of the manuscript may be sent out once more. If the ribbon is always fresh, there will be no difficulty in matching the retyped pages with earlier versions. Professional work calls for careful matching. A different type-writer should not be used for the retyping unless the entire manuscript is done over. Soiled or torn pages will in all cases be replaced. Generally a manuscript can make two or three round trips before a complete retyping is necessary.

If a third trip must be made, the same steps demanded by the second trip must again be taken. The manuscript should always be typical of the writer's highest efforts in form as well as in content. Editors are prone to be prejudiced against the obvious rejects of other magazines.

The Unsalable Article

No article should be given up as a bad job as long as a market exists that might use it. Sometimes an article will sell after it has gone to a dozen or more markets. If the idea is basically sound and the article well written, it may be exactly what some editor needs. The only way to bring the two together is to keep the article circulating in the mails, typing a fresh copy as often as required, and reslanting the material for each new market according to its requirements.

Eventually the entire list of possible markets may be exhausted without a sale, though this should not happen to as much as 10 per cent of written articles for which queries have originally been used. When the list is run through and there is no possibility of broadening it, the writer should put the article away temporarily. There is frequent possibility that the article may yet be salvaged through revision.

Getting a new angle or point of view on an idea may result in selling a previous reject. For example, an article telling of the fun and adventures two girl students had on a bicycle tour through New England was often rejected. But rewritten to explain the preparations anyone should make for a bicycle tour, it sold on its first trip to *Mademoiselle*. Another general article on the old-fashioned square dance was a "dud" until rewritten to tell how a young women made spare-time cash from teaching this dance. A hobbies magazine was delighted to print what was otherwise headed for the wastebasket.

Don't abandon an idea until you have explored all of its possibilities. If your article is rejected, perhaps you've done something wrong.

Perhaps you can salvage it. This leads us now to examine why articles
are rejected.

Why Articles Are Rejected

Good articles as well as bad ones are rejected. By no means is a
rejection a guarantee that the article is worthless. Among reasons for
rejection a writer may often find a clue that suggests a remedy and a
revision leading to a later sale.

VALUELESS ARTICLES. An individual writer may never turn out a completely valueless article. Nevertheless, tens of thousands of worthless
manuscripts are dumped upon the desks of magazine and newspaper
editors monthly. These have to be opened, examined, and returned to
the sender — if possible. Probably no one has ever accurately estimated
the percentage they are of the total group submitted. It certainly is very
high. This fact should encourage the trained free-lance writer because
it decreases the number of articles with which his own better-written
manuscripts must compete. The cure for this type of rejection is to learn
to write better.

BAD TIMING. At this point let us rephrase some remarks made
earlier. Some excellent — as well as poor — articles are returned to the
writer because they arrived too late to be used. Articles that grow out
of news events often become quickly dated. Most magazine material
has a timeless quality that makes it good reading during any month
of the year. This is the type to which it is well to devote most of one's
energies. Articles based on news events should be written only after
receipt of an okay from some editor.

Except for seasonal material, editors do not like to buy articles that
must be held over until another year. It is occasionally done, but it is
not considered to be good editing. The practice may also be detrimental
to writers. Once a newly-appointed editor told this author that when
he took over he found enough purchased material on hand to fill his
magazine for the next three years — and much of it already was too
out-of-date to be used. In many articles all that was usable was an
occasional scenic photograph. When an editor buys so loosely, he later
must close his columns to free-lance writers until he has used the supply
on hand.

ALREADY SUPPLIED. An article may be returned to the writer simply
because the magazine has a similar article on hand. The rejection slip
may not indicate this, and the writer will be puzzled to know why the

article came back. A query will always reveal when a magazine is supplied, and so help the writer avoid the rejection. There is no avoiding this type of rejection on later trips to market, unless they are preceded by queries.

RECENTLY HANDLED. It is unwise to submit an article that covers the exact idea published in the same magazine within the year. Both the query and article should be preceded by careful examination of recent back numbers of the proposed market. When such study reveals that a magazine has dealt with the same idea, two courses of action are possible: a new angle may be developed, or a new market may be sought for the original idea.

Note that these remarks concern similar articles on the exact idea. *Good Housekeeping* for instance, will use during a year's time many articles on health, but only one article telling about a specific drug or a new type of Xray treatment.

CARELESS COPY. Under this broad classification we may include manuscripts that are physically unattractive. Poor typing, single spacing, dirty and torn pages, and other such unsavory qualities disqualify many an article at first glance. The way to avoid rejection from this cause has already been discussed.

INEPT HANDLING. An article is inept if it is too long or too short, if the beginning is too long or irrelevant, if the ending is too long or unrelated to the rest of the article, and inept if the point of view is wrong. There are a thousand and one types of ineptitude. They are to be found even in the work of professional writers, and the beginner can only strive the harder while rewriting as often as time allows.

POOR ILLUSTRATION. Articles that demand illustration will surely come home if the writer has not provided adequate pictorial illumination. While some magazines will illustrate free-lance articles in which they see unusual promise, the best course is to send abundant illustration from which the editor can pick and choose.

UNKNOWN WRITER. The beginning writer should not fear "big names." Though the appearance of the so-called big names on magazine covers means usually a guarantee of a first-rate performance, it is cheaper to buy from beginning writers. Most magazines, therefore, scrutinize the mails and other magazines for promising talent. The editors of the *Saturday Evening Post* once stated that it had introduced to the reading public as many as 50 new writers within the space of 12 months.

By the way he conducts himself a writer can lessen the distrust that magazines have of unknown writers. Once he has sold an article, he no longer is unknown to that particular editor. From then on gaining a foot-hold is increasingly easier.

Learning from Rejections

Some magazines have developed rejection slips that make it possible for them to indicate briefly and quickly why the article is being returned. *Better Homes and Gardens* is among that group. By placing a check mark inside a square, the editor can indicate which of a dozen reasons has caused rejection. If he indicates that the fault is with the illustrations, the difficulty may be within the power of the writer to remedy. Similarly, a few of the other faults are possible of correction, so that the proper changes may be made and the article submitted to this magazine.

The editor of *Esquire* frequently writes a brief note to indicate what is wrong. Occasionally, articles are so badly written or poorly aimed that they are undeserving of the time it takes to dictate a note of rejection.

Sometimes editors are unexpectedly helpful. On one occasion the editor of *Outdoor Life* wrote a note to this writer saying an article lacked unity and that he was returning it. This defect was removed by rewriting, but the editor now objected to certain paragraphs because they broke up the narrative. When these were removed by another rewriting, he accepted the article. This was an unusual case, but it does indicate that it pays to profit from the advice given in notes of rejection, and shows that an article should not be discarded until every effort has been made to sell it.

When editors reject an article after having given a go-ahead sign in answer to a query, they almost invariably write a brief note to indicate why they are forced to return the piece. This is the general rule following queries. *It is an exception* when an editor writes a personal note of rejection for an *unsolicited* manuscript.

Understanding Magazine Practices

A knowledge of the routines in a typical magazine office will help the beginning writer in the business aspects of his writing. He will better understand why he must be businesslike in his own methods. He will also come to recognize the reason behind the various suggestions made in this text for arranging his manuscript and protecting the illustrations.

Mail reaches the average magazine by great sackfuls. A magazine with only a million subscribers would, on the average, receive 3,000 letters each day regarding new subscriptions or renewals alone. Scores of other letters arrive daily from advertisers, responsive readers, job applicants; and hundreds come from would-be contributors. The first step is to sort the mail into three categories, if the firm publishes only one magazine. If more are issued, then the mail must first be sorted by magazines. The three categories represent the advertising, circulation, and editorial divisions of the magazine. Each of the three may be and usually is further subdivided.

From the editorial group are selected the bulky and larger envelopes, which obviously contain manuscripts. These bulky items are opened by hand, though smaller manuscripts may possibly be opened by a slicing machine.

Routing the Manuscript

The next step is to make a record of when the manuscript was received, the writer's name, his address, the title of the article, and the number of illustrations. This card is filed away and kept as long as the manuscript is in the office.

Then a second card is usually filled out, bearing the same data as above, but offering space to record what happens to the article on its way through the office. This card records also the amount of return postage, and whether it was sufficient or inadequate, as well as the condition of illustrations.

If the manuscripts have been addressed to a specific departmental editor, they now are carried to the proper desk. Quicker action thus comes from use of the query and from knowing the name of division editors.

If the manuscripts have been addressed to "The Editor," usually they will be examined by a first reader, who may have the authority to reject or pass along to a higher-up, depending on the merits of the article. Most manuscripts addressed to "The Editor" never get past this first reader, but eventually first-rate manuscripts reach the proper desk.

Role of the Editor

Manuscripts approved by departmental editors usually have to be okayed by the editor-in-chief, and perhaps by a majority of other departmental editors. It is common practice to hold regular staff meetings to accept or reject the items approved by department editors. These latter may have full power to reject and do so in perhaps 90 per cent of all cases.

When a manuscript is purchased, the editor sends an order telling the disbursing agent how much to pay for the item. The manuscript then goes back to the departmental editor. Payment may be made immediately, or later, according to the policy of the magazine.

Manuscripts that are rejected usually go to a clerk, who detaches the routing cards, and notes whether the return postage was adequate. If it was sufficient, the manuscript is returned usually with a printed rejection slip. If the postage was inadequate, the manuscript may be left to wait until the writer inquires or sends additional postage. A few magazines contribute the additional stamps.

Most editorial offices reserve the right to make slight editorial changes or to boil articles down to fit a particular hole. *Outdoor Life* and *Parents' Magazine* are among the magazines that have submitted such alterations to this author for approval before putting them on the press. It is advisable for writers to cooperate with editors as fully as possible on this point, because space requirements can be rigid. The easiest way to make a particular piece fit any tight spot is to trim the article.

When to Write to the Editor

Occasional manuscripts get misplaced or held up in magazine offices. This is more likely to occur in the smaller offices than in the larger ones. If the article is timely and likely to lose its values, the writer should drop a note to the editor, asking pleasantly whether the article is being held for further consideration. If so, the writer states, he will be glad to let them keep it longer. But if not, he would like to have the manuscript returned, so that he can try another market. It is bad business to show anger at a magazine that holds an article too long. The writer in all likelihood will wish to submit future articles to this market. And it is easier to do business with friends than with enemies.

How much time should be allowed to lapse before writing is difficult to decide for all cases. The writer must use his best judgment in view of the time element involved. Three weeks should be long enough in most cases, though some magazines do take longer than this. A magazine's reputation for promptness in handling manuscripts must be considered before items are submitted to it. No magazine, unless it has written that it is definitely holding an article for further consideration, should be allowed to keep a manuscript more than two months. Few items of merchandise are more perishable than magazine and newspaper articles. However, magazines are busy places, and editors are often overworked. So a writer should not expect to enter into long correspondence about his work.

Keeping a Manuscript Record

Manuscript records are valuable to anyone who sends out even an occasional piece — whether article or short story. They show how much publications pay and how long they keep manuscripts. They record titles, numbers of words, and illustrations. And they show how diligent the writer has been in sending his rejected work to market.

Keeping the record is an important part of the business of writing, but it is a simple step. An example of a satisfactory type of manuscript record follows. For this type of record any inexpensive tablet or looseleaf notebook will be satisfactory. A single sheet should be devoted to each item. The two sides will be ample to record all the data necessary.

Other types of records can be devised. Some writers use 3 X 5 or 5 X 8 cards, alphabetized and kept in filing cases. Manuscript records may be more or less elaborate than the above example. Often the whole story of a writer's success is told by the difference between the date of return and that of remailing. This should be kept as short as possible. The writer should go to great pain to put aside other work if he can. Any manuscript kept at home is a dead loss to its owner.

Title	Market	Date Mailed	No. of Words	No. of Illust.	Cost	Date Accepted or Returned	Payment
Map Making by Air	Field and Stream	M. 1/10	3,500	7	$15.00	1/20	
Map Making by Air	True	Rev. 1/23	2,500	7	----	2/7	
Map Making by Air	National Geographic Magazine	Rev. 2/10	2,500	10	3.00	2/28	
Map Making by Air	Popular Science Monthly	Rev. 3/5	1,500	10	----	3/26	$350.00

Illustration 12 — Manuscript record

Foreign Markets

Only a few markets outside the United States are of consequence to the American free-lance writer. Among them are Australian, British, Indian, Canadian, English, and New Zealand markets. Contributions must be confined to those magazines of which copies are available for study unless the writer sends abroad for sample copies.

A few magazines from these foreign markets are found on the major newsstands. Additional magazines can also be located in public or college libraries. The market guides listed in Chapter 23 will supply some of the basic general information about such markets, but in all cases the data are at least a year old. Some of the magazines will send copies upon request.

The handling of return stamps is somewhat cumbersome. Although cash can be sent, this practice forces the foreign magazine to deal in currency of another nation. A better method is to purchase at the local post office so-called "International Reply Coupons." These recently cost 15 cents to cover the return of a 1-ounce item. United States mail to Canada costs 5 cents an ounce, but the first ounce to England costs 11 cents. Since rates vary with the weight of the manuscript, all manuscripts should be weighed and the cost of return checked by the post office so that adequate coupons can be purchased for possible return.

Canadian magazines in particular have long been interested in the American point of view, and in what occurs below their southern border. Right now there is an expanding market for articles by American writers. Free-lance writers should profit from exploring this market. There are some excellent Canadian magazines, a number of which are quite as good as similar publications in the United States.

Value of Author's Representatives

The writer early in his career learns of author's representatives and of how they sold this short story or that novel. And he wonders whether they could help him. The answer is usually disappointing.

In the first place, few good representatives will handle the work of unknown writers without a reading fee. Most beginners usually have so little of merit to offer that any attempt to market their work would be a complete waste of time. Representatives prefer to try to sell the work of mature, established writers who by this time need little assistance.

All a representative can do is to save the writer some of the time it takes to mail his work, particularly a piece that meets with several rejections. The representative cannot afford to, and will not, reslant an article. And often it is the reslanting that sells a manuscript on its second or third trip.

Finally, few representatives are willing to handle articles. They prefer fiction, because resale opportunities are so much greater for fiction than for nonfiction. Motion-picture rights, radio rights, television rights, and secondary publication possibilities exist for fiction; whereas, except for digest magazines, few such opportunities can be found for nonfiction. In any case article writing requires much direct correspondence with editors over queries and revisions, which could not be so easily handled by a representative.

Correspondence Schools and Critics

Another type of promised help likely to lure hopeful but inexperienced writers is the correspondence school or institute. In most cases this will prove a complete disappointment. The young writer is advised to save his money and time.

Critics of writing who advertise in writers' magazines are also likely to turn out to be failures in teaching article writing. They offer various kinds of services — collaboration, criticism, and marketing help. Nearly all charge a "fee" for reading, retyping, or criticizing the manuscripts, and in most cases this fee is the only item in which they are interested. Occasionally they sell an article, a fact which is almost certain to be mentioned in their glowing advertisements. There are enough aspiring young writers who patronize such services to provide a good income for their operators.

An incident from this author's early writing experience will perhaps illustrate the type of advice likely to be purchased from critics. A certain New York advertising critic, who charged the author five dollars for criticizing a piece of work, recommended changes to make it salable. When the changes were made, the copy was returned (with a second fee) to determine how well the advice had been followed. The critic replied that the new version was now nearly perfect and should meet with ready sale. However, the author had inadvertently returned the carbon of the first version, instead of the carbon of the second, which he had intended to forward. Consequently, the critic was writing of the identical piece in both cases. Completely cured, this writer has relied upon more substantial help since then.

Two Sources of Help

Two sources of real help are open to beginning writers, in addition to the acceptable texts in this field. The first source is an established writer. If the beginner can find such an individual in a local newspaper office, or elsewhere, he ought to cultivate that individual's friendship. A few words of expert, pointed advice from such a source are worth more than all the advice to be obtained from advertising critics over months of writing and at the cost of many dollars. Even at the risk of becoming a nuisance, the novice owes it to himself to dig up objective criticism that is free from flattery wherever he can find it.

The second and best source is a well-run class in article writing, taught by one who knows how to prepare articles for national markets. Such classes can be found in many of the larger universities and in some colleges. Arrangements can frequently be made to audit these classes or to do the work at night sessions, so that it is unnecessary to take additional courses in order to get this one type of instruction.

Writing along with other beginners in such classes is always stimulating. With a few words the experienced writer-instructor can frequently set a novice's feet on the right paths that would take him months or years to discover working by himself. Usually the checks start to arrive to some members of the class within six weeks or less after the first class meets — a type of demonstration that is a priceless experience for an aspiring writer. When a young writer sees checks paid to those who have no more ability or experience than he has, he gets a type of encouragement that can come in no other way. Writing is almost always a lonely business. Contacts with practicing writers can be a great source of inspiration and help.

Training Steps

1. Examine a copy of *Field and Stream.* Can you tell how many articles were contributed by staff members? How many by free-lance writers?
2. How many articles are definitely keyed to the season and could not easily have been printed another time?
3. Make a list, using a standard market guide, of magazines similar to *American Home* that might use an article on remodeling a home.
4. Make a second list of trade magazines that might be a source of information for anyone writing on home remodeling.
5. Which of the magazines listed as a result of Training Steps 3 and 4 are indexed in the various guides to current literature?

6. Examine the March issue of any woman's magazine for three successive years. What subjects do you find repeated? Make the same survey for the September issue.

7. Study the early career of Rudyard Kipling in America. How many editors and publishers rejected his writings before his work first began to be accepted?

8. Study the field of trade publications. Can you find a single trade represented by only one magazine?

9. Which of the writers' magazines do you prefer after a careful examination? Why?

10. Which market guide is most recent and most useful?

11. Watch as many magazines as possible for articles by writers in your locality. Try to make contact with them and to discover how they can be of help to you.

12. What magazines are published in your area? What facts can you uncover that would make good articles for them? Begin to study them now.

13. Make contact with the newspapers in your area. If they buy from free-lance writers, how do their rates compare with magazines for which you can write?

14. Become acquainted with local newspapermen and cultivate their friendship. If they are not writing for other publications, find out whether they will give you occasional tips for your free-lance writing.

CHAPTER 14

Types of Articles

Article have been variously classified by authorities on the subject. But the business of classifying articles by strict types can be overdone, for mutually exclusive categories do not exist. Most articles will fall at least in part into two or more classifications.

Types Are Not Clear-Cut

It is sometimes difficult to distinguish between the confession and the personal-experience article. Often the only difference is the extent to which intimate details are included. In addition, the interview and the personality or character sketch are more alike than different. The first usually includes more quotations or opinion than the second, but again the difference is one of extent. The process articles and the personal experience have much in common, as do the narrative in the third person, the character sketch, and the interview.

The student of article writing must not expect clear-cut types. Few people who produce articles are interested in turning them out according to types. What they try to do is to put together an interesting piece. In the process they borrow techniques that suit their purposes, regardless of the type to which it may be most readily adapted.

Elaborate plans for handling each type are unnecessary. The methods of making an inventory and of outlining explained in Chapter 8 can be used in every type of article with the possible exception of one told in strictly chronological order. The best advice to follow is to make each as fascinating as possible by whatever means come to hand. Additional help on this point will be found in Chapter 15, Techniques for Humanization.

Classification Yields Benefits

Some benefits are to be derived, however, from trying to classify and analyze the articles one comes across. Recognition of the general types occasionally yields an idea for an article. Knowledge that there is a confession article may suggest doing a confession for the magazines. The interview article may suggest a piece about an interesting person among the writer's acquaintances.

A collection of articles, classified by types, may also be an aid. When an especially appealing article is found, it should be clipped for future analysis. Then when the writer has made up his mind to do an article of that type, he can study the examples he has filed. Nothing is more helpful than to discover how some first-rate writer has solved a similar problem. Imitation of the manner of development is a legitimate practice, though one does not copy subjects or basic ideas.

This analysis can be carried far enough so that the writer knows what types his markets prefer, as well as the subjects that appeal most to them. Eventually he may become so expert in the process that when he sees an unusually good subject, he knows for which of his markets it is a "natural."

Types of Articles

In offering the following list of article types, the author realizes that many readers will eventually work out a different group for themselves. That would be a first-rate idea. Each writer's classification should be slanted to suit his own needs, for it will make the recognition, filing, and later use easier.

At the outset of his career the writer may classify articles as 1. personality sketches, 2. narratives in the first person, 3. narratives in the third person, 4. confessions, 5. interviews, 6. essays and critical writing, 7. processes, and 8. collectives.

About half of the selections on the following pages of this chapter are the work of student writers, some of whom were writing their first articles. These are not presented as perfect pieces of work but as examples of what beginning writers can do and sell to magazines of national circulation.

Personality Sketches

The personality sketch differs from the interview in that emphasis is on the individual and his achievements in the former, and in the latter on what he says. Information for both is obtained chiefly from the interview and personal acquaintance.

The popularity of personality sketches was demonstrated decades ago by *The American Magazine,* which developed to a high degree the rags-to-riches theme. So successful was the magazine that scores of other magazines adapted the type to their own purpose, and newspapers used it in their Sunday issues.

The basic appeal is the interest of human beings in each other. If the characters are successful or prominent, the interest may be taken for granted. But they do not have to be either; they need only be interesting. The widespread popularity of the Ann Landers type of column is based on this appeal. How deep the interest is can be seen in the success of the gossip columns.

The personality sketch has a wide range of form, as does the confession. It is to be found at its best in such organs as the Sunday magazine of *The New York Times, Reader's Digest, The New Yorker, Look, Life, Newsweek,* and *Time.* Its purpose also varies from entertainment to guidance and inspiration. These ends are reached by focusing attention on the personality and accomplishments of the character under scrutiny.

The article may or may not be accompanied by illustrations. In any case the writer strives to give an accurate word picture of the individual. This is done through mention of physical characteristics, habits, dress, mannerisms, interests, biographical data, opinions of others, and through the character's own words. Readers want to know the intimate details of what people think, feel, and believe. It is the writer's problem to bring these details to life on paper.

Beginning writers will find it easier to do personality sketches of individuals they know well. The personality sketch calls for skill in painting word pictures. Other than to an experienced interviewer, brief interviews usually will not yield enough information for a good portrait. Most writers have within the circle of their acquaintances one or more individuals worth writing up for the proper market. It would be well to start with these less difficult subjects.

Before undertaking to handle an article on a famous individual, the writer should obtain a favorable reply to a carefully-framed query telling of his proposed interview. Painstaking reading should precede the actual interview. A list of helpful biographical sources of information will be found in Chapter 23. They are numerous, and are frequently of great help.

All the devices of fiction are available to the writer of personality sketches. Anecdotes, particularly helpful if they involve the interviewee because of the clarity with which they reveal personality, can be gathered from friends or neighbors. Minor incidents and major experiences can be used to show the character in action. A special effort should be made to get direct quotations.

Chief reliance for developing an interesting article should rest upon the quoted words of the individual portrayed. The style should be swift and sure. Rambling, verbose explanations and descriptions ruin the personality sketch. Words that grip or stab are the most effective. For instance, an individual might be described better with a single word such as "mousy" than with a dozen poorly-chosen adjectives.

Slanting is as necessary in the personality sketch as in other types of articles. Some magazines use the personality sketch purely for entertainment, while shunning the uplift article. Some of the "movie" magazines use many sketches of a highly polished type that can be duplicated only by careful study. The trade publications purchase an entirely different type — one that puts the emphasis upon accomplishment and experience. As always, the writer must study his markets.

The two personality sketches that follow are widely different in treatment. The first is based entirely upon research in quite early sources. The second quotes material obtained from a number of sources, including at least one interview. Whereas the first writer omits reference to himself, the second brings the writer into his article at several points. The first piece is based upon an historically famous character; the second describes an individual scarcely known beyond her own community. The two show that a wide variety of techniques may be used in personality sketches.

THE TROUT AND DAN'L WEBSTER[1]

By Nicholas Karas

The village of Brookhaven, N. Y. is a quiet, reserved little town, tucked among harbors and sand dunes and hidden beneath majestic elms on Long Island's South Shore. It is much the same as many other small communities on Long Island except for its one ancient Presbyterian church, founded in 1740. Age alone can often be enough to make a church famous but this one has a special claim to fame: on a Sunday morning 139 years ago the congregation saw Daniel Webster catch the world's largest brook trout a short cast away from the pulpit. All that remains today of this historic event are some obscure records and diaries; a wooden fish, a facsimile of a trout Webster caught; a brass nameplate inscribed "The Suffolk Club" on a pew in the little church; and a Currier & Ives print that shows Webster catching a trout, with a caption that reads "We hab you now, sar."

Webster, like almost everyone born in the mountains of New Hampshire, fished for trout from boyhood days. As early as 1820, he started visiting the then famous trout streams of Long Island and was a regular patron at Sam Carman's tavern at Fireplace. In Carman's custoday, Black Dan, as he was affectionately called by many in Congress, was able to satisfy his two greatest hobbies: trout and rum, and often both at the same time. However, come Sunday morning in the acutely religious America of Webster's time, both men could always be found across the road in the little white Presbyterian church in the pew that they had reserved for their Suffolk Club. Often they were accompanied by other famous members of the fish club, among them Martin Van Buren, President-to-be, Philip Hone, soon to be mayor of New York City, and Inventor John Stevens.

When Webster was a Senator, he maintained his law practice with offices both in Boston and New York City. One of Dan'l's closest fishing cronies in New York was Philip Hone. And it was Hone who first excited Webster about Long Island fishing with rumors that a monstrous trout, "bigger than any seen before," had been spotted in the little Connecticut River.

According to Hone's diary, they caught the Friday stage one spring afternoon in 1823 and arrived at Sam Carmans' tavern after dark. They fished the next day from sunup to sunset without sight of the big trout, though, according to Carman, the fish had been seen but a few days earlier in the pool and "was 20 pounds if it was an ounce." The next day their luck changed slightly and Webster saw for the first time the fish that was to plague him for years to come. But no matter how the two men cast, they couldn't induce the trout to take their Mayflies.

Webster returned often to Fireplace to quench his thirst and to search out the big trout, but he didn't see it again for several years. Sam and his slaves did see it from time to time and kept alive the desires of Webster. It wasn't until the spring of 1827 that both Webster and Hone were again at Carman's, and by now the fish had become an obsession with Webster.

---

[1]Reprinted by permission of *Sports Illustrated* and the author, currently a freelance writer and former student of this author.

Webster and Hone fished hard the first day, Saturday, without sighting anything, and that night they drank even harder than they had fished — Webster had to be carried to bed.

But the next day, after the bell on the church across the road had tolled, the men were on their way with pounding heads to do penance for their self-indulgences. Before they entered the church, Sam gave his slave Lige solemn orders to sit guard at the pool and watch for the trout. If it should appear he was to call them immediately. Webster, Hone and Carman made their way to their pew, beneath the scowling eyes of the preacher, Ezra King, also a devoted trout fisherman.

Sermons in those days were short if they lasted but two hours, and King was known as a notoriously long speaker. His righteous voice droned on and on about the eternal faults of man and the wickedness of his life. Suddenly the shuffling of feet behind them caught the attention of Carman and Webster. It was Lige.

"He's heah, Mistah Carman, he's heah in de pool," said Lige. "Ah left Ephraim awaitin' by de watah, alookin' at de trout."

No matter how one tries, there is no inconspicuous way to leave a forward pew of a church, and knowing eyes were on the men as they walked out. At the river Webster, Sam and Lige jumped into a rowboat and Lige guided it slowly toward the spot where the trout had been seen.

One by one the men of the congregation also found excuses for slipping out, and within a few minutes the church was almost emptied. King had left the pulpit and was delivering his sermon from the aisle, slowly working his way to the rear. After an unexpected and hasty benediction, he ran for the pool, with the rest of the congregation at his heels.

The congregation lined the bank of the pool and watched while Webster cast from the rowboat. Suddenly there was a dimple on the flat surface and then the fly disappeared. Webster set the line taut, and a small trout broke the surface. A dull moan of disappointment came from the onlookers, almost in unison, almost as if Ezra King were leading them in choir.

After half an hour the watchers along the bank began losing interest — but before many drifted away a dark massive swirl broke the placid surface of the pool close to the cast fly. It was the big fish. Webster saw it and so did Sam and Lige in the boat. Rather than work the fly, Webster snatched it up again and re-presented it with a longer cast and renewed interest. It was the most eloquent cast that he could muster and the most important that he would ever have to attempt; it was more than just fishing, it was a trial of life.

The Mayfly settled once again upon the water and floated as if it had just spent the last ounce of its ephemeral life. Nothing happened for the longest time, or it seemed like the longest time for the three watching men. Finally the fish struck. It was wild, and as it took the fly the momentum of the charge carried the fish clear of the water. It landed with a splash that startled even the witnesses who lined the banks.

What followed was a real trial in every sense, the trial of two combatants — the fish fighting for its life, and Webster for peace of mind, which at times can be more dear than life itself. It was a trial that wasn't decided until the very last, until the final appeal was made from both sides. The fish gave up only after a long, drawn-out struggle that held the congregation spellbound. Finally Lige slipped a long-handled net under the fish and pulled it into the boat. The behemoth had turned almost black from its long life in the dark waters of the river, but the underside flashed orange and red and the white trim on the fins left no doubt as to the pedigree of the trout.

Webster held up the fish for the people to see, and suddenly the somber, reserved crowd broke out into cheers—unthinkable on the Sabbath. Some even jumped and shouted wildly as they crowded the banks of the river. Records have it that Squire Harmon's team of horses was alarmed by the noise and took off down the road without the driver.

Lige carried the huge fish to Carman's store, as everyone tried to guess its weight. Sam shifted the weights on the scale until the arm gingerly balanced at 14 pounds 8 ounces; Webster had just caught the world's biggest brook trout, whether he knew it or not. A fish that large couldn't go unrecorded, and Carman placed it against a wall of the store and drew its outline. Philip Hone copied the outline, and the next day it was transferred to a solid cherry plank to eventually serve as the church weather vane. It was increased in size by one-third, however, so that when the sawed-out fish was viewed in its position on the church spire it would look closer to life-size.

There are varied stories about what happened to the fish. One goes like this: when Webster arrived in New York City that evening, he, Martin Van Buren and Philip Hone went to Delmonico's where they ate the trout. Though Webster continued his fishing exploits on Long Island, as well as in other parts of the country, he never again caught a trout as large as the one from Sam Carman's pool. Nor did anyone else until 1916, when a Canadian caught a brook trout in Ontario that equaled the weight of the fish caught by Webster.

Modern recording of big fish started well after Webster's time. But the fish Webster caught was authenticated and witnessed by a President-to-be, a mayor of New York City and a member of the clergy and his congregation and was entered into the church's records. The fisherman himself was, of course, both an attorney and Senator and later Secretary of State.

The fish weather vane remained on the church for many years until, as the story goes, "a late-summer thunderstorm, as big for a storm as that trout was for trout, came down on the little village of Fireplace. There was a tremendous peal of thunder, preceded by a blinding flash of sputtering, crackling blue-green light, which struck the church spire, knocked the wooden fish off into the gutter, went down through the pipe organ and killed a mule that had taken shelter from the storm beneath some trees in the graveyard below — quite a proper place, as it turned out."

The Connecticut River still flows on Long Island but has been renamed after Carman. The big pool at the base of the mill yielded trout as late as 1956, when it was decided to build one of the many superhighways on Long Island. The pool, in the right-of-way of progress, was destroyed and the mill torn down. If Daniel Webster were still alive today, one might wonder if he could have once again saved the pool, as he did in 1845 when he came to Sam Carman's aid and had the Long Island Rail Road remove a bridge it had put up across the river. The culvert had been built with too small an opening and had dammed the stream back to the pool.

Carman's tavern lasted until 1936, when it was torn down. Even the historic little church that witnessed the event has felt the hand of progress. Fireplace, or Fireplace Mills as it later was known (it is now called South Haven), no longer prospered at the crossing-over place when a bridge was built. Over the years the congregation dwindled to the point where the church was of little use. A few years ago it gave up its location, abandoned its graveyard and was moved two miles to the village of Brookhaven.

The heavy cherry weather vane has better stood the test of time and the elements and, though suffering a little from wear, it can still be seen in the parsonage. Today, as one walks down its aisle, one can almost hear Ezra King delivering his sermon on that warm May Sunday, 139 years ago. And in the center pew, one can see the spot, marked by the brass plate, where Daniel Webster sat and listened to the word of God — and waited for word of the big trout.

A.

ARIZONA'S "AUNT ADALINE"[2]

The Greathearted Woman Who Vanquished
The Frontier and Mothers a Whole State

————————

By Oren Arnold

Early one morning in 1929 an airplane landed by mistake near a farm home outside Phoenix, Arizona. A sweet little old mummy of a woman saw it. Without waking her relatives, she had slipped out to pet a newborn colt. She was barefoot, and wore a tattered bathrobe through which the lace of her nightie peeked saucily. But she crawled quickly under a barbed-wire fence and ran to the confused pilot.

"Could a body get a ride in that contraption?" she greeted him eagerly. "It'd be a celebration. Today's my 83rd birthday."

He beheld her face, lined with much living; her hair, snowy and blowy and short as a child's. He could see that the fire within her was still flaming. "Now I know where I am," he said. "This is Gray Mansion, for you are bound to be Adaline Gray."

Thus Mrs. Gray, who on her honeymoon had ridden 2,000 miles westward in a covered wagon, got her first and last flight over Arizona's Valley of the Sun. As a celebration it was entirely proper; she looked down on a rich desert oasis which she herself had done most to pioneer. The half-million irrigated acres comprised one of the world's most successful reclamation projects.

[2]Reprinted by permission of *Reader's Digest* and the author. An original contribution to the magazine.

Her valley was oval, walled in by red-and-purple mountains, lush with grain and fruit. She saw the river twinkling like a fallen thread of sky, and the 5,000 miles of canals making silvery filigree. Gems sparkling on the green velvet were towns. Phoenix, which she had founded and "bossed" for four decades, had become a city of rare beauty. She came down beaming like a ten-year-old.

To me, "Aunt" Adaline Gray will always be a symbol of what our pioneers accomplished. She was a last priceless link with frontier days, when audacious American dreaming flourished as never before. She was not content to carve out just one cabin home for one family. Childless herself, she mothered a whole state.

Arizona was populated mainly by Indians and wild animals when she got there. But as the cactus was being cleared for Phoenix village in 1870, she spoke up in meeting. "First public house you men build has got to be a school. Get a teacher with some sense and pay him a fair wage."

A bride at the time, she made the bearded frontiersmen mind her. An educated man named J. D. Daroche was brought in as master at the unheard-of salary of $100 a month; most teachers in that era got $15 to $40. Through the 70's and 80's Adaline Gray made frequent trips of inspection on horseback. She'd ride up to an adobe schoolhouse and ask if firewood was low, if spelling books were worn out, or if the teacher's ability seemed only mediocre. Her precedent in demanding efficiency still holds. Today the Phoenix school system ranks among the best in the nation.

When the roof of that first schoolhouse was completed, Adaline called a church meeting there.

"Why shucks, ma'am," a workman objected, "it ain't a soul in this valley that can preach."

"But every soul in this valley can pray," she countered.

When bandits, gamblers, rustlers, and murderers drifted into booming Phoenix, Adaline Gray again went into action. One night a thief tried to get away with one of her saddle horses. She picked up a rifle, and at about 200 yards by moonlight knocked him sprawling. Then she doctored his wound, gave him a meal and pointed down the road.

"Now git!" she ordered. "And if I ever catch you in Arizona again, I'll shoot and do no doctorin'."

That same week two farmers were robbed and slain. Nobody seemed to do much about it, so Adaline called on ten leading citizens. "Haven't you men got the stomach to clean up things?" she challenged. "You want us women to take over and run this valley?"

Shamed, they quickly rounded up about 50 outlaws, and identified two who had murdered the farmers. These they hanged from tree limbs. With the bodies still dangling, the other undesirables were brought one by one to the spot and noosed. As each pleaded for mercy he was given a canteen and ordered not to stop running until he crossed the Arizona line.

That became another precedent. Phoenix grew up renowned as a "Sunday-school town" — this in the same era and region that spawned such helldorados as Tombstone, Bisbee, and Prescott.

Adaline was reared in gentility on an Arkansas plantation before the Civil War. When that war was over, the plantation had been destroyed, the South was heartbroken and hopeless. Adaline Norris was 19.

One day, Columbus Harrison Gray, an old friend, came to see her. He was heading for California. "My, my, my!" he whispered to her. "Nobody was ever so pretty and proud! Out West everything's clean and new and promisin'. Now I could scrape up mules . . . a wagon . . . if you—"

They dropped out of a wagon train after entering the Valley of the Sun in 1868. Lum Gray had heard about mineral wealth in Arizona and wanted to prospect. But Adaline, farm reared, told him, "It's more gold in this soil than it is in the mountains. And look at these old abandoned canals — why ancient men must have irrigated hundreds of acres here!"

Actually, ancient men had irrigated thousands of acres. Their canals, though long dry, were 30 feet wide and 6 feet deep, and extended 20 miles from the Salt River. By the time Lum returned from a fruitless hunt for ore, Adaline had turnip greens ready to pick. Lum hitched his mules to a turning plow.

An adventurous bachelor named Jack Swilling had preceded them into the valley by a few months, living in a brush lean-to. He was lazy and given to drink, but he too saw the possibilities in irrigation. The Grays pitched in with him to clean out one old canal. Jack did little physical labor, but he'd go hunting and bring in deer and quail and doves; he'd play a *git*-tar and —"sin-n-n-ng, law me, he could sing like the winds of morning," Aunt Adaline told us, decades later. The Gray's mules and Swilling's music and gun enabled white people for the first time to divert water from the Salt River onto farms.

Travelers scoffed at first, then became interested. Many begun to unhitch, people with such fascinating names as "Pumphandle" John, "One-Eyed" Davis, "Lord" Darrell Duppa, a scholarly fugitive from England. Within 12 months a boom was on. Twelve more months and the village had a flour mill, the school, a church, two "right good" saloons, a blacksmith, an undertaker, a hotel, two stores and a butcher shop.

Adaline made the butcher, Peter Holcomb, hire an Indian lad to fan flies off his meat. Self-service was introduced. Peter would hang half a steer carcas on his front porch and stick a knife in a post. Any customer could. cut off steaks or a roast to suit himself, then call through the door, "Charge me with about seven pounds, Pete."

Hundreds of acres had been brought under cultivation by the simple magic of turning water from the mountains onto the thirsty earth. The villagers prospered, and the time came for a naming. "As the phoenix bird of mythology rose from its own ashes," orated Darrell Duppa, "so will a great city rise here on the ashes of a past civilization. This valley once supported thousands of people. It will support thousands again. Let us name our town Phoenix."

"Talking through yore hat, ain't you, Lord Duppa?" "Pumphandle John" scoffed.

"Hush up," Adaline Gray ordered. "He's right. I bet a peck of potatoes I live to see 10,000 people here."

When she took her airplane ride Phoenix had 110,000 population. It has nearly 200,000 today.

One night in the early days, when Lum was off on a trip, a band of Pimas came to steal her mules. Her stable was a long adobe with flat roof and parapet walls. From 10 P.M. until after dawn she stayed up there with her rifle.

"I'd shoot over the wall at one end, run and shoot over the other," she said. "I never knew how many I kilt because they'd take their dead and wounded away. When Lum got back, nary an animal was missin'."

Later, Indian braves clad in approximately nothing, started coming into town to trade. The town's white women were distraught. Adaline Gray went from house to house, taxed each family one pair of old pants, then called a Pima interpreter named Mary Manytracks.

"You tell them redskin braves if they don't want their skins punctured they better keep them covered when they tramp our streets."

She hung the trousers on a mesquite tree near the edge of the community. For years naked Indians stopped there to dress on the way in, then left the trousers on the way out.

One year Lum Gray sold a mine for $60,000 cash. Whereupon Adaline made Lum build her a two-story red-brick mansion, its ceilings 14 feet high, its seven bedrooms rich with oak panels and tinted glass transoms. Landscaping included a swimming pool, boating lake, tall sentinel palms, rose gardens, lawns for croquet, stables with high-stepping horses.

All of this was a perfect prelude to the modern Arizona resort hotels, one of which charges $65 a day. But Aunt Adaline offered approximately the same hospitality free. She knew frontiersmen hungered for refinement and she wanted to give it to them. Gray Mansion developed as the social and political headquarters for Arizona Territory.

Hundreds of couples were married there. If Arizona today has an abundance of Adalines it is not surprising. I mentioned Mary Manytracks, a Pima. Her daughter, granddaughter, and great-granddaughter all are named Adaline. When Mary's time with her first-born came she was put to bed in the whitest sheets in the prettiest room of Gray Mansion, and Adaline herself delivered the little papoose. John Fremont, governor of the Territory in 1881, sent a young woman 240 miles by stagecoach to have her baby in Adaline's home "because it will be a source of pride for you in years to come."

"There were times," Aunt Adaline once told me, "when 40 or 50 people would be guests in and around our house, and we all loved it. When our beds filled, people would drop bedrolls on porches or in the yard. The brought buffalo meat, venison, wild turkey. We'd doctor each other's sick, bury our dead — law, I bet a hundred funerals were preached in our place — we'd bring lovers together and have big parties to help 'em marry. Governors and Congressmen and little pig-headed politicians would make their plans at our big table. Cowboys and miners, trappers and soldiers, would set for hours on end, just looking at the inside of my house. I'd see 'em touch a lace doily like it would break. They'd handle a book like it was holy. And if I played the piano for 'em — law, their eyes would shine like panthers'. Once an old woolly-bearded hunk of a mountain man tried to thank me when he was leavin'. 'Miz Gray,' he rumbled, 'it's worth a fortune just to smell you!' "

I can understand him. He found her sweet of person and sweet of mind, just as I did half a century later.

When she grew old and had become everybody's "Aunt Adaline," she'd sit for hours, looking afar. Skyscrapers loomed now on the spot she had made men build the first little school. Doubtless she was reliving her past, as many old folks do. One day I dared to ask, "What's on your mind, Aunt Adaline?"

She replied instantly, "I'm studyin' about water. We're using all of this Salt River, but that Colorado's a whopping big stream too. A body could ditch that water across Arizona to our valley lands, I bet. Our country's growin'. People need more vegetables. If I just had my strength—"

Living in the past? She was pioneering in the future, even though 80 years old. And a newspaper headline before me now says: "Valley Irrigated Area Soon to Be Doubled by Colorado Water." Adaline's second dream of empire is coming true.

When Lum Gray died, Aunt Adaline forgot sorrow in service — the only way in which it can be forgotten. She loved people, especially the "bad" ones, who most needed love.

She tried to cure Jack Swilling of drink and narcotic habits, nursing him in her own home. She who had no love for Indians as a group cherished them as individuals.

When a Maricopa woman stole a dress in Phoenix, Adaline rode 32 miles to her brush home, made her return the stolen dress, then gave her two new ones and shoes as well.

One day in 1915 a cowboy, hat in hand, approached Adaline Gray in her rose garden. For a long moment he just stared. "My name don't matter, ma'am," he finally said. "But in 1885 my pappy brought me by here, right after my mother died. You held me on yore lap and talked to me all one morning. Nobody's ever done that to me before or since, and I been wantin' to come see you again."

He had saved up $100 as a gift, and she accepted it. "When a body wants to repay a heart debt," she counseled me, years later, "you let him. That cowboy needed to give it to me, and I needed to have his gratitude. It made us both feel free and fine."

Ten years ago, Adaline Gray died in virtual poverty, so freely had she given of her possessions as well as her talents. Yet she died rich. She herself said so, in a last benediction which I shall treasure always.

"Let me tell you a thing, son," she said. "Only way you can ever be happy is to look at people without seeing their clothes or their manners. Look inside them, and you can love them every one."

Narratives in the First Person

The narrative in the first person is usually the personal experience of the writer, though it may be that of someone else. In the latter case it frequently makes use of the "as told to" device. This technique is to be seen in *Outdoor Life* and many other outdoors magazines. The article is written in the first person and signed by the principal character, but it also carries the above legend. The title and signatures would appear as follows:

CAPPING MT. EVEREST

How The World's Tallest Mountain
Was Conquered

———————

By Capt. Charles S. Worder
As Told to Ray Thomas

The first-person narrative differs little from the third-person narrative, except in the point of view of the person telling the story. Its field is quite as wide. A certain freshness of style is inherent in this type that is lacking in the other. Its single drawback is the apparent necessity for frequent use of the word "I." This handicap may be overcome by occasional resort to impersonal discussion of events and things not directly involving the writer. This involves a shift to third person, which may be used as frequently and as fully as seems necessary.

The first-person narrative is not intended to reveal secrets of personal living, nor intimate details usually withheld from print. It may reveal secrets, but these are secrets of state rather than of person. The articles below should be compared to those cited later as examples of confessions.

Narratives in the first person differ among themselves greatly. The examples that follow reveal the range of this class. The first is based on personal experience but is much like an essay. The second suggests the how-it-was-done article. Note use of the pronoun "I" in the first article, and how it has been replaced by "we" in the second. Each article was illustrated by several photographs.

A.

GARDENING IS A WAY OF LIFE[3]

A Profoundly Happy Way of Life

———————

By Lew Sarett

For better or for worse, I am an inveterate amateur gardener. I shall die one. I am a bit "touched" about every green-growing thing on earth. This queerness has not put me in any institution; it has kept me out of one.

———————

[3]Reprinted by permission of *Better Homes and Gardens* and the author.

Dahlias are my specialty. Annually I grow over a thousand plants from seed, with the hope that I may turn up a new one now and then, fit to go into commerce. Sometimes I do. But the profit on it pays me only a fraction of what it costs me to produce it.

I grow scores of tuberous begonias. I go to much trouble: special soil, special watering; coddling them all season. Strawberries — the time and money I spend on them is considerable. I fight constantly to keep the robins from harvesting my crop, and to stave off rot. The story is much the same with my muskmelons, iris, vegetables: expense, time, trouble.

Then why bother?

I can tell you why bother. I bother because gardening is a superb way in which every man who has the use of a patch of ground can solve many of his personal problems in living. Gardening is a way of life, a profoundly happy way of life.

Gardening Is an Exciting Sport

Growing anything — strawberries, cauliflower, roses, even cabbage — is an intensely exciting competitive sport. It is a game in which you pit your strength and your wits against Nature; you match them against her sometimes grudging soil, her bitter winds, and weather, against her drouths and floods, her bugs and blights, her fickleness and perverseness. A man gets a big kick from outmaneuvering Nature when she tries to throw him for a loss with epidemics and blights, with hordes of leaf hoppers, thrips, and red spiders, with unseasonable weather.

When you can take the cards which Nature deals you in any growing season — a few high cards and a lot of low ones — and play them so skillfully that you really make a killing with that poor hand — well, it is a source of deep satisfaction.

Take the soil in your garden, for example, when you set out to build a high-powered garden. It is on top of a hill. It is miserable yellow clay, stiff and poor. A chemical analysis of it shows a tragic lack of food elements: no nitrates to speak of, no phosphorus, no potash. In the first year when you grow glads and dahlias on that sickly yellow clay, your plants are spindly and blooms minute. So you spit on your hands the next year and set out to build up that soil. You spade in coarse sand, or coal ashes, and humus. You spade in well-rotted manure, broadcast three inches deep; and you spade in a good balanced plant food — four pounds per 100 square feet. The next year you add more humus and sand, another feeding of a balanced plant food.

Then comes the year when you plan to grow dahlias in a big way, to go into the dahlia shows and shoot for the blue ribbon with big perfect blooms, you hope. On a May day you reach down for a handful of the earth you've been working on; it doesn't stick to your hand the way it used to, like a ball of yellow putty — or like a yellow rock; it crumbles and sifts thru your fingers and filters back to the ground. It is perfect in its physical structure. It is friable. Now air and rain and food elements can get down to the roots of your plants. The frail roots can penetrate the soil and develop properly. And you smile, because you know how it was done.

In July the foliage in your young dahlia plants has a deep dark clean green that tells the world that those plants are getting a lot to eat — especially a lot of nitrogen. In September you go into your patch and find it loaded with huge blooms ready to cut for the dahlia show: one bush of Glamour, bearing three gigantic purple and violet blooms which measure 13 inches in diameter and 9 inches deep; a bush of Margrace, a flame informal decorative loaded with huge fiery blooms, like a bonfire; and a hill of Darcy Sainsbury, a beautiful pure white decorative, so heavy with show blooms that it looks like a white waterfall.

You know that those long symmetrical stems and that healthy dark green foliage are not accidents. You know also how you got those superb roses, delphiniums, vegetables, and fruits. Bigger than the thrill you experience when you win a handful of medals is the thrill — that feeling of power — you get from knowing that you fastened your hands on that stiff miserable yellow clay and made it disgorge an avalanche of breath-taking beauty.

That is what makes gardening an exciting sport, a great game.

Time and again Nature gets tough with you, rocks you on your heels with a heavy infestation of leaf hoppers, red spider, thrips, aphids, or with some other unpredictable insect — which may sicken and stunt your garden. Every season produces a new menace, an unusual attack from some bug or blight, an uncommon drouth. But whatever the current menace may be, you meet it. You stand toe and toe with Nature and you slug it out with her. You fight with spray tank and duster, sprinkler and hose. It's a joy to go through your dahlia patch at dusk with your spray tank and blow a cloud of leaf hoppers to the hell for leaf hoppers. You get a sense of conquest when you beat red spider and thrips and when you dispatch a horde of plant lice.

Gardening Is a Series of Adventures

There is something of primitive man in the human being; he likes a fight and he likes adventure. Gardening is a succession of adventures. It is quiet emotional adventure when your seeds begin to germinate in the seed flat and the first frail green pops out of the soil. It is a disastrous adventure when some of them damp off. It is a dark adventure when you find a young green plant of one of your most expensive varieties cut down at the base of the stem by a cutworm — because you forgot to sink a paper collar around the stem.

Your heart skips many a beat in adventures in delight in April and May, when your eyes fall on the bed of golden crocus you planted, the blue squills, the scarlet tulips, and the daffodils. It is a sweet adventure when you see your hollyhocks in July march along the split-rail fence like a regiment of soldiers.

It is a sweet moment when you harvest your luscious Pride of Wisconsin melons and the Golden Jubilee and Scarlet Pritchard tomatoes. It is a rare adventure when you walk through your dahlia patch in September and note the cascades of white flowers, the pillars of flame-colored blooms, the blanks of orange and yellow. And you pause a moment before the pompon varieties loaded with 2-inch blooms that look like perfect buttons — like shining brass buttons, white buttons and pink buttons. You experience a thousand adventures with beauty when you grow anything that has roots in the earth.

Gardening Is a Road to Riches

But there is more to matter than even all this. How can I express it? I can suggest it, perhaps, and trust that all people who really know life, its bitter and its sweet, will grasp what I am talking about.

Let us start this way. Some of us feel — as the result of a good deal of experience — that the material world and the flesh are of small consequence, speaking relatively. We do not find in the material world and the flesh our most constant and deep joy. Some delight we find — oh, yes — maybe a great deal; for this we are grateful. We take it in our stride. But some of us know that the material world also has its share of weariness, worry, heartbreak, and disaster. Soon or late we stumble upon a fact that changes the course of our lives: we discover a world that strikes us blind with the splendor and range of its possibilities, that gives us serenity instead of turmoil, quiet delight instead of pain, a zest for life instead of weariness.

What world? It is the world of ideas and beauty. It is the world within your own skull. It is the country of the mind — the country one lives in when one reads a good book, or listens to good music, or plumbs the reservoirs of Nature in a laboratory of science, or follows a good hobby — color photography, painting, the art of flower arrangement, hydridizing glads, iris, dahlias, day lilies.

There are dozens of good roads into that country of the mind — activities that deal constantly with ideas and beauty. Creative work of any kind — writing, painting, interior decorating, devising dresses and menus, planning gardens, architecture — that is one road. Music is a road. Religion is a road — a royal road for millions. Scientific research, law, teaching, medicine, business — these may be roads when intelligently controlled to big ends. One's home — and all the dear people in it — this is a road. Oh, there are many others. And all the roads are good. But for some of us, gardening is a never-failing road.

And so, for some of us, gardening is more than a pleasant hobby; it is a way of life — of living happily.

To conjure out of the black earth the rich hues of pansies, iris, glads, roses, tuberous begonias, and tulips, of peppers and eggplants; to transform the odor of the dirt into the fragrance of peonies and lilacs, of ripe melons and apples; to transmute the tasteless earth into the flavor of a Bartlet pear and of Concord grapes, and the succulence of Bermuda onions and tomatoes — this is worth doing. This is a road — a road into the country of the mind, into a world sweet and complete in itself.

In winter when one cannot work the soil there are a dozen vicarious roads into that world of ideas and beauty: the study of books on horticulture, chemistry, etomology; the study of journals devoted in whole or in part to these matters; the study of seed catalogs; the planning of gardens; the propagation of plants. There are scores of minor roads that lead into one big road: gardening.

And that is why some of us garden. That is the reason, way down deep, why some of us garden furiously, passionately, and happily. For us, it is a way of life — a way of living richly in an otherwise dark bewildered world. We go about our work, living realistically, fighting toe to toe with life as it is lived in a hard-boiled, materialistic world. But we are sustained and renewed constantly in body and spirit because we know and we follow a road into an amazing and lovely world, one of the oldest and one of the richest roads in human experience.

B.

HOUSE OF A DIFFERENT COLOR[4]

———————

By Jacqueline Judge

What would you do if your house was 142 years old and it was really showing its age?

The Thomsons decided that their 22-room farm home, which was built in 1798, and was one of the first frame houses in Holland Patent, Oneida County, N. Y., should be brought up to date. When the house was first built, it consisted of just the main part and porches; but a few years later, a wing was added with another porch. At that time, lines and symmetry were more an accident than intentional, but its contour was excellent, and we realized that it was something that should be emphasized. Its situation on a hill with a beautiful view was a location architects dream of, but the house needed rejuvenation.

Fairview looked tired — even neglected, as if those who owned it didn't appreciate its lovely lines. So, a couple of summers ago, when the family was all together, we decided to glamorize it. Because workers were difficult to get, the whole family pitched in and went to work, and we completed the job in a short time. We left the heavy, more difficult tasks to the one experienced man on the job, while we scraped off paint, gathered suitable rocks for the steps and terrace, and painted shutters.

We started on the front of the house, and removed the attic gable that gave a yawning effect. This change gave the roof a simple, straight line that accented the construction of the house. The porches seemed no longer necessary across the front of the house, and they were getting the sun that the living rooms, dining room, and office needed to wake them up. So the long porch on the wing and the porch on the main part were torn down. The two little upstairs windows that made the house look sleepy, were removed, and dormer windows were added. This gave the wing new height and made the house look perky and wide awake. Now, the bedrooms are getting more of the cheery east sun.

The front of the house wasn't our only concern when we renovated Fairview; we also considered the back. In the corner of the L formed by the

———————

[4]Reprinted by permission of *Better Farms* and the author.

contour of the house, we built a terrace out of flagstones taken from an old stone fence in one of the pastures. At one end of the terrace, we built a pool for goldfish and lilies, and painted the inside of it aquamarine to create a light background against which the fish and colored lilies could be seen. Nasturtiums, marigolds, and zinnias were planted along the sides of the terrace against the house. Floodlights made the patio a favorite gathering spot for the family both day and night.

We didn't forget a thing to add to our outdoor enjoyment of Fairview. About five yards from the terrace, we used the smaller stones from the sur- rounding fields in an outdoor fireplace. The picnic table tucked "in the shade of the old apple tree" completed our outdoors-but-home plan for summertime. We were so proud and pleased with the results that we are willing to spend all our summers at home.

Once we got started, there was no stopping us. We could not have the new Fairview be just an outside job, so we renovated the inside too. We went to work on the kitchen and bedrooms.

In the kitchen we replaced the old, bulky black wood stove with a small, compact oil stove. This left space for a large work table, and removing the wood box left space for another smaller work table. A shelf added from the cupboards, across the width of the room to the sink, made the kitchen an easier place in which to work. New linoleum on the floor, and linoleum coverings for the tables and shelves with aluminum edging to hold it down, gave added color and a modern appearance.

The bedrooms were cold and dreary, so they were the next thing on the program. The whole family had a gay time removing the many layers of wallpaper from the bedroom walls. We repapered with yellows and light greens that would catch and reflect the sunlight, and we painted the wood- work an off-white color. Heavy furniture that made the rooms appear crowded was another problem. We solved that by cutting the headboards off the beds. Then reversing the beds we used the smaller footboards as head pieces. . . .

When we finished the face lifting job on Fairview, we were pretty proud of our summer's work. The old grey shingled house with dull green shut- ters and white trim around the windows had not been at all inviting. How- ever, the freshly-painted white house with bright green shutters is something anyone would like to come home to. . . .

Our farm home now looks years younger and promises to be a place of enjoyment for years to come. We had fun bringing our 1798 home up to date, and you can have fun rejuvenating your house, too. Why don't you try it this summer?

Narratives in the Third Person

The third-person narrative article is at its best in the telling of a tale — the story of some adventure. The narrative might be concerned with a single incident such as a fire, or a series of incidents, such as might occur on a canoe trip, a visit to Mexico, or during the course of a college education.

Frequently this type is the result of personal experience, but always the experience of someone other than the writer. It is essentially the story of what happened to someone or to something. As a story, it may incorporate all the dramatic devices of the short story, including description, conversation, and suspense.

One of its purposes is to entertain, and in this respect it differs from the process article. It also differs from the latter in its use of extended description, supense, and adventure. It may tell how something *was done*, but not how *to do* something.

Every field of activity is open to the narrative in the third person — politics, science, invention, exploration, farming, industry, or the classroom. Almost any series of incidents or facts which can be fitted within a time sequence or chronology may be turned into a third-person narrative. It is a useful type. Because it does use the devices of fiction, it allows the writer considerable freedom of expression and affords training to the fiction aspirant.

The rules for this type are the same as for fiction, with one exception. The narrative article must be truthful. It may be intriguing, mysterious, or dramatic. It may be gay or sad. It may be ponderous or light. But it must rest on fact, or else the writer must indicate to the reader where it enters the realm of conjecture.

The first of the narratives below is typical of numerous modest articles for which there is a market. The second is far more ambitious, and required mature talents. Use of quotation and dialogue is outstanding in the latter. The second item is also one of those articles for which anyone might have spotted the subject. In this instance an alert mind recognized its possibilities. The writer made a good article out of it because he saw a good yarn in it, which proves that articles rise no higher than the minds that create them. The article will repay considerable effort spent on analysis.

A.

SHE'S PAID TO LISTEN TO THE RADIO[5]

Checking Commercial Announcements
Provides Growing Source of Revenue
for Shut-ins throughout the Country.

———————

By Hilda Dunn

Three years ago Miss Josephine Saya of Syracuse, New York, found herself with nothing but spare time on her hands. Encased in a cast from her neck

———————

[5]Reprinted by permission of *Profitable Hobbies* and the author.

down she turned desperately to the radio as a source of amusement. Today she earns regular fees as one of approximately 250 physically handicapped persons throughout the nation who are paid to listen to the radio. And the people who pay Miss Saya are eager to put more like her on their payroll.

Just about the time that Miss Saya, who for almost twenty years has suffered from the effects of infantile paralysis, was turning into a confirmed radio fan, a young man named George Reid was working in New York City on the idea that many national advertisers might be interested in knowing how their commercial announcements were being handled on various local stations.

Before Reid could develop the idea into anything tangible he was inducted into the army. Receiving a medical discharge he returned to New York and, joining the staff of Radio Reports, Inc., proceeded to figure out just how to make the idea work.

He knew that his first requirement was devoted, conscientious radio listeners throughout the country who would not mind inconvenient hours and who would not want to be off somewhere else just at the time they were supposed to be checking commercial announcements. Persons confined to their homes because of physical handicaps struck Reid as the most likely candidates for the monitoring jobs. He placed advertisements in magazines and newspapers that reach shut-ins and received more than 1,000 replies. One of those applying for a job was Miss Saya, who had been told by a friend of the opportunity.

Still confined to a hospital Miss Saya dictated to a nurse her application for a monitorship. It was accepted almost immediately and she became one of a nucleus of radio monitors which has grown into a smooth efficient unit operating in virtually every state in the union.

Now almost three years old, the spot monitoring service is being used by many of the most important radio advertisers. In the words of Reid: "Its present scope has broadened beyond our original expectation, due in a great degree to the interest and dependability of our physically handicappd monitors. Success of the service depends entirely on them — how accurate they may be and how conscientiously they fulfill their assignments. I have not had any reason to doubt their honesty in the last two and one half years. We make every effort to train them and to furnish them with as much information as may be required, for we realize that the results of their work depend to a great degree upon how well prepared they may be."

Radio Reports is now employing an ever increasing number of shut-ins.

"Our business demands," explains Reid, "have required us to branch out into every major market of the country. There are a number of cities, especially in the South, in which we have been unable to get monitors or to hold them. We require shut-ins who are mentally alert and who can be depended upon to fulfill their assignments."

Reid emphasizes that Radio Reports is in no way a philanthropic organization concerned with social welfare. Describing the whole arrangement as strictly practical he simply says:

"We find that the physically handicapped are the best possible sources of obtaining the results desired."

Miss Sabina Kopf of his organization backs Reid up. She says the monitors "do a tremendous job because their minds are exceptionally alert."

Most of the work involves checking spot commercials, the short transcriptions which are sent to local stations to be played between programs. Sometimes Miss Saya just checks to see that they go on as scheduled. Often she is provided with the original copy and she must "proofread" the commercial, seeing that it is word perfect and that the advertiser is not slighted.

Beside her radio a clock with a large second hand times exactly the length of the commercial announcement. Standard time for covering a spot announcement is eleven minutes, five minutes before it goes on and five minutes after.

Miss Saya must indicate the sponsor of the preceding program and the following one, to show the spot advertiser whether or not his announcement is in a desirable position. She must tell whether the time announcement is presented by the station or sponsored by a watch or clock manufacturer.

Radio Reports supplies her with the proper forms on which to register this information.

Because most monitors are intelligent individuals, they are often asked to supply their opinions of the commercial. Was the transcription scratchy? Did it end ebruptly? Was it clear and comparatively loud? Did it create a good impression generally? This information is important to the advertiser, and Josephine is painstaking in expressing her views.

About once a year Radio Reports undertakes a service called "logging," which is a full-time job for the monitor. For eight hours at a stretch Miss Saya and her coworkers throughout the country listen to their radios with undivided attention. They must record the names and sponsors of all programs, and in some cases list all musical selections played. Her family doesn't need to consult a newspaper to find out what time a favorite program is broadcast; Miss Saya has the schedule down pat.

Among the things Miss Saya likes best about her profitable hobby is the fact that she can do it while resting in her room. Sometimes she is assigned to cover a commercial before seven in the morning. Then she has a friend telephone her about five minutes before listening time so that she can switch on her radio, take notes, and go back to sleep. If she has assignments late at night, she can settle down long before the appointed hour for the job.

When she was in the hospital in the big cast, she found it impossible to fill out her reports lying on her back. When it was time to write, she had a nurse turn her over on her face. She was almost completely disabled but still she made her hobby pay.

Once a month Miss Saya receives instructions from her employer. Often a letter is included telling her what a fine and accurate job she is doing. This personal encouragement means a lot to her, as it would to any worker so completely isolated from her boss.

Miss Saya has found other ways to make money in spite of her handicap. An independent research firm employs her to telephone people and see whether or not they are listening to their radios, know the name of the program, and the sponsor. She loves this, since talking on the phone is one of her favorite diversions.

Miss Kopf from her New York office is in frequent touch with all the monitors, who range in age from 19 to 65. She receives volumes of correspondence from them. She has discovered that just as in the case of Miss Saya, it is not only the money the monitors earn for engaging in a pleasant pastime but the feeling of being a useful part of a successful organization that makes their jobs profitable, not only from a monetary but from a morale standpoint.

B.

TRAFFIC ROLLS IN PHILADELPHIA[6]

With the Help of the Man in the Street,
a Progressive City Solved Its Parking Problems
and Really Got Things Moving

———————

By Henry D. Steinmetz

If you have ever floundered in a city sea of cars, cops and horn-happy drivers, count yourself another victim of America's No. 1 urban ailment — hardening of the traffic arteries. Cities everywhere are fighting the insidious affliction — with small results. Growing worse each day, it exacts a staggering cost in time and money from every metropolitan center in America.

Street congestion in New York robs merchants of $1,000,000 a day. Boston figures its annual forfeiture to the trucking trade alone at $40,000,000. In downtown Detroit, real-estate values have tumbled a billion since 1934, twice the combined property losses of the historic Chicago fire and the San Francisco earthquake. Pittsburgh, Los Angeles and scores of other metropolises report business concerns fleeing from mid-city areas which are slowly dying of traffic strangulation.

From Philadelphia, however, comes significant and encouraging news . . . a determined citizens' committee, created by the municipal government, set out to blast log-jammed streets in the heart of town. Within a few months the worst aspects of the problem were licked. Today, traffic really rolls in the Quaker City.

Hero of the victory is Robert A. Mitchell, Phiadelphia's supercharged traffic engineer. . . Philadelphia's 2,000,000 population is packed into a relatively small area, and its centralized stores, offices and theaters are a magnet for 1,000,000 suburbanites. Moreover, the city itself is a traffic man's nightmare, with most of its downtown streets no wider than the horse-and-buggy lanes of Ben Franklin's day.

Mitchell knew what steps were necessary. He also knew that selling them to politicians and the public was something else. Of one thing he was

———————

[6]Reprinted by permission of *Coronet* magazine.

positive: traffic reform had to spring from the people — it could never be imposed on them. How he got Philadelphians to back his program is a study in modern Machiavellian tactics with a benign twist.

For years Mitchell had been building friendly contacts with progressive spirits in the local street-transit company, the real-estate board and other traffic-conscious organizations. In July, 1945, he called them together for a strategy huddle. Then, while he lay low, they tackled the City Council.

The upshot was the Council-appointed Committee for Relief of Traffic Congestion, with Mitchell as chairman. Besides transit and real-estate men, it included representatives of the Council, Police Bureau, Chamber of Commerce, Merchants Association, hotel and theater groups, two auto clubs and the largest taxi company. Mitchell had pulled strings in advance to insure this broad participation, and it later paid off in the enthusiastic cooperation of all local interests.

But getting that cooperation also took diplomacy. The merchants, fearing a blow at business, gagged at the curb-parking ban which Mitchell prescribed to remedy traffic ills. So he rolled the pill in sugar coating — a preliminary survey of shoppers' driving and parking habits. The committee had no funds for this, but Mitchell's persuasive powers were as good as a blank check. In short order he jollied the merchants, together with the transit company, into financing the project themselves.

National Analysts, Inc., an independent research group, buttonholed 5,000 shoppers in stores, mailed questionnaires to another 44,000 curb-parkers. The survey returns were startling. Less than one shopper in ten, for instance, use a car to get to downtown stores. Only 2 per cent of these shoppers parked their cars on the streets. Further, all the cars curb-parked in the crowded mid-city section carried only 3 per cent of the people visiting the district daily on business, pleasure, or shopping jaunts.

With these figures, Mitchell easily swung the merchants into line and won from the Council what he had long wanted: "No Parking" signs throughout a 100-square-block area at the city's teeming core. "No Stopping" signs also went up, effective during morning and evening rush hours.

Mitchell, who knew that even an army of cops couldn't enforce unpopular parking rules, took democratic pains to consult the people on his plan. Two months' publicity and open discussion preceded its adoption. . . Results were immediate and electrifying. Plain citizens backed the police, jeered at violators. Soon there were no violators.

Traffic spurted and auto speed through the center of town jumped 75 per cent. Trolleys bonged along 20 per cent faster, cut headway time between cars to less than two minutes. Street accidents dropped 15 per cent. And business for midtown merchants was better than ever.

Philadelphians toasted Mitchell. Cab drivers, deprived of stands, more than made up the loss in greater-freedom of movement. Trucking concerns hauled more goods in less time. Complaint letters to the newspapers totaled exactly one. A local columnist, originally critical of the scheme, publicly retracted. A few merchants moaned over the prohibition of curb loading and unloading during rush hours, but Mitchell quickly helped them solve their problems.

There have been few other difficulties, unless you count the affair of the carrot, the horse cop and the kind-hearted motorman. A minor jam was holding things up on 9th Street near Market, around 4:30 each afternoon. Investigating, Mitchell's men witnessed a touching scene. A streetcar was halted, impeding traffic. After some minutes a mounted cop joggled up. The horse, with a practiced air, poked his head in the car door and received from the motorman a fine, fat carrot. Mitchell straightened things out with a tactful suggestion to the cop that hereafter he and his steed meet the trolley more promptly.

No traffic tickets were handed out in Philadelphia the first 10 days. After that there was little need of them. Initially adopted for a 90-day trial period, the new scheme was made permanent in April.

Success of the Philadelphia venture stems directly from the spirit of cooperation kindled in the man in the street — or, as a case in point, the lady in the streetcar. A sedate, middle-aged woman, about to alight from a Walnut Street trolley, found her way blocked by an illegally parked car. Opening the door, she plunked herself in the driver's seat. Soon the owner returned. But it was a full five minutes before he regained possession of his car. At length he drove sheepishly away, no doubt a better citizen for the bracing lecture he had received before an appreciative sidewalk audience.

Word of the "Mitchell Plan" is spreading. Experts from New York, Boston, Washington and elsewhere have come to stare at cars speeding through Philadlphia's narrow streets. Other centers have consulted the Quaker City engineer — New Orleans, for instance, whose troubles he has recently tackled with a similar plan. Among traffic men, Mitchell is the man of the year, if not of the decade.

At 47, Bob Mitchell stands at the top of a profession he entered by economic accident. A Cornell graduate in architecture in 1921, he practiced till the early 30's, when the big slump hit building. Casting around for a draftsman's job, he landed one with Philadelphia's Bureau of Traffic Engineering. By 1936 he was head of the department.

Mitchell's . . . clean-up of Philadelphia isn't his first whirl with the city's traffic problems. Years ago he adopted the progressive signal-light system which is now widely used elsewhere. It enables drivers on main arteries to drive without hitting a red light, simply by maintaining a speed of, say, 30 miles an hour. He also originated the "four-phase" signal for three-and-four-way intersections — an intricate gadget that regulates lights in relation to the direction of heaviest traffic flow.

Most amazing of all, however, is a mechanical monster — the "triple reset master control" — which he designed and installed in the basement of City Hall. This device, hooked up to 60 per cent of the town's lights, automatically adjusts them three times daily to give maximum in-town traffic flow in the morning, an even two-way movement during the day, and a maximum outflow in late afternoon.

As his reputation grew, the Philadelphia traffic wizard lectured at Harvard, Yale, and other colleges, served ODT as advisory expert during the war, and co-authored a manual on traffic-control devices that has since been written into the laws of nearly every state in the Union. All of which should entitle him to a fairly imposing manner. Instead, he is a slangy, easygoing, unassuming fellow, sometimes mistaken by visitors for one of the clerks in his own department.

The final installments of Mitchell's Philadelphia traffic story are still to come. Next step will be to provide Philadelphia with additional off-street parking facilities to permit a further extension of the ban on curb parking in the mid-city area.

Figuring that parking demand will rise 25 to 30 per cent in the next five years, Mitchell and his committee have mapped an off-street facilities program for execution. . . Its main feature is the creation of a Parking Authority to condemn and acquire properties, build garages, and lease them to private operators on terms assuring reasonable parking rates. Other projected steps include enactment of an ordinance requiring built-in parking facilities as well as truck-loading facilities in all major new buildings.

Dovetailing with all this, the Philadelphia Transportation Company is replacing much of its present equipment with 895 sleek modern cars, busses and trolley coaches. Since one trolley coach can whisk 75 riders into town, the company's program will help thin out traffic and ease the parking crush.

Mitchell himself is by no means complacent over the job he has done. Starting over, for instance, he would pitch into curb and off-street parking problems at the same time. Nevertheless, his accomplishments are hailed by outside experts as well as grateful Philadelphians. For the city is on the move again, the worst of its traffic troubles a thing of the past. The same phenomenon can happen in any city, says Mitchell — if the people really want it.

Confessions

Nearly all general magazines occasionally print confession articles. *Harper's Magazine* and *The Atlantic* are likely to be good markets for this type of article, as are those that use "true" adventures. The confession article varies widely in type as well as in quality. Almost without exception it purports to be the personal experience of the writer, and some magazines require a signed statement to that effect.

Several decades ago a type of "true story" or "actual experience" magazine was developed for the sole purpose of printing articles of intimate revelation. Among leaders in that field are *Modern Romances, Personal Romances, True Romance, True Confessions,* and *True Story Magazine.* Although none ever gained a reputation for literary quality, vast circulation was achieved. And such publications became both popular and profitable.

Confessions in the true-story magazines were very different from the dignified and restrained tales to be found in such magazines as *The Atlantic*. However, both types had much in common. Both told secrets or expressed feeling of an intimacy and depth not found in other types of articles.

Success in contributing a confession article depends upon a careful study of the requirements of that magazine. *The confession article requires more careful slanting than any other type.*

Confession articles in *The Atlantic* or *Harper's Magazine* may rank as first-rate literature, and a writer must give an excellent performance to appear therein. The range of contributors is wide, from the confessions of a college professor's wife to the real life experiences of a farmer's wife on an isolated ranch in Western Canada. A writer will not be barred because the contribution is his first, but the piece must be gripping, realistic, and dignified. It may be intimate and factual, but it must be in good taste.

The true-story magazines, on the other hand, frequently throw restraint to the winds. This fact should not lead any writer to believe these magazines are without standards. On the contrary, they are meticulous within their own range of expression. Emotional description is given a freer rein than in other magazines, but no writer is allowed to uphold wrongdoing or antisocial conduct. "Sinners" must be repentant and have learned the errors of their ways. Furthermore, reference to immoral or unlawful conduct is generally barred today by these magazines. Careful study of the market is absolutely necessary.

The confession is told in the first person, even when the experiences are those of another. Newspapermen have been frequent contributors to the confession magazines. They sometimes have used the incidents uncovered in their line of duty. Some of the true-story magazines permit this, but require writers to vouch that the incidents related were the experience of at least some individual. The "as told to" device is seldom used on this type of article.

Even though the confession makes repeated use of the first personal pronoun, the writer's name is frequently suppressed. This anonymity permits the writer to reveal facts he otherwise would not reveal. He may thus attack conditions and institutions or individuals without danger to himself. This will be done within the libel laws and the rules of the magazine itself. For example, a physician might tell why he believed in socialized medicine in an anonymous article, when he might not venture to do so in a signed piece.

For the true-story magazines which circulate most among readers of limited education, style must be simple and direct. Facts must be clear and gripping. Study of the type of individuals who read these magazines will reward the writer.

The writing of a few confession articles of the true-story variety has frequently helped the style of first-rate novelists. Writers occasionally suffer from ingrown emotions, and their style becomes stilted. One of the best ways for "emotion-bound" writers to relax is to try their hand on the confession article.

An example of one of the better types of confession articles is "The Forgotten Woman," cited below. It is not exactly intimate, but it does reveal a situation which the writer would hesitate to discuss over her own name. In much lighter vein is the sceond article. This confession succeeds in being humorous. The effect was aided by humorous pen-and-ink sketches. Note in the third article that the use of the personal pronoun "I" gives no offense. Writers need not be self-conscious in using the first person in confessions.

A.

THE FORGOTTEN WOMAN[7]

———————

By a Faculty Wife

If it's still bad form for college professors, who with clergymen might be called the last survivors of the 18th century gentleman, to ask for an increase in salary, or even for a subsistence wage, it is worse form for that silent and hard-working lady, the college professor's wife, to complain. I shall complain anonymously and even then with a sense of violating a sacred code. But I have seen closely the lives of many of them, and I am moved to write what they might wish to say but do not.

There is a professor of history I think of — rather he is only an assistant professor. He is married to a girl who once taught chemistry at Smith College. He makes . . . a year, and after the income tax and pension tax is deducted, much less. He lives in a cold, rawboned house . . . there is no use hoping for a larger furnace although the kitchen is heated only by a coal stove, nor for new screens in the windows since his landlord, the college, doesn't provide screens.

His wife cannot afford even the cleaning woman whom the wives of the full professors sometime hire. She herself does all the cleaning, the washing, the ironing, the cooking and the care of her two children, except once in a while when her husband comes home for an hour, "so Amelia can go marketing." She has given up all clubs except the Faculty Wives' Club, which it is

———————

[7]Reprinted by permission of the *AAUP Bulletin*.

diplomatic to attend for her husband's sake. In spite of all her efforts the children often have colds, and there is little sun in the house and little joyfulness. Her husband feels all this to be his fault, but his very frustration makes him surly and abrupt sometimes with the college administration. It is doubtful if he will ever achieve anything very different.

They try. Even as I write, they are about to entertain the President and his wife for dinner. Amelia started a week ago to polish the silver and to freshen her old evening dress that dates back to her own senior year at college. Her husband's "tux" has been cleaned "at home" and is hanging out on the line to air. The two children are to be bribed to stay upstairs. All the day of the dinner Amelia will be cooking, dusting, and setting out her best linens and china. At seven o'clock her husband must, come what may, open the door to the guests. (The President and his wife have four servants including a chauffeur and a gardener, and an "entertainment allowance" from the college equal to half the professor's whole salary.) Tired as she probably will be, and tense over the impression they may be making, Amelia must act as her own cook, waitress nad gracious hostess.

Well, the critic will intercede, what of it? Only one in ten American women has any "help," so why should the wife of a college professor expect anything better than the rest of the nine-tenths? Does she want to write or paint or "have a career of her own?" And then the critic may add that college education for women is the "hooey" and only makes women discontented with the stove and the clothesline. Anyway, the "efficient" woman should have plenty of time for herself after the housework is done.

But what is expected of the faculty wife as part of earning her husband's salary? She is expected to contribute as much to charities as the businessman's wife, whose husband may be earning $10,000 a year. The Community Chest, the Red Cross, the college itself (toward a new dormitory or gymnasium) expect generous contributions from the faculty. But not only is the faculty wife expected to contribute funds to the charities of the community, she is also expected to assume the leadership of clubs, drives, educational projects, student entertaining, social groups, study groups, to sit on charity boards, to raise money for the hospital and the Girl Scouts, to foster music, art, schools, to take the Presidency of the Red Cross or the League of Women Voters, to work in the church, and most important of all to labor for the college in all kinds of small services such as managing teas and entertaining visiting celebrities, for which she is paid in no way except that nebulous thing called "helping your husband's career."

And in addition to these she should, if she is wise, "help her husband write a book," and that helping usually means all the way from actual research and criticism of style to typing the manuscript or shoveling the snow and stoking the furnace that he may have not only the time but also that freedom from distracting chores which is usually necessary for the best creative originality to flourish.

Well, again the critic remonstrates, "Some of the older faculty wives manage to do all the social and charity things and play bridge too." My impression is that behind this lies a secret which it is also bad form to mention. Either these professors or, in most cases, their wives have *outside* *incomes*. Mrs. Evans, wife of the distinguished Professor Evans, was the daughter of a "steel man." She has a large beautifully furnished college house for which as a matter of fact she pays less rent than Amelia. When cooks are to be had, Mrs. Evans has a cook; at the very least she has her "regular cleaning woman" and a man who comes around to garden and to run the furnace. If she is giving a dinner party, which she often does, she hires a woman to come in and do the work. . . Of course Mrs. Evans has someone in to wash and iron, she sends "everything" to the cleaners without a moment's thought of economy, she buys attractive and expensive clothes, she travels. Again it is bad form to question how all this is done on the little salary of Amelia's husband or even on the grand full professor's salary. . . The answer is, were you so crude to ask, it isn't. Mrs. Evans has an income from inherited investments about equal to Amelia's husband's whole salary. And as our best economists sometimes observe, to those who have less, less is given.

The business mind, however, asks further, "If the fellow is any good, these college professors, why aren't they paid more? Why, I pay the man who sweeps up the factory more than that. He just can't be much good. I'm sorry for his little wife though."

This is an interesting question. People are really puzzled by it. Even college presidents, who are chosen these days generally for what is called "business ability," wonder. A college professor is a lot easier to get, and cheaper, than a man to paint the buildings, or to act as treasurer, or to coach the football team. Why? Most administrators just accept it as good luck for them.

Recently a professor consulted the President of one of our colleges on a new appointment. "I can get a first-rate instructor in physics for . . ." "Then get a second-rate one for . . . ." replied the President. And he did. When someone remonstrated that a college *is* its faculty and a second-rate faculty means a second-rate education for the students, the President laughed and remarked, "Oh, we'll pick up the first-rate professors cheap when the depression comes along!" This President knew perfectly well that he could find a man with a Ph.D. to teach for a low salary. Administrators — presidents, deans, treasurers, and the like — come high. So does manual labor. So do athletic coaches. So does the urging of alumni to contribute to new buildings which cost most of all. But teachers? Why, there's the place to economize. And it works.

Behind everything — the poor salary to start with, the mean raises, the hard-working wife — lies what the President unconsciously trades on and the businessman doesn't understand at all — a true devotion to teaching, to scholarship, to knowledge. For *its own sake*. This cannot be measured. It *can* be got cheap. It doesn't know how to defend itself nor to organize in defense. Its influence on the minds of students cannot be added up in account books.

In the days of Abélard, when universities began, the young, who were eager to learn, begged the teacher to teach. A room was afterwards found, and each gave as he could. Now there are high-salaried administrators, fine buildings, big football — and the professor is the least of these.

Or not quite the least. For his wife is dedicated also and silently to the service of teaching, that indirectly through her labor others may come to have what she too values higher than money and comfort, knowledge more to be desired — and given — than much fine gold.

But oh, a decent salary would be, to the faculty wife, not "sweeter than honey in the honeycomb" but very sweet.

B.

WELL — YOU'VE TRAPPED ME![8]

Aunt Melinda Wouldn't Dream of
Stuffing the Sewing Machine
with Red Geraniums . . .

————————

By Eileen Jensen

I guess I'll have to admit it. I am an unimaginative soul. To me, a laundry stove is a place to heat the wash water — not a thing to be painted white and stuffed with gay, fluffy-ruffle petunias. I like it as a stove.

When I see a telephone booth, I am apt to think: "Now, there is a convenient place to make a phone call" — not, "Gee, what a dining room table those panels would make!"

If you observe me in the dime store buying a load of ten-cent mirrors, I am probably going straight home to look at my funny face. I wouldn't dream of gluing them in gleaming rows on a modernistic cornice! Not I!

If I purchase a number of bamboo blinds, you'll find me hanging them at my windows, not pasting them vertically around the walls of the rumpus room for fun.

No imagination.

I probably "get it honest," though. Aunt Melinda has a charming old farmhouse set back in the hills of West Virginia. You won't believe me, but at Aunt Melinda's, all the furnishings are carrying on in the tradition to which they were born. Monotonous, isn't it?

Take the cradle: there's a baby in it. Not firewood. And the firewood is in the firebox — a real firebox — not an old dresser drawer mounted on spools and painted á la Peter Hunt. Just a nasty old, lovely, old firebox! With wood in it!

The quilts, strangely enough, are on the beds — not upholstering the Early American settee. Aren't we dull?

The coffee mill isn't a desk lamp, either. Aunt Melinda grinds coffe in it. And Grandpa looks down benignly from his gilded vantage point in the fancy frame on the wall. Oh, sure, that frame would make a lovely coffee

———————————

[8]Reprinted by permission of *The American Home*.

table — what doesn't these days? — but where would we hang Grandpa? You can't go around scrapping your ancestor's photographs. Not at Aunt Melinda's!

The old treadle sewing machine whirls away merrily as Aunt Melinda patches her sheets. She wouldn't think of painting that machine white and planting the pulled-out drawers with red geraniums. She doesn't fill the bean pot with gaillardia, either. She bakes beans in it.

The last time I visited Aunt Melinda, we sat deep in our rockers and talked late into the afternoon about the strange ways of the "functionalists." She brought out the old cider jug, and we had a drink, and laughed at that woman who bent her good wire coat hangers into plant brackets. (I'll bet she's busy bending them back into coat hangers again. Coat hangers are a novelty!)

To make a pleasant afternoon perfect, Aunt Melinda gave me the empty cider jug to take home with me. I wish you could see it! It's a luscious, warm, deep, rich, shining brown.

I can hardly wait to get to work on it: you see, I'm planning to make it into a study lamp. I saw the idea in a magazine somewhere. Oh, yes — it was the *American Home!* Wouldn't you know!

C.

WHY I GAVE UP LIQUOR[9]

Even for a Moderate Drinker,
Alcohol Can Be a Costly Bargain

————

By Channing Brewster

I am no alcoholic. I was what is called a moderate drinker — that is, a blend of the social drinker and the serious drinker, with a dash of bitters. And I finally gave it up. The results have been all to the good. I am not a saver of other people's souls, but if anyone else can benefit enough from my experience to try it for himself — well, it's a free country.

In my business, drinking during business hours is frowned on — unless you can think up a good excuse, such as Christmas or somebody's birthday. Like most moderate drinkers, I began my potations after five o'clock. But unlike the majority I have never found drinking at a crowded bar or in a cocktail lounge tolerable. And if I tarried in such places, people might say there must be trouble between Charlotte and me. So, after work I would grab the first bus home.

I would find Charlotte in the kitchen, Jeremy, our seven-year-old, would beg me to play with him. Somehow, the kitchen clatter and my son's begging might rub me the wrong way. What I needed was a cocktail. So I would shake up a few.

[9]Reprinted by permission of *Reader's Digest* and the author. An original contribution to the magazine.

"Pour me one, and I'll be out in a minute," Charlotte would say — and always she would end up sipping her dispirited affair all through dinner.

Meanwhile I would settle down with the newspaper and the shaker. By the time dinner was on the table I would have emptied the shaker. Charlotte would invariably say something scathing about my drinking too much. I would answer in kind. What were a couple of cocktails? Of course, it was hard to say exactly how many a couple were — having downed my share of the shaker and what was left of Charlotte's share (I always counted her in for half).

But it would be inaccurate to say that I was drunk. I could talk coherently, though with more than normal animation. I could eat with gusto, though with little sense of taste. After dinner my head would grow weary. Whatever I attempted to do — read, play with Jeremy, go to the movies with Charlotte was ruined by a dull desire for rest.

If we went to a party, it was the same only more so. I would swallow enough pre-party drinks to get in the mood to face it. At the party, after I had had a couple more, strangers would look familiar, and some neighbor's wife would assume an exotic strangeness. After that I would be so impressed by the new-found human qualities of the guests and by my own wit that there would be no time for counting drinks. The fog would roll in.

What happened later depended on a number of variables — mainly solid food, fresh air, and more drink. The hangover might wait for its traditional morning-after or begin operations in the middle of the night. But its visitation was as certain as death and taxes, and just as funny.

If a Sunday followed the party, the hangover would be hugged to my bosom in the privacy of my bedroom. If a work day followed, the shaking hand, the blinding headache, the effort of concentration and the fear of making errors made the hangover twice as nerve-racking.

Such were my drinking habits. I should add that there were many days when I had only one or two drinks.

Then one day I quit drinking. And, since that day I have done without alcohol. I have known no craving for liquor, no envy of those who quaff highballs while I guzzle orange juice. Twice I have deliberately broken my abstinence. These tests strengthened my resolve. It was like trying to reopen a canceled love affair.

My abstinence was self-imposed. No public disgrace drove me to repentance. I took no pledge. I simply considered the problem in its totality and made my decision. The decision, like most of the important ones we make in life, was merely the culmination of a sort of ripening process. It was the same procedure I have followed in all my adult dealings — entering a new field of business, getting married, buying a home.

Considering the overall picture, I had to admit that drinking, as a contribution to the enjoyment of life, was for me a bust. It cost a lot of money, even though I was no big operator. But I was spending at least a dollar a day for drink, even though I had an aversion to bars and night clubs which were nonexistent in our town. Thirty dollars a month is a very substantial fraction of a middle-bracket income. That much saved for ten years — and just as Jeremy was ready for college, I would be ready with cash instead of alibis.

On a level of greater significance, I said thumbs down to liquor because I was kidding myself about it. I lacked the classic excuse of the alcoholic — I was not escaping from anything. My life contains no deep maladjustments. I love my wife, my wife loves me. I like people, people like me. My job keeps me on my toes. My excuse was the usual defense of the moderate drinker: that I was tired and tense. Of course, by the end of a busy day I suffered a bit from office fatigue. But I have found during the past year that I am not so tired that a brisk walk or an hour's workout on the school grounds with Jeremy's four-man baseball team won't un-tire me. Alcohol gave me a lift and then let go, and I was tired-er and duller than before.

Of course I suffer from the *malaise* of the modern world — tension. No doubt alcohol removed my tension. But it acted like a spot remover that takes the cloth with it. I came to see that I should do something more intelligent about the tension than to pour jiggers of rum over it.

It was a myth I was embracing when I thought alcohol was going to turn a party of my townfolk into a gathering as witty as a Noel Coward first act. My neighbor's wife, tight or sober, is neither witty nor wanton. Nor are the rest of the people of our town. Nor am I. Whatever capacity to amuse my conversation may possess is drawn forth not by alcohol but by the stimulation of imaginative minds. If I fortify myself by reading a book that has some meat in it, and then seek out a friend who is not allergic to ideas, a brilliant conversation may not necessarily ensue, but at least I return home with a clear head and the feeling that I have not wasted time in utter stupidity. For the true enjoyment of life, I find, a muddled head is no asset. I want to grasp the quality of an experience or the meaning of an idea in its natural state, not refracted through the obfuscating haze of a pint of gin and vermouth.

Why did I give up drink? Above all because I resented its power over me. Yes, I was a moderate drinker. I did not crave drink. Yet liquor was my master. One or two drinks could make me see the world as the world is not. Several could convince me that I could dance the rumba and drive a car exceedingly fast with the greatest of care.

I guess it was really pride that put me on the wagon. I have the reputation of being "independent." I resist vigorously even fancied attempts to boss me around. Yet liquor was acting as my boss. I didn't like the idea of not being my own master.

So I went dry. And as the saying goes, I am suffering no pain. I have felt constantly a wonderful sense of freedom — the way I used to feel when school let out and I took off my shoes and went barefoot. The pay-off came when a big organization took over my company and for three months I was out of a job. Those were tough days, but I blessed my new-found freedom and full reliance on my own self without the danger of treachery from a

glass crutch that might skid out from under me. I weathered the crisis and
am now doing better than before.

I have no desire to persuade anyone else to discontinue the use of alcohol.
But I do believe that anyone who wants freedom from a great deal of expense,
headaches and lost time, freedom from one more thing that complicates life,
may have it simply by doing what I did.

Interviews

The interview takes its name from the fact that most of the content
of the article was supplied by the interviewee. It is always based upon
one or more conferences usually arranged by the writer. The completed
article often resembles the narrative in the third person.

It usually, though not always, presents some of the quoted words of
the person interviewed. His opinions form an important part of the
article. These may be given greater emphasis by the addition of biographical facts. More than one individual may be presented, in which
case the article is likely to be a *symposium* with *opinion* forming a
large part.

Considerable advance preparation is desirable, particularly if the
interview is to be with but one person. The writer should have a good
knowledge of the personality, education, training, and accomplishments
of the person to be interviewed — even when these do not appear in
the article. This knowledge is certain to make the work of interviewing
easier.

Furthermore, the writer should have in mind the questions he intends
to ask. This he cannot do on a subject of which he is fundamentally
ignorant. The writer who intends to ask a noted judge his opinion on the
causes of juvenile delinquency for an article to be submitted perhaps to
Parents' Magazine should spend a few hours reading the material already
written on the subject. This study will be reflected in the questions he
asks. It will also be shown in the understanding he reveals of what the
judge tells him, as well as in the way the article later is handled.

The question often comes up whether a writer may put quotation
marks around words that are not exactly those of the speaker. Yes, if
the phrase or sentence quoted reflects the meaning of the person quoted.
For instance, one might ask, "Do you believe in capital punishment?"
And the judge might answer, "No." The writer would omit the question
from his article and simply write, "I do not believe in capital punishment," said Judge Sebastian. When the writer can tell himself that the
person interviewed would be glad to verify the accuracy of the quotations, then he may feel assured he has done a good job of reporting.

The interviewer should usually keep his own personality out of the article he writes, as well as the questions he asks. The spotlight should be focused on what the *interviewee has to say*.

Many cautions have been written for writers contemplating this type of article. Most of these are matters of common sense that will naturally occur to any writer. Advance preparation, tact, and accuracy must be present, and it is wise to make an opening for a later visit if that becomes necessary.

Use of the query in advance of the interview is also advisable. Nothing paves the way for a talk with a busy or famous person more quickly than being able to say that an editor has indicated interest in having the proposed article. Most individuals are ready enough to give an audience to a responsible writer, because the published article may be a help in their careers. This is true of almost everyone in the public eye, except the physician, who has to be handled more carefully. Frequently the latter can be persuaded to talk by showing the need for public information on a certain subject, and by promising to keep his name in the background.

The first article below was based upon several interviews with the newspaper editor concerned. The second is an elaborate piece that makes use of the "as told to" device. It is a true interview told in the first person.

A.

HE'S NEVER SEEN HIS OWN FRONT PAGE![10]

————————

By Edith Handleman

The editor of the Watkins Glen (New York) *Express* has never set type, never read proof or penciled one copy-reading symbol on the stories which come to him. Though he has planned the make-up every week for 36 years, he has never seen his front page.

Eighty-five-year-old Frank Severne, editor and publisher, has been totally blind since he was eleven.

Nor is his newspaper work the only field in which the slender, courteous old gentleman has achieved success. "Most people, when they're planning to run for office, seem to think it's right to come up and talk it over with me," is how he expresses the fact that he has been a political power in county and state for half a century. Governor Dewey called him on the phone personally last month to inquire if he would accept reappointment to the board of managers of the Batavia School for the Blind. He has seen the school grow from the one-building affair where, in 1872, he slept in an 18-bed

—————————————————————————

[10]Reprinted by permission of *The American Press* and the author.

dormitory, to a large school, to which the very newest addition will be the $700,000 Severne Hall.

Granddaughter on Staff

Mrs. Severne (they celebrated their golden wedding last week) works with him as business manager, and Severne is teaching the headline writing, make-up, and news judgment which he has learned to a granddaughter, who recently joined his staff.

He sets job prices himself for the publishing company, which serves a town of 4,500. He interviews advertisers and finds new subscribers — "twenty-five within the last three weeks," he says proudly. "And look at this week's paper — 100 per cent local news." He writes the editorials, not regularly, but as circumstances dictate — on . . . the world food situation, the need for community or county action on some matter.

"And whenever something of a political nature comes up, I try to get into it."

Struck in Eye

Struck in the eye by a flying walnut shell when a boy, he was put under the care of a country doctor. "Today," he explains, "we have reduced the average loss of sight from such an injury to as low as 3 per cent. But country doctors in those days didn't recognize the need for specialists." He lost the sight of both eyes, and was taken by his father to the Batavia school. It had been founded just four years previously, so, he says, "we started off together."

He encourages people to talk about what many regard as "handicaps." "One of the greatest mistakes a blind man can make," he avers, "is to encourage false sympathy. I always try to lead the conversation right to my blindness and clear that up so that the other fellow knows how I feel."

Entered Politics

He was graduated from the Batavia school at 18, and joined his father, who ran a hotel and restaurant in Watkins Glen. Gradually he entered politics, attending his first county convention when he was 37. He went to every county convention from then on until the institution of the primary system. "And the primary system," he protests, "is a fraud and a fake. I was trying to convince Governor Dewey of that just last week during a talk we had in Albany."

In 1902 he was nominated for the post of county superintendent of the poor. ("Welfare" was not yet a fashionable word.) When one man got up to protest that "instead of a man with no eyes, we need a man with four eyes for this post," a civil war veteran stood up and maintained that "Frank is a fellow who can beat every sighted man in Schuyler county at checkers — he can do the job."

Served Two Terms

He served two terms in the post. While he was doing this work, a group publishing the *Express* called upon him, asked him to take over the paper. They had hired a city man with a great deal of experience to run the *Express* the year before, but "a home newspaper is as different from a city paper as the little schoolhouse over in Milo is from Syracuse university." The city man was not succeeding, so Severne and his wife, neither having spent more than an hour at a time in a newspaper office, walked in and took charge of the debt-ridden sheet. Editors from neighboring towns gave him advice, sent their printers down to show him the ropes. Gradually he worked out his theories for a home newspaper — a column or so summarizing world news, lots of home news, and no material which lacks local interest.

After 12 years, the group was dissolved, and for the past 24 years Severne has been owner as well as editor.

Charles Evans Hughes, when governor of the state, gave Severne his first appointment to the board of managers of the Batavia school nearly 40 years ago. He was then, and is still, the only blind member. He is fond of talking about the school. "It has 8 or 10 buildings now — even a swimming pool. I brought that back from a convention in Colorado 25 years ago. How? In my head. I decided it would be a good thing, and after a few years the board was kind enough to see things my way. The students really enjoy it." His calm, firm manner, indicates that many people, eventually, "are kind enough to see things his way."

As a member of the American Association of Instructors of the Blind he has represented the school at conventions all over the United States and Canada.

His talk is full of references to old friends with whom he campaigned during their careers or during the time when he ran for state senator. "Most of them are gone, but it just seems as if I go right on. Friends have made my life full. Seneca was right — to have friends one must be worthy of them."

Five years ago the Young Republican Club of the county gave him a dinner in the century-old Jefferson hotel in Watkins Glen. It was to be a surprise, but like a good journalist, he found out about it two days before. Messages came from Joe Hanley, Herbert Lehman, the late Al Smith, editors and public men through the state. Publisher Frank Gannett praised Severne for "aiding every good cause, striving for good government." Judge Olin T. Nye, of Watkins Glen, keynote speaker, described the editor as one who "is a good neighbor and has never allowed his paper to become an avenue for scandalous matter."

Gifted with a remarkable memory, he is often called up in the middle of the night to settle disputes. He is the local authority on parliamentary procedure, proper ways to display the flag, and such matters.

The Severnes have two daughters, each of whom was graduated from college. One grandson was killed in the war; a granddaughter, Mrs. Alfred Johnson, helps with the paper; another granddaughter is being married this summer in Rhode Island. As usual, Mrs. Severne will drive the family car on this trip.

Severne's desk is bare and neat. It contains only some bulky Braille volumes on the *History of American Politics.* But his outer office is continually crowded with townspeople, whom he greets courteously, always remembering their names as soon as he hears their voices.

People in Watkins Glen tell how Irv Brown went out of town, stayed away about 10 or 12 years. One day he came back and walked into the *Express* office — quite unexpectedly. "Hello, Mr. Severne," he said hesitantly. The answer came instantly.

"Why, hello, Irv. Haven't seen you in some time, have we?"

B.

IF I WERE 21[11]

To Perplexed Youth One of the World's Greatest
Scientists Gives the Pithy Wisdom He Has Gleaned
from His Vast Experience in Adventurous Living

————————

By Dr. Willis R. Whitney
As Told to Hubert Kelley

If I were 21 or thereabouts, . . . and uncertain of my future and my career, I think I should buy a typewriter. The typewriter is one of the world's greatest inventions, not merely because it provides a facile method of rapidly communicating your ideas to others, but because it also helps you to communicate your ideas to yourself. It clarifies your thinking. It can talk to you, and it can even advise you.

I know a young man who is uncertain whether to be a boat builder or an accountant. I suggested, when he asked my advice, that he sit down at a typewriter and write two essays addressed to himself — one on the advantages of being a boat builder, a marvelous outdoor occupation, the other on the advantages of being an accountant. Then he should write two more on the disadvantages of each calling, and study what he has written. One never knows what is in his mind until he gets busy and lets it out. However, before the young man does any of this, he must learn to write on a typewriter. When he has done that, he will find that he already has one marketable skill — typing.

If I were seeking a job and could not call upon each prospective employer in person, I should prefer to apply with a typewritten letter. Print is always more impressive than handwriting, which, in some respects, is unfortunate, considering some of the untruths in print.

This brings me to another good use to which a youngster can put a typewriter. He can examine the truth of print with print. That is to say, he can write an essay on some impressive piece of advice he has just read — even this — and discover by experiment whether it is true or not.

————————

[11]Reprinted by permission of *The American Magazine.*

Say he has just read an interesting article on some great man who made good by sticking to his job. The moral of the article is that a rolling stone gathers no moss. Well, who wants moss, anyhow? One way to find out what you want to do in life is to try all kinds of jobs. If you don't like working in a filling station, try a store. Try an ofice, a shop, a farm. Not only will you find out what you want to do, but you will pick up, as you go along, an amazing amount of useful information.

Nearly every school child in America is required to memorize Polonius's advice to Laertes from Shakespeare's *Hamlet*. "Neither a borrower nor a lender be." That is palpable nonsense. Our whole economic structure is based upon borrowing and lending. Beware of such proverbs. Think. Sit down and write a letter to yourself about the age-old advice every restless kid is getting these days. See whether it is true. Walk around it. Take it apart. That goes for this advice. Maybe you can prove that you shouldn't change horses in midstream, even if your horse has a broken leg.

You don't have to be smart to see through things. All you need is a lot of curiosity about truth and some ambition.

Hundreds of thousands of veterans in their late teens and early twenties are wondering whether to go back to school. The Government has made it easy for them to return under the financial provisions of the GI Bill of Rights. Some of them have told me that they don't like the idea of being an "old man" in a class of kids. Others who have been driving jeeps and piloting planes in Europe and Asia, or who have been manning warships at sea, are fearful of boredom, of dreary hours of classroom confinement under professors who, all too often, are teaching because they are incapable of doing anything else. I sympathize with these boys, and to them I say:

"The colleges have no monopoly on education. Truth is all around you. Look for it. Your business on earth is looking for truth and using it to the advantage of yourself and others."

"But I want to study nuclear physics — atomics," one young man countered. "You have to go to school for that."

It is true that much of the expensive apparatus used in atomic research is to be found in some of our universities. An individual inquirer could not afford to buy similar equipment for experimentation. Sooner or later he probably would have to go back to school for some special work. But anybody can begin to study nuclear physics without school. I explained to my young friend how I had recently taught a little child the principles of this new and revolutionary science without laboratory equipment.

I gave the child three boxes, each full of paper wads and a handful of pins. One box, I told him, was full of neutrons; the second, protons; and the third, electrons. All he had to do was to take a wad from each box and pin them together to have an atom.

All matter is made of atoms. We arranged some of these paper-wad atoms in a little design.

"That," I said, "is oxygen — a molecule of oxygen."

We made iron, hydrogen, a number of things. We could have made 92 different elements and, no doubt, we will.

Then I suggested he make a pattern of his own. He made a very nice molecule, indeed, but I discovered, after some calculation, that the new substance he had created would last only one-billionth of a second before it flew apart. We agreed that we would have to make something a little more enduring if we were to contribute some new substance to the world.

We now have our hands on these invisible particles of all matter and force. We can rearrange atoms and make new substances, maybe an infinite number. . .

A young man can read all about it in books. Maybe he can get a job in an atomic bomb plant. If he wants specific questions answered, he can sit down at that typewriter I told him to buy, and write to experts in the field. I never knew a great man who wouldn't answer an intelligent question from a youngster . . .

I happen to be a kind of a monkey. I have a monkeylike curiosity that makes me want to feel, smell, and taste things which arouse my curiosity, then to take them apart. It was born in me. Not everybody is like that, but a scientific researchist should be. Everybody has his peculiarities; therefore, it would be impossible for me to advise the average young man whether to enter this marvelous new field of nuclear physics. There is a danger that the very wonder and mystery of it may attract somebody who would have a much better time designing, manufacturing, or selling the incredible number of new substances and objects which atomic rearrangement is already producing for us.

If I were 21 and did not feel scientifically inclined, I would not disdain a job selling plastic dishes, for instance, from house to house. It is outdoor work for a young veteran conditioned to an out-of-door life. Such a salesman would learn so much about people, more than I have an opportunity to learn in a laboratory. He should make money, have fun, and be cut in on the atomic age all at the same time. He might write a book about his experiences. He might learn some new things about what people want to buy that would help the researchist, the designer, or the manufacturer. It is not the job you take that matters so much, as what you do with it.

I heard the other day of a young colonel who was embittered because his former employer gave him his old job back — sealing envelopes. The colonel, still a youngster, had been flying a bomber in Asia. Sealing envelopes is not a bad job. Some bright young man might derive an invention from it. Are envelopes made the way they should be, or does an envelope look the way it does because we're used to the way it looks? I don't know. What about the glue, our methods of stamping and addressing? Should they be improved?

Stenography is not a bad job. One should learn something from everything one copies or hears dictated. I wonder whether any stenographer has yet devised a new way of putting on a typewriter ribbon. Or should there be a ribbon? Maybe it would be better to ink the type with some sort of roller operated by a key. I do not know. That's really a thinking job for a good stenographer. I loathe changing ribbons.

What I am getting at is that some people are inclined to shoot too high and arrive too quickly. If I were 21, I think I would be willing to take any kind of a job to see where it would lead me. . .

"What's the use of trying to do anything or be anything?" one young veteran said. "The world is going to pot. Some columnist said the other day that we were back in the Dark Ages."

This attitude may be quite prevalent among some of the disheartened young men who have come back from the seas and battlefields. I do not share it. I never was more hopeful.

The other day I was eating oysters, when it occurred to me that I could be eating oysters with complete serenity in Kansas City, Houston, or Chicago. I would not have the slightest fear of poison, although an hour's mishandling of an oyster before it reached me might endanger my life.

My oysters had been handled by a dredger, a sorter, a buyer, a shipper, a trucker, a hotel attendant, an opener, and a waiter. There they were, cold, pure, and delicious. What a triumph of ethics! All of the men who had handled them had played square with me, whom they did not even know. They may have been disgruntled about their wages, working conditions, a fall of price. But they guarded those oysters every minute.

You cannot tell me that the world is going to pot when men in all walks of life have so much responsibility, are so devoted to the common good. These are not the Dark Ages. They are the most enlightened of all times. We have evolved upward since we were cells in the sea. We are kinder, more intelligent, more able to survive. I say this in spite of war or threats of war.

I think young men should consciously take the attitude that we are growing. It may be difficult, considering the suffering which some of them have undergone, but hopefulness and faith are certain to pay out. . .

If I were 21 I think I should be active in politics. One of the things I would advocate would be a URO to be incorporated with the UN — that is, a United Religious Organization. I would ask scholars, thinkers, ministers, students, scientists, and good, everyday people to help select from the religions of the world all of the ethical truths that make for the public good. I have worked out no procedure, having neither the time nor the strength. But it can be done.

When superstitions and points of conflict are eliminated from the religions of the world, we shall have left a shining nucleus of truth that will bring all of us closer together. . .

A lot of people seem to think that a man learns only in his teens. Boys get this impression from their elders and, on emerging from the armed services at the age of 22 or 23 imagine themselves too old to take up such a noble science, say, as medicine.

I was in my early seventies when I studied medicine, not for a degree, but to enable me better to experiment with a "fever machine," which we invented in our laboratories. It is used to cure or alleviate certain types of disease with heat therapy.

While studying medicine I made a strange discovery. I found that all the things I already knew were related to what I was studying. I learned very rapidly. Sometimes I merely had to translate my special words into special medical words to understand what the doctors were talking about. A boy who has studied jeep motors, liquid fire, or navigation already knows some medicine, chemistry, physics, and psychology, and a lot of other things.

Two years ago I took up hydrogen-electric welding and became a pretty good welder. I was trying to find a means of eliminating the sputter. I relate this in no spirit of boastfulness. I just want youngsters to know that they are never too old to learn. Even at our best, we use just a tiny bit of our brains. If half of mine were calcified, I still could learn with a little bit of the other half.

If I were 21 and wanted to study medicine, I don't think I would pack off to school. I would get a job as an orderly in a hospital, carrying out bed-pans, if necessary, and look and listen. After a year or two of that, I might know what kind of medicine I wanted to study. Maybe I would find that I preferred to become an expert in hormones, rather than a surgeon. I might even end up as a druggist or a maker of surgical equipment. I would see where the job led me. . .

We are making more and more new things. The more we make, the more men will work, the more people will buy. The more they buy, the more transportation we shall need, the more stores and warehouses. Employment will snowball. There are more opportunities today in this land than there have ever been. They are increasing in number. I think they are infinite.

If the UN is successful in maintaining the peace, it may yet devolve upon the United States to feed the world. We'll have to if we put the world back on its feet. We can't produce too much food. There are innumerable opportunities in agriculture for a young man, and, with modern farm machinery, he won't find the work back-breaking. If I were 21, I would consider apprenticing myself to a farmer. Agricultural school isn't necessary. Pick a good master and earn while you learn.

"I know," one young veteran told me, "but I want to get married. I don't want to support a wife on an apprentice's wages."

"Then marry a nice farm girl on a run-down farm. Clear out the rotten old orchard with a jeep and go to work. The county agent and the government experiment stations will tell you what to do. If you don't want to farm, then put up a motorcar repair shop on her land. When motorcars and farm implements begin to roll off the belt, you and thousands of other young men are going to have more work that you can do. . ."

The older I get the more I realize that the highest good is the good of the people. If I were to choose an occupation again I should consider three things: how well it served the public; how much fun there was in it; and, of course, whether its financial reward would meet my need.

I know a young fellow, God bless him, who goes around the country selling birdhouses made in the shape of little white churches. He makes them. I now have 14 or 15 of them. I put the wren-houses in different locations at different heights to find out where wrens prefer to nest. I haven't found out much yet, except that they don't like to be near trees from which cats and squirrels can leap to the birdhouse roof or platform. This young man is having a glorious time going about the country, meeting good people who love birds. He makes money, has fun, serves the public good and the good of birds. The simple and humble things are not to be overlooked in this world of boundless opportunity.

Essays and Critical Writing

Essay articles are of many varieties. They are argumentative, humorous, critical, and explanatory. Frequently, they depend for sale upon the way they are written. The writer need not be a master of style, but he must present interesting material.

The humorous article is found in many magazines scarcely suspected of handling humor. Yet even the most staid magazine may occasionally relish having a little fun made of things it usually considers serious business. Among these magazines are *American Home, Good Housekeeping,* and *Woman's Day.*

No one can tell you how to write burlesques of serious subjects. Study the markets, use the query, and occasionally let the streak of humor in you give birth to an uproarious piece. While humor is hard to do, magazines welcome well-done items and pay good rates for them.

In the argumentative articles the writer has a chance to marshal arguments against his "pet peeves," his hobbies, or upon matters of public interest. Knowing that readers like a good scrap, editors frequently jump at the chance of getting a controversial article that they can safely handle.

The writer's purpose is to change his reader's point of view. This he does by deciding what his own point of view is. He brings together the facts and arranges them in a convincing manner. Facts speak louder than opinion, and it is well to make sure that they are on the writer's side before beginning the piece.

An able discussion of critical writing is presented by Wolseley in his *Critical Writing for the Journalist.*[12] Extensive analyses in this work can be of real help to interested writers.

Two essay-type articles in the home-decorating field are presented below. The first was done in serious vein, the second in humorous manner. The latter was illustrated with pen-and-ink sketches. Both show what can be done with everyday material by those who can see it in a new light. Among the advantages of using this type of material is that it's always at hand.

---

[12]Wolseley, R. E. *Critical Writing for the Journalist.* Chilton, Philadelphia, 1961.

A.

TATTLE TALE HOMES[13]

The Rooms You Live In
Mirror Your Personality

————————

By Lillian B. Allen

Your home is telling tales about you. Does it tell the best or the worst? The personality of you and your family is deeply engraved on the rooms you live in. Your habits, the way you live, the way you keep house affect your scheme of decoration.

You can think of homes so neat they are boring, or so untidy they annoy you. Expensive ones that are dull and cold. Or little ones bursting at the corners with warmth and friendliness.

What makes them that way? The people who live in them as much as the scheme of decoration. And the person most responsible for the impression they make on the outside world is you, the woman of the house.

You play the biggest part in creating home background. After all, you're the one who buys the furniture in good taste and to suit the needs of your family. You're the one who uses color wisely because you know what an important influence color has on your family's well-being. You're the one who blends the individuals into a family pattern. And you're the one who fuses all these elements into the home by which your friends and neighbors judge you.

You and I both know people like the Martins, the couple who moved into your neighborhood last fall with their two cute little girls. You did wonder about the careless way the children were dressed. And you heard there was discord at home. As far as you could see, Mrs. Martin was charming. So you were inclined to put the blame on the husband.

That was until you were actually invited into their home. And there's where you felt something wrong. The furniture and decorations had been nice once. But apologies didn't take the place of care. You caught a glimpse of things dumped into a messy kitchen. And everything ran behind time, causing tension and strain. So you came away understanding why Mr. Martin, a home-proud man, might be a little discouraged about his home life.

I play a little game when I call on people. Through it I've learned a lot about decorating. And I've learned a lot about my friends and neighbors. Their homes tell stories of drabness and charm, pretentiousness and courage.

It was on the prairies I found courage in a home.

Everyone in town had told me about Mary Welch. How she courageously kept up the morale of her husband and two children while they lived in a one-room house. Now with a thriving farm they had a small and unusually attractive house. A great part of this attractiveness was in what you felt of their love, pride, and achievement.

————————

[13]Reprinted by permission of *National Home Monthly* and the author.

Mary told me that strict organization of space and family cooperation had made living in small quarters possible. And that paint was her best friend. I could see evidence of the paint all around me. Color still took the place of fabrics and luxuries she couldn't afford. It was those colors, that clever planning, and a lot of Mary herself that helped to keep her family cheerful through those trying years. As a matter of fact, her ideas and ingenuity have been an inspiration and help to the whole community.

Helen was the friend I made because I fell in love with her living room. It sounds silly. But it happened. Right in Boston.

I had been asked to look her up. So she invited me over. While she was detained on professional work, I had time to size her up from her surroundings. Her room was as fresh as spring with lime yellow walls, and grayed turquoise and persimmon in the fabrics. There were lilacs on a low table near by. Her furniture was graceful but cleanly cut modern. Her accessories were unusual. And what was more important, the room looked lived in and loved. Who was it said all modern rooms were cold and clinical?

But it was her pictures that won me completely. That's where you can tell most quickly about people's taste and interest. Her four were different. Two sunny water colors, and two oriental prints. All carefully chosen and more carefully framed.

Then Helen came in. She laughed when we talked about her decorating. "It's pretty easy if you follow one idea," she said, "and have only yourself to think about. I like subtle but cheerful colors, and I don't like frills, so here it is."

Perhaps I should mention Yehudi. I call him that because, like the song, he was the little man who wasn't there. But I found out enough fine qualities about him to know he would be an interesting and probably congenial friend. A friend and I wanted to rent a houseboat for a stay on the West Coast. And his weather beaten craft was available.

Outside in the mist the craft looked discouraging. Inside, a subtle indefinable atmosphere of charm took hold of us and made us forget the room was shabby. The colors were dark and rich. The deep chairs were the kind men like when they stretch out leisurely to light a pipe and read a book. The furniture was simple, well-designed, and rubbed smooth as satin. Books on philosophy, poetry, and fine literature were everywhere. It was a room meant for study and work, for friendship and long-into-the-night talks. Everything in the room showed discrimination and sincerity. Our careful inquiry about the owner showed only that he was a writer who perferred his identity to be undisclosed.

It's a far step from sincerity of decorating and living to pretentiousness, a pitfall from the old business of keeping up with the Joneses. Each person who ventures out to buy furniture should hold this motto in front of her. "If you can't afford the real thing, leave imitation alone." A great deal of the furniture offered for sale to the unsuspecting and often uninformed public is poorly designed or poorly adapted from the historic period. It comes under the glamorous titles as Louis XV bedroom suites, Jacobean dining room suites, and now, Waterfall Modern. It suits no one's home, yet thousands are likely to buy it. And thousands of homes are doomed to become more or less alike and uninteresting before the family even gets a chance at them.

From this monotonous style, it's an easy step to the lethal or deadly atmosphere.

One young bride was actually afraid of her mother-in-law because she had to visit with her in one of these deadly rooms. The colors were drab. The furniture was ugly and poorly arranged. There were no magazines or ash trays. It was fussily neat. The atmosphere was so constrained even conversation was forced. The tragic part was that the older woman, naturally quiet and shy, didn't know she had created something that was overpowering her. She thought she had the proper kind of home for her position, and resented the fact that her son had left it.

People like the Munroes who do things are most likely to have the interesting, cheerful homes where everyone likes to go. Mr. Munroe is a high school teacher. His wife sings, and her hobby is hooking rugs. The boys do woodworking in a basement room. They all like music and dancing. They live enthusiastically and congenially on a salary that needs careful budgeting. Their home centers around a combination living room and dining room which gives space for the piano, their one home luxury.

Open bookshelves flank the wide fireplace. Tall wrought iron candlesticks hold big candles which are lighted on special occasions for music and conversation.

The room isn't a period or antique room. But because the Munroes like to pick up the odd pieces of glass and have two old chests, they chose welldesigned maple furniture to build around. Their basically warm color scheme was built up around the tawny color of the maple. Not too cluttered, their rooms look lived in. They form a truly Canadian background where two growing boys are gaining a knowledge of what constitutes a fine home life.

You can't create a home by merely copying someone else's furniture and colors. You have to find furniture and colors to suit your own needs and interests. When you do that you begin to create that quality which belongs to no one else but you and your family. No matter whether your home consists of two rooms or ten, if it has that spirit, then you know you need have no fears. Your home is telling the world the best things about you.

B.

DE-BUNKING YOUR HOUSE[14]

By Marjorie Seal

Consider the case of Augusta Wind. One morning she was awakened with a boom, bang, crash! There was her sister, Agatha, in the middle of the floor. Agatha had blithely crawled out from under the covers of her upper bunk, which was of course directly above Augusta's. She had oh! so carefully and

[14]Reprinted by permission of *The American Home* and the author.

quietly felt with her foot for the ladder by which she could descend. For some reason the ladder wasn't attached securely — and you know what happened!

Thinking her sister mortally injured, Augusta rose to her aid. This proved to be a foolhardy move; she rose too suddenly and too high and cracked her pretty skull on the upper bunk. So there you have it: they both were up, ready to start the day — one with a near fractured skull, the other with an almost broken neck.

Then there's another case. Miss Lotta Length slept in the "lower" as she was biggest. Tiny slept above.

Lotta struggled to make her bed; she bumped her head and back twelve times before the ordeal was complete. Now, Tiny had to pull a chair (one of mother's best antiques) over to make up her bunk. And, with two dictionaries on top of that, she was able to make up one side, then down to the end, and finally to the other side. Mother's antique was too old for this and collapsed.

If these troubles sound familiar to you, I have one suggestion to make: SEPARATE YOUR BUNKS!

Process

The process article is also known as the utility article and the how-to-do-something. Its purpose is to tell the reader how to decorate a room, do hand-tooled leather work, arrange flowers, make a dress or bake a cake, do contour plowing, build a fish pond, decorate a store window, lower a golf score, overcome bashfulness, improve nature, repair broken china, stencil a chair.

In every case a process is explained. The intention is to make the explanation so clear that the reader can successfully duplicate the process step by step. In fact, the process article has no other purpose. *It is not* written to entertain or amuse, though it can be handled with a light touch. Articles intended chiefly to amuse fall into the class of essays.

This article can be handled in two ways. It may be told as a how-to-do-something, or as how-something-was-done. The latter treatment is generally best because it carries more conviction. It is the easiest type of article to *write and sell*. It is easy to sell, because more process articles are bought than all others combined. And it is easiest to write because it does not seek to entertain or amuse and because it has concrete facts with which to deal.

The sole problem of the process article is that of being understood. Processes should be broken into the simplest steps possible, with complete explanation of each. An excellent check on the success of the explanation is to have the first draft read by two or three persons previously unfamiliar with the process. The trial readers should have the same characteristics as those of the proposed market. They should be asked to explain the process to the writer. If they can make a satisfactory explanation, the writer has succeeded in his purpose.

Following are some do's and don'ts for process articles.

D O N ' T S

1. Don't tell at great length how much pleasure will accrue by following your advice.
2. Don't tell at great length how much fun you yourself had.
3. Don't attempt to describe the process until you understand it yourself.
4. Don't describe more than one step at a time.
5. Don't write more than is necessary to explain the process.
6. Don't use technical terms unless you explain them at once.

D O ' S

1. State the main idea in the title and first paragraph.
2. Suggest briefly the reasons why the process is worth-while to perform.
3. Keep all directions as simple as possible.
4. Give directions in a basically logical order, such as the chronological.
5. Be definite, precise, and concrete.
6. Use tabulations and check lists whenever possible.
7. Give your reader credit for understanding the desirability of following your advice.
8. Point out all pitfalls, and tell how to avoid them.
9. Check with trial readers to make sure all questions have been answered.

The process articles quoted below include two examples of student work and are of a quality that beginning writers may expect to do. The articles compared favorably with those by professional writers appearing in the same magazines, and hence offer encouragement to writers who hesitate to compare their work with that of established writers. In most published process articles it isn't the quality of the writing but the helpfulness of the idea that makes the sale.

This type of article must be illustrated by photographs or drawings. Item "A" was illustrated by 6 photographs and 3 drawings; "B" with 2 photographs and 4 drawings; and "C" with 13 photographs. All important ideas or steps should be illustrated in the process article. Note references in the articles to accompanying illustrations.

A.

LEATHERCRAFT IS A PROFITABLE HOBBY[15]

This Ancient Art Is Good for Money Making and Enjoyment

––––––––––

By C. M. Green

Leathercraft, an art handed down from father to son since earliest times, has become a popular hobby. Anyone can learn the craft of making useful, attractive objects from leather.

This craft has become a source of enjoyment to many who find it both instructive and profitable. After you have purchased your equipment, it will not be long before you are more than reimbursed for your initial investment, for the possibilities of sales are unlimited.

The tools used in leathercraft are simple and inexpensive. Absolutely essential are the modeler, lacing punch, a sharp cutting instrument such as knife or razor blade, and a tracing tool. Other pieces of equipment may be added as you progress in your work. Some of the desirable tools are the wheel tool, snap-applying outfit, stamps, and dividers for marking lacing holes. The bare essentials are included in sets priced between two and three dollars. For a more complete set you will pay from five to ten dollars.

The best leather for tooling is Russian Calf. It works up easily. There are many kinds of leather, but the beginner would do well to start with this one on simple articles, working gradually into larger pieces and more intricate designs.

Do not try to imitate factory-made goods. You cannot possibly profit by competing with mass production. The superiority of hand-made articles is the personal touch that adheres to them. Monograms personalize an article, and it is possible to make designs characteristic of the person who will receive the gift.

For instance, if you know a young man in college and he wants a billfold with a secret compartment, you can make him one with the seal of his college on it. Or if friends of yours are getting married, make them a monogrammed table mat. A young bride might be decorating her new home to match, say, her favorite season, autumn. A circular table mat with a ring of autumn leaves in bright colors would be sure to please her.

A skin of Russian Calf measures about 11 to 14 feet, and costs about 60 cents a foot. You can purchase a half skin, or you can buy leather by the square inch. Of course it is less expensive in large quantities. W. A. Hall and Son, of Chicago, is one of the reliable leather firms that can furnish the necessary materials.

Lining leather can be purchased at about two dollars for a whole skin. Lacing varies in price according to its width, but the most commonly used is about five cents a yard. This all sets the price of an average-sized coin

––––––––––

[15]Reprinted by permission of *Mechanix Illustrated* and the author.

purse or key case at approximately forty cents. You can judge by these prices the cost of making other items. Small articles can be made from scrap leather for fifteen and twenty cents.

It is advisable to prepare your leather at least 24 hours in advance of tooling it. Soak the piece you are going to use in cool or tepid water for three minutes. This will soften the leather and make it easily workable. If it is wrapped in oil paper for the night, it will remain soft and pliable until you are ready to tool it.

First, select a pattern. For convenience, suppose you have decided to make a coin purse. Cut a piece of leather lightly larger than the pattern you want to use, and prepare as above. Place this piece smoothly on a board. Lay your pattern on the damp leather, and go over all the lines of the pattern with a pencil or tracing tool to make an impression on the leather. Use a ruler for all straight lines in order to produce a craftsmanlike article.

A design is made to stand out by tooling. A pleasing effect is accomplished by raising with the modeling tool the body of the design from the back of the leather. The background may be embossed with either a deep impression or with dots, like stippling. After the design has been raised, use the modeling tool around the edges to give it a finished look.

If you purchased a natural leather you can use color in your designs. This is the most pleasing effect of all. Use a small water color brush and special aniline dyes, which may be obtained from leather companies. To prevent streaking, the leather must be wet while you are applying the dye. Dark leathers are tanned in such a way that they will not take dyes.

If you make a coin purse, you will want to line it. This is done with a special thin leather, called skiver. Cover the backs of the tooled piece with Sphinx paste, a gelatin adhesive, obtainable from the leather companies. Place the skiver over it, press the two parts together firmly, and rub smooth. When the paste is dry cut the edges of the leather to the pattern line.

The edges are often laced together. Marking for lacing should be done very carefully, setting the dots for punching the width of the lacing in from the edge, and the width of the lacing apart.

The simplest lacing stitch is the over-and-over stitch, but there is also a loop stitch that is more decorative and covers the edges of the articles.

In punching lacing holes on a piece which must be folded, or where two edges must be laced together, it is necessary to punch through both pieces at once so the two parts will fit together.

Snaps may be obtained from any leather company, and every full set of leather tools includes a snap-applying outfit. Apply the snap after the lacing is finished, and with a little polish from a good wax your coin purse will be ideal for use as a Christmas gift or for sale to a gift shop.

Patterns can be made up for bookends, table mats, book covers, coin purses, handbags, card cases, key cases, wallets, bracelets, and belts. Patience is the prime requisite of proficiency in making leather articles. It is impossible to hurry your design or tooling or dyeing without sacrificing some of the artistry of the craft.

Your first attempts should be with small simple items, like coin purses or key cases or rectangular table mats, for in working with a new medium even an artist will make mistakes while acquiring a new skill.

When you have become proficient at designing, tooling, dyeing and lacing, you can start making objects for sale. If you want instruction in the craft, it can usually be obtained through art departments of high schools and colleges, and very often in summer camps.

B.

BUILD A WELL-HOUSE[16]

———————

by Charlotte Mathes

Fountains and wells of old were not only places of utility and beauty but important social centers. Yet today in America they are possessions almost forgotten, certainly neglected in frequent cases.

While modern life does not often include leisurely congregation at community and household sources of water, nevertheless your own garden might benefit from the architectural interest which a harmoniously-designed and -built well-house or well-head can give the planting scheme. And presence of a gushing spring or a dug well is not at all necessary, of course, to justify the planning and construction of such a decorative feature.

As examples on these pages show, the present-day well-house can be built in grounds where a piped supply of water eliminates dependence on naturally-occurring water. Yet it can serve the practical purpose of concealing a desirable, but otherwise unsightly, incinerator; or hide the faucet, hose and accessories for watering the lawn and garden. An attractive well-head (that is, roofless structure over a "well") could admirably hold the pile of leaves and grass raked up for compost.

Wells and well-heads readily lend themselves to various types of gardens. Style of course should be in accord with the character of the garden; there ar so many usable types that no problem is presented, whether the garden accompanies a home of modern, traditional, or regional architecture.

If yours is an informal garden, the well-sweep or the rustic well are particularly appropriate. The well-sweep represents one of the most picturesque yet primitive devices for raising water from wells. Its construction is very simple, being based upon the weighted lever principle.

The rustic-type well with a shingled roof and rough masonry and hewn timbers will form a charming vista in your garden scheme.

Wells and well-heads used on patios and terraces as decorative features are particularly effective. These can be constructed of cast stone or cut stone and designed along lines similar to those used by the Corinthians,

———————

[16]Reprinted by permission of *Mechanix Illustrated, Lawn & Garden Handbook*, and the author.

Romans, or Spanish. Attractive canopies of wrought iron and marble may be used if desired.

If you have been lamenting the fact that you have an old hand pump in your garden, build a small rectangular pool to catch the water and hold a few lovely water lilies. Give the old wood pump a new dress of paint or set an ivy plant to climb it and you can enjoy a beauty you never suspected it could present.

Choose a design more distinctive for the formal garden and place the well at the intersection of principal garden walks.

Still another use to which wells can be put is to use them to reflect the simplicity and fine lines of your home. For example, if your home is of brick, use brick for the well, carrying out the lines of the house on the roof of the well.

Why not make a simple garden well yourself? It is not hard to do, and requires only a minimum of ingenuity. The accompanying drawing . . . suggests a simple style and construction. Bricks, stones, fossil rock, and wood are but a few of the possible materials. The most inexpensive material is stone if you collect it yourself — and usually the most attractive choice, too.

For the inside lining of a well-house simpler than the walk-in type, use an old oil tank or barrel .You need not go to any great expense here, for an oil tank or barrel can usually be obtained as a discard or from a junk yard or gasoline station for a few cents. The tank simply acts as a solid foundation around which to place the rocks. A tank of 50-gallon capacity is ideal for this purpose. For solid foundation sink the tank at least three feet into the ground, according to its height. There is now no chance of its tipping over.

You can connect the well with your home water supply before setting the oil tank or barrel in the ground, if you like. Be sure to drill a hole in the metal the size of a waterline pipe before sinking it into the ground. Water can then be admitted and become a source of water for your plants.

After the tank has been placed, remove an inch or two of soil around the well. Place enough concrete, made of one part cement and three parts sand, so that part of the first layer of stone is imbedded in the cement foundation. Keep placing stones around in layers, using enough cement to hold the stones in the foundation.

After the cement has set for about an hour, remove the surplus with an old kitchen knife, trowel, or stick. This adds a decorative line. When the top is reached, if it seems rough and uneven, level it off with a layer of cement.

The roof, if one is planned, is easily constructed, following much the same lines as those in the illustrations. Side posts of wood or pipe may be used. These can be set up by cementing them into the wall.

Sling the old oaken bucket from a chain running around a channeled, rimmed wheel. The wheel is easily supported by a rod.

C.

MAKING POTTERY[17]

In the Kitchen

———————

By Marguerite Dodd and Kay Morrissey

If you can bake a pie — even a mud pie — you can make pottery. The twelve how-to-do photographs will give you an idea of how simple it is even for a beginner. A kitchen table with a wood or linoleum surface is good to work on, or you can make a work surface, called a bat, by pouring plaster into a pie tin to harden. A block of clay and a few simple tools are all that are needed.

Before you begin, these general facts about clay may be helpful: soft clay is never added to stiff clay — it will not stick. Handles and spouts are attached in the leather-hard (stiff but damp) state. Fit them carefully, score the edges to be joined, cover both joints with a liberal coating of slip (clay and water mixed with a spatula to a whipped cream texture) and press the pieces firmly together. Wipe off all the excess slip after the handle has been set.

The steps used in making a large crock like the one at the left of the photograph are as follows:

WEDGING.   Prepare the clay for use by working it into a uniform consistency. The clay is kneaded (much as you would knead bread) then it is shaped into a block and cut with a wire. The uncut edges are slammed hard together, the whole mass pounded and slapped into a smooth loaf. Repeat the process until the cut surfaces appear smooth, solid and free from air bubbles and foreign matter.

THE BASE.   Pat a lump of clay into a round cake with the heel of the hand. With a compass, mark off a circle the size you desire and cut it out with an orangewood modeling stick. Make sure the compass leaves a good center impression, then turn the base over so the mark will show on the bottom.

THE EDGE.   Score the edge of the base by making piecrust-like flutings with your stick. Clay welds more firmly to a roughened surface.

THE COIL.   Shape a portion of the clay into an oblong. Dampen the table and begin to roll the clay, using only the fingers and bearing down lightly. Stretch the clay out as you roll until it is twice the thickness you want the finished wall to be. Keep a damp cloth over the portion not in use.

RAISING THE WALL.   Press your first coil firmly around the base, placing it halfway up from the bottom, and weld the ends firmly together. Blend the top of the coil toward the base and smooth off the whole piece. Continue placing one coil over the other, welding the ends of each and stacking them so that all the joinings do not come on the same side.

———————

[17]Reprinted by permission of *Woman's Day* Magazine.

HALFWAY.   Add coil on coil, firming and smoothing inside and out as you go. Don't leave any crevices between the coils where air locked in will cause the piece to crack or explode in firing.

THE TEMPLATE   is cut from a piece of cardboard in the shape of the finished piece. Use it to determine where each coil should be placed, and firm the clay wall against it to obtain a uniform shape.

THE BOTTOM.   Turn the completed shape upside down and with a compass placed in the original center hole draw a circle smaller than the base to be cut away. A base that is left solid is apt to warp in the firing and not stand evenly. Make a pencil mark on your modeling stick the depth you want the base to be cut out and using it as a guide, mark off the surface into squares, then chisel out the small cubes of clay. The clay should have reached leathery consistency for easy cutting.

FINISHING.   Using a flexible steel scraper, scrape the rough surfaces lightly and smooth out the bumps with a wet sponge. Round off the sharp top edges. The piece is now allowed to dry thoroughly for its first firing.

INSIDE GLAZING.   For the fired piece, called the biscuit, mix your glaze according to the directions below. Pour the glaze into the piece and pour it out again, revolving the biscuit as you pour to make sure all inside surfaces are covered.

OUTSIDE GLAZING.   Place the piece upside down on a rack over a bowl and pour the glaze evenly around the sides. Touch up with a brush any spots you miss. Allow the glaze to dry thoroughly before it is fired again.

ABOUT KILNS.   Most towns have a pottery factory or craft school where you can have your pottery fired for a small fee. It is possible, of course, to buy kilns such as are used by professional potters. . . .

There is a type of synthetic clay now on the market called Ceramite which can be fired in your own kitchen oven if you can keep it at 250° or lower. Special synthetic glazes to be used with it can also be fired at this temperature. In using these materials it is absolutely necessary to have the piece thoroughly dry before each firing for successful results. . . .

ABOUT MATERIAL.   Look around in your own locality for companies that supply pottery materials. . . .

ABOUT GLAZING.   Most glazes come in powdered form, usually with directions for applying it. In general, mix the powdered material with water until it has the consistency of cream, and sieve out any lumps. Add a tablespoon of gum Arabic or tragacanth or a teaspoon of Sevco Gum to a pint of glaze. If the gum thickens the glaze too much thin with water. The gum keeps the glaze from powdering off before the piece is fired.

Generally the thickness of a coat of glaze should be about the thickness of the back of the blade of a silver knife. Test it by cutting into the glaze with your fingernail or a sharp knife. Many glazes are poisonous so wash your hands well and never glaze if you have open cuts on your hands. Glaze should be applied more heavily at the top of the piece as it tends to run a little.

Collectives

Collective articles are of several varieties. For the most part they consist of a number of brief items, more or less related, brought together in a single article. Frequently they appear under a single title, though not always. Common varieties include both one- and two-page spreads. Women's magazines and the popular mechanics type are among the commonest users of this article.

For example a group of new, timesaving devices for the kitchen might be incorporated into a single article. In such articles it is customary to provide a photograph or sketch for each device. A single, summarizing paragraph may introduce the entire group with one or more paragraph devoted to each item.

Menus, lists of Christmas gifts, examples of budgeting, personality analyses, information tests, as well as numerous articles prepared by magazine departments belong to the collective group.

The literary style is terse, and explanations are condensed. Queries should precede preparation of collective articles, and the pattern of display should be as simple as possible. Make-up is usually left to the magazine staff.

Item "A" below is a modern treatment of one of the oldest subjects. It was unillustrated, except for decorative background for the title. Both form and content should suggest further adaptation possibilities; for instance, an article on other superstitions.

A.

WHAT DO YOU KNOW ABOUT THE WEATHER?[18]

You're Always Talking about It But . . .

––––––––––

By Willy Ley

Since weather affects all of us all the time it's not surprising that there are countless rules, proverbs and rhymed jingles in all countries and all languages which pretend to prophesy what's to come from certain signs, real or fictitious.

A few of these more or less ancient adages contain some scientific truth, others have been kept current only because the average person remembers a prophecy that comes true and forgets those that fail. But even adages which are more or less true in one country cannot be transplanted to another, as many immigrants and refugees have found to their immense surprise. Even the way of talking about the weather varies from country to country.

[18]Reprinted by permission of *Woman's Home Companion* and the author.

For example, most Americans do not hesitate at all to say to friends and neighbors: "Beautiful day, isn't it?" and it is then, as a rule, a beautiful *day*. Few Englishmen — and few continental Europeans from countries north of the Alps would ever be that careless. The customary greeting over there is "beautiful morning" because the afternoon which follows a beautiful morning may be quite unbeautiful. Our weather hangs around longer without change.

Here are a few sayings and beliefs that prevail in America. Do you know the true from the false?

Rain before seven, clear before eleven.

False. The sooner you forget this jingle the better; it has no foundation in reality whatever. Of course it does happen that early morning rains are dissipated during the forenoon, but oftener the day keeps right on being rainy. The only basis for this prediction is that in English "seven" and "eleven" happen to rhyme. The two numerals don't rhyme in French, German or Russian; consequently, the saying does not exist in those languages.

A rainbow in the morning is the shepherd's warning.

Usually true. This old maxim is based on the scientific fact that the rainbow betrays the presence of showers some distance from the observer, even if it fails to rain at the actual locality of the observer. Here (in straight contradiction to the preceding rhyme) the saying takes it for granted that a rainy morning indicates a rainy day.

Red sky at dawning, sailor's warning; red sky at night, sailor's delight.

False. This is another of those jingles which are remembered mainly because they rhyme well. If a very red evening sky has any meteorological significance at all it might point toward a tendency to be rainy during the night and possibly through the next day. Why this should delight a sailor is hard to see because rain means poor visibility. A yellowish evening sky usually means dry weather and heat in summer. The redness of the morning sky has no significance.

Frogs and especially tree frogs are reliable weather prophets.

False. Although the belief in the weatherwise qualities of the green tree frog is so deeply imbedded in European countries that little glasses with small wooden ladders and a tree frog in them can be bought almost anywhere, the tree frog rarely prophesies correctly. Its call, which is said to be a sign of approaching rain, is usually just a mating call.

But it is easy to understand how this belief was formed. I am keeping two specimens of New Jersey tree toad (*Hyla versicolor*) in an adapted fish tank. They have a habit of calling out during and immediately before a rainstorm and can even be fooled into calling by sprinkling the plants with water. But while they rarely call when it is not raining, they are often severely silent even during a downpour.

Changes of weather conditions can be felt in old scars and fractures.

True. This statement, oft-repeated especially by veterans of former wars with old war wounds and amputations, and equally often doubted by others is, nevertheless, generally correct. A Hungarian physician by the name of Laszlo discovered the medical explanation. According to him, healthy tissue reacts to the humidity of the air. This in itself cannot be felt, but if the reaction is interrupted in some places by old scar tissue a very specific pain can be felt which is an indicator of changes in humidity which, in turn, indicate changes of weather. Removal of scar tissue often results in a loss of sensitivity.

Some people can feel an electrical storm coming long before the thunderheads roll up.

True. Repeated investigation of this phenomenon has failed to establish whether these people are actually sensitive to atmospheric electricity or whether they react to the changes in air pressure. But chances are that the changes in the air pressure are merely contributing factors.

People who feel bodily tension and hysteria during a thunderstorm are just victims of their imagination.

False. Again it is not definitely known whether they are actually sensitive to atmospheric electricity or to changes in air pressure but the feeling is not imaginary. The same behavior can be observed in certain wild and in some domesticated animals, especially dogs. My family once owned a large German shepherd dog which was usually very lovely and brave but shivered through every thunderstorm in the darkest corner of the sub-basement. No excitement of any kind could get her to leave the hiding place. After the thunderstorm she would appear by herself looking definitely sheepish and ashamed. Cats do not seem to be affected very much, but it is known that quite a number of animals — among them some very low in the evolutionary scale — show similar behavior. Since the actual events of a thunderstorm should not influence their habits of life the guess at sensitivity of some kind of atmospheric electricity seems justified.

This reminds me of a woman I knew who claimed to be able to see flashes of lightning before a storm actually broke. She was a sound sensible woman, but her claim seemed incredible.

Investigation of all the circumstances revealed that the flashes came only at mealtimes, and that they had begun right after she acquired a set of gold bridgework in her mouth. That was the clue.

It turned out she was extraordinarily fond of salads made with a dressing containing large amounts of vinegar, and that she used an old-fashioned steel fork to eat it with. She saw the flash every time the steel fork touched the bridgework. Apparently the touch of the two metals, steel and gold, in a highly acid setting, momentarily formed a small galvanic battery in her mouth which created the illusion of a flash of lightning. Since the phenomenon started up during the summer, thunderstorms were blamed.

When dogs eat grass it is going to rain.

False. When a dog eats grass it merely means that the dog has an upset stomach.

When swallows fly high the weather is going to remain beautiful; when they fly close to the ground a change can be expected.

Generally true. The scientific explanation is quite simple. Swallows eat insects of all kinds which they catch on the wing. During good weather periods the insects have a tendency to fly fairly high, up to one hundred to two hundred feet. When the air cools off because of an approaching cold front bringing rain the insects come down to weather the storm in their hideouts. We are not able to see the insects, but we are able to see the birds. The time interval between the flying low of insects and swallows and the beginning of bad weather is often short, however.

When the groundhog emerges on groundhog day and sees his shadow he gets frightened, goes back into hibernation and there will be another six weeks of winter.

False. The groundhog has other things to think about.

One of the primary factors influencing the weather is the moon.

False. It has been claimed that the atmospheric tides caused by the moon influence the movement of warm or cold fronts. It has also been claimed that the majority of all electrical storms occur at high tide. Both these claims could not be proved and it can now be taken for granted the lunar influences — if any — are so feeble that purely local factors can upset them at any time. The only major influence of the moon is on the tides.

Lightning never strikes twice in the same place.

False. But the saying is so deeply rooted by now that I have heard it repeated by people who only hours before pointed to an old blasted oak tree standing outside the village on a small hill, telling me that it was struck by lightning every summer.

There is one beach near New York City where lightning has struck the same spot repeatedly — and on occasion killed bathers — so that the suspicion has been entertained that this spot may mark the site of a buried mass of meteoric iron.

Tall buildings, like the Empire State Building, run up an impressive record of being struck by lightning every year. The saying is therefore not only untrue, but is considerably more truthful when reversed. Lightning shows a tendency to strike again and again at landmarks of any sort which are electrically exposed.

Item "B" below is a new way of displaying an old subject. It sold to this market for two reasons: the usable chart (pages 253-254) in which it appears and the stressing of the economy angle. The article was written by a student, who drew on information available in various works of reference. The student made no original contribution, but did present the information in such a form that it could be tacked to the wall for quick reference.

Stains	Silks, Rayons, Woolens	Linens, Cottons
Alcoholic beverages	Sponge with a mixture of two parts water and one part denatured alcohol. Pour glycerine on the stain and rub between the hands. Let stand half an hour and rinse with water.	Soak in alcohol and water solution about 20 minutes. Wash as usual.
Blood	Sponge with cold water. If stain is old and dried, salt added to the water helps (2 cups of salt to 1 gallon of water).	Soak in cold water. Wash in warm sudsy water.
Chewing gum	Sponge with carbon tetrachloride.	Soak in carbon tetrachloride and wash as usual.
Chocolate, Cocoa	Sponge with carbon tetrachloride. Dry thoroughly. Sponge with water and dust with pepsin powder, work powder in, let stand for 30 minutes. Sponge again with warm water.	Regular laundering will usually remove it.
Coffee With Cream	Sponge with lukewarm water. Apply glycerine and rub lightly between the hands. Let stand for half an hour. Rinse with warm water. In addition, sponge with carbon tetrachloride.	Pour boiling water from a height of 2 or 3 feet. Wash in warm soapy water.
Fingernail Polish	Wet with carbon tetrachloride. Apply a drop of banana oil. Brush lightly with a soft cloth using an upward motion to pick up the dissolved polish.	Sponge with acetone.
Grease	Make a paste of cornstarch and carbon tetrachloride. Spread it over the spot. When dry brush off. Repeat if necessary.	Wash in warm sudsy water. Use plenty of soap on the stain and rub well. Soapless shampoos are good to soften grease spots. If spot persists, dip into carbon tetrachloride.
Lipstick	Work vaseline into the stain. Sponge with carbon tetrachloride.	Loosen stain with glycerine. Launder as usual.
Ink	If stain is still wet, sprinkle cornstarch, salt or talcum to remove excess ink and keep it from spreading. Work into	Pour glycerine or soapless shampoo on stain (as quickly as possible). Rub lightly between the hands. Rinse and repeat

Stains	Silks, Rayons, Woolens	Linens, Cottons
	stain. Shake off as it becomes soiled. Repeat several times. If stain still persists, make a paste of cornstarch and one part water to one part denatured alcohol. Allow to dry and brush off.	as long as any ink comes from the stain. Rinse with clear water. Wash as usual.
Iodine	Sponge with solution made of two parts water to one part denatured alcohol.	Soap and water will often remove the stain while it is fresh. Moisten with water and place in the sun.
Paints	Treat paint immediately. Scrape off as much as possible. Sponge with carbon tetrachloride. If paint is already hard, apply to both sides of the spot and allow it to soften.	If stain has dried, soften with vaseline and wash as usual with plenty of soap and water.
Perspiration	Sponge with warm water to which a few drops of vinegar has been added.	Same treatment . . . followed by thorough laundering.
Rouge	Sponge with carbon tetrachloride. If stain persists, sponge with a solution of one part denatured alcohol and two parts water.	Loosen stain with glycerine. Launder as usual.
Smoke and Soot	Brush the stain, Sprinkle with corn meal or salt. Work it around until soiled. Brush it off, Sponge with carbon tetrachloride.	Brush the stain. Sprinkle with corn meal or salt. Work it around until soft. Brush it off. Launder as usual.
Tea	Sponge with lukewarm water. Apply glycerine and rub lightly between the hands. Let stand 30 minutes. Rinse out with water.	Pour boiling water from a distance of 2 or 3 feet over the stain. Launder.
Tomato Juice and Catsup	Sponge the stain with cold water. Work glycerine into the spot, and let stand for 30 minutes. Rinse out with water.	Soak in cold water. Apply glycerine and let stand 30 minutes. Wash as usual.
Water Spots	Dampen entire material evenly, either by sponging with clean water, or by shaking in the steam from a briskly boiling teakettle. Press while still damp.	Cottons and linens are not spotted by water.

B.

ON THE SPOT[19]

If It Can Be Removed at
Home, a Trip to the Dry
Cleaners May Be Avoided

———————

By Irene Johnson

The first element that enters into the successful removal of stain is speed. The longer you wait, the more difficult it becomes to remove.

Many of the ingredients suggested here as stain removers — cornstarch, corn meal, salt, vinegar, and vaseline — are already in the home. All of the others can be secured at any local drug store at a small cost.

If it is possible to discover what caused the stain, it will, of course, be easier to find out what will remove it. Work promptly.

Before attempting to remove any stain, however, always experiment on an unexposed area of the garment. A good place to do this is on the inside seams or under part of the hem. The test will decide whether the original color will stand up under the effects of the stain remover, and whether the fabric is strong enough.

Training Steps

1. Classify each of three consecutive issues of *Reader's Digest* separately by types of articles. What generalizations can you make from your analysis?
2. Similarly, examine three issues of *Woman's Day*. Compare your findings with those of Training Step 1.
3. Read carefully several confession articles from *The Atlantic* or *Harper's Magazine*. Now read several in *True Story Magazine* or a similar magazine. Write a 300-word analysis, stating all the differences you found.
4. Examine the various lists of article types to be found in the following texts:

   Bird, George L. *Modern Article Writing*, Chapter 14.
   Bond, F. Frazer, *How to Write and Sell Non-Fiction*. See chapter titles 6 to 9 inclusive.
   Brennecke, Jr., Ernest, and Clark, Donald L., *Magazine Article Writing*. See chapter titles 13 to 20 inclusive.
   Patterson, Helen M., *Writing and Selling Special Feature Articles*. See chapter titles 3 to 8, inclusive.
   Which list most perfectly meets your needs? This one should be the basis for your filing system.

———————

[19]Reprinted by permission of *The Woman* and the author.

5. Study several issues of *Life* and *Look*. Do their articles fall completely into distinct types? Or do the same articles belong in part to different types?

6. Which one of the other seven types (see page 195) does the process article resemble?

7. What percentage of essays do you find in your general reading of articles?

8. How many personality or character sketches do you find in an average issue of *Reader's Digest*? Of *Harper's Magazine*?

9. Study a number of process articles in *Woman's Day*. At what income group are they slanted? What educational level?

10. How would you state the differences between a confession and a narrative in the first person?

11. To what type do most humorous articles belong?

12. What type of article has the clearest-cut pattern? What variations do you find in this type? Examine a number of articles before answering.

13. Examine several issues of *This Week*. What types of articles predominate? Compare and contrast with articles appearing in the *Christian Science Monitor*.

14. Compare *Air Progress* with *Popular Mechanics Magazine*. Is there any type of article used by both magazines?

15. Compare *Music Trades* with *Music Journal* and *Musical America*. Do you find any evidence of specialization by types? By subject matter?

16. Prepare complete inventories of at least one article of each of the types cited in this chapter.

17. Prepare your own outlines from these inventories, and then compare them with those used by the various writers. How do they differ? Do you find any parts of these articles upon which you could improve?

CHAPTER 15

Techniques for Humanization

Facts are the stuff of which articles are made. But facts are likely to be dull unless a deliberate effort is made to brighten them. Even when an article is a prosaic explanation of how-to-do-something, the readers understand a great deal more if the article has been subjected to a "humanizing" process.

In earlier chapters emphasis was placed upon simple writing. The writer was urged to use short words, short sentences, and short paragraphs. Out of such writing the meaning flows with greater ease. Simple writing is good writing, and it needs no apologies.

Articles Need Sparkle

But in addition to simplicity, writing needs something else. An article may be carefully done, but unless it is also interesting or entertaining, it is unlikely to sell. Readers who come with a long-time interest in the subject matter may wade through a heavy, poorly presented article, but they would enjoy it more if it were entertaining. Most readers, whatever their interest, are ready to drop any article that lacks the sparkle of life.

It is not the presence of scientific and technical terms alone that kills off readers. These can be controlled by deft explanation. Rather, it is the lack of glamour or romance, and by this one does not mean love interest. A writer must first believe his own subject to be interesting and picturesque or glamourous. This inner feeling should find expression in his choice of vocabulary, through which the same feeling will be conveyed to his readers. Without this feeling many an otherwise excellent article will prove unmarketable.

The extent to which humanizing must be carried out will depend upon the type of readers to which the article is addressed. *Popular Mechanics Magazine* demands one type, *Reader's Digest* a second, and *The Atlantic* a third. Do not make the mistake of believing that readers of the intellectual *Atlantic* are prepared to digest endless data. They are not. Highly educated though the readers may be, they come to the more literary magazines expecting entertainment — and *clarity*.

Requirements of the prospective market must always be kept in mind. The extensive humanizing necessary at the level of *True Story Magazine* would ruin a manuscript for *The Atlantic*. The degree of education and sophistication of the reader is always important. The devices illustrated below should be used, therefore, with judgment and discernment.

Using the "You" Factor

Among the most valuable techniques for making an idea appear important to a reader is to show how it affects him — if it does. Scores of magazine articles deal with subjects that more or less directly affect the reader's health, his business and social interests, or his family and home.

Such articles may or may not make use of the term "you" as in direct address. This latter is a useful technique to attract the reader's attention, but showing how an idea affects a reader goes far beyond mere address.

If, for example, a certain city government proposes to raise the tax rate by 15 mills, the local newspaper could show how it would affect local citizens in terms of a percentage of the old rate. If the percentage were applied to various classes of homes — $5,000 to $10,000, $11,000 to $20,000, etc. — the reader could tell roughly at a glance how much it would cost him without figuring it out for himself. This humanizing would be of considerable help to that high proportion of newspaper readers who cannot figure percentages.

An article on inflation could be made far more impressive by showing explicitly how it affects the items every reader buys — his food, his clothes, his rent, his luxuries. The analysis should be carried as far and made as exact as possible. Thus, the increase on a pound of meat, a loaf of bread, or a pair of shoes might be presented.

Inclusion of the "you" factor is not to be confused with slanting. An article aimed at *Successful Farming* may be correctly slanted for that magazine stylistically and typographically, as well as being written with an understanding of the rural point of view, without development of the "you" factor. Consider an example. A writer could deal with a high protective tariff on imports by showing how it would affect the agricultural population as a whole. But the article would lack humanizing unless the writer introduced the "you" factor by showing the cost of the tariff to the individual farmer.

By means of the "you" factor the writer tries to show how forces or situations affect the individual rather than large or small groups.

Tying to a News Item

One of the oldest and still one of the best devices to arouse interest is to tie an article to a "news peg," an event recently reported by newspaper or radio. The device is as good as the news item was important. It will stir the reader in proportion to the degree to which he was moved by the item itself.

An article on fire or storm insurance can be tied to a recent disaster important enough to have attracted wide interest. The writer usually does not have to look far to find such an occurrence. Names of cities, localities, public buildings, and important individuals involved help the reader recall his earlier impressions. Since most events of this type have affected the life and welfare of numbers of human beings or of landmarks which individuals have made important, readers will be moved by the emotional content of the old reference. The writer must seek out news items in which this element is high. They are usually better if quite recent and if they were of widespread interest when first reported.

The defeat of a long-time politician can be tied to an article on the rise and fall of political careers; a bad fire in a state or national park, to an article on fire prevention; the accidental death of a well-known personality, to a need for a national campaign to prevent accidents; or the recent preservation of the birthplace of a national hero, to the neglect of scores of others. For illustrations of this point see Chapter 18.

It would be difficult to ascertain the number of times the sinking of the *Titanic* or the Johnstown flood have been used by writers. These references are hoary with age but still of value. In most cases the writer should not turn back more than a few months for news events upon which he intends to put heavy reliance. The old sensational stories must be kept in minor roles. Old news is history. The best references are to current affairs.

Photographs Add Human Interest

The use of photographs for illustrative purposes has been discussed in Chapter 11. It is the intent here to emphasize their use in humanizing abstract and difficult subjects. The simplest and easiest way to do this is to use photographs of individuals. Such photographs should be interesting in themselves and of high photographic excellence. They are best when they tell a story or show the individuals in action — at work or play.

A picture of a complicated machine is more interesting if it shows someone pointing to a particular part, perhaps to a new gadget. The presence of all or part of the human figure enables the beholder to get a more accurate idea of size. And it is especially helpful to show a good model actually operating the machine. Add a human figure whenever possible. The picture of a drifting farm in the Oklahoma dust bowl was made more pathetic by the presence of the disheartened farmer.

Second in interest to photographs of human beings are those of animals. Any attempt to list them in order of importance would lead to controversy. Usually animals rank according to intimacy of their contact with human beings. The dog, the cat, the horse — particularly the young of the species — all rank high. Everyone recognizes, of course, that the most universally appealing photographs are those of the human infant. When proper use is made of them, they cannot be surpassed.

Using Graphic Illustration

As with photographs, charts and diagrams should be used to explain and to illustrate difficult points. The hand-drawn chart or pictograph often can make clear a situation that could be explained in no other way for the average reader. Such devices bring complicated relationships down to his level. To make the charts or pictographs effective, be

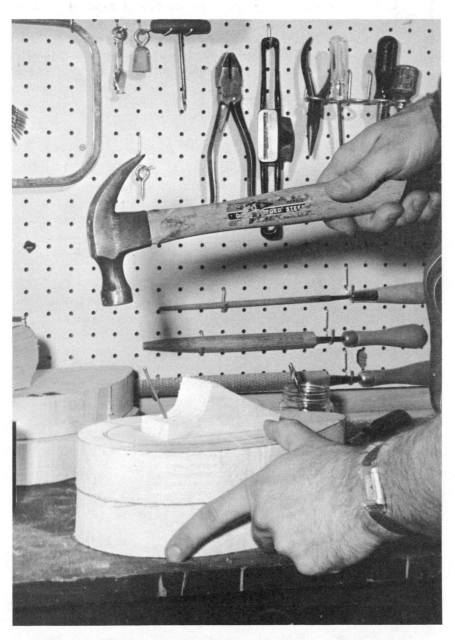

Illustration 13 — Hands may be photographed in close-ups to aid explanations. This is an excellent device to show relative size of objects. Accurate focusing is necessary so that every detail will be entirely clear. (Photo by Nicholas Karas)

Illustration 14 — Still life photographs can make an article come to life without human beings if the quality of the print and the appeal of the subject are high enough, as in this illustration. (Photo by Denis L. Rettew)

Illustration 15 — Children in action, like pups, are irresistible. The faces seem to tell a story, but the fact that they story is not clear makes little difference. The wide, grinning faces are satisfying in themselves. (Photo by Bob Kerns)

sure that they show how their subject matter affects human beings. Also in such graphic illustrations make frequent use of the human figure, and strive for simplicity.

What happens when such charts are drawn is that their creator does the thinking for the reader. The former analyzes, eliminates, rearranges, and simplifies. He drives his brain and hand in order that the reader may have an easier time. Above all he tries to show the facts in their relation to his readers.

The writer should never lose sight of the fact that logical thinking is not a natural process, but one that is acquired — and that but rarely. Whenever possible, mankind avoids thinking. Articles must carry their meaning on the surface if they are to be understood, for the average reader will not dig deeply or puzzle out an obscure paragraph. To befuddle a reader is to lose him. Writing must be simple, clear, and

Illustration 16 — The introduction of figures in the foreground, preferably not facing the camera, greatly improves the interest in scenic pictures. Trees, rocks, and other landscape objects also can be used in this way. (Photo by William Polis)

interesting. Charts and diagrams that yield their meaning at a glance will humanize difficult spots for lazy readers.

Casting in Story Form

Cast your material in story form if you want to make it interesting. Tales of adventure are always interesting. Among the subjects easily handled in this manner are camping and canoe trips, bicycle hikes, fishing trips, travels abroad, or unusual types of travel in the United States. Instead of telling how to do these things, tell how somebody has done them. Use hypothetical individuals if necessary.

It is posible to make a story out of almost any connected series of events — baking a cake, making a dress, remodeling a house, buying a farm, living in a trailer, an unusual operation, and thousands of other events.

When the story form is used, it is possible to introduce dramatic suspense, dialogue, climax, characterization, and other narrative techniques. By developing an element of suspense or mystery in the title and beginning, it is possible to hold the reader's attention. The form is not difficult. A simple narrative of how something was done or accomplished is all that is required. This is an advantage that the how-it-was-done article has over the how-to-do-something type. The first also has a greater ring of truth and credibility.

Storytelling comes naturally to most people. When it comes to putting the events on paper, merely set them down as if you were talking to a good friend. Don't try to be stylish or literary. Just be natural.

Using Rhetorical Devices

PLAYING UP ONE ANGLE. A number of rhetorical devices lend themselves easily to the article writer. One is playing up a single aspect of a subject, or an individual, as representative of a group. The rest of the material is subordinated. This involves the processes of selection. The writer picks out certain elements to discuss; he omits others.

Suppose a person is doing an article on college education. Obviously, the subject is broad enough for an entire book, as has actually been demonstrated more than once. The writer must carefully choose a few points to emphasize, and he must ignore the rest. Generally he accomplishes this by selecting a single phase of the broader subject.

Another example would be the taking of the high cost of medical treatment in one area as typical of general conditions within the country. A study of crime in one city slum could be used to illustrate what could be expected in similar areas in other cities. Good judgment and common sense should be exercised to keep the conclusions within the bounds of reason.

STATISTICAL BREAKDOWNS. A second of these devices is to break down the data or statistics to show how they work or how they were compiled. An example of this process is to be found above under the discussion of the "you" factor. Lump sums are impressive, but they are not easily comprehended. If a drive is being made on behalf of a community chest or other civic welfare agency, a goal might be set at $1,500,000. This would appear to many individuals to be a huge sum to spend on charity. But a breakdown showing how it goes to perhaps 50 different agencies would alter the picture. Then, further breakdowns to tell how the various agencies spend their budgets would make the whole campaign sound more reasonable.

Similarly, a city budget would appear huge until broken down. So would the cost of a battleship until partial enumeration was presented of the items that go into making such a ship. Large figures generally can be made more understandable by translating them into simpler terms. If the federal government were sending 25,000,000 pounds of butter abroad for relief of starving peoples, it would appear like a tremendous figure. But translated, it is less than one pound per American family, or less than half a week's supply for the entire country. Anyone can comprehend this last fact.

Few taxpayers grasp the significance of a national debt of 352 billion dollars. But considerably more can understand when you write that this sum means about $1833 for every man, woman, and child in the United States. Such translations must be accurate, and they must be easier to understand than the original figures.

CONTRAST. Contrast is a third rhetorical device for popularizing situations. Frequently used by magazines in the "before" and "after" series, it appears in descriptive passages on alterations of homes, as well as in photographs of the same. Any situation that has been changed by time, such as old landmarks, or familiar buildings, or those that *could* be changed — all lend themselves to development by contrast.

The device of contrast may be applied also to individals. You may contrast a student entering college for the first time with the same individual as he graduates four years later. You may contrast medical education of the 80's with modern medical training. Keep the contrast brief and to the point.

PERSONIFICATION. Personification is the fourth rhetorical device for humanization. Speakers and writers naturally tend to attribute life to inanimate objects. A ship is often referred to as "she," but seldom as "it."

Generally such comparisons should be used briefly and then dropped. If the comparison is a natural one, so much the better. Everyone has seen human beings who suggest some animal, such as the heavy-jowled individual who suggests a mastiff. Used with a swift, sure hand, such touches make interesting what otherwise would be colorless and inert.

Localized Interviews

Interviewing is a particularly good method to use in writing features for local newspapers, or for magazines with a limited sectional circulation. It is also excellent for magazines of national circulation when the person interviewed has a wide reputation. It calls for skill in interviewing, while the individual interviewed must also be interesting, occupy an important position, or be possessed of vital information.

The writer chooses for the subject of the interview some sort of formal report, a newspaper dispatch, or an idea of his own. It might be on a national housing program, how to combat juvenile delinquency, or a new medical discovery. Subjects that can be handled this way are without number.

For a local newspaper feature one or more outstanding individuals are chosen. In every community are some who make good "copy." Your choice may be the mayor, chief of police, a colorful minister, a teacher, an old settler, a merchant, a scientist, or an inventor. A symposium interview that incorporates the ideas of a number of individuals is particularly effective, because each of the names themselves adds to the news value of the interview.

Most magazines demand a somewhat different type of interview. They want expressions of opinion from those who are authorities in the field under discussion. University or industrial scientists and experts are among the best sources of good quotable material.

Some extremely good interviews may be based on the opinions of the man-in-the-street. If you want to know what people think of prefabricated homes, for instance, you would certainly wish to talk to those who have lived in them, as well as to experts in building. The effects of inflation are not to be learned alone from economists and statisticians, but also from the men and women who do the daily buying and know at first-hand what inflation has done to their expenditures.

Humor Is an Aid

Anecdotes and the manufactured joke have an important place in humanizing difficult material. Neither should be used, as many after-dinner jokes are, merely to create a receptive mood. They should be used only when the point has an obvious bearing on the facts at hand. Their purpose is the same as that of the parable — to illuminate swiftly a complicated situation in a way that will be remembered.

ANECDOTES. By anecdotes we mean the story of true incidents in the life of an individual. Anecdotes have a wider usage than jokes. They are less likely to grow stale before they appear in print, less likely to have been heard already, and less likely to appear as if dragged in by the heels. Anecdotes make excellent beginnings for interviews, as well as for other article types. They also provide quotable phrases for title and subtitle.

They are best when they concern the individuals mentioned in the article. Anecdotes about historical figures or figures prominent in current affairs may be used if their application is apparent. Calvin Coolidge's remark that he did not "choose to run" again for the presidency, or Franklin D. Roosevelt's observation on one of the crises in Herbert Hoover's administration that it was not "his baby" are of the type with wide application.

JOKES. Jokes are difficult to handle. They depend usually upon the element of freshness for effectiveness. Few people care to hear the same joke twice. Yet it is exceedingly difficult to uncover anything new in jokes. If the writer is truly adept, he may rework an old joke until it appears new, though the results will seldom justify the expenditure of time and energy.

Typical Example

Typical examples may be either real or fictional, and the latter are often more effective than the first. Suppose the article is one attempting to persuade home owners to remodel waste space in the basement into a rumpus room. The writer should discover two or three families that have accomplished the feat, and then should present their experiences. These examples prove the workability of the plan and introduce personalities into the article. The experience of the particular families can be used to show what should or should not be done in the process of converting the basement.

Articles can point to actual homes, farms, and workshops and stores to show what examples A and B and C have done or are doing. The exact details introduced from these instances give conviction. Readers are more interested in what people have done than in what the writer believes they should do.

Fictional examples, as indicated earlier, may excel. Various methods are available for using them. A writer may say, "Take a typical home-owner"; or "Consider an average case"; or, "A common example is the man," etc. The number of variations on this technique run into the hundreds. The "young Johnnie" and "Mary" who appear in so many articles are often creatures of the writer's imagination. It is generally considered best to let the reader know when fictional examples are used.

The Case Method

The case method, a variation of the typical example, has been used annually during the Christmas season by the Sunday edition of *The New York Times* for years in presenting its "Hundred Neediest Cases." A generalized introductory statement precedes this type of development. It is followed by short, terse individual explanations of each case. The technique can be adapted to fit a variety of circumstances.

It has frequently been used in the development of books. Such works contain considerable explanatory material, and the cases are generally used to illustrate specific points. Numerous variations of this type of development will be found in magazines and newspapers. Other forms can be developed to meet unusual circumstances.

Training Steps

1. Examine any two copies of *The Atlantic* and *True*. How do they differ in the extent to which humanizing is carried out within the articles?
2. Examine copies of *Harper's Magazine* and *Esquire*. Which has the simpler style? The greater human interest content?
3. What is meant by the "you" factor? Does it differ from direct address? If so, how?
4. What is the special advantage of using a "news peg"? Run through an issue of *Reader's Digest*. How many articles grew out of news items?
5. Why are photographs with human beings in them usually more appealing than photographs of mere scenery? Which type tells a better story?
6. Study issues of *Fortune* and *Time*. Are there pictures in these magazines that suggest similar illustrations for your own articles?
7. Quickly run through issues for the same month of *American Home* and *Better Homes and Gardens*. How many articles are told in story form in each?
8. Can you cite examples of personification from your reading?
9. Write five paragraphs personifying each one of the following: an automobile, a schooner, a large city, a locomotive, a building.
10. Select ten subjects from a Sunday newspaper or from a magazine like *Time*. Name three local individuals whom it would be logical to interview concerning each.
11. Why are anecdotes better than jokes for humanizing difficult facts?
12. How many articles in any issue of *Reader's Digest* make use of anecdotes? Of jokes?
13. Name some of the standard fictional characters used by article writers.
14. Study the magazines for examples of the case method. What kinds of beginnings are used with them?
15. What type of humanization does the *Engineering News-Record* use? *American Motorist?*
16. Rank the following newspapers in order of humanization: *The New York Times,* Chicago *Daily News,* St. Louis *Globe-Democrat,* Kansas City *Star.*

CHAPTER 16

What Business Magazines Need

Business and trade publications are devoted to the gathering and printing of helpful ideas in specialized fields, some of which are represented by a score of magazines. One writer's market guide lists 74 different businesses and trades, each represented by a number of publications. The total number is in excess of 1,500, circulated within at least 200 different businesses and trades monthly, weekly, or daily.

A few examples will indicate the type of publications with which this chapter is concerned. Among them are *American Restaurant Hospitality*, *Bankers Monthly*, *American Drycleaner*, *Chain Store Age*, *Drug Topics*, *Electricity on the Farm Magazine*, *Flower Grower*, *Successful Grocer*, *Hardware Age*, and *Furniture Digest*. Anyone aspiring to a part-time or full-time career in article writing should obtain a writer's market guide and acquaint himself with the extensive opportunities offered by these publications.

Opportunities and Rewards

Because of the numerous publications in this field, the opportunities for staff positions are excellent. These usually go to trained writers who have demonstrated their abilities, and the best type of demonstration is the production of a number of worthwhile articles. If a writer seriously contemplates trying to join a staff, he should become expert in the field of his choice. The greater his knowledge and experience, the higher are his chances of success. It is not the purpose of this chapter to set forth the route to a job, but how to write for business and trade publications. Ideas that are marketable in these magazines also can be placed with local or other newspapers if the writer can develop the right contacts.

Before turning to the specific purpose of trade publications, let us look at the rewards for the free-lance writer who does not aspire to a permanent position as a staff member.

As in all lines of work, the greatest rewards go to the hardest workers. The man who turns out the greatest number of acceptable articles will earn the highest rewards. Any writer who is willing to work hard, if he can turn out good work, should be able to earn a comfortable living. That means staying "on the job" and producing a steady stream of articles. Generally, it is easier to sell consistently in the trade field than in any other.

Rates usually start at about two cents a word; few periodicals pay less. Some pay so much an inch. Shorter articles pay higher word rates than longer articles, while rates on the items called shorts are the highest. Many students studying under this author have been paid as much as 25 cents a word for these shorts. Rates also go up for regular contributors. The writer will naturally send most of his work to the better-paying markets.

Purposes of Publications

It is necessary to understand the purposes of trade and business publications if a fair amount of success is to be achieved. Their aims and point of view should be as familiar to the writer as their requirements.

This group exists for the gathering and printing of helpful ideas. Each represents a trade or skill pursued for the making of a profit. Therefore the periodicals of the merchant, the druggist, and the plumber are devoted to helping them earn a living. The readers of such publications differ from those of the general and class publications whose subscribers seek either entertainment or ideas to make life more comfortable and pleasant.

Business and trade journals are on the lookout for new plans, policies, ideas, and methods likely to increase the income of their readers.

They are, therefore, purely commercial in nature. Their second purpose is to provide a medium in which may be advertised products and services peculiar to each field. A study of such advertising will tell much about the ideas likely to interest these markets.

Why Business Articles Are Rejected

Let us consider the special reasons why some business articles are not salable and why some are rejected by this type of publication. First, the basic idea may be an old one. This is an active field, and the chances for a good idea to bloom unseen are slight. Second, the idea may be poorly written. Generally this means it is difficult to understand — that it has not been humanized. Third, it may put too much stress on trade names, thereby turning the item into publicity for one firm at the expense of others. Fourth, the writer may have selected the wrong market. A better choice might have meant a sale. Fifth, the article may not appear to be exclusive. Most trade publications expect exclusive rights to what they buy. Exceptions must be specially arranged. Sixth, they may not be the right length. Finally, the wrong ideas may have been stressed. Because of inexperience, the writer may have played up minor ideas and subordinated more important facts.

A factor that makes it easy to sell ideas is that writers do not have to originate the ideas. The writer is a reporter, who uncovers interesting facts about other people's work and puts them into article form. He is responsible for the accuracy of his reporting, but not for creating the facts.

Business articles to be salable must be accurately and carefully handled. They must tell something new and be well written; they must present ideas rather than publicity; they must reach the right market in an exclusive article; and they must present the facts according to their relative importance. All this is not as large an order as it might appear. Simple, methodical writing will eventually bring success to the person who persists in this field.

Training and Experience

Writers with newspaper training, or those who have gained other experience in reporting, already have a good start toward success in business and trade writing, though there are other routes to a career in this field. Anyone who can recognize new ideas, gather the facts accurately, and set them down simply, can learn to do everything else demanded by these publications.

Of primary importance is a fundamental knowledge of business and business methods. Books on store management, merchandising, buying, personnel management, and related problems will give the beginner considerable help. This text takes it for granted that an ambitious writer will dig himself into the field of his choice by reading the necessary literature. This consists of books, manuals, pamphlets, and current literature. The writer will naturally read regularly all magazines related to his field. Such reading will aid him in becoming acquainted with standard practices and methods, as well as with the problems faced by his prospective readers. Eventually he will come to recognize the old and established, as well as the innovations around which he will build his articles.

There is no complete substitute for experience gained from employment in trade or business. Men and women who have office or trade experience, other things being equal, will recognize new ideas and put the right importance upon them. Lacking business experience or training, a writer must study the literature, garner what experience he can, and rely upon trustworthy businessmen and tradespeople who know of what they talk.

This borrowing of brains and experience is one of the tricks of successful article writing. The writer, like the newspaper reporter, tells little of his own exploits, but much about those of other people. The article writer must also learn to employ his subjects to check the facts, so that he will be safeguarded against error. It is an excellent idea to ask his tradesman or businessman to read the article before he submits it to an editor. A note on the cover page of the article stating that the article has been read and approved by such critics will give the editor greater confidence in a beginner's work.

Salable News Items

Salable items fall into two groups: a. news and b. articles based on successful ideas.

News items fall into several groups. They may be classified as merchandising news, spot news, personal news, opinion, and general news.

MERCHANDISING EVENTS. These items are concerned with the promotion and sale of retail merchandise of whatever kind. Typical examples are special sales events, such as department-store sales of unusual

stocks of imported goods or sales tied to dates of local historical importance. The article will usually be brief, and it will consist of the event
or sale, plus the idea used to promote the sale.

SPOT ITEMS. These may be considered as the type that happens
to a business rather than occurring because of anything the business
does. Among the types are legislative acts, interstate commerce rulings,
city ordinances, and actions of chambers of commerce. The more widespread the effect of the regulation or event, the greater the interest
to trade journals. The core of such articles is an interpretation of the
significance of the event.

PERSONAL NEWS. Personal news consists of items concerning the
personnel of business and trade. The general manager of a Cincinnati
department store becomes general manager for a larger Chicago firm.
That is news. An employee starts his own business. That is likewise
news. In the latter case, if John Jones plans to start his own store, he is
obviously a prospective customer for a dozen or more firms that
advertise in the trade journals. All personal items must be tied to an
event of widespread interest. News of the individual's family or his own
personal affairs is of no interest to other businessmen.

OPINION. News of opinion is gathered through one or more interviews. If the federal government orders employers to increase old-age
pension (social security) deductions, the fact is news. Employers' opinions may be pro or con. A symposium of such opinion may make an
excellent article that an editor will welcome. The writer sees a story
in the new situation that will develop, and he obtains it by searching
out experts whose businesses are likely to be affected.

GENERAL NEWS. This classification includes such items as change of
location, a move to larger quarters, addition of new lines or departments, improvements in equipment and building, and new store openings. They are important items to watch for, and are easy to handle.
The local newspapers can be scanned for hints on what may happen
in this field. Chambers of commerce, boards of trade, city engineering
offices, and similar sources frequently yield tips on such coming events.
Many items can be picked up by watching shop windows.

Successful Innovations

The second type of salable ideas includes successful trade and business innovations. These are merchandising ideas that actually have
helped to sell goods. They may be either big or little ideas, but they
must have been successful. They constitute the easiest type of material

to sell, for they are much in demand by nearly every business publication. Although they vary in length from a few score words to perhaps 2,000, they invariably are tied to some phase of the selling program. Unless a writer has a definite order or request from an editor, he should keep his article under 850 words. The business short runs from 100 to 250 words. More of them are published in this field than all other types of articles combined.

Minor items, such as an unusual window display, should be handled as shorts. Special sales events, including unusual local celebrations, also fall in this class.

Major store policies are worth more space. These should be handled in from 300 to 850 words, depending on their importance. Such articles call for one or more interviews with store or business officials. Often they must be checked after being written to make certain the writer understood correctly.

Need for Illustrations

Good illustrations are as essential in this field of business articles as in any other. Photographs are most common, though tables and charts may also help to illuminate business trends. Frequently the photographs may be borrowed from the advertising department of the firm mentioned in the article. The value of the free advertising more than repays the cost of the photographs. Also when photographs are not already on hand, the firm may be glad to have them taken at their own expense. If the photographs are merely loaned by the owners, the writer should be sure to return them. A tactful handling of the matter may save the writer considerable expense, as well as preserve a source of future news.

Some magazines prefer photographs of individuals. Others use only dramatic photographs that tell the story back of the successful sales innovation. Magazine policy on this point is fairly easy to ascertain through a study of back copies. The writer should make this survey and then try to duplicate what the magazine uses. If expensive photographs must be taken, it is wise to wait until the article has been accepted. Usually it is possible to state in advance of the sale what photographs can be supplied if requested.

Photographs should be keyed to the article. They should illustrate some phase of the idea about which the article is written. The more striking they are the better. Informal snapshots of individuals may be better for some magazines than commercial portraits. The suitable type of photograph can be determined through a study of the prospective market.

Other good illustrative material may be provided by window cards, advertisements, letters, various forms, post cards, or counter-display signs.

Writing the Article

The business and trade article is not so difficult to write as some other types. It consists of a single, central idea, instead of several ideas, and consequently has a simple structure. The style is also simple, and conversational in tone.

Assuming that a successful idea has been uncovered by the writer, the first step in writing is to ask what would readers wish to know about the idea in order to apply it in their own business. They would also want to know how successful it had been. This step makes it necessary for the writer to put himself in the place of the reader. The act is likely to be difficult unless the writer knows something of the reader's business. This insight should be acquired if the writer intends to devote his entire time to this type of article. A good substitute is to outline the idea to a businessman or tradesman, and then ask him what he would like to know about it.

The second step is to outline or arrange in a logical order the various points to be covered. Steps in outlining have already been set down in Chapter 8. However, nothing should be included that does not bear upon the sales plan. If two or more major ideas are involved, then more than one article should be written.

In the third step the writer simply sets down the answers to the questions his prospective reader would want to ask. The first paragraph or paragraphs should either summarize the entire article, or tell as interestingly as possible what the article is about. This paragraph must convince the editor that the article will be valuable to his readers. The beginning should be followed by a more elaborate statement of what the idea is. This is followed by an elaboration of how the plan works. Here the writer gives all the necessary details.

The last step is the rewriting and condensation. In no other field is condensation so necessary. Few articles should be over 1,000 words. Many a 1,000-word article rejected because of too great length would sell if reduced to 250 or even 100 words. Every bit of padding must be cut. The article must present the facts, and nothing else.

No substitute can be found for a systematic study of the publications themselves. The length and type of article printed are the best guide to what is wanted. Although a writer ignorant of what is really desired can sell an occasional article, he will run into far too many rejections. In the end he is likely to become discouraged by his failures — so much so as to give up what might have been a successful career.

The Business Interview

Since the interview is the basis of all trade and business articles, its principle should be understood. The interview is the medium through which a writer gathers facts on an idea already uncovered. In his hunting for such ideas, the writer will of necessity ask a variety of questions. These will be directed toward finding ideas and in making certain that they are new. He may talk to a half dozen individuals before turning up a single new idea. All this is not interviewing. The interview starts when the writer sits down with a store manager, a shop owner, or a businessman, and begins to ask leading questions about an idea already uncovered.

The first step in interviewing precedes the actual interview, determining whether the idea is new and successful. The writer simply asks whether the idea is original with the firm using it. If it is not new or if its success is still in doubt, then the idea is not stable. And the writer should not seek an interview.

The second step is to learn who is responsible for the idea, or its being put into successful operation. The idea may have originated with a sales person, but he would be a minor person to interview. The major interview would come with the department manager, the advertising manager, the store manager, or some other responsible official whose words carry weight.

On occasions these people may decline to grant an interview. If their reasons can be learned, the writer may be able to overcome their objections. Some people fear what the writer may say. An offer to permit them to check the article for accuracy will frequently dissipate their fears. Other ways can be found to change their minds. But when this can't be done, the idea should be dropped. To persist is to waste valuable time.

The interview should be informal. In fact, don't call it an interview. Merely ask if you may talk to so-and-so about his new counter display. Keep your pencil and paper out of sight as much as possible. Ask as many questions on the subject as you need, but arrange to call back if that should become necessary. The conversation must be *steered* by the writer, or his executive may wander from the point until the interview is over.

The main thing to remember is to find out how this idea differs from other similar ideas. Remember, there is absolutely nothing new in merchandising or manufacturing. Every "new" idea is only a variation on an old one. If eventually you decide the idea is not new, keep the businessman as a friend. You will want to talk to him another day.

Training Steps

1. Take a walk through the main section of your city. How many general news items, such as the signs of business moving to new quarters, can you find?
2. Repeat Step 1 at a later date. What changes do you see? Explore these possibilities for articles.
3. Walk slowly through your favorite department store. Can you note any changes in method of stock display from what you formerly have seen?
4. In this same store can you see any change in location of stock? Can you tell from observation alone whether there is a salable idea back of it? If not, make appropriate inquiries.
5. Continue the walk. Do you see any unusual window displays? Are they original? If so, you have found a salable idea. Can you obtain illustrations?
6. What local businesses are engaged in enlarging their quarters? What type of salable news item is this?
7. Read an entire week's editions of the local newspaper. What tips for business articles do you find?
8. Visit six different drugstores. Study each carefully. What differences do you perceive in their sales methods? Is there an article in them? Try this method on other stores.
9. Can you find a neighborhood grocer surviving in the face of chain-store competition? What is the secret of his success? Probably this is a salable idea.
10. Watch for businesses started by former members of the armed services. Follow the local press. There may be salable articles in these new businesses.
11. What manufacturing concerns are building, moving, altering, or improving products? Use the formula given in this chapter, write the article, and send it to the proper market. Be sure to study the publication first.
12. Begin to get acquainted with business in your area. Learn who the leaders and inventive minds are. Watch their innovations and report them for the business and trade publications.

CHAPTER 17

Writing the Science Article

The scientist is about the only one left who asks why his field should be used by magazine and newspaper writers for purposes of popularization. His indifference or aversion usually stems from the fact that news of science has at times been badly handled. Also the unwritten principles of the professions stigmatize those scientists who become involved in sensational publicity. Scientific reputations have been blighted and careers ruined by too frequent appearance in the sensational press. Generally, the scientist's interests in publication extend no farther than his own professional magazines.

This lack of interest in publication in simple form accounts in part for what social scientists call "cultural lag." The lag, or difference between the date of an invention, discovery, or other innovation and its common acceptance, is greater in some fields of knowledge than in others. It is to be found in medicine, physics, chemistry, botany, biology, zoology, engineering, and geology — in fact, in every area of scientific investigation. Any lag, however great, represents a condition probably detrimental to the public. Actually, in many cases the public is not at fault, for the facts may have been buried under a mass of highly technical vocabulary in some scientific journal which the layman seldom, if ever, sees.

Dissemination Lags in Many Fields

Common examples of the lag in assimilation of scientific knowledge are seen in the unbalanced diet of great parts of the population, in absence of sanitary provisions in villages and rural areas, in antiquated sewage disposal systems in many larger towns, and lack of medical attention everywhere. Reasons other than ignorance contribute to this backwardness of great segments of the population, but lack of public knowledge, and hence public demand, contributes its full share.

Business Debt to Science

Modern business owes a tremendous debt to science. In fact, most businesses ultimately rest upon scientific investigation. Even distributive agencies, such as retail or department stores, depend both directly and indirectly upon scientific research. The same observations might be made in the field of government. Much, perhaps most, of the unwise legislation grows out of lack of scientific knowledge of the relationships of various causes and effects. There are few individuals who wouldn't be better for a more accurate and extensive knowledge of the available scientific facts in their field.

Any writer should be able to take considerable satisfaction in striking at each body of ignorance. To cut off a few years of cultural lag in some field of knowledge is no mean achievement. Nor is the general opportunity the scientific writer has to contribute to improvement of the social and aesthetic ideals of the country to be overlooked. This is the opportunity facing the writer, and it is as challenging as any existing elsewhere.

Advantageous Position of Writers

Writers, more than anyone else, are in position to promote the spread of scientific knowledge, for the greatest instrument for adult education is still the press. The hundreds of magazines and daily newspapers and the thousands of weekly newspapers are the chief field of adult reading and the source upon which adults draw for general information. If the coverage of scientific developments, innovations, and the consequences thereof is incomplete or inaccurate, the mass of readers must inevitably fall behind in knowledge of what is happening, and therefore be at a disadvantage.

Another reason for writing in this field is the fact that it is profitable. Competition is lower than in almost any other area of writing. Hence, opportunities to step from reporting of other types of news into reporting of news of science are particularly good. The newspapers and magazines alike are able to absorb far more well-written news of science than they receive. Except for a handful of well-known names, the writer coming into this field well trained would have exceedingly little competition.

Why Many Scientists Write Badly

There are two schools of thought on the question of what kind of training is best for the popularizer of scientific news. One holds that ability to write is sufficient. Belief of this school is based upon two assumptions: that scientists write badly because they know too much science and too many technical words; and that the fewer technical terms the writer knows the more able he is to write for the general public.

Both assumptions are fallacious. Some scientists write obscurely not because they know a special, technical vocabulary, but because they have never been trained to write simply. Writing clearly is an art that requires as much practice and intelligent thought as many of the laboratory techniques acquired by the scientists. Actually some of the simplest and finest writing has been done by such world-famed scientists as Fabre, Haldane, and Eisley. The assumption that a writer can do better work if the technical names and techniques are unknown to him is another way of saying that the writer can do the best work where he is the most ignorant.

Special Training in Science Required

The second school of thought holds that a thorough understanding of the basic principles of science plus special study in a limited area are necessary for a successful career. This latter point of view is generally considered to be the sounder. The basic training can be self-acquired, though it comes easier in the colleges and universities. It should include groundwork in chemistry, physics, and zoology. The broader this basic work is, the more likely the writer will be to understand the implications to the individual and society of whatever writing he later attempts to market.

Beyond the general training there should be additional work in whatever field the writer intends to make his specialty. For instance, the writer on agricultural problems should be acquainted with the science of agriculture as well as the ordinary practices of farming. The writer on health and medicine should certainly know modern theories on diet, exercise, rest, and have a good understanding of diagnosis and prescription. This does not imply that the writer should be able to go into the laboratory and make a soil analysis or diagnose an illness. It does imply that he will have sufficient training to be able to apply his commonsense in judging the merits of the written and spoken statements pertaining to his specialty. Similarly, it would be difficult for anyone to write on the problems of child rearing unless trained in child psychology, or of public education unless educated in the basic principles of that field.

Borrowing Scientific Brains

In exceptional circumstances a substitute for formal training can be found in what might be termed "borrowing brains." The writer, if skilled in interviewing, can draw material for articles from qualified experts. The process demands that the writer know what he wants to get from the expert. This requires advance reading and study. The writer is forced to rely heavily upon the accuracy of the interviewee. Frequently second and third call-backs are necessary, and these may be difficult to obtain. In the end the writer cannot be certain that he has gotten the most significant facts. He must take the interviewee's word for that. Obviously, there is no genuine substitute for a thorough working knowledge of the field of specialization.

Simplification and Specialization

In addition to his scientific training the writer needs to be trained in the simplification or popularization of professional writing. The language of the man-in-the-street and the limited range of his vocabulary must be as well known as the technical jargon of the research worker. The writer needs to understand the limitations exacted by publication in newspapers and magazines. These are matters of style, vocabulary, space, and time — or deadlines. It is the purpose of this book as well as this chapter to help the popularizer set his feet on the right paths.

Repeating earlier admonitions, the writer must specialize in some one field, or in fields very closely allied. The writer on agricultural problems should not expect to switch effectively to child training, modern medicine, or public education. And if he attempts it, editors are unlikely to give him much of a hearing. The writing jack-of-all subjects is a hack, and editors want very little from him. Let the writer choose his specialty and stick to it. In this way he can build a reputation as enviable as that of any other professional man.

For the man who must earn while he learns to perfect his mastery of the art of simplification and while sharpening his judgment, an editorial position on a newspaper is an excellent solution. Newspaper training itself is good for the writer. It has never hurt any writer's style, and it has helped hundreds of writers perfect themselves in the techniques of writing. Newspaper training alone is not enough. It must be accompanied by a self-directed plan for increased mastery of simplification and humanization.

The Reading Program

The writer of scientific articles can be neither a hack writer nor a hack thinker — unless he intends to write for the cheap, sensational syndicated Sunday press, of which there is only one important example in America. Neither the great Sunday and daily newspapers nor the magazines of important circulation will knowingly print deceptive or inaccurate stories of science. A few minor magazines are careless of their reputations, but the writer cannot achieve an enviable career writing for them, nor is he likely to graduate therefrom to a publication in a higher class.

A thorough acquaintance with all of the best markets must be taken for granted of the science writer. If he wants to free-lance for a wide variety of magazines, he should know not only magazines of the *Popular Science* variety, but also *True* and its class, *Redbook Magazine, Cosmopolitan, Parents' Magazine,* and similar publications. Not only must he know their policies, but he must watch all issues as they come from the presses. He should also know fully two-score publications somewhat less given to printing news of science. Typical would be *McCall's Magazine, Ladies' Home Journal, Better Homes and Gardens,* and *Good Housekeeping.* Not only may they be markets for his work, but they are sources of ideas for other articles.

Because a man must specialize, the task of following the professional and scientific journals likely to print material suitable for popularization is not so great as it would be otherwise. Suppose a writer is going to contribute articles on scientific developments in agriculture. He will keep track of all publications by the United States Department of Agriculture and by leading colleges of agriculture and forestry. He will also keep up with the monthly and yearly issues of *Agricultural Index,* which lists titles, authors, and sources of most articles on agricultural subjects. By using Ireland's *An Index to Indexes*, the writer can learn of other indexes that are likely to be of service to him. These will save a great deal of widespread searching, though they are always behind the first announcement of new discoveries, which usually are made in the professional journals.

Newspapers also frequently carry original announcements of innovations, inventions, and discoveries. Regular study of the daily and the Sunday edition of *The New York Times* and the weekly *Time* magazine or *Newsweek* will uncover frequent tips for broader and more complete later treatment.

Another type of reading should also be done — chiefly to broaden the writer's education and background. This is composed of the books and similar material written by and about scientists. Nearly all of these will be found listed in the *Cumulative Book Index*, published by H. W. Wilson. Many of these works — probably most of the important ones — wil be reviewed in the Sunday editions of *The New York Times* or other Sunday newspapers.

In short, the writer should know what is happening in his field, and he must expect to discover it at as early a date as possible. This forces him to do some digging on his own behalf. In the end the capable writer of science must become quite an erudite and scholarly person.

Levels of Popularization

Science articles differ in the degree to which they must be popularized, because magazines and newspapers vary in the average educational level of their readers. Newspapers with mass circulations require articles done in the simplest terms. And yet such newspapers as *The New York Times* have a reader level probably well above that of *Popular Science, Mechanix Illustrated,* or *Pageant.* Such newspapers are read in a somewhat limited area by a selected group that want all the news with all details, whereas these three magazines strive for mass appeal on a national scale.

Recent studies of newspaper and magazine readability reveal that both types of publications are more difficult to comprehend than their publishers thought possible. For our purposes certain of these may be ranked in order of increasing difficulty as follows: *This Week* (the Sunday newspaper supplement); *Popular Science Monthly; Reader's Digest; Parents' Magazine* and *Today's Health; The Atlantic* and *Harper's Magazine;* and *Science* and other professional journals.

When writing for readers of any of these publications, the writer must not reach above their level. It is better to err on the side of oversimplification than to take a chance on the readability of any paragraph. A study of the publication itself is necessary. This, however, is not sufficient, for most periodicals are written somewhat over the heads of their readers. Few writers today understand thoroughly the complete task of simplification.

Value of Scientists' Name

Few popularizers of science are themselves authorities in any field — unless they ranked as authorities before they took up the pen. It is true that some free-lance writers do write authoritatively, but this is quite a different matter. William L. Laurence of *The New York Times* might be taken as an example. His career was almost entirely devoted to philosophy and journalism. He had done no advanced research, nor did he hold the rank of scientist in any field. Yet whatever he put his name to in scientific writing may be said to have been authoritatively written. That is why he was chosen by the armed forces of the United States to write the story of the atomic bombing of Hiroshima in 1945.

Not all writers have the background and soundness of judgment of Laurence. The names of few writers carry the same weight. But on most subjects these others can interview scientists whose names carry more weight than that of *The New York Times* staff member. This may be done to lend authority to certain points made by the writer. Such a device is not to be confused with the interview article in which the entire piece grows out of one or more interviews.

The names of scientists like Eisley, Conant, Bush, and others have appeared so frequently in the magazines and newspapers by their own choice that the academic isolation of research scientists is becoming a thing of the past. They have come to understand that they can no longer live in a world apart from other men. Consequently, it is becoming easier for the writer of science to approach such men for their opinions or for corroborating evidence. Any writer who has made a reputation for careful, painstaking work should find most scientists quite approachable. Willingness to let these men check the final article draft for accuracy will go a long way toward removing their doubts.

Handling Scientific Terms

Constantly at work exploring new fields or modifying old techniques, science keeps reaching out for new words and phrases to describe its innovations. These descriptive terms are usually based upon or coined from the Latin and Greek, though occasionally from other tongues such as the German, as in the case of rocket and nuclear research. Many new terms are far from simple borrowing. Instead, they are compounded by the addition of prefixes and suffixes to word roots. These, together with complicated sentence structures, create a stylistic "fog" element. Experts in readability have proved that reading becomes increasingly difficult as the "fog index" rises. Thus, words that incorporate prefixes and suffixes, words with vague meaning, and complicated sentences are to be held to a minimum if a readable content is to be achieved.

Upon occasion it will be necessary to use new terms that are complicated. Immediate definition or explanation should follow. This can be accomplished without interrupting the article. One way is to set off the definition with commas, as an appositional phrase. For instance, "When a *positron,* the particle of mass that carries a charge of positive electricity, collides with. . . ." Here the explanation is introduced smoothly. The use of the definite article also implies previous speaking acquaintance. While the implication is unnecessary, it does nicely avoid the air of condescension sometimes found in scientific writing. Definitions always should start with what the reader knows, and then add no more than he is able to comprehend.

Avoiding Exaggeration

Exaggeration is a pitfall into which beginning free lances sometimes stumble. Actually, the facts of science are so startling in themselves that they do not need to be exaggerated. The writer who goes beyond the facts is not likely to get a second chance in a reputable publication. Nowadays, there are so many individuals who know the truth in every field that false statements are certain to be recognized. It is better to be too conservative than too optimistic in handling science news.

To see how many problems of handling science news are solved study the work of men of outstanding reputation. Analyze their work with respect to different levels of simplication, and note how the writers handle definitions, how they cite authorities, how they simplify at the various levels. Note the caution with which they make predictions. Among those writers whose work it will pay to study are Wolfgang Langewiesche and J. D. Ratcliff of *Reader's Digest,* and Watson Davis of *Science Service.*

Rules for Writing about Science

The best set of rules for handling the many aspects of science writing was compiled by Edwin E. Slosson while director of *Science Service,* Washington. A part of it is cited below.[1]

Don't overestimate the reader's knowledge and don't underestimate the reader's intelligence. He may not know as much as you about this particular thing — let's hope not, anyway — but otherwise he may be as bright as you are — let's hope so, anyway.

Don't try to tell all you know in 500 words. Leave some over for another time. The clean plate rule does not apply here.

Don't think that because a thing is old to you it is known to the public. Many of your readers are still living in the nineteenth century; some of them in the eighteenth. Anything new to your readers is "news" to them if hung on a timely peg.

Don't imagine that the readers of a paper are, like your pupils, obliged to pretend to pay attention to you no matter how dull you may be. 'First catch your reader' is the rule of successful writing.

Don't leave out the human interest. Your reader is a human being even if you are only a scientist.

Don't forget that your reader is interrupting you every ten lines to ask, 'Why?' 'What for?' or 'Well, what of it?' and if you don't answer his tacit questions he will soon stop reading.

Don't think that you can make your topic more attractive by tricking it out with fairy lore or baby talk or irrelevant jokes or extravagant language. Bring out its real and intrinsic interest as forcibly as you can. Set off the red fire if you like, but be sure it lights up the object instead of drawing attention away from it.

Don't say 'this discovery is interesting' unless you can prove it is, and if you can prove it, you don't have to say it.

Don't suppose you must give bibliographical references to all the literature of the subject, but don't fail to give a clue by which the interested reader can get on its trail.

Don't fail to put your best foot forward. Otherwise, you may not have a chance to use the other foot. Note the construction of the news story in any first-class paper. It is built upon the same logical system as the symphony or opera overture. The opening paragraph gives in succinct fashion the main point of interest, the gist of the story, just as the first movement of a musical composition expresses the theme or motif.

Don't expect the editor to explain why he objects to your manuscript. He is probably right in his verdict, but if you would make him give a reason for it he will have to invent one and it would probably be wrong.

Don't say you can't find anything to write about. Every number of a scientific journal contains from $15 to $25 worth of good POPULAR STUFF.

---

[1]Reprinted by permission of *Science Service.*

A man can make a good living translating doctors' dissertations into English. As Chesterton says: 'There are no uninteresting subjects; there are only uninterested persons.'

Don't back up too far to get a running start. Remember the man who wanted to jump over a hill. He ran a mile to work up momentum and was so tired when he got to the bottom of the hill that he had to sit down and rest. So will your readers. Ninety per cent of the manuscripts that I have handled in twenty years as an editor would have been improved by cutting off the first page or paragraph. Yet, authors, like hens, kick on decapitation.

Don't imagine that you must add a pretty but superfluous paragraph at the end, like the coda of a sonata. The most effective close is to quit when you get through.

Don't shoot in the air. Aim at somebody. You may miss him, but you are more likely to hit somebody else than if you aim at nobody. Look out of your window and note the first person coming along the street. Imagine yourself stopping this man or woman on the sidewalk, and, like the Ancient Mariner, holding his or her attention until you have told your tale to the end.

Don't forget when you are writing for the papers that you are broadcating to a million potential readers. But how many of them are listening in depends on how you write.

Don't regurgitate undigested morsels. It is a disgusting habit.

Don't refer to notes or books while writing. Read up on the subject as thoroughly as you can, and take as many notes as you need; then put away all your notes and books out of reach and next day or at least an hour later lay clean sheets of paper on a clear desk and write out what you know about it, in your own way. Afterwards, preferably the next day, read over your manuscript critically, verify your facts, correct your data, revise your English and add any essential points, but don't expect the reader to be interested in what is so uninteresting to you that you cannot keep it in mind a single hour.

Don't define a hard word by a harder word. Vladivostok is a hard word. But when a press correspondent arrives at Vladivostok he goes right on inland without stopping to explain that 'This is a city south of Khabarovsk and east of Tsitsikhar.' So you, if you want to say 'Calorie,' say it, but don't make it worse by 'explaining' it as 'the quantity of heat necessary to effect a rise of temperature of one degree Centigrade of a cube of water each dimension of which is one-tenth part of the length of a bar of platinum and irridium alloy lying in the observatory of St. Cloud.' If you think you must define the calorie, say casually something like this, 'that 100 calories of energy can be derived from three cubes of sugar or from a small pat of butter,' or explain that a man needs to expend a hundred calories an hour to keep his body running, and 160 calories if he is working hard. . . .

Rewards of Scientific Writing

Learning to handle science for the country's leading magazines is slow work, though in the end highly profitable. Other more modest markets are available to the beginning writer. These are the juvenile and religious magazines, scores of which regularly print brief items on natural history, geography, and other scientific subjects.

It will pay the writer to study needs of these magazines, for many of them hold out open arms to beginning free lances. Some have printed booklets telling exactly how to write for them; and frequently they write letters of advice, a rare occurrence in the rest of the magazine world. Some of the best writers in America got their start contributing to the juvenile and religious publications, and many of them continue to write for them to this day.

The Sunday newspapers are also excellent markets for popularization of science items. Even weekday and special Saturday editions may be open to free-lance writers. The various departments of the *Christian Science Monitor* and the Sunday magazine of *The New York Times* are typical of the best publications in this field, and both pay good rates. Although many newspapers pay only modest rates, the writer for newspapers has the satisfaction of reaching readers who might not be touched by other types of periodicals.

Training Steps

1. Procure a copy of the Sunday edition of *The New York Times*. In the column titled "Science" mark every technical word and phrase. Note how many of these were defined or explained the first time they were used. What was the percentage? What does this tell about the reading ability of followers of this column?
2. In either *Popular Science* or *True* mark as above any article dealing with science. How many technical terms were defined when used?
3. Take the first 500 words in each item in Questions 1 and 2. What is the percentage of technical terms in each 500-word sample? Which has the higher reading level as revealed in your analysis?
4. How many similar translations of scientific fact into popular imagery were used in each 500-word sample?
5. Which article used the highest percentage of suffixes and prefixes?
6. Now take an article on a scientific subject as it appears in the *This Week*. How does it rank on the above points in comparison with the magazines in Questions 1 and 2?
7. Rank the articles in the order of care and caution exercised by the writers.
8. How many different literary devices, such as quotations, contrast, repetition, were used in developing the articles examined?
9. How many types of illustrations can you find in use in articles on the subject of housing?

10. Begin now to clip examples of popularized science. Classify them according to reading level, based on your own system or that suggested in this chapter.
11. In what ways do tabulations contribute to the readability of science articles?
12. Locate examples of the popularization of science by *Science Service*. These are intended for average newspaper audiences. Also examine articles in *Reader's Digest*, intended for average magazine readers. How do the two types compare in use of technical terms and understandable definitions?
13. In what field do you expect to specialize? What experts are there in your area who could be interviewed as authorities in your field?
14. What scientific magazines are subscribed to by your public library that might suggest ideas for popularization? Examine several of these and make a list of potential article subjects. For each subject write the names of three possible markets.
15. Study the Sunday editions of the newspapers in your area. These are likely to be your best popular markets. Get acquainted with the Sunday editors, if possible. Find out whether they buy from free-lance writers, what length the articles should be, and what photographs they want.
16. Make a list of the outstanding newspapers with Sunday or equivalent editions. Watch for local angles that can be developed into articles and sent to them. Among such papers are the San Francisco *Examiner & Chronicle*, Portland *Oregonian*, Kansas City *Star*, Minneapolis *Tribune*, St. Louis *Globe-Democrat*, Chicago *Tribune*, Detroit *Free Press*, Baltimore *Sun*, Atlanta *Journal-Constitution*, and New Orleans *Times-Picayune*.

CHAPTER 18

Selling to the Newspapers

The mechanical evolution of newspapers and magazines and the force of competition between the two are wiping out many of the physical differences that once existed between them. Magazines are achieving greater speed in production, while newspapers have added color equipment, once possessed solely by the magazines. Not long ago only the daily newspapers made use of radio, cable, and telegraph for dispatches. Many magazines today use all of them. Currently the newspapers are drawing nearer the magazines in typographical excellence.

Similarity of Newspapers and Magazines

The newspaper and the magazine also steadily grow more alike in style. Short sentences and short paragraphs characterize both, though the newspaper generally is the more telegraphic. Even literary magazines now realize the value of simplicity, and are making greater efforts to print material on the level of understanding of their readers. Although general magazines do not use that peculiar structure knows as the news story form, hundreds of trade and business publications and some religious magazines print news matter related to their respective fields. Some of these stories appear under standard date lines.

Magazine and newspapers show fewer differences today in content and subject matter of articles than at any time in the past. Newspapers have borrowed such magazine developments as interpretative articles, personality sketches, recipe columns, crossword puzzles, poetry columns, and fashion advice. Such differences as still exist grow noticeably less.

Slanting to the Newspapers

It is safe to say that anyone who can write acceptable articles for the magazines can also do articles for the daily or weekly newspapers and for other publications using the newspaper format. The same techniques of analysis and slanting that make one successful in writing for the first will serve equally well in writing for the others. In fact, all the steps of outlining explained in Chapter 8 work quite as well with the average feature article for the newspaper. While the opening paragraphs may be different in some cases, the body of the article is frequently the same.

For the free-lance writer the most profitable contribution to the newspaper is a long article, variously called a "feature," "special feature," or simply "special" article. Other material is likely to be shorter. This means it will be less remunerative, because the amount of space filled is generally one of the chief bases of payment. The additional regard of having one's name signed to a contribution will be lost in many cases. This signature, known as a by-line to the newspapers, should be affixed, nevertheless, just below the title or subtitle. It may be allowed to remain through all the editing processes.

FOLLOWING THE RULES. Most of the larger newspapers possess printed versions of their typographical and style rules, and will be glad to give a copy to a free-lance writer. Study and practice of these rules will make his work more salable. Examinations of the individual paper will reveal the most usual and acceptable types of headlines. While one need not expect the local paper to employ the version offered, the key idea incorporated may well be used — and with thanks, if it has the necessary journalistic "oomph."

If the writer finds that shorter sentences and paragraphs are used by his local journal than he customarily employs, the shift can be easily made. The newspaper paragraph consists of about three sentences of not over 15 words each. Sentences and paragraphs are both somewhat shorter than in the average magazine.

It is well to give at least a brief glimpse of important facts in the early paragraphs; for in the process of making-up, some of the last paragraphs may be dropped, as with news stories. Special understanding with the editors may, of course, eliminate such cutting. Strong paragraph beginnings are important, but the summary lead frequently used on news stories is not so common in feature articles. Subheads, described elsewhere in this book, should be supplied for those papers that use them.

The writer might remember that the newspaper is no place for subtlety of expression, or irony of statement. Let him stick to the obvious facts, and be as clear as he can.

ILLUSTRATIONS. Most often the illustrations will be photographs. Line drawings and graphs may be used, but wash drawings and other finer types of illustration are difficult to reproduce on newsprint. If the writer has to hire them done, he will seldom get their cost back from the price paid for the entire article. Dramatic, storytelling photographs are what the newspapers want, or clear, close-ups of individuals mentioned in the articles. Since many newspapers are careless of photographic prints, a free-lance writer should not submit borrowed or otherwise valuable prints that must be returned. It is much better to have them copied.

Syndicates and the Newspapers

The characteristics that distinguish non-news from news material are more likely to be recognized in items purchased from syndicates than in locally produced features. If we ignore the obvious comic strips, such differences mostly will be seen in syndicated columns of gossip; health talks; political or news analysis; humor; poetry; advice on fashion, food, love, manners; and many similar subjects. The longer feature articles are more like than unlike those in the magazines.

One can, of course, try to compete with these highly specialized newspaper features by developing one's own syndicate, and the effort may prove less difficult than would appear at first glance. The best ways to undertake this step are explained in the next chapter. Although much syndicated material is easily recognized, a great deal is not. Credit lines — the notation on sources — are frequently omitted. The information may be picked up by making inquiry of newspaper staff members.

Yet it may be said that generally the profits in producing these specialized items depend upon syndication. The individual newspaper can obtain through the syndicates features equal to what the local writer can produce and at a fraction of what he would feel his products were worth. Unless such items are a by-product of other more remunerative effort, the writer may be forced to stick to the full-length article. But both long and short pieces can be syndicated by the free lance and these rather easy multiple sales are the best way of compensating for the relatively low rates of most newpapers.

Working with Local Newspapers

The first step in selling material to a local or near-by newspaper is to visit it. The writer should inquire of the Sunday editor concerning Sunday features. The sports department often handles its own affairs. For other local weekly features either the city editor or managing editor will usually have authority to buy or reject — or will direct the free-lance writer to the buyer. Next the writer finds out what the paper is willing to buy — if anything — and what the rates will be.

RATES. In most cases rates will be rather low. Newspapers vary so widely that it is almost impossible to quote average figures. In recent years regular "stringers" have been getting as little as 35 cents per column inch, but rates usually go up with the size of the community. Times do change, however, and some newspapers are beginning to pay free-lance writers on good hourly rates that vary with writing ability and importance of the subject. At the top, rates may be as high as $15 or $20 a column, though there is not much writing of this type to be done.

It may be that better markets among the newspapers are to be found in nearby cities than at home. When outside newspapers enter the local market, they frequently are glad to obtain well-developed features based on the local scene. This grows out of the fact that out-of-town papers may not have adequate correspondents in the local field, and welcome help in increasing their competition with the local paper.

Ayer's *Newspaper and Periodical Directory* and Editor and Publisher's *International Year Book* list the daily newspapers of the United States as well as the Sunday editions. Either volume will help the free-lance writer as he begins investigation of the local or area markets. The former also includes country and community weeklies, some of which pay for suitable free-lance offerings.

As indicated elsewhere, it will seldom pay a professional free-lance writer to complete a full-length article unless he has a commitment from his local "boss." If his local or area newspaper is willing to buy from free-lance writers, the writer's next step is to get a go-ahead sign for a definite article. The understanding with a local editor should be considerably more binding than one with a distant magazine editor.

This is a good arrangement for both, though such a commitment is unlikely to be repeated with one who has fallen down on an assignment.

In contrast to the magazines, many newspapers are as careless with article copy as with photographic prints. Frequently they fail to return unused material even when the writer has made provision for its return. Because only the largest newspapers use printed rejection slips, reasons for a rejection by a newspaper are seldom revealed to the free-lance writer. Occasionally it pays to visit the editor and so to learn first-hand what is wrong.

WHAT IS WANTED. Newspapers want what they want — just as magazines do. And the best index is what is printed. Highly marketable are personality sketches of men and women in interesting occupations, even when the individual is relatively obscure. A surviving blacksmith, a druggist who won't serve sodas or sandwiches, an old wood carver, a person with an unusual hobby, an inventor, successful workers in scores of occupations, pioneer settlers — all these and more may be possibilities if the necessary pictures can be obtained.

The fact that these people are local citizens will add interest to the sketches, and make them salable when a magazine with national appeal might turn them down.

Narratives of murder mysteries, important burglaries, sensational divorces, or unsolved disappearances can be told through the person of a local policeman or a private detective. The same ideas may occur to newspaper staff members, but the free lance will have to outsmart them by digging up a new angle. Historical yarns are always good if the new angle can be found. Most of the data are in the files of the local historical society, or in back issues of the local newspapers.

Each of the eight types of articles commonly used by general magazines without exception can be placed with local newspapers. No type is barred. But each article must make the grade against the usual hazards under which free lances submit their yarns.

LOCAL ANGLES. Among the types of material that can be developed for newspaper editors are the local angles; that is, those phases of stories arising beyond the local area that have local applications capable of being further developed. They grow out of many different subjects, but they are of broad, general types: 1. local angles discovered in the local papers under out-of-town datelines; 2. local angles found in out-of-town newspapers in items either local or foreign to those areas; 3. local angles uncovered in magazines, bulletins, or other printed sources; and 4. those angles come across perhaps by accident while the free-lance writer is traveling.

Examples of the *first* and *second* angles are rare. News items affecting local areas are frequently announced in the state capitals or in Washington. They may involve city, county, or local state employees, or local offices of the federal government. Decision to transfer a state or federal agency to or from the local area is an example. Or the news might include action of state or federal government to acquire areas in the writer's neighborhood for through highways, parks, airports, or game refuges. Often the first announcement that a local man is being called to a better job elsewhere is brought to local attention by a dispatch under a "foreign" date line.

Types One and Two

a. *Local angle under date line in local Syracuse newspaper.*

ALBANY, April 13 — Detailed plans for construction of flood control projects at several points in the state were released today by the state department of public works.

Among the projects included are the Black River project, Watertown, the Upper Hudson Valley project . . .

b. *Local angle without date line in New York City newspaper.*

Under the will of Francis R. Held, filed here today for probate, an estate valued at more than $1,000,000 was left to Syracuse University. The house and grounds containing valuable paintings, antiques, and other collector's items are included in the gift.

Mr. Held, who died . . .

The first item can be expanded into a full-page feature for a local Sunday edition. With appropriate pictures of the site of proposed work and drawings showing dams and interviews with local officials or people affected, this would provide a first-rate spread. Written from a broader point of view, to include similar projects, the feature would appeal to the editors of several national magazines.

The second item could be built up by the free-lance writer through interviews with University officials on prospective use of funds to be derived from settlement of the estate, expected contests of the will — if any — and student suggestions on what they would like to have done with the money. Possibilities for pictures are present in this news story. It also suggests a magazine article on trends in gifts to educational and charitable institutions.

Under the *third* type of news angle may be found items of social, economic, or scientific interest. Among them are the "inside" stories of political deals and manipulations, or the "story behind the story" frequently seen in Sunday editions. New products put on the national market by local concerns occasionally are first spotted in advertisements in national magazines. Releases from such divisions of the government as the Department of Agriculture at times contain rulings that affect local businesses. News of import or export restrictions, or import shortages may first be found in releases from the controlling department. Similar in origin are announcements of scientific discoveries or developments affecting local manufacturing or processing firms.

Type Three

From a homecraft magazine.

> A portable washing machine small enough to sit on a table top has just been put on the market by an upstate New York manufacturer. The picture to the right shows that the machine holds . . .

The picture with this item revealed the name of a local manufacturer of a well-known washing machine. Investigation showed that production had been kept a secret to achieve dominance of the market. When developed for the local paper, the story told the number of employees working on the model, the name of the designing engineer, the length of the experimental period, a roundup of other data on the machine, its prospects, and general information about the manufacturing concern.

Under the *fourth* type of news angle may be included items concerning local characters who are away from home — if they have not yet found their way into print. Some of these will be tips for personality sketches or tales of achievement by those who are better known outside their own city than in it. Such individuals are far more common than generally realized. Of this type was a feature done for the Sunday edition of the Atlanta *Journal* by this author on a game sanctuary established in Florida by a former Atlanta resident. Written as a dispatch to the *Journal,* and illustrated by photographs, the item found ready acceptance. The lead is shown below.

Type Four

> One of the most beautiful retreats in Florida is Camp Manywings, a game and bird preserve near Grandin, in Putnam County, created by W. E. Browne, who is perhaps

better known in Atlanta for having decorated and furnished some of Georgia's finest homes.

DEVELOPING LOCAL TIPS. Of a different kind are items arising locally and printed locally. These may be news stories that have been held to brief treatment either by lack of staff writers to develop them or by lack of understanding of their news value — of which the first is more likely.

Unfortunately, on stories of this latter kind the free-lance writer has to compete with staff members who may be as competent as he is and as well acquainted with local conditions. Because a great deal of article writing is done by reporters and special writers as part of their regular duties and without extra compensation, newspaper editors are naturally reluctant to buy local stories from free lances. The easiest items to sell, therefore, are those from off the beaten track, or those overlooked by staff writers.

a. *A brief item buried on the financial page.*

> The Krens Bat Co. has recently installed infra-ray apparatus to speed up seasoning of hickory for its nationally-famous autographed bats. Drying period is cut from seven months to a matter of days.

b. *Picked up on a fishing trip.*

> A local man of wealth had recently bought a famous chateau on one of the Thousand Islands. The house was built in the 1870's by a New York railroad baron. It had later figured in seven scandals and at least one murder. It was said to hold fabulous paintings and tapestries.

SELLING NEWS TIPS. Some newspapers, particularly metropolitan dailies, pay good rates to anyone who turns in a tip for a story that has not been picked up by a staff member. An additional bonus may be given for the best tip of the day. The work of gathering the facts is ordinarily done by staff reporters, and payment is made after verification of the accuracy of the tip. Tips on accidents, fires, human-interest possibilities, crime, acts of heroism, and other unusual occurrences are among ideas that may be purchased.

Writing for Press Associations

Writing for local bureaus of the press associations has some points in common with free lancing for the local paper and also with working for the syndicates. The writer competes with local reporters and possibly the bureau manager, and consequently has to dig up items overlooked by fellow craftsmen, or develop angles touched on but lightly by other reporters. At the same time he may have to take and supply photographs as he would for syndicated material. These he delivers to the local bureau for transmittal.

"SCOOPS." The free-lance writer cannot hope to achieve many big "scoops." Newspaper coverage is generally too efficient to be easily beaten, and Big Events are usually carefully covered. Also he has the task of playing a lone hand against the entire resources of perhaps one or more well-run newspapers. When he does get a hard-earned exclusive news story, generally he won't be paid any more for it than for the average run of daily news. Nor will he have the satisfaction of seeing his name signed to a story. That treat is reserved for staff members of the leading press associations. *Editor and Publisher* occasionally records exceptions to this rule, but they are no more common in the life of the average free lance than Christmas bonuses to staff reporters.

HUMAN INTEREST. Occasionally sales of human-interest items may be made to local press bureaus, budgets permitting. These are the stories that draw a laugh or bring a lump to the throat. Every newspaperman knows the type and is under pressure to produce them as frequently as possible. But human interest is where you find it, and a free lance may dig it up as well as anyone else.

Because the recording of human affairs is mostly canalized, many human-interest items may be found at such news sources as fire stations, police stations, the S. P. C. A., lost-and-found departments of public and private agencies, juvenile courts, and welfare bodies. Included among old standbys are the little yarns of pets — lost, strayed, stolen, or in trouble — tales of wildlife exploits, and always stories of young children doing unusual things.

Standard texts on news writing usually devote some space to discussions and illustrations of this type of news items. A list of such texts will be found in Wolseley's *The Journalist's Bookshelf*, cited in Chapter 23. A good sense of humor and a sympathetic attitude are of much help in writing human-interest stories. Some writers have a flair for handling this type of material, and some find it impossible to do. When local newspaper budgets are flexible, the free-lance writer may be able to dispose of some such items without going to the wire services.

Writing for the Future

For the free lance who accurately knows his local newspaper markets, the local press bureaus, the wire services supplying features, and the syndicates, there are possibilities for doing articles or features with potentialities against the day when some break in the news makes it possible to release these to the right market. This is one of the very few exceptions to the rule for use of the query, and it pays only when using spare time and where one is master of the market. The practice is not recommended for articles aimed at the general magazines.

By way of example, the free-lance writer might learn of a resident of the community who once occupied a prominent place on the front pages. He can get the facts together (mostly from local newspapers), whip up a story, and procure pictures, and wait for events to supply a news break to which he may tie his data. Newspapers use such "news pegs" to make their articles appear more timely. They usually come sooner or later. Another example of their use is in connection with situations where trouble may one day break — a prison riot, a flood, a disaster in some dangerous industry. The writer can make his preparations for writing about the disastrous moment. An example of this development is cited below.

In this case the free lance has noted an increasing death rate in the professional boxing ring, which he believes is caused by careless physical examinations and improper refereeing. The writer has brought together the record of deaths over a period of years; has talked to interested officials, boxers, and trainers; and waits for a spectacular ring death to which to tie his story.

The news story — or anticipated "news peg" — might be as follows:

> NEW YORK, Mar. 30. — Billy Ryan, promising middleweight, fighting for a chance at the national title died last night in his dressing room one hour after being hit on the chin by a wild left-hand swing.
> A cheering Garden crowd of 5,000 paid fans applauded Ryan's uphill battle against 163-pound Tony Palermo, who battered Ryan to the floor in the sixth. As Billy climbed to his feet, a wild punch flush on the chin . . .

This is the way our free-lance writer might begin his article, "Death in the Squared Circle," for a Sunday newspaper.

> The death last week of Billy Ryan, rising middleweight, one hour after he was carried unconscious from the ring in New York City, brings the total ring deaths to 13 in the last 12 months.
> In 1944 there were only 4 such deaths, in 1945 there were 6, and by 1950 the number climbed to 11. Recent years show a steady increase.
> The time has come to . . .

Working with Out-of-Town Papers

Although the free lance will expect to devote most of his time to articles, he may temporarily find it desirable to assume one or more correspondenceships for out-of-town papers. He obtains such work by writing to or approaching directly such papers as may be interested in news from his area. Generally there are few such vacancies, most of them being filled by local newspapermen. But if his application is in and vacancies occur, he may be appointed to take over the position as correspondent.

Similar opportunities exist in supplying news of business to some of the trade and industrial journals. A letter to the editor of any such journal will soon reveal whether correspondence vacancies exist.

When working with out-of-town dailies, more frequently than in any other type of writing, the free lance will make use of the telegraph in querying. When he learns of an important news break, he will address a query to his previous contact or to the responsible editor, such as:

> AIR CRASH HERE. TEN KILLED INCLUDING GOVERNOR.
> CAN SEND 500. PIX AVAILABLE.

Queries vary in length and content. The above query tells the editor that the writer can send newsworthy material up to 500 words, also that he has pictures of the crash. The editor then wires back to give definite orders on how much and what he wants, including directions about pictures. Where working arrangements are in effect between free-lance writer and editor, queries are usually sent collect.

Training Steps

1. Analyze five or six different newspapers, including your local newspaper and one or two near-by journals that are likely to be good markets. First, mark every story of local origin.
2. Next check every story bearing the credit mark of Associated Press or United Press-International. What types of credit lines are used?
3. Now mark the printed items other than cartoons and strips. In this residue will be found the syndicated material. To spot it, eliminate editorials, correspondence items, and all types of advertising.
4. Uncover and list all local angles in the various classes of news stories above. These will be of varying merit.
5. What local items are capable of additional development?
6. Compare the non-news features of your newspapers with the shorter features of the same number of general magazines. How many found in the magazines are unduplicated in the newspapers, and *vice versa?*

7. Make a list of a dozen or fifteen trade or union business journals that print news items of interest to their field. Use the market guides for this step.

8. State what characteristics these items have in common with news stories.

9. Make a word count in five newspapers and five magazines. What is the difference in length of the average sentence, and of the average paragraph?

10. What is the range in sentence and paragraph length among the magazines? The newspapers?

11. Analyze four or five articles in *This Week* and the Sunday magazine of *The New York Times*. What differences in slanting do you find within the same types of articles?

12. How many of these articles were tied to new pegs?

13. If the articles were not developed by means of new pegs, were they seasonal in character? What was the device used to make them appear timely?

14. List a half dozen subjects of potential articles, such as historical buildings, battlegrounds, or critical situations. For each, state one or more news items that would enable you to release an article about each.

15. Set down the types of illustrations to be found in your best newspaper markets. Do these markets use charts, graphs, or wash drawings?

16. Examine a month's issues of your local newspaper. What items do you find that might have been made into articles worth syndicating in your own name? Make this examination a regular part of your writing and study habits.

17. What out-of-town newspapers compete in your local markets? Find out if they are interested in free-lance articles from your city or area.

18. Make the acquaintance of some local old settlers, public officials in office a long time, police officers about to retire, librarians, or elderly tradesmen. What mysteries — murders, scandals, burglaries, or disasters — do they recall that might now be retold? List these and file them. Watch for the news peg that will make them timely.

CHAPTER 19

Multiple Sales to
Magazines and Newspapers

Syndicates perform a number of useful services in the newspaper world. Because of overlapping circulation, however, all of the general magazines and most of the others have to be excluded. Though competing newspapers may be served by the same syndicate, it is a general rule that newspapers whose circulations overlap shall not be allowed to buy the same items.

Syndicates Aid Press and Writers

Newspapers profit from patronage of the syndicates because they can get higher-class material in greater quantities than if they employed their own contributors exclusively. Syndicate features cost but a fraction of that of locally developed features. The result is that newspapers achieve wider circulation and greater profits, a fact that suggests continued growth of the syndicates.

From the point of view of the writer, syndicating is also desirable if the item is a signed piece. Unfortunately much syndicated material does not carry the name of the writer or of the syndicate, a factor that makes this type of feature difficult to identify. Syndicates generally pay higher rates than the individual newspaper, even when they buy outright. On signed pieces, such as columns, cartoons, or unusual articles, the greater advertising given the writer's name may eventually be of considerable commercial value.

The syndicates have become an important factor in newspaper publishing. A study of some weekly newspapers reveals that 60 per cent of the content originated in syndicates. Though few if any dailies depend to this extent upon syndicates, it is common to find daily newspapers in which from 20 to 30 per cent of the editorial matter comes from such sources.

Types of Syndicates

Syndicates are as varied in character as the newspapers they serve, but can be grouped together under two main types. The first group is operated by a newspaper or its subsidiary. The second is operated privately. Both types exist for the profits they return to the owners.

Newspaper Syndicates — These ordinarily handle a wide variety of material. Among the outstanding syndicates are those of *The New York Times,* the Chicago *Tribune,* the Chicago *Sun-Times,* and the Des Moines *Register and Tribune.* Newspaper syndicates, like that of the Chicago *Tribune,* are famous for their cartoons and comic strips. The Chicago *Daily News* made newspaper history in World War II with the syndicated writings of its foreign correspondents. Others in this group are noted for fiction, columns, or spot news. One of the most widely circulated Sunday newspaper magazines is *This Week,* published by the *United Newspapers Magazine Corp.* Its chief competitor is now *Parade.* Both magazines buy from free-lance writers.

Privately Owned Syndicates — There are several hundred syndicates of this type. Some are one-man organizations, operated from a single office. Services of the latter type may be limited to a single kind of material supplied by the owner-editors. Many of them are not in the market for contributed material. Some others employ scores of clerks, writers, artists, and editors. They also buy freely from unknown writers, but generally prefer well-known names. A list of syndicates can be found in Editor & Publisher's *International Year Book.* As with magazines, the needs of the syndicates must be learned from first-hand study, such as the writing of queries, personal visits, scanning the newspapers, and reading of all other material available.

SPECIALIZED SYNDICATES. Some syndicates handle only photographs. And some of these even limit themselves to photographs of disasters, such as fires, floods, storms, or accidents. Other syndicates specialize in interviews with celebrities, finance, fiction, sports, fashions, women's page features, or popularization of scientific developments. Since every writer must eventually specialize within limited fields, he should get acquainted with the syndicates that are his best markets. This is a job that each writer must do for himself. The care and pains taken will be repaid by successful contacts with the proper syndicates.

Syndicate Policies

As mentioned above, syndicates are operated for profit, and they attempt to follow those policies that will bring them the greatest return. Two items are favored by these organizations: famous names and multiple-part features.

APPEAL OF FAME. Famous names and "big" names are attractive to the syndicates for the same reason they are attractive to readers. The name of Churchill, for instance, immediately after the close of World War II suggested the possibility of inside information, of the telling of long-kept secrets, and of the divulging of important international pacts. Naturally, readers jumped at the chance to see what he was able to reveal. Walter Winchell's column is popular with tens of thousands, because he reveals so-called secrets about the famous or near-famous. It is a fundamental trait of human nature, known to all editors, that people will read whatever purports to tell the secrets of those in the public eye. When free-lance writers can get famous names into their copy, they increase the chances of selling it.

By "big" names is meant something else. The "big" names are the individuals who have already arrived in the writing profession. It used to be said while Irvin Cobb was alive that his name on the front cover of *Saturday Evening Post* would sell thousands of additional copies of that issue. Successful writers build up a following that means extra sales to the magazines when their names appear. But beyond this, "big" names are important to editors because they are usually a guarantee of successful performance. Put yourself in the place of an editor. Which would you rather trust, the work of an unknown, unproved writer, or a piece by one whose name stands for years of successful work?

The unknown writer has his handicaps, but he also has certain advantages. Many editors prefer to buy his work because they can get it for less. In much syndicated writing, the author's name never appears, anyway. Where the writer's name itself means little, a way to avoid this handicap is to interview and quote from famous people and from experts.

SERIAL FEATURES.   Other things being equal, a feature that can be run day after day over a period of months or years is likely to appeal to syndicate editors more than the item that appears but once. The cost of exploiting the long-run feature grows proportionately less with each appearance, while the return goes up. Such a feature also builds up a following with the passing of time. The good will or interest of a group of readers in a particular feature may be worth hundreds of thousands of dollars to the newspapers, the syndicate, and the originators. Syndicates dislike to lose to a competitor any feature that has an established following.

The great bulk of syndicated material, however, is not of the perennial variety. Some features run for months, some only for weeks. If interest in them begins to wane, the syndicates are quick to look for a substitute. This fact is the bane of the established writer, but a source of comfort to the beginner. Writers have to be nimble about uncovering new ideas, and they should be able to recognize when an idea has grown stale.

USING MARKET GUIDES.   The market guides are good indexes to syndicate policies, particularly if they print information that comes directly from the editor. However, syndicates change from time to time, and printed information becomes out of date. It is more difficult to learn what syndicates need and want than to get the same information about magazines. Constant study and querying are needed to keep a writer's information up to date. Writers must remember that newspapers exist to print items that are timely, and it is the business of the syndicate to anticipate these needs. Lucky is the syndicated writer whose material is relatively free from the pressure of the calendar or of current events.

If you have an idea that seems worthy of syndication, be sure that it has widespread appeal. Syndicates generally deal with clients from coast to coast. Hence the broader the appeal of your proposed feature, the more likely it is to attract a syndicate.

Value of New Ideas

The literary world is full of writers who hope to achieve fame by imitating outstanding successes. But most of their hopes are quickly buried, for imitation is soon spotted. None of the scores of imitators of the late George Ade's "Fables in Slang" ever met with recognition or financial success. Thousands have aped the style and techniques of O. Henry, but no one else ever rode to fame on his literary innovations. Imitation is valuable as a device for training, but it also is the shortest path to oblivion for any aspiring writer.

Syndicates do not want imitations of someone else's style, technique, or basic ideas. What syndicates desire, and are willing to pay well for, are new ideas and innovations that no one else has thought of, or new approaches to familiar subjects.

Adaptation versus Imitation

A well-known weekly once published a series of articles by a famous New York chef, who toured America to write of noted restaurants and their finest dishes. The series was billed as "A Cook's Tour of America." No other magazine would be likely to consider sending some other noted chef on a similar tour in imitation of this series. But a shrewd competing editor might send a famous writer like Arthur Schlesinger, Jr., the historian, on a sweep about the country to write of important historical places.

This latter process is not imitation, but adaptation. It is both legitimate practice and shrewd editing. The second editor simply allows a good idea to suggest something quite different for his own use. He does not imitate style or technique of development. In fact, he is certain to try for as great a difference in treatment as possible. Similarly, the prospective columnist who admires a daily column on "Rambling about New York" had far better try his hand at doing one for the weeklies on "Unknown American Heroes" than to imitate the first. The strip illustrator who wants to imitate "Superman" with an "Atomic Man" will be likely to achieve better results with a brand-new idea.

The slogan for the syndicate writer should be: "Don't imitate; originate." He should dig deeply into his own experience for something unique and unconventional. If what he turns up is interesting, and if he can sustain it over a considerable period, some syndicate will give the idea a hearing.

Working with Syndicates

Several plans for handling financial arrangements with syndicates are open to contributors.

FLAT PRICE. The least common procedure is to state a flat price for a piece of work. This protects the writer against sale at a rate he would consider too low. But it also eliminates sales when the asking price is considered too high by the syndicate. And as the writer may not be in a position to know how much it is worth to syndicate, he may well ask more than its value.

"USUAL RATES." A second method is to submit the item at the "usual rates" and trust to the fairness of the syndicates. This generally works out satisfactorily, for square dealing with writers is necessary if a syndicate is to stay in business. Shady dealings soon become publicly known, and the operator is thereafter shunned by free-lance writers.

These two methods are frequently used when a single contribution is being offered. The second is held to be better than the first, but neither should be used when the offering consists of a series of items, such as a plan for a comic strip or a column.

FIFTY-FIFTY BASIS. A third method should be followed when the contribution includes a number of items. The heart of this is to make the offering on a 50-50 basis. The writer states that he expects to receive 50 per cent of the gross returns from syndication. If the first distributor isn't willing to work on this basis, then another agency should be approached. Some syndicates offer 50 per cent of the net profit. But this is not a good bargain for the writer, since he has no way of checking or determining the cost of advertising and distributing his work. It is possible to load many miscellaneous or nonexistent expenses onto a good-paying feature. If 50 per cent of the gross return is insisted upon, then the agency will have an incentive to keep expenses as low as possible. However, in some instances a writer may have to settle for less than 50 per cent in order to get the services of a syndicate.

Some syndicated writers make fabulous incomes, and numerous others earn more than editors of the papers in which their work appears. Almost without exception, the peak returns go to those who are innovators in the field. They are the ones who originate an idea and ride it to fame. A world of hard work, perseverence, and intelligent effort is required in every successful case.

Starting a Column

SUBMITTING SAMPLES. There are three roads open to syndication of a regular feature of your own. The first is to do a number of samples and then submit them to a syndicate. You have then only to persuade the agency to try them out. This is a gamble for you, but a bigger one for the syndicate, for it has to put up the money for advertising, duplicating, and selling. Some writers have got their start this way, but it is a difficult route. Hundreds of beginning writers are turned down for every one who gets the nod. Most syndicates refuse to take an untried, unproved feature, because they know from experience that most offerings will prove to be duds.

ON THE SIDE. The second method is to get a job on a newspaper and then do a column on the side. The newspaper may or may not pay for the column. From one point of view the writer is fortunate to be able to get his material into print where it can be tried, improved, or dropped at no expense to himself. If his idea appears good, and he has both originality and productivity, the writer can ask his readers to tell how they like the idea. From their response he will know whether he has something really good, or just a "flash in the pan." If a number of favorable letters come in, the writer can take these, together with clippings of his best work, with plans for future columns to the syndicate of his choice. The final decision will be made by the syndicate or one of its competitors.

DIRECT SALES. A third method requires a visit to one or more daily or weekly newspapers to persuade them to accept your trial efforts without charge. If you can persuade an editor to take a chance on your homespun column or comic strip, the next step is to furnish him, in the case of a daily feature, with a week's supply in advance. Then arrange to have galley proofs made of the entire lot. These can be mailed to noncompeting newspapers together with a good sales letter. Bills can be sent monthly to those newspapers that use the material. This can be checked by inspecting the papers after they are published. Eventually the writer may build up quite a string of papers that use his output regularly.

If the business transactions become too troublesome, then clippings from the various newspapers using the idea, with letters from admiring readers, can be used to convince a syndicate that it should relieve the writer of the physical labor of mailing out releases and collecting fees. If the feature is of widespread interest, the syndicate will more than earn a 50 per cent commission.

The weekly press offers some advantages over the daily press as a medium for trying out ideas. Weekly newspapers are more likely to appreciate a free offering, and they are usually more willing to cooperate with a young writer. Nearly all daily newspapers use more or less syndicated material with which the new feature must compete. Urgent demands on daily space also may prevent a tryout that is sufficiently long to allow the writer to hit his stride.

Syndicating a Single Item

For the writer who wants to use the mails on rare occasions to syndicate his own articles, another method is possible. Whereas the first three methods were aimed at achieving ultimate syndication through some previously existing distributive agency of national scope, this latter method aims at setting up a country-wide plan for the syndication of a single item.

STEPS TO FOLLOW. The writer starts with an idea he believes to be of interest to a number of newspapers. He then puts the idea through the following steps.

1. The idea is written in newspaper style. The piece is kept on the short side, rather than the long. It is slanted as carefully as possible.

2. The writer next makes a list of the newspapers that may be interested enough to pay for the item. He then makes certain, by consulting some such aid as the state maps in Ayer's *Directory*, that the circulation areas do not overlap. For instance, he might include a Chicago paper and a Minneapolis paper, but not a Minneapolis paper and a St. Paul paper.

3. Next he makes as many duplicate copies of the item as there are newspapers on his list.

4. Duplicate sets of photographs (if these are required) are obtained for each newspaper.

5. Cover pages are made as for any other type of article, but in addition the cover page carries these words: "Exclusive in your circulation area."

6. A release date is typed on the cover page, such as "Released to all papers dated August 29."

7. The item (with pictures, if any) is sent about ten days in advance for weekday editions, or about three weeks for Sunday editions. For important releases this period can be somewhat shortened.

Ideas that other newspaper reporters and free-lance writers have missed are best, though syndicating of rewritten material is done. Checking of facts and adapting additional information are usually essential for rewrites.

The rate of pay will vary widely from a few dollars upward, depending upon the newspaper, the length of the item, its importance, and the number of illustrations. Payment of ten dollars from a single newspaper is not uncommon for average items.

A typical cover page is shown in Illustration 18.

DIFFICULTIES EXAGGERATED. The difficulties of self-syndicating an article and of breaking into big-time syndicating have been exaggerated. Actually, it is being done constantly. The greatest obstacles have always

Charles E. Bellman
807 Euclid Avenue
Syracuse 10, N.Y.

Submitted at usual
rates. Exclusive in
your circulation area.
For release to all pa-
pers dated August 29.
About 900 words.

WHAT IT TAKES TO MAKE

A CHAMPION IN ANY SPORT

—

The Top Men in Five Sports Reveal
Cost in Pain, Self-Denial and
Long Lonely Training Hours

—

This article has been prepared from interviews with national champions in five amateur sports.

They differ on whether the great sacrifices made in becoming a champion are worth the acclaim, the medals, and
other awards. They do not think they have lived normal lives,
and they tell whether they would want to start over again—if
they could.

Enclosed are photographs of the men taken at one of
their winning moments.

Illustration 17 — Sample cover page for syndicate article

been that writers have not known how to go about it, or that they have submitted shoddy imitations of established features. The writer with a good idea can get a hearing and a trial by following the steps outlined above. It need hardly be said that inferior ideas will probably be stopped by the first editor who meets them. Let the writer depend on originality, and let him shun imitation as he would plagiarism.

Training Steps

1. Study a list of syndicates from a market guide. Secure copies of four different metropolitan Sunday newspapers. List the names of contributing syndicates found in each.
2. Examine copies of the two Sunday magazines, *This Week* and *Parade*. How many feature articles are found in each? How many seem to be of the type you could have done?
3. From a newspaper office or city library get four country weeklies from separated points. List the features appearing therein. How many are of the type you think you could learn to do?
4. You are interested in doing a series of newspaper articles on "America and Its National Monuments." A. Make a list of 15 titles for different articles to be written, i. e., "The Alamo — Sacred Heart of Texas." B. Compile a list of references in which necessary data could be found on each monument. C. Make a list of photographic syndicates from which pictures could be obtained. D. Write title, beginning, and outline for first article.
5. Study sufficient issues of your local newspaper to discover and list 10 local items that could be rewritten for syndication to other newspapers.
6. In a single sentence state the basic idea for a new type or syndicated column. Now draw up a list of content for 15 different issues of this column.
7. Make a list of characters for a new type of comic strip or story continuity. How could you get someone to illustrate it?
8. Ask a dozen or two people what type of articles they would like to find more frequently in their newspapers. Could you supply any of them?
9. What are the outstanding natural beauty spots of your state? A. Make a list of these. B. List the steps you would take to syndicate a single article on the subject to each of ten leading newspapers circulating mainly in the state. C. Now write such an article, or another equally salable. An article or series of articles on outstanding athletes of your state would make an acceptable substitute.
10. Would a gossip column about Washington political figures appeal to a widespread public? A. How would you go about determining this fact? B. How would you undertake to start such a column?

CHAPTER 20

Handling the Technical Article

The technician who has spent months or years on a research problem may throw together an article explaining the results. Many scientists and engineers believe they are not obligated to produce easy reading when they turn to scholarly reports. Even trained technical writers fall into this erroneous attitude. Among publications that illustrate the occasionally baffling results are such journals as the *Journalism Quarterly, Public Opinion Quarterly,* and *American Political Science Review.*

This chapter is intended to point out how to produce copy that is readable within the sphere for which it is planned. The remarks that follow can be applied to many types of technical writing.

Technical Piece Defined

Those who have studied this book thus far should have no difficulty in distinguishing between the popularized technical article for magazines of mass circulation and the unpopularized technical article intended for the limited audience of the professional or scientific journals. Both types of technical piece are based upon scientific data, part of which may appear in tables, in charts, diagrams, or other interpretative form.

If the piece is intended for publication in a magazine, it should be classified as an article. It can, however, be handled in other forms, which will be mentioned later. Further, it may vary in reading difficulty depending upon the audience for which it is written.

Scientists, engineers, technical writers, and advanced students all have difficulty in writing for a mixed audience, especially if these writers have a limited knowledge outside their own fields. This grows out of the fact that these men usually write of a new process, invention, discovery, or development which brings out little-known facts in scientific or technical language. Many of them are not trained in the techniques of simplification, and frequently use the slang or jargon of their own laboratories. Many technical expressions or abbreviations have limited circulation. And, finally, many of these men write ungrammatically and unclearly.

Readers of Technical Pieces

The technical piece has a number of different kinds of readers, chief among whom are the following: 1. fellow scientists or engineers within the same organization; 2. readers of a professional, trade, or hobby magazine; 3. the "higher-ups" in industry and government; and 4. technicians who may try to put into operation the instructions given in the technical piece.

The first group of readers includes those of wide interests. They are the type who read *Science* and *Scientific American* or such trade magazines as *American Engineer* and *Engineering News-Record*. There are scores of such magazines, many of which are interested in the offerings of free-lance writers. Their readers are a mixed group, most of whom are scientifically or technically trained.

On the fringe of this group are the readers of the well-known *Popular Mechanics* and *Popular Science,* which are in the mass reading field. In addition there have been added in recent years journals on boats, automobiles, high-fidelity recording equipment, photography, television, and many other areas — all of which carry technical articles and are interested in free-lance offerings.

The third type of reader is found among those who give research contracts to outside firms or to the scores of American universities now doing contract research for private business or various branches of the federal government. In many cases the finished report is strictly confidential — not for publication.

The fourth type of reader is the engineer or technician who takes the finished explanation of the technical writer and puts the directions or explanations into practice. Depending on education and experience, they are able to read and use manuals of greater or lesser difficulty.

Forms of Technical Writing

The *explanatory document* is of greatest interest to the general writer, and is the chief topic discussed in this chapter. However, other types of writing also exist and will be examined briefly. One of them is the *descriptive manual*, whose purpose is to explain the construction, operation, and purpose of a product, to offer maintenance information to keep it functioning, to describe repair techniques, or to list spare parts. A common example is the automobile operator's manual supplied with new cars.

The *progress report* that records accomplishment or work done to date is another type; so is the set of *specifications* that gives instruction on quality and kind of material used in home construction or in the building of a factory. The *inventory report* is still another example.

Publications intended to help *train* employes and brochures to explain *innovations* or *new products* are among other types. Still others include *technical advertisements, lectures,* and *publicity.*

Who Does Technical Writing?

Anyone who produces a technical article or other form of technical piece may be called a technical writer. On this or on any other basis there are good writers and bad ones. The scientists, engineers, technicians, and other research workers may or may not prepare for distribution an *explanatory* article on their experiments, but they generally do put together some form of written report from which a technical writer later prepares a more usable and understandable account. This latter piece, written from the earlier notes, often forms a vital bridge between the researcher who supplies the original ideas and the production engineers who put them into successful operation. If it is written in article form for a professional or mass magazine, it is a true technical article.

Some of the largest American engineering concerns are known to employ as many as 150 technical writers in a single plant. As often as not the management hires college graduates with majors in English, history, or possibly economics. These untrained writers are usually expected to learn of technology and writing by trial and error. The system has not been satisfactory, and in recent years a considerable number of these would-be writers have come to the schools of journalism for realistic instruction in writing and simplification techniques.

Ideally, if you want to be a technical writer, you should have a bachelor's degree in a pure science or engineering, and post-graduate work in writing that includes instruction in organization, clarification, and readability. Of course, few are so trained. Instead, most writers who do the technical writing for electronics, biology, pharmaceuticals, and mechanics and structures are either trained engineers who have left these occupations, or the pick-me-up college graduates mentioned above. The good technical writer, in addition to a solid basic education, should have intellectual curiosity and ability for self-instruction, and he should be meticulous with details.

Some out-of-plant free-lancers also are among the technical writers. They have to be technically competent, and they usually have built a reputation by working their way up from simpler types of writing. Some magazines, such as *Fortune*, employ staff members with demonstrated competence to do technical articles. For such writers technical writing is a full-time occupation.

Another group of growing importance includes the technical writers employed by firms whose sole business is producing technical pieces under contract for concerns without an adequate technical writing staff. These writing agencies are usually located in cities with sufficient electronic and engineering concerns to create local support for their services.

Handling the Technical Job

The bsaic steps in handling a technical piece are the same for all types of technical writing, although the steps do vary in length or importance from item to item. These basic steps include 1. acquiring an understanding of the task, 2. research, 3. organizing and outlining, 4. writing, and 5. rewriting and editing.

UNDERSTANDING THE TASK. The *first* step is to get a general knowledge of what comprises the task. Are you preparing an article, up-dating an assembly manual, or producing an entirley new manual? Somewhere will be an official document that tells exactly what you are expected to do. It may be a government contract, an in-plant memo, or a set of instructions from another firm with which your department has a writing contract. If there are earlier versions of the assignment, as in the case of a construction manual to be rewritten, you should study these until you understand as much of them as you can with your current background.

RESEARCH. You may then take the second step to supply missing information by beginning a research or study program in whatever information sources are available, including talks with experts in this field. The search may send you to an in-plant, local, or university library for checking purposes. Among the reasons for research are verification of data upon which the piece is to be based, discovery of parallel or similar work, estimating the value of the new work, finding additional facts for inclusion, or pursuing definitions of new terms or workable knowledge of the basic concepts involved.

The research may also send the writer to interview one or more out-of-plant specialists. If this becomes necessary, he should first undertake his own education on the subject by reading a few simplified or popular presentations — if they are available — and then a few more advanced treatments in scientific journals or technical books or monographs.

This early reading program and the library research — if well done — will supply much of the basic knowledge needed for an understanding of the problem involved in the new writing job. You will likely know what questions to ask scientists or engineering collaborators and what question *not* to ask. When this point is reached, you are ready to start the first of a number of interviews with the knowledgeable men who are to help you.

In the first talk it may be well to try to get only a general understanding of the innovations or processes to be explained. Later other interviews will be in order. If the proposed task has not been undertaken before, original notes and reports should be obtained to form the bulk of the finished article.

This preliminary research will help a writer avoid mistakes, which will occasionally occur in the interpretation of a scientist's work. This is to be expected. The writer is an expert in one area, while the engineer or scientist is expert in another. The average scientist will expect the writer to have some difficulties, and will be prepared to cooperate with him.

Elsewhere the author has written of working with scientists (Chapter 17). It should be pointed out that if the two work for the same firm, or if the writer is doing a contract job for the scientist's employer, the scientist will be duty bound to help the writer. Hence, the writer may take as many notes as time permits in the presence of the scientist and in whatever manner is best adapted to the job, including the use of a tape recorder. If the writer has properly prepared himself on this subject and its vocabulary, he should have little difficulty that successive interviews cannot remove.

ORGANIZING AND OUTLINING. These comprise the third step. By organizing is here meant the bringing together of all necessary data and the proportioning of the subdivisions according to their importance. The important points to be considered include the following: the readers, purpose, funds and space available, deadline for completion, and type of publication.

The reader determines the extent to which technical material should be simplified, what vocabulary to use, what terms to define, what kind of and how many illustrations to use, and such other considerations as length.

The purpose can be as varied as any other writing aspect. It may be to entertain — if it is to be presented for popular reading — but more frequently it is to inform, to explain, to compare, to show change and improvement. Whatever the purpose, it should be clear in the writer's mind.

The extent of funds and space available influence length of presentation, the number of illustrations, perhaps even the kind, the weight and quality of paper, which printing process to use, extent of distribution, and other items of varying importance. If space is limited, condensation and a tighter style will be necessary, and illustrations may have to be limited or omitted.

The deadline, or date for completion, also may determine how much work can be done, whether extra help must be employed, how much "midnight oil" must be burned, etc. When speed is necessary, some steps or elaborations may have to be skipped.

Type of publication must be considered, whether a magazine article, monograph, leaflet, advertisement, or other form. These items influence length and also are related to the type of reader.

The interrelations between these items are obvious. If the technical writer himself is not expert and knowledgeable in all of the writing and publishing techniques, then someone else must supply the basic information, not only before the writing is begun but also before the outlining or organization is started.

Organizing and outlining work together like the right and left hands. In discussing outlining this author means the formation of an orderly presentation of all the parts of a technical piece in a logical manner. It isn't enough that the manner of presentation be orderly; it must be the most sensible, which means the one best fitted to the purposes and circumstances involved. An alphabetical arrangement would be orderly, but not necessarily logical or sensible. In an index or glossary the alphabetical list is both orderly and logical. But in a set of directions on how to assemble a piece of machinery, first things must come first and all other items must be in the order in which they are to be assembled.

The process of outlining was explored on pages 318-319. The same method can be applied to the technical article, monograph, or book. When the research and interviewing are done and one faces the task of arranging notes in orderly fashion, you should put all major topics on easily shufled cards, such as 3″ x 5″. Some sort of logical order exists in every aggregation of parts, and what is good order for one group is not necessarily good for another. The best order is determined by the purpose of the piece, and will be that order in which the reader would wish to use them.

WRITING PROCESS. This is the fourth step, and its goals are accuracy and clarity for the description and exposition involved. The writer is not concerned with entertaining his reader, nor with such elements as dramatic suspense. Instead, he must be able to explain his subject with simplicity and accuracy, both of which call for a good understanding of the subject.

It is customary to begin some technical pieces with a summary, possibly of what has been learned, of what the new device can accomplish, or of how the new model is different or better than the old. However, it is not necessary to write the summary first; the summary can be written last. Instead, begin writing at a point at which you feel most sure of yourself and of the facts. As you progress from part to part, your knowledge and understanding of the job will increase. For the parts about which uncertainty arises, reference to experts or resort to research may be necessary.

Most technical writing consists of descriptive and expository passages, in which the sentences should be as simple and as forward moving as possible. Declarative sentences are the greatest source of strength, and they should follow each other in orderly fashion. Writing then becomes a process of setting down one clear sentence after another.

REVISING AND EDITING. Few, if any, writers can produce good work without revision and editing — certainly not their best work. Rearrangement, rephrasing, and substitution are all necessary for the sake of accuracy, clarity, and logical sequence. After the first draft has been completed, the manuscript should be put aside for a few days, if possible. Then with a refreshed point of view the writer begins to rearrange words, phrases, and paragraphs. He reconsiders his readers, whether

experts in the same field, other scientists, or a popular audience. He
debates his choice of words and perhaps changes them. He asks himself
whether every phrase, paragraph, and step is clear. He also checks
grammar, punctuation, spelling, and capitalization.

If a summary section is needed, he may now add that. He looks to
historical aspects if reference should be made to them, and whether
credit should be given to another and earlier worker. If so, credit lines
are usually footnoted or brought together at the end of the piece.

Other items for consideration include length of paragraphs and order
of their arrangement, as well as length of sentences. Both paragraphs
and sentences may need to be broken up to improve readability. Only
well-known abbreviations should be used either in footnotes or in the
body of the article. If there is any doubt, the abbreviation should be
spelled out the first time used. Abbreviations that need no explanation
are published in a list by the American Standards Association.

Some consideration should also be given to eliminating the jargon of
the men who produced the notes and data being explained. This jargon
goes by such names as engineeringese, gobbledegook, bafflegab, sciench,
etc. The terms refer to debased English. They do not refer to the indispensable words properly coined to name or describe new processes
or inventions. Jargon is bad because it decreases clarity and intelligibil-
ity, and so destroys the purposes of the technical piece. Users of jargon
write of *finalizing* instead of finishing, of *writing-wise* instead of the
writing, or of checking the data *plant-wise*. Twisted phrases and literary
adornment should be considered jargon in the technical piece. The
majority of official documents, including university bulletins, reek with
jargon. Watch for it, and eliminate it from your writing.

Illustrations

As the writer is seldom an artist or draftsman, he often cannot
originate the necessary illustrations. So he consults with the drafting
staff and possibly the scientists or engineers. Together the illustrations
are planned. Many laboratories and manufacturing or engineering concerns maintain their own staff of technical illustrators. So do such
magazines as *Fortune, Popular Science, Popular Mechanics,* and many
others. When a free-lance writer works with this type of publication,
he is expected to help with the illustrations by supplying blue prints,
photographs, and sketches whenever possible.

You can add to your usefulness by getting acquainted with all the
illustrative possibilities in your field, and by keeping up with the best

being published by other firms. You should know the potentialities for illustrating what you write although you cannot do the art work yourself.

Printing Knowledge

The reader has learned considerable in earlier chapters about preparation of manuscripts — margins, double-spacing, and other details. All of this is usable when writing the technical article, because the rules and practices are much the same in all printing shops. Some new techniques must be picked up for technical writing. For instance, it is sometimes necessary to draw by hand certain mathematical symbols or Greek letters. The *first* time such are used they should be circled lightly in pencil and then explained in the margin with the explanation also circled. This is for the benefit of editors and printers who are to handle the manuscript. The beginner should study the carbon copy of other technical pieces written for his firm. He will, of course, keep a permanent carbon of his own manuscripts. He will need one for his own files and at least one carbon and the original for his employer.

Beyond such basic information you should learn the commonest printing practices and terms, so that you can anticipate the expectations of printers or magazine editors. This brief treatise on technical writing cannot go into detailed explanation of printing aspects. Such books as Edmund C. Arnold's *Ink on Paper* (Harper & Row) will give you all the necessary information, or will indicate where it is to be found. With this subject, as with most others, you must expect to be your own instructor, self-directed and persistent, looking into all the sources you might expect to be useful.

Training Steps

1. Define a technical article. How does it differ from a technical report?
2. What indexes list the contents of technical and scientific journals?
3. List 5 different forms in which technical material appears.
4. List 10 different magazines that use only technical articles.
5. List 10 different magazines that use popularized versions of technical articles.
6. What are the purposes for which technical articles and other technical material are used?
7. What are the 5 basic steps in writing the technical piece?
8. What is a simple way to get started on an outlining task?
9. What important items should be considered before outlining a technical piece?

10. In suggesting illustrative material for a technical piece why is it valuable to study similar pieces of writing?
11. Why is a knowledge of printing useful to the technical writer?
12. Define jargon. How does it differ from ordinary slang or colloquialisms? In what areas of public life is it most common?

CHAPTER 21

Seasonal and Anniversary Articles

From the point of view of the writer or editor who plans his work, articles fall into two classes: those subjects that cannot be anticipated and those that can.

Most common among the first class is the article based on such unexpected events as accidents, great storms, serious fires, or spectacular crimes. Articles so based are usually handled by only the newspapers, which rush them into print before their timeliness wears off.

The second class is composed of those subjects that can be anticipated and for which long-range plans can be laid. Four distinct types are found in this class. They are the seasonal article, the holiday item, the anniversary remembrance, and the article dealing with fads and crazes. This chapter discusses the last four types.

Seasonal articles, holiday pieces, and anniversary remembrances are quite obviously tied to the yearly calendar. The fad or craze may or may not be. Nevertheless, the success of all four types depends in large part on the timeliness of their appeal, and all attempt to treat their subjects with a new approach or a new angle. The monthly magazines do not as a general rule attempt to compete with the newspapers in presenting the early facts on such events. They frequently do assign

special writers or staff members to do articles on the consequences of
these happenings.

Calendars and Editors

Pressed by the timeliness of the newspaper, as well as by the imme-
diacy of radio news broadcasts, magazines must print some articles
closely related to the date of issue, or be consigned to a role they have
long avoided — that of being behind the times. That is why so many magazines give top priority to articles in step with the calendar.

Only a few newspapers have developed sections that compare with
similar material in the best magazines. Perhaps there are no more than
a dozen newspapers whose articles rank with the thoughtful, carefully-
prepared presentations that appear in scores of magazines. This is to be
expected, for magazines and newspapers alike survive because of specialization. The public looks to the latter for immediate presentation of
important events, but thoughtful people seek more careful analysis and
more complete background in the nation's magazines.

Long ago magazine editors turned to the calendar to find a source
for article subjects that would help them compete in timeliness with
the newspapers. The magazines eventually trained their readers to expect
certain kinds of articles in certain issues. Now readers demand that
magazine editors keep up the practice, and few editors would risk what
might happen if they abandoned the practice. Newspapers also use
many articles based on the calendar, and it is this type of material which
free lances may find easiest to sell to the daily press.

Seasonal Articles

The seasonal article, an excellent example of how the practice of
timely writing has worked out, is simply an article tied to one of the
four seasons. It can be sharply differentiated from the anniversary item
because no specific date can be assigned it. For instance, the February
issues of several monthly magazines have regularly presented one or
more articles on vegetable gardening. The same issues frequently carry
articles dealing with the birthdays of Lincoln and Washington. The
former type is keyed to an entire season or perhaps longer, whereas the
latter's usefulness may be limited to a single day — the anniversary of
the birthday.

PLANNING AHEAD.   Editors are forever making plans to anticipate the
seasonal demands of their readers. Some of the necessary articles are

assigned to staff members, because editors must know for certain that they will have on hand satisfactory treatment of required subjects when it is needed. They are usually delighted to come across such an item in their mail, for it means the staff can turn to something else equally pressing. Furthermore, the free lance usually has a fresher viewpoint than that of the staff member.

NEW TREATMENT. Usually *the writer's chance of selling will rest on his ability to suggest a new type of treatment for a familiar subject, or a new approach to a hoary problem.* Remember that there are no new subjects — merely new approaches to old ideas. Simply avoid the angles used in previous articles.

PROCESS ARTICLES. Among the seasonal articles easiest to handle are process articles. Every magazine reader recalls articles that have told how to make spring salads or store furs during warm months; how to plan a summer picnic, select a summer camp for the children; how to winterize the house, get the children ready for school, protect shrubbery against winter freeze; and how to guard against fall colds, fires in leaky chimneys, or bad accidents on icy pavements.

It may appear strange that the seasonal writer should be always about six months ahead of the season, but such is his program. In July when thermometers soar, he is doing articles on winter sports or on cleaning the furnace. Then when winter rolls around, he is already planning pieces on summer vacation trips or on how to teach timid children to swim.

USING LIBRARIES. An adequate public library can be of great help to anyone interested in writing the seasonal article. Practically all of the general, the women's, and the first- and second-class magazines use such material. To learn what is salable, one need only study back copies.

INTERVIEWING. Still another approach is to interview merchants and tradesmen on seasonal trends in their occupations. Merchants must plan months ahead in order to have the right items on hand for each season. This fact fits in well with the working schedule of the writer of seasonal articles, who also must be planning ahead. He may discover salable ideas too late for whatever season is current, but he will be in touch with them and can write them up for the same season next year.

In some cases editors will be glad to print how Big Town Emporium doubled its sale of overcoats, even though it is too late to help other merchants before another fall and winter season. The successful promotion idea when printed will be remembered until the proper time to use it, or the idea may be translated in terms of other articles of merchandise.

Holiday Articles

The writer of holiday articles may not require a book of dates to tell him what lies ahead, but he will need access to magazine files to discover what holidays are worth writing up. Additional help may be secured by consulting such indexes as *Readers' Guide to Periodical Literature*. Christmas and Thanksgiving are so important that some magazines devote the entire December and November issues to them. Although each holiday period centers in a single date, their observance is normally spread over a longer time. Appropriate themes are found on cover pages, in the editorials, and in the articles, not to mention the fiction and the advertising.

The extended observation is true also of New Year's Day, Fourth of July, Leap Year, Labor Day, Memorial Day, and Easter. The fact is proved by the interest shown in these dates by the monthly magazines. Any one of them is important enough to attract the interest of various magazine departments. Numerous articles can be keyed to these dates, among them articles on fashion, food, entertainment, new slants on the significance of the dates, unusual or old-time observance, or similar customs in foreign lands.

Anniversary Articles

It has been stated that certain subjects are inexhaustible sources of materials for articles. Actually, first-rate subjects are not quite that plentiful. One of the best sources of subjects for articles is the almanac or yearbook of dates. So many interesting characters have lived and died and so many important events have occurred, all of them recorded in accessible books, that the writer need not look far to find a date worth writing about again.

WARS. Recollect how many articles have been written about the American Civil War! How many about the Battle of Gettysburg alone! And how many on Lincoln's address in commemoration of that event! Probably no one knows what the totals have been, but many articles will be written about these same events in years to come in spite of the Hundredth Anniversary celebrations.

The battles and the wars of mankind around the globe will long be an important source of salable articles. The anniversaries of the Revolutionary War, the Civil War, the Spanish-American and Mexican Wars, many notable Indian battles, and of World War I and World War II will not long remain out of the columns of the magazines and newspapers.

DISCOVERIES. Anniversaries of inventions, too, are first-rate jumping-off spots for a recapitulation of their development, history, and contribution. Every reader of this book will recall numerous articles on the cotton gin, the telegraph, the Atlantic cable, the linotype, the steamboat and steam engine, and the automobile and airplane. The anniversaries of important medical discoveries similarly can be used for first-rate articles. Fundamental discoveries in the sciences — chemistry, physics, geology, or astronomy — can also be relied on for their possibilities.

OTHER DATES. The historical importance of landmarks should not be overlooked, and anniversaries of the erection of well-known buildings or their destruction may be worth noting. Dedication of state and national parks and the preservation of homes and birthplaces of national heroes are opportunities for articles. Many writers have done excellent articles on the anniversary observance of outstanding disasters. Typical of the events so observed are the sinking of the "Titanic," the Johnstown flood, the San Francisco earthquake, the Chicago fire, the Eastland disaster, the burning of the zeppelin "Count von Hindenburg," and the Iroquois Theater fire.

ANNIVERSARY AIDS. Any of these occurrences is worth mention in national magazines, but for each event of this type there are scores of local events that can be handled for local newspapers. Most public libraries keep a file of clippings of outstanding local happenings. These can be consulted by interested writers. The historical societies present in many counties are equally good sources of article material. So are the records in county courthouses and in published county histories.

Most events of national historical importance are recorded in such books as *The American Book of Days*, and Putnam's *Handbook of Universal History*. The first reference presents dates in calendar form by month and by day of the month, so that it is easy to discover what has occurred on any date in the year — a necessary procedure in writing articles that are tied to the calendar. A third work, *Anniversaries and Holidays*, not only lists holidays but tells how they are observed and how the custom started. Complete reference to these volumes is given in Chapter 23.

TYPICAL EXAMPLE. Typical of the manner in which historical facts may be turned into marketable items by tying them to an anniversary was an article by this author on John Brown of Harper's Ferry fame. Two sandstone grave markers found in a Pennsylvania buckwheat field indicated the burial place of one of Brown's wives and one of his sons. The owner of the country store not far away collected small fees to be used for the erection of a monument calling attention to the two graves and the near-by ruins of Brown's tannery. These were all the facts available at the site, though two photographs were later taken.

Information which would have been available in almost any public library provided the body of the article. Tied to the anniversary of John Brown's death, which was on December 2, the article sold to a New York Sunday newspaper in mid-November. The anniversary of Brown's birth on May 9 might also have been used. The other date was nearer to hand and so was chosen. The opening paragraph was as follow:

> While the death of John Brown of Harper's Ferry on Dec. 2 will probably go unobserved by most of America, in the rural community of Blooming Valley, Penn., Thomas R. Cooney, a country storekeeper, will make a pilgrimage to the graves of John Brown's wife, Dianthe, and his son, Frederick, near which Cooney hopes to erect a monument.

The new facts available were not important in themselves, but they permitted a tie-in with a retelling of old and well-established facts, which sold because of the timely connection with the anniversary. Some ingenuity was called for and some reading in the public library. None of it was difficult. In much the same way, free-lance writers can write and sell articles on important subjects to national publications, or less important items to local newspapers.

WHICH ANNIVERSARY? Hard and fast rules cannot be laid down to determine which anniversary dates are important. Some facts are celebrated every year. Some are celebrated on the tenth, twenty-fifth, fiftieth, seventy-fifth, and hundredth anniversaries. But almost any anniversary can be used if the new angle is clever, the article well done, and the subject of importance. Recent events may be observed each year for the first decade, and less frequently thereafter.

As indicated by the John Brown incident, articles sell most easily when their relation to current events or ideas is emphasized. *Encyclopaedia Britannica* and *The Encyclopedia Americana* will prove invaluable in supplying the background for many of these historical or biographical treatises.

Interviews can be used at appropriate anniversaries to retell the facts in the lives of famous or remarkable living people. Statesmen; authors; celebrities of the stage, motion pictures, and radio; famous athletes; inventors; and occasionally obscure people connected with important events are among those who represent possible subjects for marketable articles.

Fads and Fashions

Not so important as the foregoing type but nevertheless productive are the fads, crazes, and fashions that sweep the country from time to time. Some are connected with the seasons of the year, while still others are involved with recurrent social, economic, or political phenomena.

STYLE TRENDS. Perhaps of first importance are fashions for men and women. It is necessary to point out only such magazines as *Esquire, Seventeen, Mademoiselle, Harper's Bazaar,* and *Vogue* to demonstrate the influence of public whim in the publishing world. Furthermore, nearly all of the women's magazines except professional journals maintain departments devoted to display of forthcoming fashions. As much money is usually spent by these magazines on the fashion department as on any other of the departments. Color pages, salaries, and scouting trips at home and abroad make this an important division. Countless women's pages in the newspapers and trade magazines devote a part of their content to reporting fashion changes.

Fashion trends are fairly easy to anticipate. Hints come from such centers as Paris, Hollywood, St. Louis, and New York City. Fashion scouts scan the preview fashion shows to pick up advance tips, while buyers from stores everywhere ferret out whatever they can learn of future trends. Most fashions are of sufficient duration to allow magazine handling. Even those born to last but a single season are known far enough in advance to permit magazine treatment.

ABILITY NEEDED. Unless writers are expert in their ability to spy out and make accurate forecasts, they cannot hope to do much with the best fashion magazines. Most of the writing for these magazines is done by staff members, fashion designers, or by other experts upon assignment.

FREE-LANCE OUTLETS. Only a few possibilities exist for free-lance writers who have not yet made a reputation for themselves. Perhaps the best of these is with the daily and Sunday newspapers through arrangement *in advance* to report or cover fashion shows, or to pick up feature items on local high school or college fads. It is the local angle that is important with these items. Since they are usually covered by regular staff members, a previous commitment from the editor is essential.

As the free-lance writer's knowledge and reputation are built up, there may be some chance for a position on the staff of such magazines as *Mademoiselle, Seventeen,* and *Harper's Bazaar,* or special assignments from the editors or to do features for them.

FADS. In handling articles on fads and crazes, beware of those that are so short-lived as to be out of date before your article can reach the newsstands. If there is such danger, try to sell your work to a Sunday newspaper rather than to a magazine. It is possible to develop on these items certain angles that are of a less perishable nature. For instance, one might do an article on the development in recent years of the bicycle's popularity among youngsters. There is probably a market for an article on safe conduct for bicycle riders. Often a great deal of prestige goes to the youngster who is quick to pick up new fads, and quite often such prestige creates a problem. Those who do not or cannot follow popular practices suffer deeply in various ways. *Parents' Magazine* and some of the teacher's journals are markets for mature discussion of this and similar problems.

ELECTIONS. Writers might also watch the passing elections and preceding campaigns for article ideas to be used in following years. Such subjects become timely each year on the same dates, and so are easily anticipated. Given a new point of view, the writer can set out in plenty of time to interest some editor.

When to Begin Writing

Among the aims of most magazine editors is to keep their publications as timely as human ingenuity and foresight can make them. But because few magazines are equipped for printing articles on short notice, a great deal of staff writing and buying in advance has to be done.

In order to be able to fit into the magazine routine set up by these practices, the free-lance must know something of the time schedule in the various types of publications. The more accurate this knowledge, the easier will be the business of selling to specific magazines.

Editors, like writers, keep files of ideas. Some of the ideas may not be used for a year; some for two, or three. This is particularly true of seasonal ideas that are unlikely to grow out of date or otherwise become valueless. Editors do not dare wait until the approach of their deadlines before arranging with staff or free-lance writers for seasonal and anniversary material. General plans are often made a year in advance, while in monthly magazines specific and final plans are seldom made within four months of the publication date.

WORKING AHEAD. For the free-lance six months generally is none too far ahead to begin the campaign to place a seasonal article in a monthly magazine. It takes time to write the query and get an answer, and perhaps to write and hear from a second or third editor if the first was not interested. It takes additional time to get the facts together and to write the article — possibly two or three weeks. Also the editor who writes favorably in response to a query may not like the article when he sees it. If he turns it down, then the article must be sent out until sold, or until there is no longer a time to get into print while it is still timely.

This time-scheduling means that on an article for Washington's birthday for a February issue that will reach the newsstands in late January, the writer should begin work by the first of August. Then, if the editor isn't interested in buying, there is still time to send the article to other markets.

Articles for weekly magazines should be underway not later than from 6 to 8 weeks before publication is expected. The query should be sent out at an even earlier date. Any writer working closely with an editor should be able to obtain more precise information on magazine deadlines than suggested in the preceding paragraphs. Obviously, the lag between buying and printing varies with the individual magazines. The news magazines, *Time* and *Newsweek,* have an exceptionally short production period, but they are not good markets for free-lance offerings. Such a weekly as *The Saturday Review* more nearly approximates the average in terms of time lag.

Experience with editors, with rejections and subsequent efforts to reach other markets, and with manuscripts that grow stale will teach the writer how important it is to work far ahead of publication — as well as how long that period should be.

Using Magazine Files

The best guide to what a magazine will buy in seasonal and anniversary articles is to be found in back copies. Most magazines are edited in accordance with formulas that call for certain types of articles. Magazines hesitate to alter their formulas if they have proved successful. Consequently, it is possible to count on a high degree of uniformity in the annual schedules.

If magazines use seasonal articles, they will ordinarily be found in the same issues each year. Having fixed the month or appropriate week when a magazine prints articles on football, for instance, a writer can arrange his own writing schedule to be in step with the schedule of the magazine. This should begin with a query preferably six months in advance of the date of publication.

While duplication of subject is desirable, duplication of treatment, angle of approach, and content are not. A new angle must be found, new treatment should be worked out, and the actual content should be as unlike that of preceding articles as possible.

When studying magazine files, any writer should be on the watch for workable ideas in his field. He may be running down one type of item, but he should not pass up any hint or suggestion that he may be able to use later. Either a clipping should be made — if that is possible — or enough of the idea should be copied out to satisfy future needs. These should be put away in the writer's permanent file of usable ideas.

Success with anticipatory articles depend on knowing what will be of interest later on. It depends also upon accurate timing and cooperation with the editors. Foresight is required, but the extra effort is worth while, for editors are especially glad to have seasonal articles offered to them.

Training Steps

1. Examine the files of *American Home* for any three consecutive years. In what month did the first garden article appear each year? In what other months each year do garden articles appear? Compare issues for the three years.
2. How many football articles are printed yearly by *Sports Illustrated?* Make a timetable of their appearance for three years.
3. Visit your local library, historical society, or country courthouse. Discover what historical records are available. What notable local events can be worked into magazine or newspaper articles? What are the best markets for them?
4. What are the outstanding newspapers with Sunday editions in your state? Inquire of the Sunday editors to see what historical features they would care to see, including battles and natural disasters.
5. Ascertain whether your state publishes a magazine. Usually these are devoted to the historical, cultural, social, and economic interests of the state. Nearly every state has such a magazine. Write to the editor to see whether you may submit articles on your own area. Also study the magazine for ideas to be tried out on national magazines.
6. Take a walk about your city or consult your friends about the current fads. Make a list. Which are on the way out? Which are beginning?
7. Ask a few merchants how they handle items for which fads create sudden demands. See if there is an article in this idea for a trade publication.
8. Familiarize yourself with *The National Geographic Magazine.* Note how this magazine handles historical articles of a regional nature. Examine the photographs. These are an excellent guide to both subject matter and treatment.

9. See if you can work out a new angle for an article for Lincoln's birthday, also for Washington's birthday.
10. Try to discover some neglected American hero whose anniversary should be celebrated.
11. Make a list of historical characters hailing from your community. Find out whether papers in your locality or area would buy articles on these people.

CHAPTER 22

Selling Photographs

The purpose of this chapter is to point out some possibilities for marketing photographs taken by writers who own a camera and understand its uses. It does not attempt explanation of the techniques of taking, developing, and printing photographs. That task is well done in the works referred to later in the chapter.

Because photography is often a part-time job, it fits in well with free-lance writing. The two complement each other ideally. While taking photographs to illustrate shorts or full-length articles, the writer often can with but little greater effort take additional shots of the same subjects to be marketed separately, or he may turn his lens toward different subjects in the same neighborhood. Still a third source of revenue will be found among pictures from articles that failed to sell. Many such prints can be placed if properly edited and captioned.

In the process of studying and uncovering photographic markets, a great deal of information will be picked up that can be turned to account in article writing. The pursuit should take the writer into new fields where salable article ideas will be turned up and new markets found. At the same time he will have opportunity to keep abreast among his own article markets. It may happen also that turning from one of these occupations to the other will serve to lift him out of the doldrums into which even the best writers occasionally drift.

Growing Importance of Photographs

While the value of illustrations appears to have been recognized as early as the beginning of printing processes, their adoption did not keep pace with that of unadorned type matter. Limitations of paper, ink, and engraving processes, as well as the demand for speed in press operations, combined to hold them to a minor role.

The greatest impetus to the use of photographs since 1900 has possibly been given by the reorganization and redesign of *Life* magazine in 1936. Instant adoption by the public of its new format and the group of magazines launched upon the tide of its success, including *Look* and *Ebony*, proved that what the public wanted was more pictures. Readers desired magazines that were easier to read, quicker to yield their content, and more interesting. Hundreds of editors and editorial workers knew this at a much earlier date, but it took *Life* magazine to show how the demand could be satisfied.

The success of such news periodicals as *Time* and *Newsweek* also is in good part dependent upon the alert and skillful use of timely news photographs. If denied the use of up-to-the-minute photographs of dramatic quality, neither of these publications would have such great reader audiences as they now enjoy, nor would their articles so easily convey their meaning.

Evidence of the influence of the picture magazines is to be found in nearly every publication that regularly uses photographic illustrations. One might not think of *Better Homes and Gardens* as coming under this influence. Nevertheless it has, and in a way that is typical of a host of other magazines. In the average issue will be found at least one how-to-do-it article, complete with pictures. Other illustrated articles will be used in the various departments, and in all of its chief competitors in a similar manner.

Although some articles are merely accompanied by photographs, numerous articles today consist entirely of photographs, explained only by brief captions. Among the scores of users are the women's home magazines, fashion magazines, and business and trade publications. Such pictorial sequences appear in more and more magazines as time passes.

Cameras for the Writer

Though this chapter is intended for writers who possess and operate one or more cameras, the following remarks may prove valuable to other writers who will one day enter the camera market.

Anyone buying his first camera should take three steps: 1. he should seek the advice of experienced photographers, in addition to the help of those who sell cameras; 2. he should procure and master at least one book for the novice; and 3. he should buy only a low or medium-priced camera.

Before buying a camera, the novice should seek the aid of the amateur or professional photographer. Since most owners become enthusiasts about their own cameras, it is well to talk to a number and so to survey the field. Once a camera has been purchased, then the advice of dealers on its operation is likely to be invaluable.

Many advantages are found in a used camera purchased from a reliable shop. It is less expensive, it should be as good as a new one, and the buyer usually gets most for his money. Lacking local opportunities for purchasing a good second-hand camera, the prospective buyer can usually obtain what he wants through one of the photographic magazines. In them will be found advertisements of dealers of established reputation. These firms can usually be counted on to stand behind any sales they make.

If a new camera is preferred, then the beginner would do well to purchase one under, say, $75. For that figure a fairly accurate camera with sufficient range of operation can be had. Although it will not have the highest speed and certain other advantages, it will be good enough to practice on. After the owner has used it a few months, he will know whether a camera fits into his career. If not, he has not lost too much. If the use has proved successful, then he can make plans for obtaining a better camera.

Books on Photography

Among books that may be useful are those cited below. Some of them may be picked up at sceond-hand bookstores, or borrowed from city or college libraries.

Where and How to Sell Your Pictures, Arvel W. Ahlers, (New York: Amphoto, 1962).
    A list of American and foreign markets.

Feature Photographs that Sell, Edmund C. Arnold, (New York: Morgan & Morgan, 1960).
> Collection of 365 daily picture ideas.

Portrait of Myself, Margaret Bourke-White, (New York: Simon & Shuster, 1963).
> An autobiography of the author. Illustrated with her photographs.

Images of War, Robert Capa, (New York: Grossman Publishers, 1964).
> Collection of excellent photographs by the author.

Photographs, Henri Cartier-Bresson, (New York: Grossman Publishers, 1963).
> Photographs by Cartier-Bresson. Essays on his methods.

Photography and the Law, George Chernoff and Hershel Sarbin, (New York: American Photographic Book Publishing Co., 1958).
> Legal aspects of taking photographs. Rights of privacy. Copyright.

The Minolta Manual, Joseph David Cooper, (New York: Universal Photo Book, 1959).
> A manual on the Minolta.

Color Photography, Eliot Elisofon, (New York: Viking Press, 1961).
> A collection of Elisofon's work.

The Complete Photographer, Andreas Feininger, (Englewood Cliffs, N. J.: Prentice-Hall, 1965).
> Complete summation of Feininger's previous works.

Creative News Photography, Rodney Fox and Robert Kerns, (Ames, Iowa: Iowa State University Press, 1961).
> How to communicate news, ideas and information.

On the Creation of Photographic Ideas, Philippe Halsman, (New York: Ziff-Davis, 1961).
> How to get ideas.

How to Shoot and Sell Money-Making Pictures, Walter L. Harter, (New York: Amphoto, 1961).
> A practical book, somewhat on the commercial side.

A New Guide to Rollex Photography, Fritz Henle with H. M. Kinzer, (New York: Viking Press, 1965).
> A teaching manual on how to use the Roliflex.

You Can Test Cameras, Lenses and Equipment, Herbert Keppler, (New York: Amphoto, 1962).
> 124 ways to check cameras before buying.

Press Photography, Rhode and McCall, (New York: Macmillan, 1961).
> How to report with a camera.

Photojournalism: Pictures for Magazines and Newspapers (2nd ed), Arthur Rothstein, (Philadelphia: Chilton Books, 1965).
> An updating of his earlier book on this subject.

The Art and Techniques of Journalistic Photography, Otha C. Spencer, (Wolfe City, Texas: Henington Publishing Co., 1966).
> A survey of photography as an art form and form of expression.

A Life in Photography, Edward Steichen, (Garden City, New York: Doubleday, 1963).
> A collection of superb photographs. Some text.

Visual Persuasion, Stephen Baker, (New York: McGraw-Hill, 1961).
The effect of pictures on the subconscious.

Salable Prints

Back of every salable print is a definite idea. The idea is first conceived by the photographer, and then *visualized*. This means that the
photographer has to dramatize his idea by means of people, animals,
scenery, and items of furniture or other props. Nearly all first-grade
photographs are carefully planned to convey an idea or impression.
Even if some dramatic situations have been come across accidentally, no
one can depend upon mere chance to supply ready-made subjects with
all the desirable qualities present.

A vast difference exists between different photographs of the same
subject. What is it that makes one print memorable and another a
failure? Among the necessary qualities are 1. good composition, 2. freedom from irrelevant detail, 3. proper centering of points of chief interest,
4. animation, 5. wide range of color value, 6. human interest, 7. dramatic value. These are among the qualities that make a print pleasing
to the eye of the magazine or newspaper reader.

Just as slanting is necessary for articles, so is it necessary to slant
photographs. Slanting of the latter is somewhat easier than of the
former. Mostly it is a matter of selecting the right market. If numerous
issues of the prospective market have been studied, it will be easy to send
the right prints to the right market.

Why Prints Are Rejected

Reasons for rejecting good prints vary. The chief reasons are as follows: 1. they went to the wrong market; 2. they arrived too late to be
worked into the schedule; 3. the magazine was already stocked; 4. they
failed to tell an interesting story; or 5. they lacked the proper restraint.
This last fault is likely to be true of prints other than in the class of
"leg art."

Technical reasons for rejection include diffused focus, weak tones,
insufficient contrast, scratches and bad holes, light-struck areas, too small
size, uninteresting foreground, and cluttered composition. The foregoing
by no means include all the technical reasons for rejection. The experienced amateur and the professional photographer can tell at a glance
what is technically wrong with a print. But only those who have studied
the markets and know how far to submit in advance of publication can
know why good prints are returned.

Some monthly magazines select photographs as far as eight months in advance of publication, others only six. Few work as close as four months to the date of publication. Seasonal prints also are much in demand. They are more readily tied to the calendar than articles. Unlike the latter, they usually have to be done twelve months in advance if the out-of-doors is to be introduced. From four to six months later they are taken from the files and submitted to the magazine editor who uses that type of print. Newspaper editors can be approached at a later date.

Subjects for Photographs

Whether or not a subject is interesting usually depends upon what the reader brings to it. Similarly, whether an idea is usable depends upon what the photographer can see in it. While the manner in which some ideas may be developed often is obvious, at other times ingenuity and rare originality are required. This latter situation is the real test of the photographer's ability.

ANIMALS. Interest in domesticated animals is perpetual. The subject is always good, always new; and the market is wide. The Sunday rotagravures seldom go to print without one or more photographs of household pets or farm animals. Such subjects also appear on magazine cover pages, in the advertisements, and in the story and article columns.

Tens of thousands of pictures of cats and kittens have been and will be printed. Cats hunting, nursing, playing, fighting, or merely yawning have in their photographic likenesses entertained countless millions of readers. Dogs come a close second to cats in point of interest, and horses in third place. All domesticated animals make good subjects — suckling pigs, grazing sheep, feeding chickens, and the perennial Thanksgiving turkey.

ARCHITECTURE. A more sober business is the photographing of homes and monumental buildings. Some photographers have made a profitable business of photographing nothing but homes. A large percentage of home owners will buy a well-taken picture of their home if the price is right. The free-lance writer who specializes in articles for the home-and-garden magazines might well see what he can do with this branch of photography.

Photographs of homes are best when taken with a three-quarters profile — either left or right. They should be snapped when the sun is shining against the front — if possible — and the view of the house should be framed by trees or shrubs. The common "before" and "after" pictures of remodeled homes are usually taken in fall or winter and in summer, respectively. In addition to sales to owners, possibilities include sale to Sunday newspapers, house-and-garden magazines, trade journals, historical societies, museums, and private collectors.

BABIES. Babies have long been the favorite camera subject of photographers everywhere. More than pets, even more than pretty girls, they have consistently appeared in more places in more magazines than any other single subject. When combined with an animal, such as a young dog or kitten, they have frequently been irresistible.

Babies make good subjects for many reasons. Interest in them is universal, and they are naturally good posers. Yet it is not enough that baby pictures be of attractive youngsters. The society sections of the newspapers are full of such pictures, most of which *would not* be salable to the rotogravure sections or to the magazines. Baby pictures must show the subject doing something — if merely expressing an unusual mood, such as wonder or puzzlement. Props of some sort are almost always necessary, though a parent, a companion, a pet, or a toy may serve in that capacity. Somehow the photographer must make the picture tell a story. Such is likely to occur when the youngster is faced with something new within his experience. Ingenuity will go a long way in helping the photographer contrive new situations and new types of adventure for the very young.

BEAUTY SPOTS. The rotogravure sections of the Sunday newspapers, the syndicates, and such publications as *Audubon Magazine* have long been good markets for photographs that were recommended chiefly by their beauty. Waterfalls, lush meadows, woodland trails, winding creeks, snow and ice scenes, are fit subjects in this class. While it is somewhat more difficult to make them tell a story, they should express such moods as tranquility and serenity. The quiet of early morning and evening may be captured in carefully-planned shots. Other moods and feelings have been beautifully expressed by pictorial and scenic views found in numerous magazines and newspapers.

FARM AND COUNTRY. The authentic farm scene is in demand in a wide variety of markets. While the farm journal usually wants photographs devoted to new inventions for the farm, new crops, new ideas in agriculture, horticulture, and animal husbandry, or improvements for the barn or the house, general magazines prefer the farm scene that tells an interesting story. So do the rotogravure sections.

The usual farm routines of plowing, planting, cultivating, and harvesting offer limitless opportunities for dramatic, storytelling photographs. Human interest and beauty alike are in these everyday chores — if the photographer can see these qualities.

Illustration 18 — Action is one of the elements that makes a successful picture. Participants in the picture should not be looking directly into the camera. In this way the posed look is avoided. (Photo by Norman B. Moyes)

HOME AND GARDEN.   No photographer need go out of his own home or beyond his own garden to find subjects for his camera. A sense of humor is a great help in seeing the familiar routines and objects in a new way. Variations on the old chores, such as "dad" in "mother's" apron while washing the dishes, are photographic "naturals." But they must tell some sort of story. Even sweeping and dusting can be made interesting if imagination is used. Canning, redecorating, upholstering, repairing, remodeling, and similar active processes are suitable for picture sequences.

Outside the house are rock gardens, pools, herb and vegetable gardens, flower beds, arbors, pergolas, fireplaces, flagstone walks, stone retaining walls, decorative wells, and massed shrubbery. Close-up, crystal-clear pictures showing details of construction of such subjects are much in

Illustration 19 — Street scenes are especially useful in travel articles. Such pictures should be taken when pedestrians or vehicles are present. Cars and costumes may "date" such shots, but increased interest offsets this fact. (Photo by Norman B. Moyes)

demand. The general, distant, scenic shot is more difficult to sell. Here, also, are opportunities for picture sequences and "before" and "after" shots of repairs and alterations.

NATURE. A study of *Audubon Magazine* will show what is meant by the nature picture. Most rotogravure sections are steady users of this type of photograph. These are the pictures that show various aspects of natural history — the pollination of a flower, gathering of honey, building the bird's nest, feeding young birds, close-up of insects and flower parts, bursting of the milkweed pod — any of the life processes of plant, insect, or animal.

From the first swelling bud of the pussy-willow in spring to storage of the last nuts by the ever-present squirrel, the out-of-doors offers an endless variety of subjects. Certainly, it is one of the pleasantest of occupations — this pursuit of pictorial nature. Few photographers have specialized in this field, for it requires patience, expert knowledge of camera and natural history, as well as willingness to spend long hours in

Illustration 20 — Scenes that transport their viewers to distant places bring interest and strength to articles, both in the eyes of the readers and of those who may be prospective article buyers. Note the appeal in this photo. (Photo by Bob Kerns)

the open. A writer-photographer can build an enviable scientific reputation in the field of nature, for the demand is great and the competition slight.

Illustration 21 — Close-ups of people are always better than middle distance shots, because they give the beholder a greater feeling of being present. And they improve sales chances of accompanying manuscripts. (Photo by Bob Kerns)

A word of caution might be dropped concerning one point. The day when magazines and newspapers are interested in faked pictures of nature is past. Humorous associations and interpolations are possible if so indicated; but few publications will knowingly buy falsified pictorial facts.

SHORE SCENES. The sailing schooner, the freighter, the liners, the trawlers, dorymen, lobstermen, clam diggers, oystermen, seine menders, and the endless items of ocean traffic and deep — sea fishing — all are important to the photographer because they hold great interest for landsmen as well as for seafarers.

Bathing beauties, shore picnics, and sculptures, games, beach conversation and gossip, odd characters, toddlers — these are what editors want. As one writer says, "What is a beautiful picture of a sand dune compared to a shot of three pretty girls playing leapfrog on the beach?"

SPORTS. Because sports involve struggle, adventure, and glimpses of the unusual, photographs in this field are perennially interesting. Sports fall into two groups: organized and unorganized. Many organized sports — baseball, football, basketball, and track — are amply covered by staff photographers from newspapers and magazines. Nonprofessional gatherings in the same sports are better sources of salable photographs. Sand-lot baseball, marble games, and other sports involving youngsters up to the mid-teens are prolific sources of good pictures. These are best when marketed so that they can be published in advance of or at the beginning of the proper season.

Among unorganized sports, fishing is by all odds the most important. Trout fishing, surf casting, bass fishing, deep lake trolling, and the immortal boy with his homemade outfit — these bring a breath of the out-of-doors, a moment of relaxation, or a brief vicarious vacation to those who cannot get away from their duties. Good pictures in this class are difficult to take but rewarding. Editors seldom get enough good pictures of this sort that are free from publicity taints. Resorts, hotels, railroads, and bus lines are good market for such photographs.

TRADING AND MANUFACTURING CONCERNS. From the business and manufacturing districts of the cities and towns come the photographs that fill the hundreds of trade and manufacturing magazines. Pictures of attractive store windows, new departments, remodeling, new stores and new locations are wanted by magazines that cater to trades involved. A good picture, 50 or 75 words of copy, or a picture sequence often suits the editor best. Most frequently overlooked are the wholesalers.

They also are served by trade journals. So are the manufacturers. Not many writers or photographers understand the needs of these last two groups; consequently, competition is relatively light. The writer who specializes among the trade journals will find literally hundreds of markets for carefully-slanted photographs.

Photographic Magazines

The writer needs the encouragement and market notes of the writer's magazines, and the writer-photographer needs the aid of a good photographic journal. Articles by experienced photographers will help solve many a problem in exposure, developing, printing, and marketing. The annotated list below includes the most outstanding magazines of value to the amateur. Some will be found in the average city library and need not be purchased. Others may be available in photographic supply stores for occasional study, but for clipping the photographer needs his own.

Modern Photography. Monthly. Jacquelyn Balish, Editor, 33 W. 60th St., New York.
    Good advice for amateurs and professional photographers.
National Press Photographer. Monthly. Joe Costa, Editor. National Press Photographers Association, 235 E. 45th St., New York.
    Press photography and all related fields. News items, trade news.
Popular Photography. Monthly. Bruce Downes, Editor. 1 Park Avenue, New York 16, New York.
    General and technical articles. Emphasis on amateur work. Combined with other magazines in recent years.
U.S. Camera Magazine. Monthly. Ed. Hannigan, Editor. 9 E. 40th Street, New York 16, New York.
    Excellent picture sequences. Beautifully illustrated.

Photographic Markets

Nothing surpasses personal contact in selling photographic prints. For the writer-photographer in the small town this means careful cultivation of local newspaper editors and regional magazines. If he lives not too far from larger publishing centers, he can make the round of editors every few weeks.

These office calls are best because they are more likely to reveal why prints are rejected, as well as more likely to uncover what the editors are looking for. A few visits to editors are worth more than all the current market notes in existence. Orders for future delivery are the natural outgrowth of editorial conferences. However, when free-lance writer-photographers have become known to editors, queries or direct submission of prints may be completely satisfactory.

One authority states that 85 photographs are sold by free-lances for every 15 sold by commercial studios, and that free-lance photographers furnish most of the photographs purchased by magazines. One magazine alone purchases more than 6,000 annually. Magazines of small and medium circulations may be better markets than more imposing magazines, because the latter frequently have their own highly-organized staffs.

PRICES. Prices paid for photographs vary so widely that it is not possible to give an accurate average. *Life* magazine pays a minimum of twenty-five dollars per print for free-lance photographs. Many rotogravure editors pay much less. Prices in the last decade have doubled or trebled in most markets. Black and white prints bring much less than color prints or transparencies. Advertising agencies, makers of calendars, and publicity bureaus sometimes pay fabulous prices for outstanding pictures. Two, three, four, or five hundred dollars is not an exceptional price for a cover photo even on a modest magazine, while top prices go up to fifteen hundred dollars and more. Prices paid by most markets can be found in the writer's market guides listed on p. 357. Beginners can learn what their photos are worth from them.

RIGHTS. The photographer is the exclusive owner of any picture he takes when acting for himself — until he sells all or part of the rights. In selling a print to an editor, he also sells the right to reproduce it; consequently, the seller should state what rights he intends to sell. If the sale is of *exclusive* rights, the print should so state. Similarly, any rights reserved should be mentioned.

Since the right type of picture may sell to several markets, it is often wise to state that you are offering only "newspaper rights" within the circulation area of the prospective buyer, or single publication rights if the buyer is a magazine. Thus, the same photograph may be sold to a newspaper, a magazine, postcard firm, calendar publishers, and perhaps an advertising agency, if the respective rights have been properly reserved. Such widespread sales are limited by the fact that some editors will buy only the exclusive rights of a photograph.

MARKET GUIDES. A number of helpful guides are at hand to aid the free lance in selling his photographs. The information they offer should be supplemented by first-hand study of magazines, and by personal visits to agencies and editors when possible. Below is a list of such guides.

Directory of Newspapers and Periodicals, (Philadelphia: N. W. Ayer and Son, Inc.).
> Lists magazines and newspapers by place of publication.

International Year Book, (New York: Editor and Publisher).
> Lists all photographic syndicates, partly classified. Correspondence with firm usually necessary to determine if they buy as well as sell.

Literary Market Place, (New York: R. R. Bowker Co.).
> Brief list of advertising agencies and public relations bureaus.

The Writer's Handbook, A. S. Burack (ed.), (Boston: The Writer).
> Frequent editions. Articles by numerous contributors to *The Writer.* Market notes are good, especially for beginning writers, but should be supplemented by queries .

The Writer's Market, (Cincinnati, O.: Writer's Digest Publishing Co.).
> Best information on whether magazines buy photographs.

Mailing Prints

Prints may be sent singly or in batches. Ample postage should be placed on the return envelope. In all cases photographs should be protected by two pieces of corrugated cardboard placed in the return envelope. The cardboard should be about an inch larger than the photographs, which are inserted between the boards. The top photograph may be turned face down to protect it from scratching. Envelopes are addressed as for the mailing of an article.

Close-up portraits may be as small as 5 x 7 inches. Most of the other types should be 6 x 8, 7 x 9, or 8 x 10 inches. The latter size is preferable. A brief note may be included, and is advisable when the sender is unknown to the prospective buyer. Prints may be submitted under the phrase "at your usual rates," or a definite price may be asked. The sender's name should be penciled or stamped on the back of every print. Typewriters should never be used on photographic prints, for some of the characters strike through and may reproduce. Such defacing may cause rejection of an otherwise acceptable print.

Captions should be slanted to each market. Some publications use short cutlines; others want fuller explanation. Subject matter affects the length and character of copy, though the style tends to be condensed. The facts, of course, must be accurate. If desirable, attention may be called to points of interest in the photograph. Individuals are usually named from left to right, and the row is given when two or more lines appear.

In general supply more information than appears necessary. An editor can easily blue-pencil part of the wordage, but may be unable to increase it. Copy is typewritten on a sheet of paper slightly narrower than the print. The sheet, which should not be unnecessarily large, is next pasted to the back of the photograph at the bottom, and then bent up and over the face of the print.

Legal Aspects of Photographs

The courts have held that an individual may be libeled as readily by a photograph as by printed words. In selling prints the free lance should be careful not to offer those that hold anyone up to public scorn, contempt, or ridicule. If in doubt, the photographer should omit the questionable print.

There is an easy safeguard that can be taken, and that is to have those who appear in a print sign a brief statement saying that the picture is used with their permission. This is seldom necessary in the case of pictures of large crowds, since they are not likely to be libelous. The fact that a gathering is public is usually sufficient safeguard. Study of what newspapers and magazines print is a good guide to what may be safely offered for sale.

Training Steps

1. Analyze three issues of *Life magazine*. How many picture stories are found in each issue?
2. What percentage of photographs is used merely to illustrate text matter?
3. In how many cases does the entire text serve solely to explain photographs?
4. Examine issues of *Time* and *Newsweek*. What are the sources of their photographs? How many are dramatic, storytelling photographs? How many are static poses, such as studio portraits?
5. Make a tabulation of the list of photographic credits in any issue of *Life*. How many photographs appear to be the work of free-lance photographers?
6. Study the list of photographic syndicates in Editor and Publisher's *International Year Book*. What suggestions do you get from a study of the classifications for marketing pictures?
7. If you have been an amateur photographer, take the time to run through your files or album. How many pictures have you that you could sell after proper cropping and enlarging?
8. If *The Illustrated London News* is available, note whether it is printing photographs from the United States. If so, what are their character and where were they obtained?
9. What do you understand by the term "photographic idea"?
10. If your local newspaper has a picture page, how many of the photographs tell a dramatic story?

11. How many picture sequences do you find in an average issue of *Look?* Do these differ from the picture sequences in *Life?*
12. Study several issues of *Audubon Magazine.* What type of photographs do they use? Are any of them dramatic storytellers?
13. Make a similar study of *American Forests.*
14. Make a list of three photographs that you consider typical for each month in the year — a total of 36 photographs.
15. What are the differences between an instructive photograph and an amusing photograph?
16. Does your state have a historical magazine to which you could sell photographic stories?
17. What departments of your state government issue bulletins or magazines to which you might sell pictures?
18. Visit a newsstand. How many magazines use photographs for cover illustrations of a type that you could furnish?
19. How many sports magazines appearing on the newsstands use photographs from free-lance photographers?
20. Which of the out-of-doors magazines use photographic frontis-pieces or occasional photographs?
21. From Editor and Publisher's *International Year Book* make a list of the Sunday newspapers in your area that publish rotogravure sections. Obtain copies of these, study them, and then make inquiries to determine to how many you can sell photographic prints.

CHAPTER 23

Reference Works for Article Writers

In addition to the typewriter and its customary supplies, possibly a camera and equipment, and a few miscellaneous items, the chief tools of the writer are books, magazines, and other published works consulted in the production of articles. The content and uses of these invaluable tools should be familiar to the writer and available to him in an adequate degree.

The ordinary routines of writing will lead to the use of these tools upon many occasions: 1. in checking the accuracy of the data to be used; 2. in the correction of spelling, punctuation, and grammar; 3. in uncovering usable data or new subjects; 4. in keeping abreast of recent developments that may be adapted to the writer's field; 5. in checking the work of literary competitors; and 6. in locating quotations or anecdotes with which to illuminate the manuscript.

Using Magazines

Discovery will quickly be made that no one person can subscribe to all the magazines published. The problem is to decide which to purchase and which to obtain at other sources. Some should always be at hand so that they can be referred to frequently and thoroughly digested. With others a skimming through will be sufficient. Most of these can be used at public libraries or elsewhere without the expense of purchasing.

THE HOME LIBRARY. For the firt two or three years a beginner will find that writers' magazines afford good advice and encouragement. The occasional article that fits one's needs may more than repay the subscription price. Some writers' magazines are highly commercialized. If this defect is understood, such magazines can still be of value. The following magazines are recommended for home use, but the writer should study a few issues of each before selecting any to which he intends to subscribe.

Author & Journalist. $4 a year, Farrar Publishing Co., Monthly. Washington, D. C.
> Market notes and prize contests. Articles on writing, occasionally by noted writers.

The Matrix. Theta Sigma Phi. Austin, Texas.
> Articles on all phases of writing. The woman's slant. Published six times a year.

The Quill. Sigma Delta Chi. Chicago. Published monthly.
> Articles on all phases of writing. The man's slant.

The Writer. $4 a year, 8 Arlington St., Boston 16, Massachusetts. 02111. Monthly.
> Sound articles on writing; market notes and prize contests.

The Writer's Digest. $3.50 a year, 22 E. 12th St., Cincinnati, 10, Ohio. 45210.
> Market notes and contests. Numerous pieces by successful writers. Long on inspiration and encouragement.

If the writer's field is a broad one, he won't be able to afford all the magazines to which he may be able to sell. Yet he should, if possible, subscribe to two or three of the leaders. Whatever magazines are chosen, they should strengthen his hold upon that field and improve his writing equipment.

Beyond the confines of any writer's special field are numerous magazines that may contribute to his development. He may wish to subscribe to one because of its influence on his style, to another to broaden his point of view, and to a third because original discoveries are first mentioned in it. Chosen with care and wisdom, such magazines will help mould a successful career.

THE PUBLIC LIBRARY. From public libraries will come much additional help. There many magazines will be found that are worth following. Some may deserve only a quick skimming; others will repay study from cover to cover — advertisements included. A weekly habit should be that of dropping into the city library for a few hours spent in keeping up to date. If the writer doesn't, he may one day find that his articles are beginning to be turned down — his field has grown away from him. The writer who is put on the shelf by his favorite editors will have a difficult time getting down again.

THE PRIVATE LIBRARY. Among other sources of valuable reading material are the libraries of experts and hobbyists. The stamp collector is almost certain to subscribe to *American Philatelist*, even if the public library does not. Physicians, psychiatrists, and other professional men, merchants, and craftsmen usually subscribe to their respective journals. If need to consult them is not too frequent, the writer may ask to be allowed to study the publication at the subcriber's place of business.

THE NEWSSTAND. A considerable part of keeping up to date can be done at the newsstand. If the writer makes a friend of the proprietor of a first-rate stand, he will permit such study. The introduction of new magazines can thus be noted, as well as the disappearance of old, established publications.

Other Reference Works

Although the major works of reference will be used at public and institutional libraries because of the high cost of private ownership, every writer will want to possess certain indispensable volumes. The number and kind will vary with the writer's specialty, but there should be no compromise on quality. When buying a permanent work, always get the most authoritative. This need not be the most expensive.

HOME LIBRARY. Since the building of a reputation for soundness of judgment and reliability of statement depends upon the accuracy of manuscripts submitted, every figure, name, and statement, as well as all doubtful spellings must be checked. Below is suggested a minimum library for serious writing. Should the writer decide to explore the various possibilities for himself, *How and Where to Look It Up*[1] will offer much help. Later in the chapter certain useful references, classified by type, are cited. In *all* cases try to get the latest edition of each reference work.

The Columbia Encyclopedia. New York: Columbia University Press, 1959.
    Compact work with concise articles planned for home and office use.
    Good when exhaustive articles by experts are not needed. One volume.

---

[1]*How and Where to Look It Up*. R. W. Murphey, New York: McGraw-Hill, 1958.

College Handbook of Composition. Edwin C. Woolley and Franklin W. Scott. Boston: D. C. Heath & Company, 1958.

Newspapers: 1. The local newspaper.   2. A comprehensive daily, such as *The New York Times.*

Roget's International Thesaurus. Peter Mark Roget. New York: Thomas Y. Crowell Company, 1962.

   Most complete list of synonyms, antonyms and related ideas.

Standard works: the best in the writer's specialty should be on hand.

Webster's New International Dictionary. Unabridged. Springfield, Mass.: G. & C. Merriam Co., 1961. Including Supplement.

   Includes foreign phrases, proverbs, abbreviations, and much other useful information in addition to definitions.

The World Almanac and Book of Facts. Harry Hansen (ed.), New York: New York World-Telegram and The Sun, yearly.

   Most useful of American almanacs for miscellaneous information. Social, economic, religious, political data, etc.

PUBLIC LIBRARY.   Not one writer in a hundred can afford to own all the source books he can use. Inevitably he will turn to the nearest public library or other repository for aid. To form the habit of using the public library should be one of the free-lance writer's early resolutions. The first step is to consult the librarian and win her cooperation. Any trained librarian can save the average writer a large percentage of the hours he must spend in research. She can not only save his time but also will often uncover or recommend material that would escape a less experienced worker.

With a little encouragement the librarian will also give instruction in the use of the available facilities. Such training is valuable, the more so because it can be used in other places and times. In absence of such instruction, a great deal of help can be found in *Find It Yourself.*[2]

The selected list of reference works that follows is not exhaustive, but is intended to introduce the writer to the most important standard works likely to be of use under ordinary circumstances.

ALMANACS AND ATLASES:

Historical Atlas. W. R. Shepherd. New York: Barnes & Noble, 1956.

   Excellent historical perspective, covering shifting geographical concepts, 1450 B.C. to 1929 A.D.

Information Please Almanac. D. Gotenpaul. New York: Simon & Schuster, yearly.

   Much useful information of a miscellaneous character. Tabulated. Incorporates facts current in preceding year.

---

[2]*Find It Yourself,* Elizabeth Scripture and Margaret R. Greer. New York: H. W. Wilson Co., 1955.

Rand McNally International World Atlas. Rand McNally. New York: Rand McNally.
> Most of the maps are of North America. Some foreign countries and world maps. Many statistics. See latest edition.

Universal World Atlas. New York: C. S. Hammond & Co., Inc., 1952.
> Political maps of countries and continents. Index of towns and cities of the world.

Whitaker's Almanack. Joseph Whitaker. London: London House, revised annually.
> Statistics of the British Empire, 1869 to date. Also foreign countries.

BIOGRAPHICAL SOURCES:

American Men of Science. Jacques Cattell (ed.), New York: Bowker, 1965.
> Facts about distinguished scientists. There are similar works for educators, writers, journalists, and other professional workers. See latest edition.

Current Biography. New York: H. W. Wilson Co.
> Monthly and cumulative yearbooks. People in the news.

Dictionary of American Biography. New York: Scribner, 1933.
> Includes only those no longer living. Noteworthy persons of all periods who lived in the United States. Signed articles, bibliographies.

Who's Who. New York: St. Martins.
> Best quick reference about living Britishers. See most recent volume, also earlier editions for nonactive or the recently deceased.

Who's Who in America. Chicago: Marquis, 1964-65.
> Biographical dictionary of notable living men and women. Data supplied by subjects. Home and business addresses. Published every two years. Also publish the Monthly Supplement.

BOOKS OF DATES:

The American Book of Days. G. W. Douglas. Rev. ed. by Helen D. Compton. New York: H. W. Wilson Co, 1948
> All important and many obscure anniversaries, including births and deaths of historical characters. Arranged by day of month and year. Useful for writer who anticipates calendar events.

Anniversaries and Holidays. M. E. Hazeltine. Chicago: American Library Association, 1944.
> Holidays and how to observe them, their origin. Worldwide.

An Encyclopedia of World History. W. L. Langer. Boston: Houghton Mifflin, 1952.

The World in 1965. Associated Press. New York: The Associated Press.
> Yearbook summary of events around the world.

BOOKS ON WRITING AND SELLING:

The Art of Plain Talk. Rudolph Flesch. New York: Harper & Brothers, 1946.

Free-Lance Writing for a Living. Paul W. Kearney. New York: David McKay Co., 1953.

How to Write and Sell Magazine Articles. Richard Gehman. New York: Harper, 1958.

How to Write and Sell Non-fiction. Hal Borland. New York: Ronald, 1956.

Magazine Article Writing. Ernest Brennecke, Jr. and Donald L. Clark. New York: Macmillan, 1942.

Marketing Your Literary Material. Donald MacCampbell. New York: The McBride Co., Inc., 1950.

Spare-Time Article Writing for Money. William J. Lederer. New York: W. W. Norton & Co., 1954.

Technical and Industrial Journalism. Delbert McGuire. Harrisburg: Stackpole, 1956.

The Writer and His Markets. Paul R. Reynolds. New York: Doubleday, 1959.

The Writing and Selling of Non-fiction. Paul R. Reynolds. Garden City: Doubleday, 1963.

Writing and Selling Special Feature Articles. Helen M. Patterson. New York: Prentice-Hall, 1956.

Writing Science News for the Mass Media. David W. Burkett. Houston: Gulf Publishing Co., 1965.

Writing the Feature Article. Walter A. Steigleman. New York: Macmillan, 1950.

DICTIONARIES AND WORLD BOOKS:

The American Language. H. L. Mencken. New York: Knopf, 1963.

New Century Dictionary of the English Language. New York: Appleton-Century-Crofts, 1952.

      Based on matter selected from original Century dictionary with addition of new material.

New Standard Dictionary of the English Language. New York: Funk and Wagnalls Co., 1952.

      Serviceable one-volume work. Emphasis upon current information.

Webster's Dictionary of Synonyms. Springfield, Mass.: G. & C. Merriam, 1942.

      An alphabetical list with explanation and differentiation of use and meaning.

Encyclopedias:

The Encyclopedia Americana. New York: Americana Corp., 1964.

      General encyclopedia. Strong in recent names and subjects in the fields of science and technology. Yearly supplements.

Encyclopaedia Britannica. Chicago: Encyclopaedia Britannica, Inc., 1965.

      Arts, sciences, and general literature. See latest edition, plus yearbooks.

Encyclopedia of the Social Sciences. E. R. A. Seligman (ed.). New York: Macmillan, 1938.

      All important subjects in the social sciences. International in scope. Much biographical material. See latest edition.

INDEXES OF NEWSPAPERS AND PERIODICALS:

Business Periodical Index. New York: H. W. Wilson, cumulative issues.

International Index. New York: H. W. Wilson Co.
    1907 to date. Selected periodicals of the world. Science and the humanities.

Monthly Catalog of U. S. Government Publications. Washington, D. C.: Government Printing Office.
    All documents of Congress and the various departments.

The New York Times Index. New York: The New York Times.
    1913 to date. Monthly accumulative. Gives date, page, and column with reference to related topics.

Pople's Index to Periodical Literature. Gloucester, Mass.: Peter Smith, 1938.
    Covers 1802 to 1908. American and English periodicals.

Readers' Guide to Periodical Literature. New York: H. W. Wilson Co.
    1900 to date. Full dictionary cataloging of articles entered under authors, title, subject. Monthly and accumulative.

Times. London: The Times.
    1876 to date. Important topics. An official index.

ILLUSTRATIONS:

A.L.A. Portrait Index. Washington, D.C.: Library of Congress, 1906.
    An aid in tracing illustrations for article use. Indexes 120,000 portraits of 35,000 to 45,000 persons found in books and periodicals.

Graphs – How to Make and Use Them. Herbert Arkin and Raymond R. Colton. New York: Harper & Brothers, 1940.
    See Chapter XXII for standard works on photography.

MARKET GUIDES AND TIP SOURCES:

Author & Journalist. Washington, D.C.: Farrar Publishing Co., monthly.
    Cumulative market list.

Christian Writer's Handbook. Chicago: Christian Writer Institute, 1961.
    A guide to what religious magazines buy.

The International Guide. London: World Little Magazines, 1961.
    Markets for beginners, mostly nonpaying.

Literary Market Place. New York: R. R. Bowker Co., yearly.
    Author's representatives. Markets. Other helpful hints.

Readers' Guide to Periodical Literature. New York: H. W. Wilson Co., 1900 to date.
    Lists what various magazines have published, hence is a guide to subjects in favor.

Standard Rate and Data Service. Chicago: Standard Rate and Data Service, Inc.
    Good reference to trade and business magazines. Publishes several specialized editions. Check for edition of special interest to the writer.

Writers' and Artists' Year Book. London: A. & C. Black, Ltd., yearly.
    Best English and American markets. Rates of pay.
The Writer's Handbook. A. S. Burack (ed.). Boston: Writer, Inc., yearly.
    Similar to *The Writer's Market.* Where to sell.
The Writer's Market. Kirk Polking (ed.). Cincinnati: Writer's Digest, yearly.
    Lists 3,500 buying markets in class, general and trade magazines.
    Editors' names and editorial offices. References usually carry editors'
    approval.
Writing for the Religious Market. R. E. Wolseley (ed.). New York: Associa-
    tion Press, 1956.

WRITING MISCELLANY:

    Collection of articles by experts on religious writing.
American Newspapers, 1821-1936. New York: H. W. Wilson Co., 1937.
    Gives location of files of American newspapers available to writers.
Becoming a Writer. Dorothea Brande. New York: Harcourt, Brace, 1949.
Book Review Digest. New York: H. W. Wilson Co.
    A digest and index of selected book reviews in over 50 English and
    American periodicals, principally general in character.
Cumulative Book Index. New York: H. W. Wilson Co., 1898-
    Monthly, accumulative. Books published in United States, Canada,
    Great Britain and British dominions, and colonies up to 1928.
Famous First Facts. Joseph N. Kane. New York: H. W. Wilson Co., 1964.
How to Interview. Walter V. Bingham and Bruce V. Moore New York:
    Harper & Brothers, 1959.
The Journalist's Bookshelf. R. E. Wolseley. Philadlephia: Chilton Company,
    1961.
    Most complete bibliography of books of interest to article writers.
The Law of Literary Property. Philip Wittenberg. Cleveland: World, 1957.
Local References: Bluebooks, city directories; local histories city and county;
    telephone book.
Manual of Style, A Staff. Chicago: University of Chicago Press, 1949.
Methods of Research. Carter V. Good and Douglas E. Scates. New York:
    Appleton-Century-Crofts, 1954.
On the Art of Writing. Arthur Quiller-Couch. New York: G. P. Putnam's Sons,
    1961.

YEARBOOKS:

The American Yearbook. New York: American Year Book Corp.
    Narrative accounts, bibliographies, and statistics. International coverage
    on many subjects.
Directory of Newspapers and Periodicals. Philadelphia: N. W. Ayer & Son.
    Lists all newspapers and magazines published in United States and
    Canada. Alphabetized by title and by places of publication. Annual.
International Year Book. New York: Editor & Publisher.
    Data on daily newspapers, syndicates, press associations, and feature
    services. Annual.

Statesman's Yearbook. New York: Macmillan.
>   1864 to date. Statistics about governments of the world. Annual.
Statistical Abstract of the United States. Washington, D.C.: Government
>   Printing Office.
>   Pertinent data on numerous aspects of government and business.
>   Comprehensive.

Using the Writer's Tools

MAGAZINES.   Numerous suggestions have been made in this text on
the manner and desirability of using magazines as an important part of
the writing career. The free-lance writer simply has to keep ahead of his
field. This means that he must know of new inventions, devices, practices,
regulations, or laws as soon as they can be written about and long before
they reach the more popular press to which he contributes.

The greatest aid in keeping track of the scientific and technical magazines likely to be of interest to any writer is found in the various guides
to periodical literature. Several of these were listed under "Indexes."
Numerous additional indexes are available in well-equipped libraries.
Any librarian can help you discover whether indexes are prepared for
your own field. Time saved by using an index instead of the technical
journals can be spent studying the magazines likely to use popularized
adaptations.

REFERENCE WORKS.   When using reference works the writer will find
that often the best place to begin investigating a subject is in an
encyclopedia like the *Encyclopaedia Britannica* or *The Encyclopedia
Americana.* These usually give additional references of known merit.
Among them will be authoritative books into which the writer can go
as deeply as he has time. In addition, the various indexes referred to
will help him uncover the latest developments which have not yet found
their way into book print.

Eventually, the writer will have to master the sources of information in his field, or content himself with mediocre success. To this end
he should give himself a course in library resources. The hours so
invested will be saved a thousand times in the pursuit of a writing
career.

QUESTIONNAIRES.   One other tool is at hand. That is the questionnaire. With it the latest data or information not otherwise available can
be rather quickly compiled. Since thousands of questionnaires circulate
in the mails, those sent out by the writer should be as short and as
easily filled as possible. Confidential information should not be expected,
and stamped envelope for return should be provided. Pledges should

not be made that will be difficult to keep, such as a promise to send out copies of the tabulated results or of the article — if and when printed. At best, the questionnaire is a weak tool, and should be used only when no better instrument is available.

Training Steps

1. Go to the nearest library and obtain a copy of *Readers' Guide to Periodical Literature*. Study carefully the list of magazines indexed. Note that signed articles are indexed by title and by author.
2. Find out what other indexes are available in your library. What periodicals do they index?
3. Select three subjects that interest you. Using appropriate indexes, count by years the number of articles written on each in the past five years. Is the subject of growing or decreasing interest?
4. Study these same three subjects in the *Cumulative Book Index*. What books (if any) have been published on the subjects in the past ten years?
5. Under how many classifications is the same item mentioned in the *Cumulative Book Index?* In *Readers' Guide to Periodical Literature?*
6. What are the principles by which books are catalogued? If in doubt, ask the librarian.
7. What newspapers other than *The New York Times* publish indexes?
8. What is the best index to magazines in your specialty?
9. Make and keep a list of magazines in your field that are not listed on any index. Hereafter file all articles from these magazines likely to be of interest later.
10. Since most house organs are not indexed, keep an eye open for any that might print interesting articles.
11. What methods are used by publishers of encyclopedias to keep them up to date?
12. Begin to set up a card catalogue system of books, magazines, and other publications that have important bearing on your field.

CHAPTER 24

Knowing the Editors

Editors are buyers, purchasing articles in a market that usually is well supplied. Theirs is the problem of selecting from the heaps of manuscripts that reach them those articles that mean success for their publications. Consequently, they buy what they believe their readers will like.

Editors and Guessing

Until recent years no scientific yardstick existed by which an editor could measure accurately what was popular. Some years ago a magazine editor hit upon the idea of filling his pages for an imaginary family in Indianapolis. Because he aimed at mass circulation among the middle class his ideal was a composite of average families everywhere, but by visualizing his Hoosier family, he could come closer to supplying material that would please it. If this sounds crude, let it be known that several magazines did achieve success by similar formulas.

In recent years more refined methods have been developed. They are the reader-interest surveys, which have been rather widely adopted by newspapers and to lesser degree by magazines. By using a methodology, now on a scientific basis, an editor can find out exactly what his vast audience thinks of various articles, and the degree of intensity of that belief. He can also find out, with somewhat greater difficulty, how his magazine ranks in comparison with its competitors.

These methods tell the editor how well he has done with *what he has already published*. They do not tell him, except by inference, about what he has bought but has not yet sent to his readers. Lack of information on specific articles in advance of publication is partly compensated for by knowledge of what general types of reading subscribers prefer. For instance, most readers like articles on health. So some editors supply frequent articles of this type. Among the magazines, *Good Housekeeping* has at least one such article in every issue, while hundreds of newspapers employ syndicated health features. Readers also like articles that tell them how to be more efficient or more succesful in business, or how to attract friends. They like stories of adventure and romance. Editors try to supply these wants.

The editor must be a shrewd buyer and a shrewd businessman. Because he is a businessman, he expects those who wish to write for him to be businesslike in their dealings. The writer will, therefore, conduct himself as if he also were in business — as in fact he is. Every step in the selling of an article is a step in the business world.

It should be one of the aims of the writer to give an editor his money's worth. He can do this by offering honest products. When he presents a statement as a fact, he will have made certain that what he says is true. He will not resort to guesswork or half-truths. Furthermore, he will pack as much substance into his article as possible. If an item is intrinsically worth only 75 words, he will not spin it out to 500, or even 150. The writer will be repaid many times over for fair and considerate treatment of editors.

Following Up Queries

When, in answer to a query, an editor writes that he would be interested in seeing an article proposed by a writer, that individual should round up his facts in short order, and set about producing the article *at once*. The finished piece should reach the editor at the earliest possible date. Delay means that the editor may forget he expressed an interest; or he may change his mind, because the opening he saw may have vanished. Consideration for the editor alone suggests that the article should be sent out promptly.

Any promises held out in the query should be fulfilled in the article. If a length of 1,500 words was suggested, then the complete work should be within a few score words of that mark. Previous suggestions as to content should be carried out. If it was stated that five points of interest would be covered, then they should appear in the article.

Occasionally an article needing illustrations will be submitted without them, but with a promise to supply them if the article is accepted. This is never more than a weak substitute, for often illustrations sell an article. When illustrations are promised, they should be supplied promptly, and should be of good quality.

It is also good business, as well as excellent judgment, to be meticulous about carrying out whatever suggestions the editor makes. Frequently queries are answered without recommendations for development. But when an editor reacts favorably to the point of mentioning a particular length, angle of approach, style, method of development, or type of illustration, every effort should be bent toward exact fulfillment of his wishes. This is the surest way to obtain future orders from the editor.

Good judgment is shown also when the writer addresses his article to the editor who answered the letter. Usually this will be an assistant to the editor-in-chief. To make sure that the manuscript reaches the assistant's desk and that the query response itself is not forgotten, the cover page should carry a paragraph stating, "This is the article in which you expressed interest in your letter of . . ." Some such reminder may make the difference between rejection by the first reader and acceptance by the staff.

Making Use of Rejections

Word of rejection may come in any one of three forms: 1. a printed, noncommittal card that gives no indication of why the article was turned back; 2. a printed sheet upon which may be checked one or more of a list of reasons for rejections; and 3. a dictated note, which may or may not set forth reasons for returning the article.

NONCOMMITTAL REJECTIONS. The first type, which is the most common, leave the writer staring at a blank wall. He doesn't know whether they changed their policy, whether photographs were inadequate, whether the article was too long or too short, or whether he missed the mark because of one or more of the common faults of free-lance material.

This type of rejection card should not be and seldom is sent to anyone who writes an article in response to a query. When an editor expresses interest in an idea and finds it didn't turn out as he expected, he usually sends a note telling why the article didn't meet his needs.

CHECKING FAULTS. The second type is considerably better than the first, because it tells why the article failed to make the grade. Among magazines that have developed such devices is *Better Homes and Gardens*. While this is not the complete answer to the rejections problem, it does save the magazine time and expense when indicating why each one of the thousand of unsolicited manuscripts was returned. Free-lance writers can be grateful that at least a few periodicals have gone thus far to soften the blow of rejection.

Articles generally fail to make a market for various well-defined reasons, discussed earlier in this volume. If illustrations are inadequate, it is easy for a subeditor to put a check mark against such a statement among the list of reasons for rejections. Occasionally more than one reason influences the decision, and a free lance may find two or more items checked. Or perhaps a piece that is fairly well done simply doesn't arouse editorial enthusiasm. Then any editor may be at a loss to say why he must return it.

EDITORIAL LETTERS. Letters, the third type, can be as uninformative as a printed rejection, but usually are not. Most editors do not send a note of rejection unless the article has merited some editorial favor. They simply reject it with a printed timesaving form. *Esquire*, which is among the few exceptions to this latter practice, has been of outstanding help to free lances by rejecting nearly always with a written explanation.

The written note, therefore, is to be considered a sign of encouragement, *even when it gives no reason for the rejection*. Beginning free lances learn to distinguish between the note and the printed slip, and take encouragement from the former, for it means that they *almost* landed a check. To them it marks a step up the ladder.

When the printed list of reasons for return or letter from the editor indicates why the article was returned, there is chance to profit. If the indication is that the article was too long or too short, the writer can shorten or lengthen the piece. If photographs should have been included but were not, the writer can procure them. Often, the reason for rejection is trivial and can be quickly set right.

Whenever the cause for rejection is remediable, the writer should make the change and return as soon as possible to the same editor with a note in which he states he is resubmitting the article without obligation. He should call attention to the fact that he has made the changes and now hopes it will meet with editorial acceptance. This author once had the experience of having a magazine accept an article which it had pre-

viously twice rejected — for different reasons both times. Needless to say
the matter of resubmitting should be handled tactfully with no suggestion of forcing an unworthy manuscript upon the editor.

Visiting the Editor

Under ordinary circumstances neither the untrained writer nor the
editor has anything to gain from a visit by the former to the latter's
office. No visit should be undertaken until the writer has demonstrated
his ability to write, either by publication in a competitor or within the
publication of the editor he proposes to visit — preferably the latter.

Sooner or later, however, every trained and productive writer should
become personally acquainted with the editor of his best markets. This
is a *must* for success in writing — so much so that many writers declare
it is next to impossible to achieve a considerable success outside the
chief publication centers of the country. Although this statement has
many exceptions, it is true that editors prefer to know what their
contributors look like. It helps in sizing them up. Editors like the chance
to ask about writers' background and training, and to learn their general
philosophy and approach to mutual problems.

The writer gains much from such a visit, which should be repeated
from time to time. He learns how to deal with the editor, what kind of
ideas he likes or dislikes, as well as what his future publication plans
may be.

When calling on an editor, it is a good idea to carry along two or
three carefully thought-out ideas. If they are good (and they shouldn't
be offered unless they are) an order or go-ahead sign may result from
the interview. They can be presented orally in a few minutes. The
writer outlines what he has in mind, tells whether pictures are available,
sketches his plan of development, and mentions an estimated length.
Also a typewritten notation may be left on the editor's desk. From the
way the editor reacts to his presentation, the writer learns much that
will help him to sell ideas on future occasions.

Results of a well-planned visit are not onesided. The editor has
something to gain also. First-rate ideas are never too numerous, and
the writer who drops several on an editor's desk earns a welcome. The
editor has the chance to pick up some good material for his magazine
and to aid in its development. He also gets better acquainted with his
contributors, which is a help in editing and planning a magazine.

Both editors and writers must work harmoniously. The writer can't
hope to sell articles that the editor doesn't want. Nor should he expect

to sell merely because he has become acquainted with the editor. His only hope of selling is to produce what the editor wants, but he has a better chance of doing this if he understands the editor's point of view.

Out of such meetings may grow mutual understanding, and that much-to-be-wished-for-event — an unsolicited order from the editor for an article. And at any time it is easier to do business with a friend than with a stranger.

Contacts with Friends and Relatives

Breaking into print in a substantial way is not easy, and it is even more difficult to appear in print regularly. Consequently, a writer should make use of whatever contacts he has in the magazine and newspaper world. So-called influence carries little weight with important publications. They won't print an inferior piece merely because one of the editor's relatives wrote it. If a writer makes good, it will be because he earned it.

Having a friend or relative in the publishing business helps only to the extent that it assures more careful scrutiny of the work submitted. The better the publication, the less likely is influence to count. These remarks refer to getting material into print, not to the matter of obtaining a position. Having a "friend at court" works two ways. While it may assure more careful scrutiny, it also assures that mediocre work will be the more quickly spotted.

On small newspapers and magazines, including some city-wide and sectional publications, the matter of influence may be more important. But it is unlikely even on the less critical magazines that shoddy manuscripts would continue to be accepted. In other words, in order to succeed a writer must produce first-rate articles.

Letters to the Editors

Editors, being human, like an occasional word of commendation. When an unusually good issue of one of the magazines to which you sell has been put out, write a letter saying so. Or, if you like an outstanding article, let the editor know. Such acts might well become part of the writer's program. When based on honest conviction, they cannot fail to help to create better relations between writer and editor.

Any editor doing a good job deserves to be told so. The individual who makes it a practice to write such letters won't be forgotten. But he shouldn't be so crude as to couple it with an effort to sell the editor on an article. This author does not suggest that. He is suggesting a parallel program for establishing long-time friendly relations.

Since no staff has a corner on all the good ideas, editors welcome suggestions that can be used in their columns. These may be ideas for new features, new departments, or single articles. Almost any writer will stumble upon good ideas for articles that are outside his own field. The writer who takes time to drop a note about it to one of his editorial acquaintances will certainly be repaid by increasing cordial relations with that editor.

Pleasing Editors

While editors will excuse much in writers who turn out superlative fiction, they do not give the same free reins to the article writer. Instead they look upon the latter as a businessman, and expect him to foreswear the artistic conduct allowed the fiction writer. They expect the article writer from first to last to conduct his writing, correspondence, and personal relations as any first-rate business executive.

Among the rules of conduct calculated to reduce friction to a minimum are the following: 1. answer editorial letters by return mail if possible; 2. make your letters as attractive in appearance at least as those of the editor; 3. fulfill all implied or actual obligations, but don't promise more than you know you can deliver; 4. work on a basis of complete honesty; and 5. make every new article better than the last one submitted.

Any writer who wants to improve the quality of his work will lay out a program of study and self-education. Even the university-trained man has only begun his education when he gets his diploma. If he plans to become a writer of business articles, he will know little of actual business procedures when he leaves the university — unless he has been employed in a business. His first step is to get an education within the buiness world. He can do this by getting a position, by reading the appropriate business magazines, or by doing both — preferably the last.

This program of self-education should be made a lifetime habit. It is the only way in which any writer can keep up to date in his field. Editors are not interested in outdated ideas. Actually, they expect the writer to be a little way ahead of the parade.

Finally, the free-lance writer is urged to work hard at his calling, and to rewrite — and rewrite.

Training Steps

1. Select a magazine to which you would like to contribute. Make a list of the features you admire. Make a second list containing those you dislike, or at least find unappealing.

2. Write a practice letter to the editor commending the magazine for the items you liked. Be sure to mention them by name.

3. Weigh carefully the second list. Discuss it with friends and acquaintances. Try to find some expert whose opinion you can get. Digest all the various opinions. Have you any first-rate ideas for improving the magazine? If so, work the ideas out painstakingly and make a sample page or pages showing what you mean. Now write an accompanying letter and send both to the editor, addressing him by name. Say you are submitting it without obligation, but would like his reactions.

4. In what way can reader-interest surveys be used to guide editors in buying material for future issues?

5. Go to the library and make a bibliography on the subject of public-opinion polling and reader-interest surveys. Read at least a dozen good articles on these subjects. Answer this question: In what way can the principles of these surveys be used in sampling the work that a writer might wish to do?

6. Have you sampled public opinion when you ask a dozen men and women what they think of a subject? Explain your answer.

7. Classify the contents of three consecutive issues of *Reader's Digest* under the eight types of articles (page 196). What is the formula that makes this magazine a success?

8. Study the magazine *The Men's Digest*. How does its formula differ from that of *Reader's Digest?* How does the formula for *The Catholic Digest* differ from these two?

9. If influence is of little value to article writers, what is the purpose of establishing and maintaining contacts?

10. What local features would you like to see in your local newspaper? Can you do any of them for the editor in charge of this type of material?

11. Begin now to cultivate the editor of the publication for which you hope to write.

CHAPTER 25

Discovering Article Techniques

Writers have three purposes in reading articles written by other professional writers: a. they read to study the techniques of writing; b. they read to uncover ideas for new articles; and c. they read for pleasure. These motives are presented in order of importance, though if the article writer does much reading of articles for pleasure, he is wasting time.

Reading in One's Own Field

The most serious purpose the writer has in reading is to improve his mastery of the writing craft. Naturally he will read carefully in the field in which he hopes to contribute, and the works most painstakingly examined will be those of the best writers. It is of little value to pursue the writings of beginners because generally they have yet to master the techniques of article writing. One of the early jobs is to find out who the leaders are in the beginners' field.

Suppose a young writer is interested in writing articles on health for the home magazines. He would look into such publications as *Today's Health* and *Parents' Magazine,* for they are deeply concerned with the subject. Also he would keep up with the women's magazines, such as *Ladies' Home Journal, Good Housekeeping, McCall's Magazine,* and *Better Homes and Gardens,* because they frequently use articles on health by authoritative writers. Other clues to good articles in this field can be gleaned from *Readers' Guide to Periodical Literature.*

Studying "Big-Name" Writers

In *Today's Health* the young writer might find an article by an expert on the benefits and dangers of using new anti-biotic drugs in the home. Because of the quality of the magazine and the reputation of the writer, the beginner may safely decide that here is a writer worth studying. This is particularly true if the author is a reputable writer of science articles. So the novice begins to tear apart the article to see what is satisfactory to *Today's Health.* Probably he will need two copies of the magazine if he intends to file the article or its parts, for some of the copy may be printed on both sides of the paper.

The writer will not overlook the possibilities of writing a similar article on another subject for a second magazine. The piece by the expert may suggest an article on the danger of self-medication in general; or one on "death that lurks in the average medicine cabinet"; or even one on how to safeguard the medicine cabinet from children's hands — this one to be done for *Parents' Magazine.* Further popularization for the newspapers is also possible.

The writer's last thought in reading the article will be the pleasure there may be in it for him. If the article is carefully analyzed, there will be little time for mental diversion.

When it comes to analysis of the article for technique, the writer will apply every test and classification he knows from title to ending. He will name each technique used — if he can. A review of points to be covered will be found later in the chapter.

Operating a File

Two different files should be operated by the article writer. One of these should be for ideas, the other for examples of article techniques. Either a card system, a loose-leaf notebook, or a number of manila folders will be satisfactory containers. The chief aim should be to keep the system simple enough to work. Bulky newspaper clippings soon mount up, but usually can be handled satisfactorily if manilla folders are used.

THE IDEAL FILE.   For filing ideas to be used in future articles, 5 x 8 inch cards are excellent. Used vertically or horizontally, they provide space for clippings and accompanying comment. Appropriate data consist of 1. an accurate label, 2. source, page, and date, 3. the clipping, 4. suggestions for development, and 5. possible markets. Below is a typical example.

GREAT MEN

Syracuse Herald-Journal, 10/12

> SPRINGFIELD, ILL. (AP)—A half-dozen letters in the handwriting of Abraham Lincoln were found here today in the tearing down of an old building not far from the site of the office in which Lincoln once practiced law.
>
> The letters are said to deal with the political aspirations of Lincoln.
>
> Notes:
>
> > 1. What are the new facts revealed by the letters?
> > 2. What light do they throw on Lincoln's career?
> > 3. How can they be handled to justify a new article?

Market: The N.Y. Times Sunday Magazine

Illustration 22 — A sample idea filed for reference

As the mounted clippings begin to accumulate they should, be filed in some container, such as an open cardboard box. The label should appear first, and the card should be filed alphabetically by this key. The phrase "great men" is the key on the above card. Indexing will vary somewhat according to the writer, for what would be the significant phrase with one writer will not be with another. In any case, the index should be based on the word or phrase most easily recalled. Frequent study of the file will help to keep the ideas fresh in mind.

THE TECHNIQUE FILE.   The above method for handling an idea for a possible circle can be used with slight variation for filing notes on technique. The parts then become 1. the name of the technique, 2. the source, 3. the clipping, and 4. the comment.

If the clipping is an example of a good title, it should be labeled "Title." The name of the publication and date follow, then the clipping, and finally your own reactions. These latter might possibly include some paraphrases that would fit articles you have written or might write.

The technique file is somewhat easier to handle than the idea file and is more permanent. The number of classifications is limited. Once these are set up, the writer need only identify the new clipping and drop it into the proper envelope, or mount it and file as convenient.

This file will contain a number of alphabetized envelopes or folders for the various types of articles, as well as for such subdivisions as title, subtitle, and beginning. These latter will also be further subdivided and alphabetized since there are various types of titles, beginnings, and other parts.

Revising the Idea File

The file of ideas should be revised at least twice a year, and preferably oftener. Those that are known to be dead should be weeded out or put in an out-of-date file. There is no use letting obsolete ideas clutter up the file and steal precious minutes each time they are handled.

How often a writer will refer to this file will depend upon the type of writing done and upon the writer. Certainly he should study it frequently enough to keep its contents in mind. It is also quite important that he maintain a wide and carfeul reading and clipping program to keep the ideas flowing in. These should be marked and filed while they are still fresh in mind.

In spite of himself the writer will find that he lets some excellent ideas get away. The merits of some will not be recognized until he finds them turned into articles and published. Others may be lost because they were forgotten. This can be avoided by operating a schedule in a diary or a loose-leaf calendar. A note set down on the date when work should be started, plus a reference to the location of the idea, will protect the writer's plans from miscarriage.

Some ideas that have been overlooked may still be good because they are not tied to a particular season or date. This is the kind to use when seasonal material is scarce, though items of this latter type can occasionally be rescued if the writer is clever. He has only to search until he finds the "angle" to bring it to life.

What to Collect

TYPES OF ARTICLES.   Nearly everyone who has written about articles has classified them differently. When the student writer attempts to file them away, he should use the list that best suits his own purposes.

The effort at classification should be in keeping with his own attitude toward events, so that relocating the article will be easy.

While article types tend to remain fixed, occasionally something new is born. In recent years numerous magazines have used the collective article, which consists of a multitude of short items on similar or related topics. Usually the group is brought together under a single title and often in a two-page spread. For instance, a score of items may be combined in a single article on "New Appliances for the Kitchen," or an article may include a dozen explanations of how to make minor repairs about the house. In such articles each division is usually illustrated with a drawing or photograph.

Newspapers use a greater variety of article types than the magazines, but show less variation within the types. The occasional innovation can be easily recognized by anyone familiar with types and techniques. It is well to be able to recognize such inventions, because editors have a habit of jumping on the bandwagon of any successful experiment.

Types of articles also become out-of-date, such as the "rags to riches" theme, as developed years ago by *The American Magazine*. The place of this article has been taken by sketches of "interesting people," who may come from any trade, profession, or place. Among requirements is that they be accomplished individuals.

The writer who expects to earn a living by writing may be able to make that task somewhat easier by concentrating on those types most in demand.

If the classification given in Chapter 14 does not satisfy the writer's requirements, he might try a classification based upon the kinds of articles used by his chief markets. If he is doing pieces for the trade journals, he could add a classification for news items, a type of material that is important to these magazines. The short, for example, is more frequently used by them than by the general magazines. For the newspapers he might add human-interest items.

TITLES. Since the title first catches the eye, it must be good in order to hold the reader's attention and persuade him to read further. But first the title must convince an editorial staff that the article is meritorious.

Many an editor has a peculiar eye for titles. He may like puns, or playing upon words. Or he may be averse to both. He may like question titles or dislike them. Whatever the case, the writer should find out what his editors like, and supply them the best of the type. He will also carefully clip good titles from the periodicals for which he does write and from those for which, as yet, he only hopes to write. He will read many other publications with a hunter's eye for excellent examples that can be adapted to his own purposes. That means, of course, that they must be slanted to his own markets.

It will be remembered that titles were classified in Chapter 10 as follows: 1. striking statement; 2. provocative; 3. label; 4. paraphrase (including pun); 5. declarative sentence; 6. how, why, what; 7. question; 8. direct address; 9. quotation; 10. exclamation; 11. rhyme and alliteration; 12. balance and contrast.

SUBTITLES. No good classification of subtitles has appeared, partly because they do not readily lend themselves to pigeon-holing. Some periodicals do not use them; others do. Among magazines that use subtitles, highly stylized forms appear. Not infrequently they are found above the title, or on the opposite page, as part of a two-page spread. Collecting newspaper titles and subtitles, except in the magazine section, is not very productive, because of the wide range of typographical treatment used in the average newspaper.

The writer will have to decide for himself whether or not to use subtitles. The device gives one more opportunity to catch the eye of the staff reader, or editor, as well as an opportunity to amplify the all-too-short title. Subtitles do help in the selling job. This author believes that they should be used on most articles, particularly on those mailed without the usual query. When an article is sent out in answer to a query, the writer should follow the practice of the recipient editor.

BEGINNINGS. At first the writer may wish to collect article beginnings according to the classification suggested in Chapter 9. This is a handy list that works well, but further subdivision is possible and often desirable.

Anyone who specializes is likely to find himslef writing for a limited group of markets within which allowable beginnings may be restricted. Certain types of trade-publication articles, such as news items, are rather inflexible. Literary adornment is kept to a minimum. At the other extreme are the general magazines, which seek as great variety in structure as is consistent with good taste. Slanting to the market is the answer to this problem, as with many another in article writing.

Where opening paragraphs are combined with the title and subtitle into a single unit, the clipping is best filed under types of beginnings. If the item is a choice one, it can be copied and refiled under titles.

From time to time these clippings should be weeded out, for practice changes. New editors introduce different "musts" and "must-nots." Old patterns may be thrown out with the retiring staff. Introduction of new type faces or type sizes may increase or decrease the number of words it is possible to use, or the number of lines.

TRANSITIONS. An excellent classified list of transitional words and phrases is to be found in Brennecke and Clark's *Magazine Article Writing*, pages 192-193.[1] Practice in the use of these connective devices will show how many are required to knit an article firmly together without becoming obtrusive.

Articles that are outstanding for their use of linking words and phrases should be clipped in their entirety. Such articles are likely to be the work of first-rate writers. "Big" names are also an excellent guide to anyone hunting this type of material.

ENDINGS. Formal conclusions, or summaries, are used less frequently than formerly. This is particularly true of the process article in general publications, of the trade journal article and of the newspaper feature. When a writer has discussed his subject or made his point, it is expected that he will cease writing.

Some writers succeed in handling the matter of the last paragraph so skillfully that their example is worth imitating. Adaptation of their techniques will increase the writer's mastery of article writing.

When an ending is needed, the writer should be able to compose one satisfactorily. The greatest kick and the strongest emphasis may be needed in the last few carefully-chosen words.

NARRATIVE DEVICES. No one has ever succeeded in enumerating the entire list of narrative devices open to the serious writer, for they are almost without number. The collector of article techniques will find them in two sources: articles and fiction.

Study of articles from the best writers is important, because from them it is possible to learn how narrative techniques have been adapted to the purpose of the article. Generally, the article is a briefer piece and a more condensed and compact literary form than the work of fiction, so that techniques must be adapted to the article when borrowed from fiction. Study of this adaptation is important, and should be diligently pursued, particularly at the outset of a writing career.

In the masterpieces of short and long fiction will be found many techniques still rarely used by article writers. Intelligent analysis of the current work of leading writers of novels and short stories will be repaid. Such study will help article writers stay out of ruts of their craft by putting new techniques in their hands and by bringing to them new points of view.

---

[1]*Magazine Article Writing*, Ernest Brennecke, Jr. and Donald Lemen Clark. New York: Macmillan, 1952.

ILLUSTRATIONS, HUMANIZING TECHNIQUES. Devices for humanization, of popularizing, abstract facts were listed in Chapter 15. Among these, photographs, charts, and pictographs will be easiest to collect. It is highly desirable that the standards of pictorial excellence be learned. If any writer contributes to a field that uses photographs, he should master the business of providing acceptable enlargements in adequate numbers and of the type in use by his markets.

Examples of the pictograph are becoming more numerous. Many variations on this device are in use by magazines. Some of these charted figures are of such clarity and excellence that they tell the entire story with the help of only a little copy. For this reason special attention should be given to them. Sunday newspapers, the weekly news magazines, and hundreds of trade publications, as well as many general magazines, are steady patrons of this type of illustration. Consult your markets and file away those items that extend the range of possible illustrative devices. Later adaptation may persuade an editor to buy your article.

Other techniques for humanizing, such as the case method, should be clipped and filed. A different folder or envelope used for each variety of device will be handy for quick reference.

Taking Articles Apart

One of the best ways to learn to recognize the many techniques is to analyze the content of well-written articles that appeal to you and are of the type you wish to write. Begin with the title, writing upon it the name of the type to which it belongs — label, question, direct address, or other type. Then classify the beginning and ending and underline transitions.

After these obvious steps are taken, the more thoughtful work gets underway. This involves the recognition and labeling of style and the narrative techniques, such as conversation, flashback, hypothetical persons, and suspense.

An additional and equally significant analysis of the organization of the article can be made. First, the basic purpose of the article must be recognized. The main divisions are next marked, and the subdivisions within each. If unnecessary or extraneous material is found, this should also be marked. Ability to recognize the weaknesses of an article is as important as being able to recognize the virtues.

Finally, an appraisal of every element of the article should be made. This calls for exercise of the writer's best judgment. Fortunately, judgment improves with such exercise as this, and ability to name and evaluate mounts rapidly with the passing months. After a time the actual writing down of the many labels will become unnecessary, though at first it should be done with meticulous care. A large part of any writer's education comes from self-teaching, and such analysis as suggested above is the best instruction a writer can give himself.

Training Steps

1. Make a list of the ten most outstanding writers in your field. Learn, if you can, what was their preparation for a writing career. This can sometimes be pieced together from contributors' columns. Such works as *Who's Who in America* also help.

2. Once the outstanding writers have been selected, begin to watch for their work. Never let one of their articles go by unread.

3. Salable ideas should be collected assiduously. Take any issue of the local paper and mark every item that suggests an article. Name the type of article suggested. File these away under proper labels for future references. Make this a *daily* part of the writing program. Jot down any ideas you may have for developing these items, so that your original impressions will not be lost.

4. Study some of the good books on fiction writing. From these compile a list of narrative techniques. Then analyze ten articles in *Life* and *Sports Illustrated,* marking every technical device recognized. Which magazine uses the most narrative techniques? In which are the articles most effective?

5. Examine a dozen different issues of *Readers' Digest.* Mark every item that you might have been inspired to write by something seen, heard, or read in the past 18 months.

6. Lists of types of articles, copies of titles and beginnings and other parts, if kept at hand, are aids to quick analysis. Pinned to the wall near the writer's desk or slipped under a glass-topped table, they refresh the memory at a glance.

7. Write out a list of your favorite markets. Make a tabulation of the types of titles favored by each.

8. Examine and classify 100 beginnings from articles in your best markets. How many do you find of each type?

9. Collect a number of articles that are outstanding for their smooth transitional devices. Underline and preserve for future reference numerous examples.

10. Select three of your favorite writers and analyze three articles by each. Which one uses the greatest variety of narrative techniques? Is his writing the most interesting?

11. Leaf through a dozen leading magazines. What new illustrative types can you discover that were not in use five years ago? two years ago?

12. Analyze an article as carefully as you can. Put it away and get it out three months later. Examine each part well and mark each one upon which you would now venture a different comment.
13. How do newspaper titles, or headlines, differ from those in magazines?
14. Make your own classification of the contents of two or more newspapers, omitting advertising, editorials, and current news items.
15. How much syndicate material do you find in each?
16. Study several newspapers. Do you find any items of local interest that you might expand sufficiently to sell it to the same or a competing newspaper?

CHAPTER 26

T

Creating New Ideas from Old

The heart of every good article is a sound idea, and the final article is simply the elaboration of this idea, made interesting by humanization. The techniques of article writing were dealt with in the early chapters. Sources of ideas such as the newspapers, scientific publications, and personal observation also were discussed. Now that the reader of this text has achieved a degree of maturity and a more professional point of view of the business of being an article writer, it is time to tell of a more subtle aspect of writing — the use of the imaginative faculties in creating and developing ideas upon which to build salable articles.

What Are New Ideas?

Few if any absolutely new ideas are to be found anywhere. Most article ideas are adaptations or modifications, by one process or another, of ideas that have been around for a long time. Practically all the good ideas have been used many times. The fact that there are few new ideas is good news to young writers — rather than a cause for despair. It means that they need go to no painful and exhausting search, nor extensive travel, to uncover workable material. Actually the main sources of ideas are at hand in magazines and newspapers, in books, and in personal experience and observation.

The various imaginative processes for turning old ideas into new ideas will be handled at the end of this chapter after discussion of how to make the mind work. The writer must expect that the products of these imaginative processes will vary widely in quality. Some ideas will be excellent and worth developing; others will be discarded because of questionable value.

Also a writer may feel the need for a new angle on an old idea, but he should not mistake this need for a marketable angle itself. For example, he might believe that an article ought to be printed on juvenile delinquency. Articles have been and will yet appear on the subject. But the idea itself is too broad to be dealt with in a single article. A narrower, yet brighter, aspect, must be found, such as "Does Scouting Cut Down Juvenile Delinquency?" Or "Juvenile Crime Begins at Home." Or "Public Parks — the Hunting Ground of Juvenile Delinquents." Or "How Boy Gangs Become Criminal Gangs."

Determining the Value of Ideas

The value of any idea is determined by its intrinsic merits with respect to a given purpose. Concerning article ideas, one asks, How important is the idea? How many people will it entertain or interest? How many will it help — improve their health, prosperity, or happiness? How universal is it? How widely has the idea been used? Or how recently has it been used in the most likely markets? Also, Is the new angle adequate to make editors and readers forget previous articles? Is there something important to contribute that was not previously published?

Many such questions can be asked about any subject. The experienced writer will need to ask fewer questions than the beginner. In fact, the former may know almost by instinct that an idea is or is not worth handling. The novice can only hope that he is asking enough questions and the right ones.

The purpose of raising questions is to test the merits of the idea. Literally hundreds of these tests may be tried out before the writer finally makes up his mind. From one point of view the writer's only asset is his time. He cannot afford to devote a week or two or a month or two in processing an idea that he will later discard as lacking in merit. This discovery or judgment should be made, if possible, at the outset before extensive research and writing begin. These questions are the short cuts that aid such a discovery.

Having settled on a usable idea but before undertaking its serious development, the writer asks such additional questions as, What is the purpose of the proposed article? For what market should it be written? How important is the idea to them? How long should the article be? Does it need illustration? If so, can appropriate illustrations be obtained? Are the necessary data available? All these and many other parallel questions must be asked and answers attempted.

During the outlining process the writer keeps up a continuous barrage of questions. (This is also true during the rewriting process.) These questions help turn big problems into little problems, which are, as any writer knows, easier to solve. Also they break a long article into small units. Where it is always difficult to conceive the writing of two, three, or four thousand words, even the young writer soon learns to visualize a single paragraph unit as it is going to look.

Recording Ideas

The notebook is an indispensable aid to the imaginative processes of the part-time or full-time article writer. Into this notebook should go all the hunches, tips, and full-blown ideas. Most of these will quickly fade from the mind otherwise, and the only safe repository is a well-organized notebook.

Any scrap of paper will do for the first record, because these sudden hunches may occur at any moment — at a concert, in church, on a bus, or in a bath. They should be recorded *when* they occur — if possible — and later transferred to a permanent notebook or some other indexed system, classified in a manner most usable to the writer.

Even little ideas should be set down, because little ideas eventually may add up to big ones, and a big idea is not to be scorned. Ideas in the notebook are like bonds in the safe deposit vault. The time will surely come when they will be needed and can be cashed in. Every writer runs into periods when he is at least temporarily "written out." It is then that he can dig out from his notes the jottings from past inspiration for future articles.

Regularity of note-taking and thoroughness are both important. They tend to guarantee that the writer will not run out of ideas — that there will always be some worth-while material to work on. It it usually best to put down more than seems necessary at the time of writing, for the setting that produced the idea or its color and content may be partly forgotten. Anyway, what once seemed unimportant may later appear important. Fragmentary ideas, as well as old and new ideas, with later classification will increase in value, and they will become more useful as additional notes are added to them.

When jotting down these hunches, the writer should set them down in inventory form by adding as much information to them as he then possesses. He should "muse" about them until he has exhausted his current knowledge and his hunches. This is the best way in which to develop an angle or approach that will be original with the writer. Later, the broad research can be done with less danger of being too imitative, or of having the writer's originality swamped by the point of view of other writers.

Working with Your Mind

Not all minds work alike. What seems to be easy for one may be difficult for another. But it is true that we can chart some general principles which will make it easier for any article writer to get along with his own mind — to work with it instead of against it.

The first principle to learn is to know one's own habits of mind. Try to discover as time wears on how you work best. It is said that Alexander Woollcott did most of his writing in later years while in bed. If a writer works that way best, he probably would be foolish to try to change his own nature. Some people can only write after ten o'clock in the evening when everything is quiet; others write best in the morning before the rest of the household is up. Some must have a cabin hidden in the woods, or an office with whereabouts unknown to family and friends.

Discover *how* and *when* and *where* you write best. Work out the easiest pattern for yourself, and then follow it as completely as possible with a *regular* program of writing. Don't wait for a writing mood to hit you. It *may not*. Start to work anyway, and set out as confidently as possible. The habit of work can grow on a writer. Most writers find that having a *time* and *place* for writing helps put one in a well-worn rut that makes literary production an easier task than it otherwise would be.

Open-Mindedness

During these periods of writing when the imaginative or creative processes are at work keep an open mind on the ideas that occur to you. Don't reject anything connected with the subject at hand. Write it down. It may appear later to be better than it seemed at first sight. Also it may be a genuine hunch or inspiration of which you don't see the point. One might add that in quantity there is bound to be some quality.

Another point to remember is that one list of ideas may be the basis for another list, which will be the beginning of a completely different article. Anyway, keep on jotting ideas down. The best ones often come last. If you stop too soon, your best thoughts may never be born. Some writers find that rejection or turning back of what seems to be an inferior idea occasionally blocks other ideas from coming through.

Another tip is to use your hobbies to free the mind so that ideas will come through. The hobbies should be of the type that occupies the hands, but leaves the mind relatively or entirely free.

Getting a Picture of Your Purpose

Try to get a picture of what you want to be as a writer. Not many people can master two or more forms of writing at the same time. If you have decided to be a writer of articles, master this form of writing before you devote much time to short stories or novels.

Further, it is not enough that you want to write articles, although this is far better than merely wanting to write. Ask yourself on what subjects you want to write. Also for what magazines. These are not easy points to decide, but they are important and deserve your best and most sustained judgment.

Developing Imagination

The imaginative ability to accomplish the various undertakings suggested in this chapter can be developed through exercise, as imagination is a native talent possessed by everyone, though in different degrees. No set of rules or special exercises is needed. Simply practice on article ideas, following the methods suggested later in this chapter under "New Ideas from Old Ideas."

A wide reading program built around the writer's field of interest will give the imagination food on which to grow. Travel, observation, good listening, and good viewing also will help.

Developing Concentration

The ability to concentrate occurs unequally, but it can be developed with practice. Because it is a definite aid to the writer's imaginative powers, it is worth cultivating.

One good way to increase the power to concentrate is to deepen one's interest. It is a law of human nature that the earnest study of any subject produces an abiding interest in that subject. So the free lance can do two things: a. he can work on the subjects in which he already has an interest, i.e., in his specialties or hobbies; b. he can plunge whole-heartedly into the research of any subject to which he has newly turned his attention.

This cramming of the mind through research also has a value beyond the immediate learning of facts. From the process come good ideas later on. These ideas often are solutions to problems that previously troubled the writer. They sometimes are referred to as hunches or inspiration. In all cases they should be recorded and submitted later to the critical judgment to determine their worth.

Also the act of putting ideas down on paper helps to focus the attention on the problem at hand. The writer is helped to concentrate by working on his inventory, outline, title, a new and better beginning, or a stronger conclusion. Any note-taking in support of the proposed article helps.

An effective, if tricky, way to increase concentration is to set an immediate goal with a reward to the writer when the goal is reached. For instance, the free lance can promise himself that when he has done a good stint of work (precisely stated) he can go fishing. Or when he has finished his article, he can go to a movie. This author used to promise himself a trip to Florida if he could think out enough good article possibilities in that state to justify the trip. The process usually worked out very well, and eventually paid the expenses of the round trip. This application of "the carrot before the donkey's nose" can be adjusted for greater or lesser rewards as circumstances warrant. Try putting yourself on the incentive system, and see how it works.

Imagination and the Emotions

How many articles, novels, poems, and short stories have been writ-ten under the inspiration of the emotions no one will ever know. Cer-tainly, they have been a great motivating force. Some of the world's greatest masterpieces have been produced under the stimulating influ-ence of love, using that word in its broadest sense to include not only the love of a man for a maid, but also that of a parent for a child, or any human being for any other.

Many of the world's tenderest poems have been penned because the imagination was keyed to emotion — from the love sonnets of Elizabeth Barrett Browning to Robert Browning, and "Little Boy Blue" by Eugene Field; to "The Night Before Christmas" by Clement C. Moore. The world needs articles of finer quality, or keener discernment, of more moving force. There is no reason why the writer should not channel his deeper emotions into the production of such pieces. There is every reason why he should, for the world would be poorer without them.

The opposite of love is hate. An individual may hate a set of circumstances, certain forces at work, or a situation or condition so deeply that he is moved to write about it. Out of such deep emotion obviously came Harriet Beecher Stowe's "Uncle Tom's Cabin."

Shocking experiences also move people mightily — accidents, death, or natural disasters. The well-known article "And Sudden Death" by J. C. Furnas was so produced. The author was so deeply disturbed by the horrible spectacle of brutal, accidental death on the highways and streets of the nation that he wrote his moving piece. Its powerful quality has caused it to be reprinted again and again. The deep horror felt by Furnas cried out through the lines of his article. He could not have written so had he felt calmly about this needless slaughter. The important point for the free lance to note is that Furnas gave expression to his horror *in writing*. He could have allowed his feeling to be dissipated to wear off ineffectively. Instead, he put it to work, and he produced a splendid piece.

This emotional drive can be one of the strongest drives any writer can experience, but he has got to put it to work if it is to be productive.

Love and hate are not the only emotional drives. Anger or indignation may be just as productive. So may compassion, generosity, or pity. Curiosity about or enthusiasm for a hobby, sport, or other pastime may be the source of a good piece.

Some of the baser emotions, such as depression, or dread of being poor, have also sparked a drive to produce articles and other types of writing. Even the psychologists probably would agree that the effort to turn these "blue" moods into productive channels is an excellent way to get rid of them.

Reporting and the Imagination

The imagination can create imaginary difficulties as well as solve real ones.

If the article writer will think of himself as a reporter, he can often lessen the preconceived difficulties of the next writing job. It is true that some articles are "think pieces" in that they are mostly made up of what the writer thinks about this or that. But most articles describe or explain an object, a process, a situation, or an individual. In producing a piece like this the writer is first and last a reporter. To his job of reporting he adds the techniques of the fiction writer to make his article more entertaining.

He also has a reporting job to do in that he has to gather the facts through interviewing people and through research and study. He works with facts and generally there is a story to be told. By using the imagination to get a composite view of this story, the free lance is able to see his piece as a complete entity even before he has written it. Thus, he is able to write with direction and purpose and with as little waste effort as possible.

Creative vs. Critical Faculties

Another danger to the writer in his writing lies in the antagonistic nature of the creative and critical faculties of the mind. Often they appear to be at war with each other; and if the writer permits this fratricidal strife to develop unpoliced, eventually the sterner critical faculties win out. Then the critic in the writer may well write over the remains of the imagination, "Here lies the body of a would-be free-lance writer."

Judgment, which is the product of the critical abilities of the mind, is exercised intermittently. It is not to be used when the creative faculties are at work. Many a critic has "judged" himself right out of the creative world. How otherwise explain the extremely low production of creative works by those who devote their lives to the teaching of English and the appraisal and criticism of the creative works of others. Witness on the other hand, the far higher productivity of writers who work in or have worked in the various branches of journalism.

This writer still recalls with horror the fate of a writer who permitted duty and necessity to suppress his creative faculties. Year after year he got farther away from his one creative book, an early effort that shook the South by subtle and intuitive descriptions of the effects of its torrid climate on the people. Meanwhile, his critical faculties developed, taking complete possession of his mind. When he finally awakened to the destruction of his creative mind, he did away with himself with a revolver.

When a person tries to write, he calls upon the imaginative faculties, and he should give them a relatively free rein. He may have to guide them back to the subject at hand, but he should not be critical of what they turn up while they are at work.

Ideas and the elaboration of ideas need to be tested. The original inventory and all the drafts of each article must be tested, but the writer critically judges them after he has safely gotten them down on paper — not consciously while he is setting them down.

The second step in article writing, the production of a classified inventory, is, however, a critical process. In this the writer *does* test every word, phrase, anecdote, or group of data. This is not a creative task, though a number of new and good ideas may be thrust into consciousness during the process.

This writer believes it is wise to avoid critical friends and their critical judgments when in the process of creating. Instead, get a writing friend who will give you proper encouragement. Then draw upon various critical judgments when you are testing or revising your ideas or their elaborations.

The above paragraphs may seem to overemphasize the critical and imaginative struggle. A writer cannot help exercising some judgment as he writes, depending upon his experience and skill. Nevertheless, he will be wise, indeed, if he keeps the "dangerous" critical faculties in their proper place.

Tapping the Unconscious

The preceding pages imply that at times extra help may be had by the writer from his subconscious or unconscious mind. If so, how? Can this source of help be drawn upon at will? What preparations must the writer make?

Without going into the involved discussions of the deeper aspects of the human mind, let me say that many writers do rather regularly put their subconscious or unconscious mind to work. They do find that it gives them real help from time to time. It is unfortunate that few, if any, learn to control the subconscious mind completely. Yet important subconscious help can be received by the writer just as surely as minor miracles can be performed by the hypnotist through his own special techniques of fixation and suggestion.

How can we put to work the unconscious mind, in which is recorded all the impressions of the senses from a lifetime of living? We have some clues to the methods of releasing these memories, and of putting the *organizing* or *sorting* abilities and the inventive capacities of the subconscious to work.

DAY DREAMS. Some of the writer's most valuable efforts are made when he is sitting still, apparently doing nothing. This quiet period may be difficult to explain to the family or friends. Probably it is wisest to tell them frankly, "I'm planning (or thinking through) an article." The writer has to prevent the intrusion of others into these precious thinking or "musing" periods, because such invasion destroys the chain of thought and prevents ideas from springing into the conscious mind from subconscious sources.

You will make many false starts in these periods of musing, but the will can draw the imagination back to the original purpose of the chase, which is to get all the ideas you can without being critical of their content. However, avoid reveries or day-dreams that are beside the point. Let ideas flow freely into the mind, but see to it that they are about the idea or article with which you have to deal.

HELP FROM SLEEP.   Any one who has gotten up in the morning and has found that the problems of the night before have solved themselves while he slept will recognize that he got help "from somewhere." To get what help you can from this source simply charge the mind before you go to sleep. Run over your notes methodically and with as complete concentration as you can command. Any time of the day will do for this step, although the period shortly before retiring is best. While you sleep, the subconscious mind keeps on sorting and rearranging the data so provided and links them with what have previously been recorded. Often the subconscious comes up with surprisingly helpful results. Next morning, or later, the writer may find that his difficult problems have been solved for him. Most writers, if not all, draw help from this source, although they are not always aware of the fact.

Some writers keep a pad and pencil at the bedside to record ideas that have awakened them. In the light of the next day, some ideas will appear weird and unusable; others may be just what is needed. But good ideas that are relevant to the problem will not be produced until they have been preceded by a great deal of conscious effort and study.

INCUBATION.   When ideas appear to be unmanageable, it is often because the writer has not done enough thinking about them, and has not allowed them to incubate long enough. Think through your ideas thoroughly, then put them aside for a day or more. These incubation periods nearly always help a writer, and they often provide the ideas that later come like flashes of inspiration.

Many good angles and titles come after such a period of incubation. If they elude you at first, start at the beginning and go over all of the facts again. You might pick a quiet Saturday or Sunday afternoon for this when you do not have other pressing duties. Read your article notes carefully. Ponder every idea. From one of them eventually may come the angle or phrase that is exactly what you want. The work will have been done by the unconscious mind. Having studied your notes, put them aside and do only those things which in the past have tended to produce good ideas. For instance, go to church, or to a concert, or take a walk — something not too stimulating. Or work at your hobbies — anything that frees the mind. Eventually, you will find a solution for the immediate writing problem.

Models for the Imagination

The imagination should be trained in habits that are helpful to a writing career. The article writer, like the fiction writer, can "play the sedulous ape" to models worthy of study.

Once a writer has settled on the area or areas in which he intends to write, he ought to find out who are the best writers in that field. Either he finds out the magazines that publish material of the kind he wants to write and studies the back numbers, or he looks up articles of this type with their authors in *Readers' Guide to Periodical Literature*. Next, he begins to accumulate a file of these writings. The second-hand magazine stores may be useful here. Finally, he begins a systematic study, sharpening his judgment on *who* and *what* is best.

The purpose of such study is to reveal *what* the best writers write, *when* they write, for *what* publications they write, and *how* they write. A keen, steady analysis will reveal almost endless tips to improve the writer's style and his writing program. A mastery of these tips will shorten the period of his writing apprenticeship.

Keeping the Imagination up to Date

Timeliness is important in many articles, and this means that the writer must be a reader of the magazines and newspapers if his thinking processes are to provide him with recent angles and future trends. A number of methods exist for making sure that the writer's offerings will be timely when they hit the newsstands or arrive in the homes of magazine subscribers. Writing of events tied to the calendar, such as Washington's or Lincoln's birthday, is one. This was described in Chapter 21.

A second method of achieving timeliness is by watching for seasonal subjects, such as baseball or football yarns, or stories of gardening or house painting. This was also discussed in Chapter 21.

Another important method and an excellent source of new ideas, requiring considerable exercise of the imagination and judgment, is the divining of trends in current events. The movement of the stock market consumes a great deal of public interest — far more than is customary. Should investors get in? Should they get out? A good angle on this subject for a business journal is the control of rumor-makers. And an interesting article for a general magazine can also be done on the dangers of accepting tipsters' advice over the radio or from *any other* source.

For the agricultural journals, government support of prices for farm products is still a hot issue, and it looks as if it will continue to be for some years to come. The general public still does not understand this issue, nor appreciate the degree to which its meat and grocery problems are affected. A considerable number of articles yet need to be written on this subject.

Protection against fall-out from hydrogen and other bombs and the role of civilians in defense are unsettled problems with much to be written on each. The guaranteed annual wage for industrial workers is another problem. While much is being written on these three topics, each is likely to be a problem for some years to come.

Still another area in which the imagination needs to be properly informed is that of the basic human "drives," which center around food, propagation, security, recognition, and shelter. These items are of eternal interest. But as the writer looks around, he asks himself, What aspect of these "drives" interests the public now? What is new? What is going to be important to them in the next few months, or the next year? Certain immediate applications are always important, such as critical aspects of finances and health. If the writer can anticipate and illuminate these interests, he will have angles that will interest the magazines.

This anticipation requires the writer to make use of his imagination. He must put himself in the other man's shoes. He must ask such questions as, What will the reader be needing to know? What will he be discussing? In what will he be interested?

Some of these subjects will "be in the air," and they will interest other writers. The free-lance must simply think a little farther ahead than his competing writers, think a little more clearly, turn up a different and better angle, and use the query to the editor.

New Ideas from Old Ideas

Because there are practically no new things under the sun, you may ask, From where do new ideas for articles come?

The answer is that they are nearly always produced in one way or another from one or more old ideas. Once a writer knows that he is after new angles on old subjects and knows what the processes are for producing them, his mind almost automatically suggests what he wants. Generally, he should stay inside the areas of knowledge with which he is familiar through education or experience. It is then that he builds on accumulated knowledge and so has less research to do.

Below are cited eight different types of manipulation through which new ideas can be worked out of old ideas. Any writer who will take an issue of *Reader's Digest* and apply these eight types of manipulation ought to come up with a wealth of perfectly sound ideas for brand new articles.

The types of manipulation are: 1. addition and multiplication; 2. contiguity and propinquity; 3. division and subtraction; 4. exaggeration; 5. modification; 6. opposition or contradiction; 7. parallelism; and 8. questioning.

1. ADDITION AND MULTIPLICATION. When an article has been built around a single major idea, another writer may be able to produce a different article by adding a number of items in the same class or category. The original item might appear in the new article, but it would likely be in a greatly reduced form.

A national magazine has printed an article on the use of the medicinal weed *rauwolfia* (from India) in the treatment of hypertension. One can keep on adding similar examples of other medicinal herbs, such as quinine and belladonna, until he has constructed an entirely different article. Instead of a full-length piece about one herb, the free lance writes of 30 or 40 herbs, none of which draws more than two or three paragraphs in the new article.

Another article tells of a farm wife who has run a successful roadside stand. It describes her methods. A different article might tell of a score of farm wives who have operated similarly successful stands. The composite article on their success might well make a more helpful piece than the first one.

2. CONTIGUITY AND PROPINQUITY. At times sheer *propinquity* will suggest an article. In the early days of Marineland, the famous Florida aquarium, this author visited it and the flamingos at Hialeah Park, near Miami. Having a good vacation, he had forgotten about article writing. Later seeing an article on these self-same flamingos, he realized that a fascinating piece could be written on Marineland.

These are not what could be called *parallel* ideas, but are suggested by association or the fact of *propinquity*. In the same way other articles about the Stephen Foster Memorial on the Suwannee River, the Jungle

River cruises at Silver Springs, and the diminutive deer of the Florida keys would be suggested by other points of interest in the same state.

It is to be noted that *contiguity* or *propinquity* may of themselves suggest other ideas to the writer, but he is supposed to use this type of association as an exercise in ingenuous thinking to uncover usable ideas. He must ask himself, What else nearby is worth writing up? Or who else?

3. DIVISION AND SUBTRACTION. Occasionally a part of an idea or article can be expanded into a full-length piece. This process is the reverse of *addition* and *multiplication*. It is particularly valuable in culling ideas from the works of other writers. The writer, as he reads, keeps his eyes open for ideas that deserve fuller treatment.

An article on American national parks under this process should suggest a fuller treatment on American waterfalls, or on the continual encroachment on these parks. An article on American memorials and monuments suggests a piece on the statutory likenesses of American heroes, or an admonitory article on public desecration of American shrines.

It is not uncommon for an article on a successful business or institution to mention the names of several unusually capable individuals, who have contributed greatly to the success of the organizations. These names are tips for personality sketches or other stories of these successful careers.

4. EXAGGERATION. This type of development opens up a wide field for articles on curiosities and items that are unique. While akin to hyperbole, it relies more heavily on selection of extreme examples than upon distortion. The *Reader's Digest* series on "My Most Interesting Character" is an example. To produce a central character the writer canvasses his total experience and selects the individual who has interested him most, or influenced his life to the greatest degree. Around him he spins a web of fact and interpretation.

As pointed out earlier in this book, extremes of many kinds make usable ideas. One extreme may suggest another in a different field, as under No. 7, *Parallelism*. Here are a few extremes upon which articles have been built: the smallest book in the world, the richest man, the strongest man, the largest gem, the fastest human being, the largest animal, the most accurate gauge, the tallest or fattest human being, the tallest building. Surely, these fascinating extremes have already suggested possibilities to the users of this book for articles on other extremes!

5. MODIFICATION. Under the technique of modification we take an idea and change it a little bit here and there. This gives a different angle on an older idea. Even though the size of the angle may be a rather slight one, the difference is important, because it gives the writer a new approach or point of view from which to handle an old problem.

These changes may be made one at a time, although many changes may be made before the new idea reaches its final form. This is the same evolutionary process by which automobiles, for instance, are changed year after year until the style strikes out in an entirely different direction.

A simple example of how this process works might take the old adage, "Honesty Pays." A slight sardonic twist yields the title, "Honesty Pays — the Other Fellow." Or "Little Strokes Fell No Great Oaks — Today," in an article on modern power saws. Note the changes that have been made in the title below from *Reader's Digest*. Note also at how many different points it is possible to make changes.

AMERICA THROUGH THE EYES OF A JAPANESE WAR-BRIDE (The Original)

MEXICO THROUGH THE EYES OF AN AMERICAN PAINTER

AMERICA THROUGH THE EYES OF A LIBERIAN NEGRO

CANADA THROUGH THE EYES OF A MINERAL HUNTER

AMERICAN CHILDREN THROUGH THE EYES OF A SCOTTISH TEACHER

AMERICAN MUSIC THROUGH THE EARS OF A FOREIGNER

This process of *adaptation* or *modification* can go on almost endlessly. It is the literal truth that any of the adaptations above could well have made a printable article. Naturally, the writer uses this method until he gets an idea that fits in with his immediate needs. Some *adaptations* may have to be filed away for future use and development.

This author believes that this is a far better way to dig out a usable idea than to travel to a strange city on the blind hope that one will stumble across a good idea, a suggestion that was outlined in a recent book.

6. OPPOSITION AND CONTRADICTION. The world is full of assumptions and beliefs concerning which, in the light of today's circumstances and knowledge, a writer might question the wisdom. For instance, "Early to bed and early to rise" is much less likely to make a man "healthy, wealthy, and wise" than late to bed and early to rise. Other things being equal, long hours are almost certain to produce greater results than short hours.

Many parents and others have questioned whether modern public school instruction is as effective as that of a generation ago in teaching reading, writing, and arithmetic. The criticism is so widespread that it has become widely accepted as fact. Yet the available data seem to show quite the reverse, so there are definite possibilities here for an important article. Who is going to do the research and write this piece?

Also to every issue there are at least two sides. An article on one side calls for an article that sets forth the issue from the other side — possibly in another magazine. But if you believe in the latter side, perhaps you may have the genesis of a good article. If some one writes that the TVA program has been a complete boon to Tennessee and neighboring areas, maybe you are the one to do a more analytical piece from a wider background.

Finally, be contrary: it pays. If some one writes of the happiest person in the world, you write of the saddest. If he writes of the best ways to save time, you write of the best ways to waste it!

7. PARALLELISM. The technique of producing ideas through parallelism is occasionally like that of *opposition*. This need not trouble us, inasmuch as we are interested in producing usable ideas — not in merely classifying the methods of production.

Here is how *parallelism* works. You take any idea that appeals to you, such as an article on old-fashioned Christmases. You ask yourself, What else is old-fashioned that is worth an article of the light essay type? You come up with a number: old-fashioned box socials or pie suppers, sleigh rides, harvest dinners, sugaring-off parties, or valentines.

Also try shifting the attributes from one published article to your proposed article. For instance, if some one had published an article about the *oldest* gun or book, you write one on the *oldest* harp or the *oldest* code of laws. In essence, the writer looks at an article, selects a dominant or unusual attribute or quality and applies it to a different idea or item to produce a second article.

Or you take an idea like the one that "honesty pays." You ask, What else pays? You decide that "education pays," and "good health pays." In recent years many preachers are saying that "religion pays." Here, then, are three ideas worth considering by the best writers.

Or you remember the old admonition that mothers have given their young children for generations, "Mother knows best." By *parallelism* you could come up with the idea that "baby knows best" when he needs feeding and about what is good or is not good for him — an excellent idea for *Parents' Magazine* or *Today's Health.* By way of contrast, through the technique of *opposition,* you would arrive at a different angle that "Mother doesn't know best." This latter idea would develop the thesis that mothers (or fathers) should leave certain decisions to the experts, the dentists, physicians, teachers, and lawyers.

Also by *parallelism* you uncover neglected people, places, and things. For example some one writes about Audubon, the neglected genius. The writer should ask, What other genius has been neglected? (There is one — Brasher — even greater than Audubon and worth an article.) Also he should ask, What other geniuses in what other lines have been forgotten or have not yet been appreciated? As in each of the eight techniques, the free lance asks, Who else? What else?

8. QUESTIONING. Almost any positive idea that is commonly accepted can be turned into a workable idea by framing it as a question. This is a highly useful technique, because it starts off with a judicious attitude by asking whether the idea is true. The writer then proceeds to set forth the facts on *both* sides of the point at issue. In this respect, *questioning* differs from *opposition* or *contradiction,* which usually stick to one side or the other of a moot issue. In the idea used above, which cited the saying, "Mother knows best," we simply ask, Does Mother know best? Or, Does honesty pay? Or, Are all superstitions unscientific? Or, Do dreams come true? This last idea was once used in the *Reader's Digest.*

It is possible to question almost endlessly the adages, beliefs, maxims, semitruths, and many so-called "sayings," as well as ideas of many kinds, with the intent to produce an article based on the truth behind the known facts. A survey of magazine contents for any year will reveal scores of articles of which the basic idea could have been produced in this way.

Summary: The eight techniques analyzed above add up to the fact that the writer first should be a questioner of the accepted ideas. He should look at an article or idea and ask himself, What else? Who else? Where else? Why else? When else? How else? Every person, place, thing, cause, date, and method has its parallel, and each is subject to further dissection and inspection by one or more of the eight processes. Each of the six questions in this paragraph can and should be asked under each of the eight types of development.

Eventually, all the questions and the techniques can be applied not only to the central idea, as explained in the foregoing pages, but also to all the major and minor divisions of the article. The free lance will develop facility in these processes as he continues to work with them.

Training Steps

1. If there are actually few, if any, new ideas, from where do the ideas for magazines and newspapers come?
2. State six questions that should be asked in determining the value of a proposed idea.
3. What is the basic purpose of raising questions about a proposed idea?
4. Is it better to follow the natural working methods of your mind, or to try to reform it? Discuss both sides of this question.
5. What is meant by keeping an "open mind" on the offerings of the subconscious?
6. What is meant by getting a "picture" of your purpose? Why is that important?
7. How can the powers of the imagination be developed?
8. Name three techniques that help increase one's powers of concentration.
9. How can the imagination make use of the emotions? Cite some examples of writers who have done so.
10. Why is the article writer also a reporter? What value is there in developing this concept?
11. Describe the dangers from conflict between the creative and the critical faculties. How can these dangers be avoided?
12. Name and describe three ways to tap the unconscious mind.
13. What is the advantage of having "models for the imagination"?
14. How can the imagination be kept up to date?
15. State the eight techniques for developing new ideas from old ideas. Give an example of each type.
16. Why should article writers be persistent questioners?

Appendixes

A Typical Magazine Survey
Instructor's Rating Guide
Copyreading Symbols

APPENDIX A

Typical of Illustrations

THIS is the type of magazine analysis a beginner might make when surveying his chief markets for the first time. It calls for inspection of all the issues of the magazine for at least 12 consecutive months, an inspection of the Table of Contents for two or three years in order to recognize all types of seasonal material in use.

Instructors in journalism classes will find it usable as a model for student work. All such reports must keep up with changes in magazine policies and staff membership. There is no substitute for continuing study of current market needs. As soon as a writer becomes thoroughly acquainted with a magazine, keeping up to date with it is a simple matter.

Parents' Magazine
52 Vanderbilt Avenue, New York 17, N. Y.
Mrs. Dorothy Whyte Cotton

For Whom to Write

This magazine is published for intelligent parents, chiefly the mother, of families with average or better income. Middle-class in appeal.

What to Write

Anything dealing with problems of rearing children "from crib to college." If the writer can claim authority or personal experience, he has a better chance of selling. Technical articles by psychologists or plain pieces by experienced parents are used, and pieces on mental hygiene of parents. Short pieces on how certain problems were solved. Buys articles on play appa-

398

ratus and home improvement from children's angle. Also education and community affairs.

How to Write

Articles should be simple, clear, and free from undefined medical terms. The "homey" touch is preferred. Write as if conversing with an interested friend of good education. Purely medical or psychological articles are not wanted. Use conversation, anecdotes, examples. Titles and subtitles often are of sentimental or popular nature, i.e., "The Forgotten Father," and "They Don't Know When to Come Home." Good illustrations help. Limit 1500 words on popular articles and 2500 on thoughtful subjects. Includes nothing intended for the reading of children.

Rate of Pay

Ten cents a word to novices. More to experienced writers. Buys some photographs.

Trends and Policies

Uses seasonal articles. Articles dealing with babies are found in every issue and at all seasons. This is "sure-fire" stuff, but must be good. Other ages not always dealt with in each issue, although second place seems to go to adolescent age. College age receives least space. Articles on beauty and fashions printed sparingly.

Article Examples

"Is Your Child a Weathervane?" This article asks, "Do you know how the weather affects your baby?" It then shows by anecdote, and frequent reference to "your baby," how the weather makes a difference in a child's health, growth, and behavior.

"Who Wants a Spoiled Baby" is a recipe for a contented baby, and suggested cure for one who is already spoiled.

"Play Safe This Christmas" shows how "you" can take thought beforehand to make sure no accidents will happen to your holiday's fun.

Queries

Gives prompt attention to letters on possible subjects. Prefers one-page outline with a few opening paragraphs. Reports within three weeks.

Article Ideas

Might use article on how to build a game room or how to plan a party for young people, or an interview with a child psychologist.

Similar Markets.

Today's Health.

Instructor's Rating Guide

FOLLOWING is a list of the chief faults in the preparation of an article for mailing. Instructors may wish to mimeograph and use it in their class work. Students will find the instructor's judgment, as shown by the items checked, worth referring to frequently.

I. Envelopes

    A. Outer:

        1. Return address: missing——; incomplete——; illegible——.

        2. Magazine address: missing——; incomplete——; wrong office——.

        3. Not prepared as first class mail——.

        4. Addresses poorly arranged or balanced——.

        5. Envelope wrong size——.

    B. Inner:

        1. Return address missing——; incomplete——; illegible——.

        2. Author's address missing——; incomplete——.

        3. Not prepared as first class mail——.

        4. Addresses poorly arranged or balanced——.

        5. Envelope wrong size——.

II. Stamps

    A. Outer envelope:

        1. Insufficient——. 2. Insecurely or improperly attached——.

    B. Inner envelope:

        1. Should be clipped——. 2. Insufficient——.

III. Cardboard (if photograph or drawings are included):

    A. Too light——; too heavy——.
    B. Too small——; too large——.
    C. Should be fitted to inner envelope——.
    D. Envelopes should be labeled "Photos—Do Not Bend"——.

IV. Manuscript Appearance:

    A. Margins: too narrow——; too wide——; uneven——.
    B. Author's address: missing——; incomplete——.
    C. Magazine title: missing——; should be underlined or capitalized——; word count underestimated——; overestimated——.
    D. (More) omitted from bottom of early pages——.
    E. Does not indicate the end——.
    F. Pages badly numbered——; pages do not carry proper identification——.
    G. Too much erasing——; "X-ing"——.

V. Cover Page:

    A. Upper half unlike upper half of page 1——.
    B. Note to editor: not a good advertisement for article——; too brief——; too long——; overlooks interesting items in article——.
    C. Illustrations unlisted——.

VI. Title:

    A. Balance: not centered——; too high——; too low——; too long——.
    B. Content: uninteresting——; inaccurate——; not concrete——; unrelated to subject——; a mere label——; exaggerated——; inappropriate——.

VII. Subtitle:

    A. Balance: not centered——; too high——; too low——; too long——; too short——.
    B. Content: repeats title——; gives no additional information——; uninteresting——; not a good advertisement for article——; unrelated to article——.

VIII. Subject:

    A. Timeliness: too late to reach market——; too early——; too frequently written about——.
    B. Content: not enough information——; no new material——; not practical——.

IX. Treatment:

    A. Length: too short——; too long——.
    B. Style: too familiar——; not sufficiently friendly or chatty——; stilted——.
    C. Paragraphs: too long——; too short——.
    D. Sentences: too long——; too short——.

E. Words: too long——; difficult words undefined——; too much repetition——.

F. Punctuation poor——.

G. Spelling: too many misspelled words——.

X. Beginning:

A. Length: too long——; too short——.

B. Content: uninteresting——; not related to article——.

XI. Transitional devices:

A. Length: too long——; too short——.

B. Value: fail to accomplish purpose——; don't link beginning and body——.

XII. Body:

A. Facts: sometimes not relevant——; not interestingly presented——.

B. Pattern: not clear——, reader gets lost——; steps should be labeled——.

C. Explanation: hard to follow——.

XIII. Conclusion:

A. Length: too long——; too short——.

B. Effectiveness: fails to summarize——; adds nothing valuable——.

XIV. Market:

A. Appropriateness: does not use free-lance material——; too difficult for beginning writers——; does not use this type material——.

XV. Illustrations:

A. Need: not used by this market——.

B. Number: too many——; not enough——.

C. Quality: underexposed——; overexposed——; lack human interest——; inappropriate——.

D. Size: too small——; wrong size——.

E. Type: market does not use photos——; maps——; sketches——; charts——; diagrams——.

F. Preparation: cutlines missing——; owner's address missing——; cutlines ineffective——; not tied into article.

XVI. Humanization:

A. Needs anecdotes——.

B. Use narrative form——.

C. Translate facts——.

D. Use more quotes——.

Copyreading Symbols

THE list of copyreading symbols below includes all those that should be used on manuscripts submitted by free-lance writers to prospective buyers. Where it is necessary to make more than two or three corrections on a single page, that page should be retyped.

1. Three lines under a letter or word are an order to set it in large capital letters; as, New York   new york

2. One line under one or more words is an order to set it in italics; as, *Reader's Digest*   Reader's Digest

3. An elongated figure like an "8" encircling 2 or more words is an order to reverse the position of the words; as, Lake Erie.   Erie Lake

4. A vertical line between two words is an order to separate them; as, Flying Fortress   Flying Fortress

5. An oblique line through a capital letter indicates that it is to be changed to a small letter; as, president   President

6. A circle around an abbreviation or a numerical figure is an order to spell it out; as, a six-foot man   a 6 ft. man

7. A circle around words or figures spelled out indicates that they should be abbreviated; as, Syracuse, 10, N.Y.   Syracuse, Ten, New York

403

8. A caret is placed at the point where letters or words written above the line are to be inserted; as, John Walker was unanimously elected president.

                      unanimously
John Walker was ∧elec-
ted president

9. Semicircles are used to indicate that words or letters are to be brought together; as, Lapland

Lap⌒land

10. A small x or a period in a circle indicates insertion of a period; as, Syracuse, N. Y.

Syracuse, N$_x$Y$_x$
Syracuse, N$_⊙$ Y$_⊙$

11. Semicircles are occasionally used around quotation marks to show whether they are beginning or ending quotes: as, *He shouted, "Taxi! Taxi!" as he left the hotel.*

He shouted, "Taxi! Taxi!" as he left the hotel.

12. Two signs are available for calling attention to a new paragraph.

ℋ "What time is it?" he asked
⌐"Ten o'clock," she announced.

Index